The Criminal Justice Network

The Criminal Justice Network

An Introduction

Steven M. Cox

Western Illinois University

John E. Wade

Southeast Missouri State University

Fourth Edition

Boston   Burr Ridge, IL   Dubuque, IA   Madison, WI   New York   San Francisco   St. Louis
Bangkok   Bogotá   Caracas   Kuala Lumpur   Lisbon   London   Madrid   Mexico City
Milan   Montreal   New Delhi   Santiago   Seoul   Singapore   Sydney   Taipei   Toronto

McGraw-Hill Higher Education

A Division of The *McGraw-Hill* Companies

THE CRIMINAL JUSTICE NETWORK: AN INTRODUCTION

Published by McGraw-Hill, an imprint of The McGraw-Hill Companies, Inc. 1221 Avenue of the Americas, New York, NY, 10020. Copyright © 2002, 1998, 1989, 1985 by The McGraw-Hill Companies, Inc. All rights reserved. No part of this publication may be reproduced or distributed in any form or by any means, or stored in a database or retrieval system, without the prior written consent of The McGraw-Hill Companies, Inc., including, but not limited to, in any network or other electronic storage or transmission, or broadcast for distance learning.

Some ancillaries, including electronic and print components, may not be available to customers outside the United States.

This book is printed on acid-free paper.

1 2 3 4 5 6 7 8 9 0 FGR/FGR 0 9 8 7 6 5 4 3 2 1

ISBN 0-07-232148-2

Editorial director: *Phillip A. Butcher*
Senior sponsoring editor: *Carolyn Henderson Meier*
Senior marketing manager: *Daniel M. Loch*
Project manager: *Christina Thornton-Villagomez*
Production supervisor: *Gina Hangos*
Coordinator freelance design/interior design: *Artemio Ortiz Jr.*
Supplement producer: *Nate Perry*
Media producer: *Shannon Rider*
Photo research coordinator: *David A. Tietz*
Photo researcher: *PoYee Oster*
Cover design: *Veronica Smith*
Cover photo: *Michael Newman/PhotoEdit*
Typeface: *10/12 Palatino*
Compositor: *Shepherd Incorporated*
Printer: *Quebecor World Fairfield Inc.*

Library of Congress Cataloging-in-Publication Data

Cox, Steven M.
    The criminal justice network: an introduction / Steven M. Cox, John E. Wade.—4th ed.
      p. cm.
    Includes bibliographical references and index.
    ISBN 0-07-232148-2 (alk. paper)
    1. Criminal justice, Administration of—United States. I. Wade, John E. II. Title.
HV9950 .C69 2002
364.973—dc21
                                     2001044763

www.mhhe.com

ANNIE—THIS ONE'S FOR YOU.

About the Authors

Dr. Steven Cox is a professor in the Department of Law Enforcement and Justice Administration at Western Illinois University. He has been teaching, conducting research, and providing training for criminal justice practitioners for the past 35 years both in the United States and abroad. He is author/coauthor of numerous books and articles and serves as a consultant to a variety of criminal justice agencies. Dr. Cox received his Ph.D. at the University of Illinois, Champaign/Urbana.

Dr. John Wade is a professor and chair of Southeast Missouri State University's Department of Criminal Justice. He has more than 27 years of teaching, research, and training experience in criminal justice. He has served as a consultant to many police agencies throughout the Midwest, has conducted extensive research on rural crime and recently developed a methamphetamine education curriculum for the Midwest High Intensity Drug Trafficking (HIDTA) program. His current research is focused on the manufacture of methamphetamine. Dr. Wade received his Ph.D. from Kansas State University.

Preface

*T*he field of criminal justice is constantly changing as new laws are passed, new technology is deployed, and old social problems continue to fester and surface. The police are accused of racial profiling, they charge dozens if not hundreds of innocent people with crimes they did not commit or that did not occur, and corruption seems to run rampant in big-city police departments. At the same time, community policing brings relief to neighborhoods plagued by crime and disorder for decades. Overcrowding in the courts leads to a denial of justice for many defendants, but restorative justice offers alternatives to traditional court proceedings and holds out hope for both victim and offender. New supermax prisons are built to house society's most dangerous offenders while new and exciting alternatives to incarceration are explored. Helping students understand the nature and extent of such changes and the interrelationships among them is the goal of this text.

APPROACH

In this new edition, we again provide a comprehensive, practical view of criminal justice in the United States. We continue to believe that criminal justice can best be understood by viewing practitioners as being interrelated in a variety of both official and unofficial ways. These practitioners conduct business in various components of what is best viewed as a network of interacting individuals whose everyday decisions have consequences not only for others in their agencies, but for criminal justice practitioners in all components of the network. Thus we continue to compare day-to-day practical aspects of the network with the theoretical model on which the network is based. In our view, this approach involves an examination of the role of the public, the uses and abuses of discretion throughout the network, and the effects of political considerations on the day-to-day operations of the criminal justice network.

- Using the network approach instead of the more common systems (police, courts, corrections all pursuing identical goals) approach, we can examine the impact of politics, discretion, and differing goals on the actions of criminal justice practitioners.
- We recognize the public as a crucial player (though often neglected) in the criminal justice network. Without public cooperation, the police would be severely hampered, the courts would not be properly utilized, probation and parole would be totally unworkable, and the entire network would not be financed.
- Similarly, the importance of discretion cannot be underestimated. Discretion plays an important role at all levels of the network—from the use of discretion by citizens in deciding whether to call the police, to the use of discretion by police personnel in determining how to handle calls from the public, to the use of discretion by the prosecutor in deciding whether to prosecute a particular case, to the sentencing discretion of judges.
- Superimposed on the criminal justice network is the political structure of the society in which the network exists, and the influence of political decisions and considerations cannot be overlooked.

In the following pages, we have tried to take the practical aspects of criminal justice into consideration as we discuss the various components, procedures, and bases of criminal justice in the United States. We have attempted to define technical terms clearly when they are presented, and we have included numerous practical examples and highlights in an attempt to present the introductory student with a basic understanding of both the theoretical and practical aspects of the criminal justice network. These examples include, among others:

- "Intensive probation pays off"
- "Stench on the bench"
- "Rampart hasn't changed how criminal courts do business"
- "Juries, their powers under seige"
- "How Norfolk County aims to curb recidivism"
- "A boy caught in a legal travesty"
- "No jail for son who beat mother"
- NJ Att'y General: "We targeted minorities"

THE FOURTH EDITION

In addition to including the new "In the News" boxes identified above, we have made numerous other changes to this edition, which include:

- updated references
- discussion of recent cases which have attracted national attention
- coverage of recent trends and concerns in criminal justice

The Fourth edition also features:

- expanded discussion of ethics (Chapter 2)
- expanded discussion of some types of crimes (Chapters 3 and 4)
- discussion of the new federalism (Chapter 3)
- coverage of the rise in use of methamphetamines
- coverage of Internet crimes in our discussion of white collar offenses (Chapter 5)
- discussion of problem-oriented and community-oriented policing in Chapter 6 (a new chapter combining the old Chapters 6 and 7)
- Coverage of new issues in corrections (Chapter 12) and victim/witness rights (Chapter 11), including the rebirth of restorative justice

PEDAGOGICAL AIDS

To enhance learning, we have included the following devices in every chapter:

- chapter-opening vignettes to capture student interest
- chapter outlines to provide a road map to reading each chapter
- in-chapter "In the News" boxes to help students see the practical application of what they are reading
- end-of-chapter "Internet Activities" to encourage students to use the net as a research and learning tool
- end-of-chapter summaries and key terms lists to help students prepare for exams
- end-of-chapter "Critical Thinking Exercises" to encourage students to go beyond memorization of terms and concepts in their learning
- An instructor's manual, including testbank, is available

INSTRUCTOR SUPPLEMENTS

As a full service publisher of quality educational products, McGraw-Hill does much more than just sell textbooks. The company creates and publishes print, video, and digital supplements for students and instructors as well. This particular text is accompanied by the following instructor supplement:

- Instructor's Manual/Testbank—chapter outlines, discussion questions, a complete testbank, and more.

The Instructor's Manual/Testbank is provided free of charge to instructors. Orders of new (versus used) textbooks help McGraw-Hill defray the substantial cost of developing supplements like this. Please contact your local McGraw-Hill representative for more information on the supplements available with any of our texts.

IN APPRECIATION

A number of people have helped in the preparation of this book. For their encouragement and assistance, we would like to thank the late Dr. Donald J. Adamchak, Dr. William P. McCamey, Dr. Gene Scaramella, Dr. Michael H. Hazlett, Dr. Giri Raj Gupta, Professor Dennis C. Bliss, Dr. Michael Brown, Dr. Michael Parker, Dr. Paul Keys, and Professor Arrick Jackson.

For substantive contributions we wish to thank Professor Terry Campbell for his insightful contributions to the chapter on corrections, Professor Milo Miller who helped update the chapters on law, and Professor Jennifer Allen for her contributions in the area of restorative justice, and Professor Linda Ferrrell.

We also want to thank the reviewers of the fourth edition manuscript for their many helpful suggestions:

Charles Crawford—Western Michigan University
Patricia Campie—University of Arizona
Yenli Yeh—University of Virginia at Wise

We welcome your comments concerning the text.
SM-Cox1@wiu.edu
jwade@semovm.semo.edu

Contents

12   Corrections   264

The Criminal Justice Network

CHAPTER ONE

Criminal Justice in the United States:
A Network of Interaction

Police officers on bike patrol—a useful strategy for getting to know community residents.
Corbis Royalty Free Images/PictureQuest

J oey J. dropped out of school at age 16 because he found classes irrelevant to the world in which he lived. Joey never knew his father, and his mother worked long hours at a minimum wage job that provided no insurance, sick days, or vacation. She managed to keep Joey with her but had little time to spend with him. Joey tried to get a job after dropping out of school, but because of his age and lack of education, nothing legitimate was available. So Joey became a runner for a local drug dealer. He made good money, but within a month he was apprehended with a sizable quantity of drugs in his possession. The police tried to contact Joey's mother, but she was unable to leave her job without fear of being fired. A number of social service agencies were contacted, but none seemed to have exactly the right program for Joey. Seeing little choice, the police arrested Joey for possession of drugs.

The prosecutor, who happened to be up for reelection, was tough on drug offenders and had at his disposal a new drug law mandating prison time for possession. This law had been passed by the legislature because voters in the state were becoming increasingly concerned with the sale of drugs, wanted "something done about it," and brought political pressure on legislators. The judge, elected to office with the support of several legislators, found little evidence that Joey's circumstances warranted probation and sentenced him to the minimum mandatory time in a correctional facility for youth.

In prison, Joey learned a good deal about criminal behavior but little else. After his release, Joey again tried to find legitimate employment but now had a reputation for being a "hard case" because he had spent time in prison. Joey returned to the world he knew best to find employment and was again arrested, prosecuted, and convicted of drug-related offenses, this time as an adult. Joey spent the rest of his life in and out of prisons, never able to succeed in the legitimate economy and never able to avoid the police for long.

Key Terms

criminal justice network

territorial jealousy

crime control model

due process model

public

presumption of innocence

unofficial probation

justice

Chapter Outline

Criminal Justice as a Network of Overlapping Components
The Forgotten Component: The Public's Role in the Criminal Justice Network
Some Key Assumptions of Our Criminal Justice Network

CRIMINAL JUSTICE AS A NETWORK
OF OVERLAPPING COMPONENTS

The gap between the "ideal" criminal justice system as discussed in academic classes and the daily practice of criminal justice in the United States seems to be growing wider on a daily basis, as In the News, "Movin' On" illustrates. Among the questions being asked are: What kind of justice system do we have, or do we in fact have a system? Does the jury system work, or is it time to find an alternative? Are the police held to higher standards than the rest of us? Are any of us really protected by the Constitution? Are all decisions in the justice system ultimately political in nature? Is there no end to the discretion of criminal justice practitioners? In this chapter we begin to address some of these issues by exploring the assumptions on which the criminal justice system is based and the day-to-day realities by which the system operates.

Typical models of the criminal justice system show each component of the system receiving cases from, and passing cases on to, other components. Thus, the police process some alleged offenders and send them on to the prosecutor, who passes some on to court officials, who pass some on to correctional officials, who eventually return some to the society from which they originally came. All this is to be accomplished within a framework designed to protect the innocent and guarantee the rights of the accused. Although these models are not totally inaccurate, they are somewhat misleading in that they fail to indicate:

1. The routine pursuit of different, sometimes incompatible, goals by various network components.
2. The effects of feedback based on personal relationships inside and outside the criminal justice network.
3. The importance of political considerations.
4. The widespread, routine use of discretion at all levels of the network.

Many of these models lead us to focus on what the criminal justice system does or does not *do*, leading us to overlook the fact that it is not the system itself that acts or fails to act, but individuals who interact or fail to interact (subject, to be sure, to some structural constraints of human origin) to achieve differentially perceived goals. It is more realistic to think of a **criminal justice network,** consisting of a web of constantly changing relationships among individuals, some of whom are directly involved in criminal justice pursuits, others of whom are indirectly involved.

Perhaps the most familiar example of a network is the television or radio network in which stations share many programs, but each station also presents programs that are not aired by other stations in the network. Viewed from this perspective, the criminal justice network appears as a three-dimensional model in which the public, legislators, police, prosecutors, judges, and correctional officials are involved in interactions with one another and with others who are outside the traditionally conceived criminal justice system. The everyday business of criminal justice is accomplished, according to this model,

In the News

Movin' On, but Memories Will Stay

By Steve Warmbir

After more than three years of covering crime and the Cook County courts for the *Daily Herald*, I'm moving on to another newspaper.

Over that time, there have been startling jury verdicts, tales of injustice and stories of triumph.

Here's a brief overview of the more memorable moments in your criminal justice system.

@*@*@*

That nick was painful: Neal Allen had taken off his wedding ring and wristwatch as the jury filed in to deliver its verdict in Allen's first-degree murder trial.

Allen, a Palatine executive accused of killing his boss, figured he was going to prison.

Allen had stabbed and slashed his boss more than 40 times, and had only a nick on his leg, but claimed self-defense in his 1996 trial. The jury, though, accepted it, acquitting him of all charges in one of the most unusual verdicts ever at the Rolling Meadows courthouse.

@*@*@*

Why bring up the past?: Talk to Lizell Bryant, and he'll tell you he's not a violent man. Sure, he killed his wife and in-laws in 1981.

And, yes, he is accused of trying to kill wife No. 2 in her Des Plaines home in 1998.

But Bryant says it's unfair to see a pattern.

"Why bring up the past?" he asks.

So far, Bryant has not had bad luck with the judicial system.

In his first case, prosecutors wanted to give Bryant the needle, but he wound up serving seven years for killing three people.

In his second case, in which he was charged with trying to kill his second wife, he was convicted of a lesser charge but even that got thrown out after the judge granted him a new trial because of an error his attorney made. Bryant is awaiting a second trial on the charges.

@*@*@*

Let this be a lesson, guys: Rodolfo Tirado of Arlington Heights paid a steep price for having an affair with a married woman. Seven months in jail, to be precise.

Tirado was charged last year with criminal sexual assault, kidnapping and unlawful restraint.

Tirado's defense attorney argued the alleged victim was making up the charges to hide her affair with Tirado from her husband.

The woman didn't help her case when she recanted her allegations, then recanted her recantation. She also visited Tirado a few times in jail and destroyed trial evidence of

Continued

photographs showing her and Tirado together kissing.

The charges were dropped against Tirado.

@*@*@*

And how about . . . The Lake Zurich minister who said it was "God's will" to have an affair with a man's wife while giving him marriage counseling . . . Legendary Bleacher Bum Ronnie "Woo-Woo" Wickers triumphantly woowooing outside a Rolling Meadows courtroom when he was cleared of woowooing too loudly in Schaumburg . . . Cook County Judge James Ryan, who was caught under an avalanche of media attention for upholding a ticket against a pregnant woman speeding to the hospital to deliver a baby. Ryan caught more flack from another woman who said the judge had her held in his courtroom too long when she had to go to the bathroom. She didn't make it in time.

Chicago Daily Herald, *March 24, 2000, p. 1.*

through negotiations among any or all involved parties. In any given negotiation, the various parties may pursue the same or different goals. Interaction among concerned parties may be influenced by both overt (visible) and covert (hidden) pressures and considerations. Perhaps an example will help clarify this approach.

Suppose a drive-by shooting has occurred in a particular neighborhood. Certain segments of the public (those who live in the locality, for example) are likely to become alarmed and to demand that the police "do something." The mass media may publicize the case widely, bringing additional pressure on the police to find the offender, on the prosecutor to successfully prosecute the guilty party, on the judge to hand down a severe sentence, and, eventually, on parole board members not to grant parole. The police may want very badly to catch the offender to protect those who live in the community and to maintain or develop a positive public image. The prosecutor, who in addition to being concerned about protecting members of the community may be thinking about the effects of favorable or unfavorable publicity on an upcoming election, may want a conviction badly. Thus, both the police and the prosecutor are pursuing a common goal—crime control—but both are also pursuing additional, different goals as well. In addition, the police chief may use this case as a basis for requesting more resources, the public may demand more patrols, and political officials may call for the chief's dismissal for failing to prevent such incidents.

Let us suppose that the police arrest a person they think may have committed the crime discussed above, but they do not have what they consider a strong case. They believe they need a confession before they can present a reasonable case to the prosecutor. To obtain such a confession, they may pressure the alleged offender to talk to them so that they can clear the crime by arrest and relieve public pressure. At this point, the prosecutor may step in and tell the police not to use undue pressure, to see that the alleged offender clearly understands his or her rights, and to make certain that the arrestee has access to a lawyer if he or she wants one. These statements by the prosecutor may make it more difficult for the police to obtain their confession and may cause conflict between the police and the prosecutor. Still, both are pursuing the same goal—crime control. In our hypothetical case, the police are concerned primarily with obtaining the facts to control crime, while the prosecutor is also concerned with due process, which may at times make crime control more difficult.

Taking our example one step further, we might ask why the prosecutor would caution the police as indicated above. In the network approach to criminal justice, it becomes clear that the prosecutor is bringing the courts, political considerations, and public opinion into the interactive network. The United States Supreme Court justices have ruled that due process must be followed by all criminal justice network personnel; the Court's decisions have limited police practices concerning search, seizure, and interrogation. Further, these rulings are supposed to represent the will of the people as expressed in the First, Fourth, Fifth, and Fourteenth Amendments to the Constitution (see the Appendix). Of course, the manner in which the Constitution is interpreted at any given time depends, to some extent, on the composition of the Supreme Court, which depends on political appointments made by the president, who depends on votes from the public for obtaining office. Thus, we see that decisions in cases in other locales made by criminal justice personnel who have no knowledge of or concern with this particular case can, nonetheless, affect this case. Any case dealt with by the criminal justice network can be analyzed in this fashion, and a great many activities and decisions that otherwise appear to make little or no sense can be understood.

We believe the best way to view the criminal justice system is as a network of interrelated, but independent individuals who are subject to many internal and external pressures, and who work under (and are at the same time developing) a set of operating procedures in pursuit of similar, but not always identical, goals. While public and political influence, legal requirements, and discretionary justice pervade the entire network, each party in the network has goals and problems not shared by other parties. For example, the police are concerned with making arrests, the prosecutor with obtaining convictions, the judge with providing impartial trials, and correctional officials with custody and/or rehabilitation. Although the judge may also be concerned with rehabilitation and custody (in terms of sentencing), she or he is not directly concerned with the physical act of making an arrest, prosecutors are not directly concerned with keeping people in custody, and correctional officials are not directly concerned with obtaining convictions (except in incidents occurring within the prison walls). Each party, however, is indirectly concerned with what all the other parties do.

The following example may help make the network approach employed in this book easier to understand. Over the past several decades the relationships between drugs and crime have been emphasized by law enforcement and the media. Drugs have been portrayed as direct causes of crime (individuals behaving violently as a result of the influence of drugs) and indirect causes (individuals stealing to get money to buy drugs). As a result, powerful segments of the American public determined that something should be done about the "drug problem." These powerful (in terms of monetary and political resources) groups elected representatives who voted to pass new legislation making drug-related crimes subject to mandatory imprisonment. Prosecutors, judges, and corrections personnel, guided by these new laws, imprisoned numerous offenders who, while not involved in violent crimes, were in some way tied to drug possession, distribution, or manufacture. The police began seeking forfeiture of cars, boats, airplanes, and houses of those who were found to be in possession of illegal substances, and the courts became involved in deciding the legitimacy of these forfeiture procedures.

The number of drug-related convictions increased significantly, as did the size of the prison population. The vast majority of those imprisoned were not major buyers, importers, or sellers of drugs but the small-time criminals working for them, a point not lost on the media or the public. As the number of inmates receiving mandatory sentences for drug-related crimes grew, prisons became increasingly overcrowded.

In response, some inmates whose crimes were far more serious than those of the drug offenders were given early release to make room for those serving mandatory sentences. The media began to focus on offenses committed by those receiving early release, and the public became concerned about dangerous offenders being set free. To avoid further overcrowding, prosecutors and judges began to use alternative charges to deal with drug-related offenders to avoid mandatory sentencing. Law enforcement officials, taking a hint from prosecutors and the courts, began to modify their behavior with respect to drug-related behavior, and politicians began to reconsider legislation requiring mandatory sentences for drug offenders. The public began to breathe easier because fewer serious offenders were receiving early release, and the media found new issues to present to the public.

Criminal justice, as the example above clearly indicates, is not a one-way street with cases and information flowing only in one direction. It consists of a network of relationships in which any party can both influence and be influenced by any or all other parties, and all may be influenced by public opinion and other factors that are not directly involved in criminal justice, as indicated in In the News, "No Justice."

Criminal justice, in this respect, is like an intricate spiderweb. Pulls or pressures on one part of the web may cause changes in all other parts. Special interest groups define socially harmful activity and persuade voters to elect political officials who represent their interests; the performance of these officials is evaluated in the area of criminal justice. In a variety of ways, both

In the News

NO JUSTICE IN A SYSTEM THAT WON'T ADMIT ERRORS

By Molly Ivins

Have you noticed that the system of criminal justice in this country is shutting down, piece by piece by piece?

DNA identification, which has become more sophisticated by the year, is the greatest advance in criminal detection since the fingerprint. It has enabled the system to put away criminals who otherwise would have gotten off scot-free and to find perps years after the crime when their DNA shows up after an unrelated arrest. Short of a truth serum, this is the best thing that could happen for the criminal justice system.

The problem is, DNA evidence sometimes shows that the system messed up and nailed the wrong person for a crime. In fact, it happens depressingly often.

The notorious inability of prosecutors to admit that they are ever wrong is a fact of life. What is far more horrifying is the refusal of judges and courts to look at evidence that proves innocence. Can you imagine how that must feel—to be in prison for a crime you didn't commit and to finally be able to prove it, only to have a court refuse to consider the evidence?

Most of this is a consequence of a noxious law that Congress rushed through after the Oklahoma City bombing.

Called the Anti-Terrorism and Effective Death Penalty Act of 1996, the law was aimed at the ability of federal judges to second-guess state courts and at the ability of prisoners to file endless habeas corpus claims challenging the constitutionality of their convictions. ("Habeas corpus" is a Latin phrase meaning "you have the body" and goes back hundreds of years in common law as well as being in the Constitution. It means that if you can show you were unfairly tried, you have a remedy through the courts.)

True, the right has been abused for nitpicking purposes by some lawyers, but to effectively abolish the right is a dreadful abrogation of freedom. Where in the world are the militia folks now that we need them? Where are all those right-wingers who claim freedom as their most cherished possession?

The trouble with the '96 law is that it was poorly written and has been subject to conflicting interpretations by the lower courts. The law says that a federal judge can reverse a state court conviction only if it was contrary to federal law or if it applied federal law in an "unreasonable" way.

As Justice Ruth Bader Ginsburg pointed out, reasonable jurists always disagree on constitutional issues.

Continued

The new film *The Hurricane*, with Denzel Washington, is about a case in point. Rubin "Hurricane" Carter, a contender for the middleweight boxing title, was wrongfully convicted of a 1966 triple murder. He spent 19 years in prison before he was finally released.

The movie depicts the conviction as a frame-up by one racist cop, but as Selwyn Rabb, who originally covered the story for the *New York Times*, wrote: "The actual story is more harrowing because it exposes an underlying frailty in a criminal justice system that convicted Mr. Carter not once but twice. The convictions were obtained not by a lone, malevolent investigator but by a network of detectives, prosecutors and judges who countenanced the suppression and tainting of evidence and the injection of racial bias into the courtroom."

Under current interpretations of the 1996 law, Hurricane Carter would not be free today.

A "Frontline" documentary on PBS, "The Case for Innocence," gives the most chilling case histories in a stupid and tragic trend in criminal justice.

The most thoughtful comment in the documentary came from a law professor concerned about the criminal justice system's refusal to consider its own errors. He pointed out that in most other systems, when something goes horribly wrong—a plane falls from the sky, a type of car begins bursting into flames, a hospital patient dies from gross malpractice—there is a system in place to deal with the error. There are investigations, reports and ultimately corrections made to prevent recurrence.

In the criminal justice system, there are only denials and strenuous efforts to prevent the exculpatory evidence from being presented in court. The ease with which our criminal justice system can nail the wrong person has been painfully demonstrated time and again.

Perhaps the saddest and most terrifying finding in "The Case for Innocence" is that in the 60-some-odd cases in which innocence has been proved by DNA and the accused finally freed, none of the cases has been reopened.

Chicago Sun-Times, January 14, 2000, p. 41.

direct and indirect, the goals of one component (the police) are transmitted to the other two (courts and corrections). Indirect communication is often the means employed, even though more direct communication might improve cooperation among components and the overall effectiveness of the network. Suppose, for example, a particular judge feels that personal use of marijuana should not result in criminal penalties for the user. For a variety of reasons, she does not directly communicate her feelings to the prosecutor; instead, she imposes no penalties on marijuana users brought before her. After unsuccessfully prosecuting several such cases, the prosecutor "gets the message" and refuses to prosecute such cases before this judge. For a variety of reasons, the

prosecutor may not communicate his or her disinterest in such cases to the police chief, whose officers continue to arrest marijuana users. Eventually, after
police officers see that the prosecutor will no longer prosecute such cases, they
stop making such arrests. The message has been transmitted, but a considerable amount of time and resources may have been wasted by using this indirect method of communication. Similarly, cooperation among the components
might have been improved considerably by a straightforward discussion of
the parties involved, but political considerations, personality differences, or
territorial jealousy (the desire to protect one's turf from others) often hamper
such discussion.

One of the major difficulties with viewing criminal justice in the United
States as a cooperating, goal-sharing, communicating network is that such a
network operates best when consensus about the goals of the network exists.
In our society, such consensus exists with respect to certain offenses, but is
lacking with respect to many others and with respect to the procedures to be
employed in the pursuit of alleged offenders. On the one hand, many citizens
and practitioners favor the **crime control model,** which allows for the arrest
and prosecution of individuals who are known to be factually guilty of committing a crime. On the other hand, many prefer the **due process model,**
which requires that evidence of guilt presented in court be obtained according
to legal guidelines. For instance, the police might receive a tip from an anonymous caller who states that a specific individual living in a specific hotel room
is manufacturing methamphetamine (meth) in the room. Using the crime control model, the police break down the door to the room, find meth and the
products used to manufacture it, arrest and charge the offender, and use the
meth as evidence in the ensuing trial. Under the due process model, the police
must demonstrate that the tip came from a reliable informant, obtain a proper
search warrant, and maintain a proper chain of evidence, or the meth will be
inadmissible as evidence in court and the defendant will be acquitted. That is,
even though the defendant was factually guilty of possessing and manufacturing the meth, he is not legally guilty because the procedures established to
safeguard the rights of citizens were violated in this case. The emphasis on
crime control versus due process shifts with changes in political administra-
tions, public opinion, and the judiciary, demonstrating the importance of understanding criminal justice as a network and the lack of consensus as to how
best to proceed in dealing with crime and criminals.

Similarly, when the public is uncertain about the desirability of rehabilitation, the enforcement of morality, or the best way to punish offenders, it is difficult for practitioners to cooperate and share goals. Viewing criminal justice
as a web of interacting parties, each with a set of goals that may or may not all
be compatible with those of others, makes it easier to understand how such
events can occur. This view is especially important when we realize that we
are dealing not with a small number of criminal justice agencies but with
thousands of agencies—each with its own regional variations and each with
its own personnel. In addition, we must consider perhaps the most important
party to any criminal justice network, the public.

THE FORGOTTEN COMPONENT: THE PUBLIC'S ROLE IN THE CRIMINAL JUSTICE NETWORK

The **public** is the most important part of the criminal justice network for a variety of reasons. Before discussing these reasons, we should point out that the term "public" is somewhat misleading. Actually, we are dealing not with one large homogeneous group called a public, but with thousands of different publics. These publics are divided by factors such as geographical area, race, gender, age, social class, and degree of adherence to law. Many of these publics have unique interests and concerns that separate them on most issues from other publics. In short, there is no one, united, consensual group of citizens who make up a single public. Citizens comprise a variety of different publics. As we shall see, this heterogeneity is extremely important for criminal justice. At least as important, however, is the fact that, with respect to any given issue, many of these publics are apathetic about the criminal justice network. A great deal of what happens in the name of criminal justice goes largely unnoticed by most citizens, and pressures to modify the network or the activities that occur within it are often brought to bear by small, vocal groups who have an interest in a particular issue, but who become apathetic again once that issue is resolved.

No matter which of the many publics we are talking about, it is important to recognize the role that each may play in the criminal justice network. First, the vast majority of social control in any society is performed not by the police and courts, but by various segments of the public (families and peer groups, for example). Second, these publics provide resources for and evaluations of

Members of the public frequently exercise their right to protest.
Mark Downey/Lucid Images/PictureQuest

the entire network. Without public support, police, court, and correctional officials would be helpless to achieve their goals. Consider, for example, the
helplessness of the Los Angeles police in the aftermath of the announcement
of the Rodney King verdict. Black citizens took to the streets in protest, loot-
ing, burning, and occasionally attacking nonblacks while the police were
largely invisible. Absent public support, the police cannot enforce the laws or
maintain order. Further, if citizens refuse to provide information to the police,
the police (a largely reactive body) cannot perform their duties. Successful
prosecution (or defense) is impossible if members of the public refuse to testify. Ex-convicts cannot be reintegrated into society without the cooperation of
the citizenry. Without financial resources provided by the public, none of the
criminal justice agencies could hire new personnel, develop new programs, or
improve efficiency. From beginning to end, then, there is no doubt that the
public (all the many publics or segments) plays a major role in criminal justice
and should not be overlooked when we discuss the criminal justice network,
since each segment wants and expects something from representatives of that
network. Some want:

1. Specific types of laws enforced (e.g., liquor violations).
2. Specific types of offenders taken into custody (troublesome youth).
3. Their property returned.
4. A police report so that insurance claims for lost or stolen property can be
   settled.
5. The elimination of the death penalty.

   In general, the various publics want their real or imagined problems to be
dealt with and resolved officially. In short, publics are involved in the criminal
justice network in a variety of ways, and this involvement (or lack of involvement) is crucial to the functioning of the network.

SOME KEY ASSUMPTIONS OF OUR CRIMINAL JUSTICE NETWORK

To understand how that network actually functions (as compared with how it
functions in theory), we need to look at some of the assumptions on which the
network is said to be based. These assumptions include the following:

1. The components of the network cooperate and share similar goals.
2. The network operates according to a set of formal procedural rules to
   ensure uniform treatment of individuals.
3. Each person accused of a crime receives due process and is presumed
   innocent until proven guilty.
4. Each accused person receives a speedy, public trial before an impartial
   jury of his or her peers.
5. Each accused person is represented by competent legal counsel, as is the
   state.

6. Innocence or guilt is determined on the basis of the facts.
7. The outcome of criminal justice procedures is justice.

We have already dealt with the first assumption—the cooperative, goal-sharing network—and found that cooperation is sometimes lacking and that the various components often have individual, in addition to collective, goals. We will simply add that each component in the network is continually competing with all other components for budgetary dollars.

The second assumption is that the criminal justice network operates according to a set of formal procedural rules to ensure uniform treatment of individuals. To the extent that this assumption is true, race, social class, and gender should have no bearing on the manner in which cases are handled. Similarly, each individual being processed should go through the same clearly delineated steps. There is, however, considerable evidence to indicate that blacks and whites, males and females, and middle-class citizens and lower-class citizens receive differential treatment in the criminal justice network. Blacks in particular face discrimination in the system of criminal justice, beginning with arrest and continuing through incarceration (Mann, 1993; Tonry, 1994). While not all authorities agree (Wilbanks, 1987), some argue that the poor and minorities are more likely to be arrested, less likely to have an attorney immediately, more likely to be represented by a public defender than retained counsel, and less likely to make bail (McGarrell, 1993; Tonry, 1994).

It is clear that not all defendants go through the same procedural steps when they enter the system. Some are handled by administrative review boards rather than criminal courts (e.g., white-collar offenders). Some are prosecuted, others are not. Some are involved in plea bargaining, others are not. Some are convicted and sentenced to prison, while others who are convicted of the same type of offense are not. As we shall see, public opinion, political power, and the exercise of discretion may affect what happens at all levels of the criminal justice network. Assumption number two, then, is at least questionable.

Assumption number three concerns due process and the **presumption of innocence.** No doubt, due process applies in theory to all accused individuals, but what is to guarantee that due process is observed in a practice, for example, like plea bargaining? While several formal procedures have been developed to help ensure that due process is observed in plea negotiations, a great deal of the negotiating remains largely invisible. The more invisible the negotiations, the greater the chance for manipulation by those involved. The fact that guilt is often presumed is apparent in the practice of **unofficial probation** for alleged juvenile offenders. The juvenile is told by the police, juvenile probation officer, or prosecutor that she or he must meet certain requirements for a specified period of time "or else," which means that the juvenile will be processed through the juvenile court if she or he does not agree to the unofficial probation. Note that the juveniles involved have not been adjudicated delinquent, the facts of the case have not been heard by the court, and the evidence possessed by the authorities is sometimes contested. Where, we might ask, does due process fit into such an arrangement? Nonetheless, such programs exist and are encouraged in many jurisdictions.

With respect to the presumption of innocence, we might simply note that, in general, the police do not believe they arrest innocent people and prosecutors do not believe they prosecute innocent people. There is also evidence to indicate that public defenders do not assume or care whether their clients are innocent (Livingston, 1996, p. 460). It may be that judges and juries presume the defendant to be innocent, but it certainly appears that others in the network assume the defendant is guilty.

Assumption number four, dealing with speedy, public trial before a jury of peers, is clearly questionable. A tremendous backlog of cases ensures that a speedy trial is more an ideal than the reality in many jurisdictions. Since the vast majority of trials involve a guilty plea before a judge, the notions of a "public" trial and a "jury of peers" are called into question. Even when jury trials do occur, the issue of whether the jury consists of peers remains unresolved because of the routine exclusion or excusal of certain types of jurors.

With respect to the assumption that the accused and the state are competently represented, many observers have noted that a significant proportion of lawyers practicing in criminal courts are not competent to do so. Strier (2000, p. 122) states, "It is no small curiosity that our legal system espouses equality of treatment (equal justice); yet our trial mechanism, more than any other, skews trial outcomes in favor of the side with the better attorney and more money." Mann (1993) argues that even if public defenders are effective, their clients typically believe they would be better served by private counsel. As Estrich (1998, p. 97) indicates, "The right to counsel guaranteed by the Constitution only guarantees the defendant a warm body. The issue for a poor defendant . . . is whether he'll even get to meet his lawyer for an interview" before going to court.

Assumption number six is that the facts of each case will be used to determine innocence or guilt, yet many claim that actual guilt or innocence is the least important factor in determining legal innocence or guilt. Instead, they claim, the resources of the state and defense counsel; the style, presentation, and knowledge of the attorneys involved; and various public and political pressures often determine guilt or innocence.

Finally, assumption number seven concerns the notion of **justice.** If the network or the product of the network is perceived as just by most citizens, we can expect considerable public support for the network. If, however, some groups believe that justice is not uniformly, fairly, or equally applied, we can expect opposition to the network.

In a society such as ours, where citizens are free to voice their dissent and dissatisfaction (within broad limits), it is easy to see that justice is differentially perceived. Those who have little (power, money, status, etc.) often perceive less justice than those who have a great deal. Members of minorities who have been treated as second-class citizens (officially or unofficially) tend to view the network as less just than do members of the dominant group. Both of these points are illustrated by the O. J. Simpson murder case. Because of his considerable wealth, Simpson was able to hire a "dream team" of attorneys who used every conceivable strategy to convince the jury to acquit. When the verdict was announced, it was hailed as a victory by many minority group members and received with a sense of disbelief by many whites.

Victims of crimes and their relatives and loved ones often see little justice in plea bargaining or probation. Offenders seldom see justice in the balance of power between themselves and the state. Justice is often exemplified by the courtroom scene in which the champion of the state (the prosecutor) and the champion of the defense do battle before a jury of 12 (perhaps fewer) "tried and true" persons who decide innocence or guilt on the basis of a presentation of facts with the aid of an impartial mediator (the judge). Today, such scenes are rare, probably occurring in less than 10 percent of all criminal trials. The reality of the criminal trial today involves no jury but a plea negotiated between the prosecutor and defense counsel with the consent of the accused and, sometimes, the judge. In those cases involving jury trials, counsel for the prosecution and defense would each like the jury to believe that he or she is just presenting the facts. In reality, both the prosecution and the defense present the "facts" in such a way as to make their own case look better and to sway the jury. We are all aware that jurors are not chosen simply on the basis of their good intentions. The media, at least in cases receiving national attention, may also have a major impact on both the trial and the perception of justice in general. Whether or not one believes justice is done also depends on the role one plays in the system (e.g., victim, witness, or offender). Again, the O. J. Simpson case is instructive as an example of the points outlined above.

Justice, then, appears to be largely in the eyes of the beholder. Whether or not a particular network for dealing with criminals is seen as just depends, in part at least, on the extent to which the network operates according to the assumptions on which it is based. If these assumptions are not followed in practice, a discrepancy is soon observed between the real and the ideal. As a result, citizens may not know what to expect from the network, may view it as operating on other than an equitable basis, and may believe that justice depends more on access to knowledge and resources required to beat the system than on actual guilt or innocence. Another possible conclusion is that the network simply does not work at all and is not worth supporting. Consider the following examples that call into question many of the assumptions on which our justice network is based.

The videotaped beating of Rodney King by Los Angeles police officers in the early 1990s led to an acquittal of the officers involved in criminal court, but to a later conviction on civil rights violations in federal court. (Police officers involved were acquitted of criminal charges by a jury in a venue different from the one in which the event occurred, but were later convicted by a federal jury of violating King's civil rights.) This was followed by the criminal court acquittal of O. J. Simpson on murder charges, based, it appears, in part on alleged police misconduct. (If the police can't be trusted to obey the law, should violators be acquitted whatever the evidence?) Simpson was subsequently convicted on wrongful death charges in civil court. (Does wealth provide protection for some in criminal court? Wouldn't someone with fewer resources have been convicted of these crimes? Is race really the overriding issue here, as the response to the acquittal seems to suggest?) The actions of federal authorities at Waco and Ruby Ridge led to considerable criticism of federal law enforcement officials. (Are government officials honest? Were these politically motivated and condoned attacks?) The state of Illinois suspended capital punishment in 1999 as the result of the disclosure of errors and possible police and prosecutorial misconduct. (In convicting offenders and sentencing them to death, have we been sending innocent people to their deaths? Are prosecutors and the police involved in conspiracies?) In Philadelphia, the convictions of dozens of people were overturned as the result of police misconduct and, as we go to press with this book, similar allegations have been made concerning the police in Los Angeles. Abner Louima was sodomized by New York City police officers, one of whom was convicted. New York City police officers also fired 41 rounds at Amadou Diallo, who was holding a wallet, not a weapon, in his hands. Nineteen of the rounds hit Diallo, causing his death. The officers involved were acquitted in a jury trial after the trial had been moved out of New York City to Albany. (Can we trust police officers anywhere? Can we trust the courts to oversee police conduct? Are those segments of the public lacking in political clout routinely treated differently by the police, prosecutors, and judges?) Simultaneously, methamphetamine production appeared to be growing out of control and school shootings were a regular part of the news. (Can't we even protect our children in school? Is the violence attracting headlines today so different from the violence that occurs in inner-city schools on a continuing basis? Do we care less about one than the other?) The government handling of the Elian Gonzalez case was roundly criticized by the media and the political opposition, as well as by some members of the Cuban community. (How did we single out this boy to be returned to Cuba when so many Cuban refugees are allowed to stay? Do parental rights prevail, or was appeasing Castro the intent of those actions?) Efforts to achieve gun control led to concessions from Smith and Wesson, but concealed-carry laws advance in several states. (Do we want gun control, or do we want everyone to carry a weapon?) Last, but surely not least, the president of the United States, in politically charged proceedings, was impeached by the House of Representatives on charges stemming from alleged sexual activities in the White House and the subsequent attempt to conceal the activity, but the Senate failed to indict him. (It may be all right to have extramarital sex in the White House, but is it all right to go on national television and lie to the American public about what happened? Did justice or politics prevail, or are the two inseparable?)

In our critical look at some of the key assumptions concerning criminal justice in the United States, our intent has not been to convince you that the network does not work. Rather, it has been to point out that the network often does not work in the fashion we say it does or should. As we proceed through this book, we hope you will continue to question the workings of the criminal justice network, and we hope you will continually compare what you know about the network with the material presented.

In the chapters that follow, keeping in mind certain guidelines will help you comprehend both the ideal and the reality of the criminal justice network. Unquestionably, one of the most important factors to keep in mind is the set of legal statutes and court and administrative decisions that spell out the formal procedures that guide the system. At the same time, to analyze activities within the criminal justice network, it is important to examine the influence of the media, public opinion, political factors, and discretionary justice. Unless we focus on these areas, much of what happens in the criminal justice network will be difficult to comprehend. Why, for example, do we characterize the Supreme Court (generally thought to be the most impartial, scholarly court in the United States) as liberal or conservative? Are political considerations important in this highest of courts? If so, in what ways? And what are some of the effects of such considerations?

Similarly, we might ask why white-collar offenders (who, by many estimates, cost the U.S. public more in terms of dollars annually than robbers, burglars, and other thieves) are infrequently handled by criminal courts? Do the various publics view white-collar offenders as criminals? If not, why not? And what are the implications for offenders and society?

To what extent are the police accountable for "adjusting" cases on the street or in the station? To whom are prosecutors accountable for their decisions concerning prosecution? Why do great inequities in sentencing occur among judges? Is discretion a normal and/or necessary part of criminal justice?

Satisfying answers to these and other questions can seldom be found simply by referring to formal procedures, laws, or regulations. References to these formalized procedures need to be supplemented by looking behind the scenes to determine how specific decisions are made within the broad framework of criminal justice. This can best be accomplished by using the network approach.

Summary

1. In this chapter, we have contrasted the real and the ideal of some aspects of criminal justice in the United States. We may have assumed the existence of a system that is more orderly and coordinated than the reality, which may better be viewed as a network of individuals with a diversity of goals.

2. There is little doubt that the police, the courts, and corrections form an interacting network in which changes in one component have clear implications for the other components.

3. The public is an important, perhaps the most important, component of the criminal justice network. What we generally think of as the public actually consists of many different publics with varied interests and concerns, or with no interests or concerns at all, with respect to criminal justice. It is the combination of these publics that supports and evaluates (or fails to support or evaluate) criminal justice agencies and programs.

4. Many of the assumptions on which the criminal justice network is thought to be based are questionable at best in practice.

5. Justice means different things to different people. Whether justice is done in a particular case depends on whether we take the perspective of the defendant, the victim, the police officer, or the jury. Justice, in the ideal sense as the outcome of a battle between two champions before a mediator and a jury, is the exception rather than the rule in criminal cases in the United States.

6. Several important factors are involved in understanding the criminal justice network and its operations. Public opinion, political considerations, media feedback, and the exercise of discretion are important factors in the day-to-day operations of the criminal justice network and should be recognized as such.

Key Terms Defined

criminal justice network   A web of constantly changing relationships among individuals involved more or less directly in the pursuit of criminal justice.

territorial jealousy   A concern with protecting the turf of one's own agency; sometimes makes cooperation among agencies difficult or impossible.

crime control model   A model for procedures to be employed in the pursuit of justice; based on factual guilt.

due process model   A model for procedures to be employed in the pursuit of justice; based on establishing factual guilt while adhering to legal guidelines.

public   Thousands of different groups divided by characteristics such as age, race, gender, adherence to law, social class, and geographic area; often mistakenly regarded as a cohesive whole, or "the public."

presumption of innocence   The belief that an accused is innocent until proven guilty; often lacking among police, prosecutors, and defense counselors.

unofficial probation   Probation imposed prior to a determination of guilt or innocence.

justice   The belief that various parties involved in a dispute get more or less what they deserve. To some extent, this belief depends on the role of the person doing the perceiving (e.g., is he or she the victim, the offender, or a witness?).

Critical Thinking Exercises

1. What are some of the advantages of viewing criminal justice as a network instead of using a more traditional model?
2. Do all the various components of the criminal justice network have identical goals? Similar goals? Overlapping goals?
3. Why are politics, discretion, and the public important components of the criminal justice network?

Internet Exercise

In this chapter we discussed a network approach to criminal justice. To better understand the network approach you are encouraged to visit the website of the National Criminal Justice Commission (NCJC), a section of the National Center on Institutions and Alternatives at *http://www.ncianet.org/ncia/ncjc.html*.

1. At the opening menu, click on and read the history of the commission. Using the history and the biographies of the members, available from the NCJC menu, discuss whether or not the NCJC represents a network approach to criminal justice.
2. From the NCJC menu, click on the recommendations section. Read all the recommendations; then turn specifically to numbers 1 and 6. Reread those recommendations. Discuss the impact on the public and other criminal justice components if these two recommendations are followed.
3. Now click on the summary of findings. Scroll down to the section on expenditures. How does the competition for government funds create territorial jealousies with other social service agencies?

References

Estrich, S. (1998). *Getting away with murder.* Cambridge, MA: Harvard University Press.

Livingston, J. (1996). *Crime and criminology* (2nd ed.). Upper Saddle River, NJ: Prentice Hall.

Mann, C. R. (1993). *Unequal justice: A question of color.* Indianapolis: University of Indiana Press.

McGarrell, E. F. (1993). Trends in racial disproportionality in juvenile court processing: 1985–1989. *Crime and Delinquency, 39* (1), 29–48.

Strier, F. (2000). Adversarial justice. In J. L. Victor, (Ed.), *Annual editions: Criminal justice 00/01* (24th ed.), pp. 116–23. Sluice Dock, Guilford, CN: Dushkin/McGraw-Hill.

Tonry, M. (1994). Racial politics, racial disparities, and the war on crime. *Crime and Delinquency, 40* (4), 475–94.

Wilbanks, W. (1987). *The myth of a racist criminal justice system.* Pacific Grove, CA: Brooks/Cole.

Suggested Readings

Cole, G. F., & Gertz, M. G. (1998). *The criminal justice system: Politics and policies* (7th ed.). Belmont, CA: West/Wadsworth.

Klofas, J., & Stojkovic, S. (1995). *Crime and justice in the year 2010.* Belmont, CA: Wadsworth.

Marshall, T. (2000, December 13). Drug war is much like Prohibition. *The Houston Chronicle*, p. 35A.

Mehren, E. (2000, December 14). National perspective; crime; death penalty case: Will of which people? *Los Angeles Times*, p. 5A.

Muraskin, R., & Roberts, A. R. (1999). *Visions for change: Crime and justice in the twenty-first century.* Upper Saddle River, NJ: Prentice Hall.

Neubauer, D. W. (2001). *Debating crime: Rhetoric and reality.* Belmont, CA: Wadsworth/Thompson Learning.

Ralston, R. W. (1999). Economy and race: Interactive determinants of property crime in the United States, 1958–1995: Reflections on the supply of property crime. *American Journal of Economics and Sociology, 58* (3), 405–34.

CHAPTER TWO

Politics, Discretion, Ethics, and the Criminal Justice Network

Criminal justice is always practiced within a political context.
John McCoy/Los Angeles Daily News/Corbis Sygma

A junior high school teacher was assigning group projects to her social studies students. One of the groups was assigned to gather information on the relationship between law and politics and relate what they found to the rest of the class. In an attempt to stimulate their thoughts, the teacher initiated their group project by defining politics for them and providing them with some current examples of the pervasive nature of politics in criminal justice by discussing the 1994 crime bill and the politics involved in appointing and electing key criminal justice officials.

Hadji, a foreign exchange student, started the group discussion by relating his observations on how law was formed in the United States. He was enthusiastic about a system that provided input from local citizens and remarked that in other parts of the world, law was created by a very small minority and resulted in serious conflict between the government and the police.

The class appreciated Hadji's analysis but thought they would make a greater impact if their discussion focused on a local issue. Their teacher had mentioned the relationship between power, authority, and discretion, and they wanted to apply those concepts to the issue of underage consumption of alcohol. The students noted that state legislatures had the power to establish the minimum drinking age; however, the authority for enforcing those laws rested with the police, prosecutors, and judges of the criminal justice network. They noted that public pressure often led to more rigid enforcement and that some police officers chose simply to pour out the alcohol and escort the violators home while others strictly enforced the law. One member of the group recognized that prosecutors could dismiss or plea-bargain cases, and another pointed out the latitude judges had in imposing sentences.

From their discussion the students were able to develop a presentation that recognized the politics of developing and enforcing laws that affected their local community.

Key Terms

politics

independent counsel

power

testilying

plea bargaining

ethics

authority

discretion

full enforcement

selective enforcement

Chapter Outline

Politics in Criminal Justice
 The Pervasive Influence of Politics: From the Law to the Police and Courts to Corrections
 Power, Authority, and Politics
 Recognizing the Consequences of Politics in the Criminal Justice Network

POLITICS IN CRIMINAL JUSTICE

According to Estrich (1998, p. 65), "The best that can be said of the political debate about crime in America is that it has nothing to do with crime. Politically speaking, crime is a values issue; the value is toughness . . . No one tells the truth, and the political dishonesty is distorting and destroying the system."

The relationship between law and politics has been recognized since ancient times. Yet it took the social conflicts of the 1960s and 1970s and the intense reaction to violent crime in the early 1990s for us to recognize the fact that criminal justice reflects the values of those individuals and groups with political power. In fact, among the agencies that lend themselves most readily to political manipulation are those of the criminal justice network (Chambliss, 1994; Cole & Gertz, 1998). Crime and justice are clearly public policy issues (recall the example from Chapter 1 on mandatory sentencing laws). As the headlines reflect more, or more severe, crimes, the public calls upon political leaders to "do something." In many cases, politicians respond by saying what they believe the public wants to hear, whether or not what they promise is likely to have any dramatic impact on crime (Walker, 1998, p. 14). Conservative politicians have been most successful in this respect over the years as they advocated a law-and-order approach and get-tough policies. Nonetheless, Bill Clinton used support of a national police corps and of various gun control measures as a way to neutralize the conservative approaches of both George Bush and Bob Dole in 1992 and 1996. As Walker (1998, p. 17) points out, "Nonsense about crime is politically nonpartisan."

There is a tendency when discussing the relationships between politics and criminal justice to focus on the negative aspects of those relationships. This is true perhaps because cases involving political corruption or manipulation of the criminal justice network for personal gain receive a great deal more attention in our society than the day-to-day influence of politics on the network. A moment's reflection, however, is all that is required to note that political input into the criminal justice network is both necessary and desirable in a democratic society. The intermingling of politics and criminal justice is characteristic of all known societies and so may be considered perfectly normal. In fact, a crucial distinction between totalitarian and free nations is that although both develop criminal justice networks controlled by government, governments in totalitarian societies often acknowledge no accountability, while in free societies, criminal justice practitioners are answerable to democratically elected political bodies. The recent hearings in the federal legislature focusing on the actions of federal law enforcement officers in the Waco, Ruby Ridge, and Elian Gonzalez cases clearly illustrate this principle of accountability.

The Pervasive Influence of Politics: From the Law to the Police and Courts to Corrections

Law is not written in a vacuum; rather, it is the result of political action. **Politics** may be defined as the process by which tangible (material) and symbolic rewards or resources are differentially distributed or allocated. According to Lasswell (1958) politics is concerned with who gets what, when, and how.

As we indicate throughout this book, criminal justice practitioners work in a network of reciprocal relationships, many of which are shaped by political considerations or are directly political. As Cole (1993, p. 4) indicates, "the confluence of law, administration, and politics results in a system in which officials who are sensitive to the political process make decisions at various points concerning the arrest, charges, conviction, and sentences of defendants." At one level, we are all aware of the importance of political parties in determining who the prosecutors, judges, police chiefs, and wardens will be who staff our criminal justice network. But just how important are political considerations in the day-to-day functioning of the network, and in what ways are they important? In its application, isn't the law supposed to be nonpolitical? Isn't everyone supposed to be treated the same under the law?

In his study of the relationship between politics and the police, James Q. Wilson (1968) found that there was little direct, day-to-day political influence on the police in the communities he examined. However, he found that the political culture of the communities was very important in determining the style of law enforcement employed, the type of chief selected, and the nature of departmental activities and policy. Alpert and Dunham (1997, p. 93) point out that politics are integral to any police operation. Personal politics involves using influence for personal gain, while community politics involves democratic control over the police. While the former may cause a variety of problems, the latter is essential in our society.

Observations indicate that the political form of city government (commissioner, mayor/council, city manager) makes a great deal of difference in the extent to which politics permeates police departments. On the one hand, the commissioner form of government places a political figure, who may or may not be acquainted with the complexities of police operations, at the top of the police administrative hierarchy. On the other hand, a professional city manager may make political intervention into police operations less likely. In the case of Elian Gonzalez, for example, Mayor Joe Carollo ordered City Manager Donald Warshaw to fire Police Chief William O'Brien, who had failed to tip off the mayor concerning the raid by federal authorities that removed Elian from the home of his uncle and returned him to the custody of his father. Warshaw refused to fire O'Brien, and Carollo then fired Warshaw. O'Brien then quit as chief of police, "denouncing Carollo as 'divisive and destructive' " (Hosenball, Isikoff, & Contreras, 2000, p. 32). In fact, this case illustrates as well as any the impact of local actions on the entire system. As you can see from In the News, "There They Go Again," the removal of Elian from his uncle's home in Miami (local), based on a court order (federal), led to political comment at the local, state, and national levels and to the threat of congressional hearings.

Regardless of the form of government involved, police, probation, correctional, and court administrators are dependent on the political figures mentioned above for resources. Personnel, equipment, salaries, and benefits are all negotiated through the political representatives of citizens. At the same time, of course, these criminal justice practitioners themselves, as voters and citizens, can influence the outcome of elections and thereby have a voice in selecting the political figures with whom they will negotiate.

We are all familiar with the misuses of political power in relation to police departments. Politicians who use, or attempt to use, the prestige of office to place themselves above the law have become infamous, particularly in recent decades. There are also able politicians who seek office to attempt to correct some of the wrongs that have been uncovered in police departments, courts, or correctional facilities. The police are influenced by political considerations in yet another way. The cases that they prepare must eventually be transferred to the prosecutor for further processing; thus, the policies and desires of the prosecutor influence the kinds of cases sent forward by the police, as well as the manner in which such cases are prepared.

The prosecutor is first and foremost a political figure. Prosecutors are political actors of consequence because they are generally elected with party support, they have patronage jobs at their disposal, and they exercise considerable discretion. Prosecutors are tied both to the internal politics of the criminal justice network and to local, state, or national political organizations. Since the discretionary powers of the prosecutor are considerable, he or she may be persuaded to take political advantage of the criminal justice position. So charges may be dropped to avoid the possibility of losing difficult cases (and thereby political support), disclosures of wrongdoing by political opponents may be made at opportune moments, and decisions about the types of crimes to be prosecuted may be made for strictly political reasons. A good example of the relationship between the office of prosecutor and politics is the appointment of an **independent counsel** at the federal level. When a sitting president is to be investigated for possible wrongdoing, the attorney general of the United States would normally be in charge of the investigation. However, because the president appoints the attorney general, it is feared the political connections between the president (the attorney general's immediate boss and political benefactor) and the attorney general may interfere with a complete investigation. The law allows the appointment of a private attorney to conduct the investigation in such cases. Even under these circumstances, however, there is

In the News

THERE THEY GO AGAIN

By Margaret Carlson

Two groups were ecstatic when Republicans announced Elian hearings last week: the Miami relatives and Democrats. And it's not just Congress's most volatile members giddy with excitement over reenacting The Story of Elian, but also Senate majority leader Trent Lott and Judiciary Committee chairman Orrin Hatch. Undeterred by George W. Bush's lack of enthusiasm for such partisan theatrics, Lott boasted he would get to the bottom of where the obviously hopeless negotiations stood at the time of the dawn raid. And House majority whip Tom DeLay went ballistic over the government's "jack-booted thugs." He was far more publicly incensed by U.S. marshals using guns to forestall the threatened violence of the Miami crowd than he ever was over guns used by children to slaughter their classmates.

Republicans like to chest-thump that they follow their conscience, not the polls. But it's just as likely that they're following the klieg lights out of their post-impeachment media wilderness. The Gonzalez family—who took to crossing the street to the media encampment calling out "It's time to go live," the way other families announce "It's time for dinner"—ran an enviable press operation. The loopy, frequently hospitalized Marisleysis was hysterical over supposedly doctored photos of a smiling Elian but savvy enough to overshadow the Attorney General's press conference with her guided tour through the upturned bedroom. After

Donato Dalrymple joined the Gonzalez household, so crowded with hangers-on it resembled the Marx Brothers' stateroom in *A Night at the Opera*, Marisleysis burnished his image as the heroic fisherman who saved Elian. As it turns out, he's a housecleaner who has been so hungry for the limelight that his cousin, the veteran seaman on the boat, has vowed never to see him again.

By Friday, when chairman Hatch realized that Republicans could inadvertently be creating a new voting bloc—anti-anti-Castro Cuban Americans—he postponed the hearings (forever, perhaps?) and rethought the possible witnesses. But Democrats will surely insist on calling "the Fisherman"—a cross between Kato Kaelin and William Ginsburg. It will be a priceless television moment when Dalrymple tells how he and Marisleysis let Elian lick his face. The Democrats will also relish hearing from the paramilitary group, Alpha 66, and the four guards with concealed-weapons permits who patrolled the encampment.

Waco hearings didn't work, even though 80 people died. Impeachment hearings didn't work, although the President actually had sex with that woman. Trying to show that reuniting a devoted father with his devoted son is a miscarriage of justice because the son had the misfortune to wash up on the shores of a swing state? No wonder Democrats are happy.

Time, May 8, 2000, p. 38.

concern as to whether a complete, honest investigation is possible because of the various political pressures brought to bear on the independent counsel. In the investigation of President Bill Clinton's conduct in office, Kenneth Starr was appointed independent counsel. Some were concerned that he might not conduct a thorough investigation because he was appointed by Attorney General Reno and supervised by Reno and a panel of judges. Others were concerned that he used his powers as independent counsel too broadly, costing American taxpayers over $40 million and looking into conduct that was not the immediate subject of his assigned investigation. In this case, many Republicans supported Starr's tactics, while many Democrats were critical, indicating the intermingling of politics and prosecutorial investigation at the highest levels.

The prosecutor, of course, does not have total freedom to exercise his or her discretion, since the police, the publics, and the judges all have vested interests of their own to protect, and they exert varying degrees of pressure on the prosecutor. Some prosecutors are more concerned about advancing their own political careers than providing the legal expertise required by some other components of the criminal justice network. Others, elected to office soon after graduation from law school, may have promising political skills but little or no competence or experience in the courtroom. Many others are basically concerned about providing the services required by the public in a competent, professional manner. In any case, the public has the opportunity to indicate satisfaction or dissatisfaction with the prosecutor at election time. The prosecutor who wishes to continue in office or to advance in the political arena is constrained, to some extent, by the conflicting interests of those who surround him or her, as well as by financial obstacles (Barlow, 2000, p. 366).

The next step in the career ladder of many prosecutors is that of judge, and deeds performed for a political party are often invaluable in obtaining a judgeship. In a number of states, county and circuit court judges are elected directly by the voters. In other states, judges are appointed by the governor from a list prepared by a more or less nonpartisan committee. In either case, the appointments are clearly political, and most judges have records as active political campaigners. The extent to which this remains true today is indicated in In the News, "Stench on the Bench."

Federal judges are appointed to the bench by the president with confirmation by the Senate in a highly politicized process whereby the senior senator of the president's party from the state in which a vacancy exists typically controls the appointment. When federal judges are appointed, partisan politics are clearly not set aside, since the vast majority of all federal judges ever appointed have been members of the same political party as the president who appointed them. That the United States Supreme Court is not exempt from party politics was demonstrated clearly by Woodward and Armstrong (1979) in *The Brethren: Inside the Supreme Court.* From consideration of nominees by the president, through Senate approval or disapproval of such nominees, the appointment process is clearly political. The Court's decision to hear or not

---

In the News

STENCH ON THE BENCH

Editorial

Revelations this week that federal prosecutors are investigating how judges are appointed to fill vacancies in Cook County are further evidence of the dire need for reform of a court system that has been beset by corruption, incompetence and inexperience.

Now comes word that prosecutors recently interviewed each of the three Illinois Supreme Court justices from Cook County and are seeking records of the court's appointments since 1990. The investigation was prompted by the allegation of a judge's ex-wife in a divorce deposition. The woman claimed the judge took $20,000 from their bank account to give to a politician to ensure his appointment. The judge was appointed to a temporary position in 1995, was reappointed in 1997 after losing in a judicial election, and was slated again and finally was elected in 1998.

The implication that judgeships can be bought is nothing new in Cook County, where politics is known to be a powerful force that infects the judiciary and all other branches of government. Would-be judges must go before a slating panel whose members are more interested in the lawyer's political loyalty and clout than their legal qualifications or experience. The federal investigation into 10 years of judicial appointments could take years. Meanwhile, each new allegation of corruption and cronyism diminishes public trust and confidence in our courts. The time for change in the current system of electing judges is long overdue. The main qualification for judges should be merit—both to get on the bench and to remain there.

Chicago Sun-Times, *April 28, 2000, p. 39.*

---

hear a case and the decision concerning who will write which opinion are also made in a clearly political context. Finally, we should be aware of the ramifications of changes resulting when the political ideology of the Supreme Court changes as a result of retirements and new appointments. Over the past two decades such changes have occurred, for example, with respect to defendants' rights as the Court has changed from the liberal Warren Court to a more conservative Court, and there are fears that erosion of defendants' rights might well continue. Currently, there is a clear division among the justices on most issues; Chief Justice Rehnquist and Justices Thomas, O'Connor, Scalia, and Kennedy form the conservative coalition, while Justices Stevens, Souter, Ginsburg, and Breyer make up the liberal coalition. Many observers believe the balance of power was changed with the 1991 appointment of Justice Clarence Thomas, making it clear that "the person who is in the White House with the power to nominate new justices" can shape the future of the Supreme Court

(Roth & Knapp, 2000, p. 13). It should be noted that while the president rec- ommends candidates for the federal judiciary, he does not act alone. Candi- dates are recommended to him by political associates. The senate reviews, and sometimes refuses, his recommendations, again demonstrating the interaction of politics and the justice network at the highest levels.

Before leaving our discussion of politics and lawyers, we would like to note the importance of the many local and state bar associations, as well as the American Bar Association, to the criminal justice network. These associations commonly screen and recommend candidates for positions in the judiciary and thereby play a key role in determining the level of competence and the ex- tent of partisan politics in the network, demonstrating the manner in which organizations not included in the traditional systems model influence the criminal justice network.

In the field of corrections, once again the impact of political decisions on the criminal justice network can be clearly seen. The political appointment of wardens has been a significant handicap in developing good correctional pro- grams. In addition to playing a key role in determining the type of custody or treatment an individual receives while in prison, political considerations are generally involved in determining the makeup of the parole board, which de- cides if and when an individual will be released from prison. In the majority of jurisdictions, parole board members are appointed by the governor with legislative confirmation.

Probation officers are generally appointed by the chief judge of a circuit or by a panel of judges. In locally administered probation offices, political considerations play an important role in determining who will be appointed to the probation officer's job. In state-administered probation departments, the influence of political considerations may be less apparent. Today the ma- jority of states have eliminated local administration in favor of statewide ad- ministration of probation. However, there is little doubt that local interests still play a part in the selection and retention of probation personnel in indi- rect ways.

Power, Authority, and Politics

We can define **power** as the net ability of persons or groups to recurrently im- pose their will on others despite resistance (Blau, 1964; Weber, 1947). The exer- cise of power depends on the ability to supply and to withhold rewards and/or punishment. As mentioned earlier in this chapter, politics may be de- fined as the process by which rewards are differentially allocated. Power and politics, then, are inextricably interwoven. The legitimate use of power by per- sons in specially designated positions may be termed **authority.** In other words, we agree to grant people in certain positions the right to use certain types of power. The granting of this right is a political process that involves elections or appointments by others in positions of authority. Thus, we elect an individual to the office of president, and this individual consequently has the right to exercise certain types of power based on the authority of the office.

Similarly, the president may appoint federal judges who then have certain powers as a result of their offices. The municipal fire and police commissions around the country are appointed by mayors and/or councils and then appoint individuals to the position of police officer. The police officer may then use certain types of power that go with the position.

Appointment or election to office does not give the appointee the right to use all forms of power or to exercise power indiscriminately. To the extent that an officeholder uses power in accordance with the rules of appointment or election, we consider his or her behavior legitimate. The use of powers other than those prescribed or in situations other than those specified as appropriate for the office involved is considered illegitimate. For example, the police officer who uses deadly force in self-defense while on duty is exercising legitimate power. The same officer who uses deadly force against a fleeing adolescent who has committed a minor misdemeanor is overstepping the boundaries of his or her authority and using power illegitimately.

The exercise of power from positions of authority requires that the person occupying the position of authority be granted the right to hold the position by those over whom authority is to be exercised. In a democratic society, this granting normally involves an election process or an appointment process. In a totalitarian society, the granting may be passive, as when citizens fail to resist by revolution or coup. Power and authority are not unilateral. They involve the consent (either passive or active) of those governed. A major difference between democratic and totalitarian societies is the procedure by which those exercising illegitimate power from positions of authority may be removed from office. In our society, for example, illegitimate use of the powers of office led a president to resign from office. Had he not done so, impeachment proceedings might have removed him. Citizen dissatisfaction with the performance of a public official may lead to a turnover in the presidency every four years, the recall of a judge, or the suspension of a police officer. In totalitarian societies, these peaceful means of addressing wrongs involving politics, power, and authority may be of little value, and revolution may be the only alternative available.

Recognizing the Consequences of Politics in the Criminal Justice Network

It should now be clear that political considerations are a necessary, normal, and desirable part of the criminal justice network. The most certain way for us to maintain control of the network and direct its practitioners to serve societal goals is the political process. When we elect and remove from office the individuals who control key resources in the criminal justice network, we determine the direction and practices adhered to by those who exercise varying degrees of authority over us. We control the criminal justice network to the extent that we select officials who operate openly and to the extent that we take the time to exert our political influence by monitoring the conduct of these officials and removing from office those who fail to meet our expectations.

There are, however, some very real dangers in the politics of criminal justice. There are those who argue that criminal justice is a game played by those who have wealth and political power against those who have neither. To the extent that these charges are true, we might expect to find resentment and hostility toward the criminal justice network among those who have little or no political power. That such resentment and hostility exist is clear. Studies have shown that upper-income groups hold more favorable attitudes toward the police than lower-income groups, that blacks at all levels of income have negative attitudes toward the police, and that more blacks than whites feel the police are disrespectful to them (Johnson, 1997). Studies also indicate that minorities may be treated by criminal justice practitioners in ways that stigmatize, brutalize, and reinforce minority stereotypes and oppression in our society (Feiler & Shely, 1999; Leiber & Stairs, 1999; Schaefer, 2000). Public defender and assigned counsel programs experience virtually every imaginable kind of financial deficiency. There are neither enough lawyers to represent the poor, nor are all the available attorneys trained, assisted by ample support staffs, or sufficiently compensated (Estrich, 1998, pp. 96–99). Finally, we have to assess carefully the demands from criminal justice practitioners that certain portions of their operations remain covert.

DISCRETION IN CRIMINAL JUSTICE

The exercise of discretion is another necessary, normal, and desirable part of criminal justice. But the invisibility of practitioners involved in plea bargaining and the political considerations involved in decisions to prosecute a case, hear a case, or grant parole often lead to suspicion and distrust. The exercise of discretion by practitioners in the criminal justice network has been a controversial issue for a number of years. Many students of criminal justice have been concerned about the largely invisible, and therefore uncontrollable, nature of discretionary justice.

There is little doubt that if we define **discretion** as the exercise of individual choice or judgment concerning possible courses of action, discretion is a normal, necessary, and even desirable part of the criminal justice network. The exercise of discretion in the criminal justice network is extensive. In what ways do individuals in various components of the network exercise such discretion? What are the consequences of the exercise of discretion for the network, for practitioners, and for those being processed? Is it possible to control discretion?

Public Discretion

One of the reasons we feel so strongly that the public must not be overlooked or underestimated as a component of the criminal justice network is that members of the public have discretionary powers of considerable magnitude. With respect to observed criminal or suspicious acts, each citizen may exercise discretion in terms of reporting or not reporting, testifying or not testifying, telling the truth or not telling the truth, and so forth. Evidence indicates that over 60 percent of the crimes occurring in the United States go unreported as the result of this exercise of discretion (Perkins & Klaus, 1996, p. 3). As a consequence, the police do not investigate a large proportion of all crimes committed since they do not know (except in the relatively rare case of on-view or proactive police work) that they exist. Similarly, the prosecutor is helpless to prosecute offenders in cases where testimony on the part of witnesses is required to substantiate charges if citizens refuse to come forth to testify or testify falsely.

Among the reasons for failure of citizens to cooperate are the beliefs that the police are ineffective in arresting offenders, that prosecutors give away too much in plea bargaining, that judges hand out sentences that are too lenient, and that the entire criminal justice network is too time-consuming and uncertain (Conklin, 1998, pp. 54–56).

The exercise of discretion with respect to specific criminal activities, however, constitutes a relatively small part of the wide range of discretionary activities available to the public. Voting for politicians who campaign for or against stricter law enforcement, supporting or failing to support bond issues intended to improve police services, aiding or failing to aid in the social integration of ex-convicts, and obeying or failing to obey laws are all within the scope of public discretionary activities. At the most basic level, then, members of the public serve as gatekeepers for the criminal justice network as they exercise discretion.

Police Discretion

The police serve as the second level of gatekeepers for the criminal justice network. Among their discretionary powers are arrest or nonarrest, life or death, citation or verbal reprimand, investigation or lack of investigation, and many more. Just as the police may be unable to arrest an offender without citizen cooperation, the prosecutor may be unable to prosecute if the police fail to make a legal arrest. For a variety of reasons, a police officer may decide not to enforce the law. He or she may consider enforcement of certain laws a waste of police resources. The personal characteristics of the offender, departmental regulations, the time of day, the place in which an encounter occurs, public expectations, and previous court decisions may all influence the officer's decision. The realization that **full enforcement** is seldom possible or desirable, that **selective enforcement** can be an effective technique, or a personal belief that the law is inappropriate may also affect an officer's actions.

In addition, the police sometimes take less than proper action to avoid due process of law. Observers of police departments have found that police may fabricate charges or details of incidents to benefit themselves in court proceedings. The process has been referred to as **testilying,** rather than testifying (Cunningham, 1999). This option is open to police as a discretionary aspect of

Police officers have considerable discretionary power.
D&I MacDonald/Unicorn Stock Photos

their work. Harassment, either mental or physical, can be viewed as a discretionary measure.

If laws were written in perfectly clear language, if they contained no contradictions or ambiguities, if there was no difficulty in applying the principles stated in laws to particular situations, and if all officers were thoroughly familiar with all laws, deciding whether or not a particular law has been violated would be a simple and straightforward task for the officer. Unfortunately, these conditions, taken either singly or in combination, are seldom met. The law in the United States is a huge, complex, sometimes contradictory, and constantly changing collection of prescriptive and proscriptive rules. The large number of professionally trained legal experts, lawyers, and judiciary officials who make their living arguing over different interpretations of the law gives some indication of the ambiguities and complexities involved in applying the law. A police officer is not, and for that matter does not need to be, a lawyer, but familiarity with the basics of law is required if the officer is to discharge his or her responsibilities appropriately. Even the best police training programs provide limited information on the law, however. Consequently, most of the police officer's understanding of the law is achieved indirectly. Through the informal instruction and advice offered by colleagues and supervisors, in-service training programs, cramming for promotional exams, self-initiated reading, day-to-day work experiences, and experiences in the courtroom, however, police officers quickly acquire what might be called a working knowledge of the law. For all practical purposes, this working knowledge *is* the law as it functions in the day-to-day activities of police officers. It is this work-generated interpretation of the law, which may or may not correspond with the interpretations of lawyers and judicial officials, that guides the officers as they carry out their law enforcement duties.

The law explicitly grants some discretionary powers to police officers and creates a framework within which other discretionary judgments may legitimately be made. It is one measure of the importance of discretion in police work that these are among the first items that become incorporated into the officer's working knowledge of the law. The officer understands, for example, that certain leeway is permitted in determining whether or not probable cause for a search is present (though legislation and court rulings have increased the confusion surrounding the legal latitude granted the officer in these matters). It is also common knowledge among officers that the overlap that frequently exists among laws gives police officers the opportunity to pick and choose which laws, if any, will be cited once a suspect is apprehended. Thus the officer can choose to "throw the book" at a suspect by citing violations of several laws or can charge the suspect with a more or a less serious offense than circumstances might warrant. In a variety of ways, then, the law, as interpreted and understood by the police officer, creates the framework within which, and sometimes around which, police discretion is exercised (Cox, 1996; Conser & Russell, 2000).

Deciding whether or not a violation of law has taken place is perhaps the most basic, though perhaps not the most consequential, discretionary judgment a police officer makes. If the officer decides that no violation has taken place, there are usually no further formal consequences for anyone involved. If the decision is that an offense has occurred, the officer has the power to set in motion a highly complex, very expensive, and extremely inconvenient set of procedures that may end with the deprivation of a suspect's liberty. To be sure, the officer's judgment that a violation of the law has occurred is by no means the last word on the subject. Prosecutors and judges may eventually reverse the officer's decision, but it is typically the first judgment made by an official of the criminal justice network and, as such, must be considered a basic discretionary power.

Although determining whether or not an offense has been committed is a basic discretionary decision, it is probably not the most consequential so far as the exercise of police discretion is concerned. In essence, it is a technical judgment, dependent on the officer's knowledge of the law and capacity to apply the general principles embodied in the law to the particular events that have occurred. However difficult this judgment may be (and it is difficult in many instances), it is a decision that merely sets the stage for a far more consequential one—deciding whether or not to take official action. If the police officer decides not to arrest, the remainder of the legal machinery in the criminal justice network does not normally come into play. Once an officer decides to take official action in a criminal matter, he or she again exercises discretion with respect to the number and type of charges to be brought against the defendant. The case is then turned over to the prosecutor, who makes a number of discretionary decisions.

Prosecutorial Discretion

"Viewed in broad perspective, the American legal system seems to be shot through with many excessive and uncontrolled discretionary powers, but the one that stands out above all others is the power to prosecute or not to prosecute" (Davis, 1971, p. 181). Discretionary activities on behalf of the prosecutor include deciding whether or not to prosecute a given individual, what charges to file, whether or not to plea-bargain, how much time and money to devote to a particular case, what type and how much evidence to share (under discovery motions) with the defense, and, in some cases, what type of sentence or punishment to recommend if the defendant is found guilty. Like the police officer, the prosecutor operates within a network that places limits on the amount of discretion he or she may exercise. Economic considerations, political considerations, public opinion, the law, and expectations of other network practitioners all influence the decisions made (Barlow, 2000, pp. 365–66).

Defense Counsel Discretion

Defense counsel, in conjunction with the defendant, has discretionary powers as well. He or she must decide whether to plea-bargain, what plea to enter, what motions to file, how much time and effort to devote to a given case, whether or not to accept any given case (at least when private counsel is involved), and so forth. In addition, the attitude of defense counsel toward plea bargaining (demanding or reasonable, for example) may be related to the likelihood of success in reaching a compromise. Again, there are constraints that to some extent shape the decisions made, but the exercise of discretion by counsel obviously occurs frequently and has important consequences.

Judicial Discretion

Judges decide whether objections that attorneys make to the questions asked of witnesses by other attorneys should be sustained or overruled. They decide whether evidence may be admitted or must be excluded, whether there is sufficient evidence to let the case go to the jury for a decision on the factual question of guilt, or whether a mistrial must be declared as a result of some serious error that would prejudice the case. They may have great influence over the jury through their attitudes, their rulings, and their charges. They will also have an impact on those who testify and those who are parties in the trial. Judges, too, are in positions that permit considerable discretionary activity. Some are more lenient than others in admitting certain types of evidence. Some have reputations for being "maximum sentence" judges, while others may be regarded as "bleeding heart liberals." Some are more trusting of police testimony and less inclined to pay strict attention to technicalities than others. Disparities in sentencing individuals who have committed similar crimes are yet another example of judicial discretion (Dripp, 1996). At the level of the United States Supreme Court, judicial discretion is even involved in deciding whether or not to hear a particular case. The discretion exercised by judges may not have the immediate life-or-death impact that sometimes characterizes police discretion, but the long-term effects of sentencing decisions may have the same impact.

Plea Bargaining as a Form of Discretion

Plea bargaining is a form of discretion that involves at least the defendant, the defense counsel, and the prosecutor. In some cases it may also involve the police and the judge. Since bargained or negotiated pleas account for the vast majority of guilty pleas in the United States, plea bargaining is a key part of the criminal justice process (Palermo, White, & Wasserman, 1998). The parties involved all exercise discretion in bargaining over the charges to be filed and the sentence to be imposed. The defendant may exercise her or his discretion in deciding whether or not to enter into plea negotiations. The same is true of defense counsel and the prosecutor. Once they agree to negotiate, the opposing parties attempt to gain concessions from each other. The extent to which the parties are willing to grant such concessions depends on their individual judgments (discretion) as to what may be gained in return. The judge, in some jurisdictions, exercises his or her discretion in determining whether or not to accept a negotiated guilty plea along with the attendant conditions. In some cases, the prosecutor may talk to the police officers involved in the arrest or investigation before deciding what concessions, if any, to grant in the negotiations.

As has been pointed out, none of the discretionary powers exercised is without limits. Each participant in plea bargaining is constrained by the facts of the case, resources available, and the goals of other participants. Again, the network model allows us to analyze the workings of criminal justice practitioners as they go about their day-to-day duties.

Correctional Discretion

The exercise of discretion also occurs frequently and regularly among correctional officials. Probation and parole officers decide what conditions to impose on their charges and how strictly to enforce such conditions. In juvenile cases, for example, the judgment of a probation officer can determine whether a probationer may marry, move out of state, or join the armed forces.

Although parole boards operate according to specific regulations, discretion plays an important part in determining when and if parole or early release will occur. The discretionary powers of prison wardens to make inmate assignments and to allow minor infractions of prison rules to go unpunished by instructing guards as to the type of conduct they consider worthy of note are considerable. Similarly, prison staff members exercise their discretion in determining what to overlook and what to report to the warden.

Although we have not attempted to discuss all the types of discretion in the day-to-day operations of the criminal justice network (for example, the discretion exercised by political figures in determining whether to try to influence the decisions of the police or prosecutor, or the discretion exercised by offenders in deciding when and how to commit a crime), it should be clear that discretion plays an important role at all levels of the network. Network participants, of course, are limited as to the amount and type of discretion they may employ by the factors we have discussed above. Still, the range of alternatives available at any given place in the network is sufficient to make it difficult to predict with certainty exactly what actions, if any, will be taken, except perhaps in cases involving serious predatory crimes (and even these are sometimes not predictable). Selective reporting of crimes, selective enforcement of laws, and selective processing of those against whom the law is enforced are necessary and normal activities in the criminal justice network. Criminal justice, as we know it, could not exist without discretion. We should not lose sight, however, of the fact that the exercise of discretion sometimes confuses those who participate in or observe the network. When the exercise of discretion becomes whimsical or haphazard, predictability is lost, and for those in a democratic society, the network may cease to be perceived as one dispensing justice.

ETHICS IN CRIMINAL JUSTICE

Closely related, perhaps inseparable, from notions of discretion and politics in criminal justice is the issue of ethics. The word **ethics** has a number of meanings. In its most general sense, it refers to the sum total of human duty, the moral obligation of human beings to act in ways that are good and just and proper. Applied ethics may be viewed as dealing with standards created by and/or for professionals, and specialized ethics may be seen as those that apply to a particular profession. For a specialized area of ethics to emerge, certain conditions must be met. The area must have some special features that make it difficult to bring under the domain of general, conventional ethics; that is, the ethics of the area must be in some way different from conventional ethics (Pollock, 1994; Close & Meier 1995; Delattre, 1996; Souryal, 1998).

Criminal justice practitioners possess at least two capacities whose use raises special ethical problems: They are sometimes entitled to use coercive force, and they are sometimes entitled to lie and deceive people in the course of their work. Because of these two special capacities, it is imperative that criminal justice practitioners exercise discretion within an ethical framework. The ethics of criminal justice practitioners have consequences that are of concern not just to practitioners but also to those outside the area, because practitioners who engage in unethical practices may offend the moral sensibilities of sizable numbers of people.

Ethical considerations are paramount where certain types of misconduct cannot be or are thought better not controlled by other means (law, supervisory review, or public opinion). Usually, these areas involve considerable discretion on the part of practitioners who consumers must trust to be ethical. Unethical behavior destroys the confidence of those who trust criminal justice practitioners not only in the individual practitioners involved, but also in the network itself. Governors convicted of racketeering, police officers sodomizing prisoners, juries acquitting defendants who appear clearly guilty, and presidents who are impeached do little to inspire confidence in the criminal justice network or in the ethics of governmental officials.

Of course, the actual decision to violate ethical standards comes down to the individual. Thus, the practice of criminal justice can safely be entrusted only to those who understand what is morally important and who respect integrity. Without such understanding and respect, no codes or rules or laws can safeguard other citizens from the danger of misconduct by police, prosecutors, judges, wardens, and other criminal justice practitioners.

It may be argued that so many gray areas exist in the practice of criminal justice that black-and-white decisions become impossible. While reasonable people may debate the existence of probable cause for a vehicle stop, reasonable doubt in a criminal case, or judicial dispositions of probation versus incarceration, there are some acts that are clearly unethical: stealing; brutally violating human and civil rights; planting evidence, obtaining retroactive search warrants, or forcing people to sign disclaimers; lying under oath; disclosing confidential information. Although most of us would agree that such behaviors are inappropriate among criminal justice practitioners, there is ample evidence that they occur with some degree of regularity (Dripp, 1996; Smith, 1997; Cunningham, 1999). Although the proportion of criminal justice practitioners involved in unethical conduct is probably relatively small, their conduct tarnishes the image of all practitioners.

Summary

1. The relationship between law and politics has long been recognized, but events at the close of the twentieth century indicate just how important this relationship can be.

2. Although cases involving the negative impact of politics on criminal justice receive a great deal of attention, we need to be aware of the many positive aspects of the relationship in the criminal justice network.

3. Societal values (both positive and negative) are transmitted to the network through the political process. The creation of law is a political act.

4. From police to prosecutors, judges, and correctional officials, the political culture shapes policies and practices. Prosecutors and judges are politicians, and police chiefs, wardens, and probation and parole officers are political appointees. It makes little sense, therefore, to think of the criminal justice network as outside the realm of politics.

5. Power (the ability to influence others) and authority (the right to use certain forms of power in certain circumstances) are critical components of the criminal justice–political network. Authority does not allow individuals to use power indiscriminately, and the exercise of authority requires either the active or passive consent of the governed.

6. Political considerations are a necessary, normal, and desirable part of the criminal justice network. They provide a way for concerned citizens to influence the scope and direction of the network. However, if political access is not uniformly available to all citizens, resentment and hostility among those denied such access may be expected.

7. Discretion, or the exercise of individual choice or judgment, is an important part of the criminal justice process. Although choices and judgments made by participants in the criminal justice network are limited by the resources available, the expectations of other participants, the law, and other factors, there is still considerable latitude in the decision-making process. Discretion is a normal, necessary part of criminal justice, but it can be misused and abused. When the exercise of discretion leads to unpredictability or to predictable favoritism in the criminal justice network, it is likely that the network will be characterized as unjust.

8. Ethical values are derived from many sources and range from general beliefs about life to specialized ethics applied to specific criminal justice practitioners. Specialized ethics are essential for criminal justice practitioners because they sometimes have the rights to deceive others in the course of their duties and to use deadly force, and because much of what they do is invisible to outsiders. Although there are some gray areas in the practice of criminal justice, there are also many areas where proper conduct is obvious to all of us. When criminal justice practitioners fail to engage in ethical conduct, they tarnish the image of all those involved in the network.

Key Terms Defined

politics   The process by which rewards or resources are differentially distributed or allocated.

power   The ability of persons or groups to impose their will on others despite resistance.

authority   The right of specially designated persons to use power in a legitimate fashion.

discretion   The exercise of individual choice or judgment concerning possible courses of action; a normal and necessary part of the criminal justice network.

full enforcement   Enforcing all the laws all the time.

selective enforcement   Enforcing some laws at one time and place and others at other times and places.

testilying   Police making intentionally false statements under oath in court.

plea bargaining   A form of discretionary activity in which the charges to be filed and/or the sentence to be recommended are negotiated by at least the defendant and his or her counsel and the prosecutor.

ethics   Standards of right and wrong behavior.

independent counsel   A private counsel retained by the U.S. attorney general to investigate high-ranking government officials.

Critical Thinking Exercises

1. Discuss the complex relationships among law, politics, and the criminal justice network. Are these relationships always negative in nature? Why or why not?
2. What are the relationships among power, authority, and politics? How do these relationships affect the criminal justice network? Give a specific, recent example.

Internet Exercises

The issue of ethics in criminal justice has stimulated many criminal justice organizations to develop formal codes of ethics, and some of those organizations publicize their codes on the Internet. You can access the Benton, Missouri, police code of ethics at *http://www.law-enforcement.org/bentonpd/ethics.htm.*

   Read the Benton Police Department code of ethics; then answer the following questions:

1. What are the highest priorities in this code of ethics? Are they appropriate? Are there any additions you would make if you were developing your own code?
2. What are the expectations for police officers who are off duty? Are these reasonable? Are these expectations communicated during educational and skills training?

3. What role does discretion play in the code of ethics? If you were designing a training workshop, how would you communicate the importance of these concepts to the participants?

4. The code provides no provisions for violations. What type of sanctions do you think should be imposed for violations of fundamental duty, confidentiality, and acting officiously?

References

Alpert, G. P., & Dunham, R. G. (1997). *Policing urban America* (3rd ed.). Prospect Heights, IL: Waveland Press.

Barlow, H. D. (2000). *Criminal justice in America.* Upper Saddle River, NJ: Prentice Hall.

Blau, P. M. (1964). *Exchange and power in social life.* New York: Wiley.

Chambliss, W. J. (1994). Policing the ghetto underclass: The politics of law and law enforcement. *Social Problems, 41* (2), 177–94.

Close, D., & Meier, N. (1995). *Morality in criminal justice: An introduction to ethics.* Belmont, CA: Wadsworth.

Cole, G. F. (1993). *Criminal justice: Law and politics* (6th ed.). Belmont, CA: Wadsworth.

Cole, G. F., & Gertz, M. G. (1998). *The criminal justice system: Politics and policies* (7th ed.). Belmont, CA: West/Wadsworth.

Conklin, J. E. (1998). *Criminology* (6th ed.). Boston: Allyn and Bacon.

Conser, J. A., & Russell, G. D. (2000). *Law enforcement in the United States.* Gaithersburg, MD: Aspen Press.

Cox, S. M. (1996). *Police: Practices, perspectives, problems.* Boston: Allyn and Bacon.

Cunningham, L. (1999). Taking on testilying: The prosecutor's response to in-court police deception. *Criminal Justice Ethics, 18* (1), 26–40.

Davis, K. C. (1971). *Discretionary justice: A preliminary report.* Chicago: University of Illinois Press.

Delattre, E. J. (1996). *Character and cops: Ethics in policing* (3rd ed.). Washington, DC: AEI Press.

Dripp, D. A. (1996). *Trial, 32,* 60–62.

Estrich, S. (1998). *Getting away with murder: How politics is destroying the criminal justice system.* Cambridge, MA: Harvard University Press.

Feiler, S. M., & Sheley, J. F. (1999). Legal and racial elements of public willingness to transfer juvenile offenders to adult court. *Journal of Criminal Justice, 27* (1), 55–64.

Hosenball, M., Isikoff, M., & Contreras, J. (2000, May 8). Cashing in on little Elian. *Newsweek, 32.*

Johnson, J. (1997, September). Americans' views on crime and law enforcement. *NIJ Journal,* 9–14.

Lasswell, H. (1958). *Who gets what, when, and how?* New York: Macmillan.

Leiber, M. J., & Stairs, J. M. (1999). Race, contexts, and the use of intake diversion. *Journal of Research in Crime and Delinquency, 36* (1), 56–86.

Palermo, G. B., White, M. A., & Wasserman, L. A. (1998). Plea bargaining: Injustice for all? *International Journal of Offender Therapy and Comparative Criminology, 42* (2), 111–23.

Perkins, C., & Klaus, P. (1996, April). *Criminal Victimization, 1994.* Washington, DC: U.S. Department of Justice.

Pollock, J. M. (1994). *Ethics in crime and justice: Dilemmas and decisions.* Belmont, CA: Wadsworth.

Roth, B., & Knapp, S. (2000). Taking a chisel to our rights. *AFT on Campus, 19* (8), 12–16.

Schaefer, R. T. (2000). *Racial and ethnic groups* (8th ed.). Upper Saddle River, NJ: Prentice Hall.

Smith, M. B. E. (1997). Do appellate courts regularly cheat? *Criminal Justice Ethics, 16* (2), 11–19.

Souryal, S. S. (1998). *Ethics in criminal justice: In search of the truth.* Cincinnati, OH: Anderson.

Walker, S. (1998). *Sense and nonsense about crime and drugs: A policy guide* (4th ed.). Belmont, CA: Wadsworth.

Weber, M. (1947). *The theory of social and economic organization.* London: William Hodge.

Wilson, J. Q. (1968). *Varieties of police behavior.* Cambridge, MA: Harvard University Press.

Woodward, B., & Armstrong, S. (1979). *The brethren: Inside the Supreme Court.* New York: Simon and Schuster.

Suggested Readings

Brooks, L. W. (1997). Police discretionary behavior: A study of style. In R. G. Dunham & G. P. Alpert (Eds.), *Critical issues in policing: Contemporary issues* (3rd ed.), pp. 149–166. Prospect Heights, IL: Waveland Press.

Close, D., & Meiers, N. (1995). *Morality in criminal justice: An introduction to ethics*. Belmont, CA: Wadsworth.

Estrich, S. (1998). *Getting away with murder: How politics is destroying the criminal justice system.* Cambridge, MA: Harvard University Press.

Lyles, K. L. (1996, Spring). Presidential expectations and judicial performance revisited: Law and politics in the federal district courts. *Presidential Studies Quarterly, 26,* 447–72.

McGrath, B. (2000, April 26). In circuit court races, it's old-fashioned politics. *Chicago Daily Law Bulletin,* 5.

Wahlbeck, P. J. (1997, August). The life of the law: Judicial politics and legal change. *Journal of Politics, 59,* 778–802.

Weber, M. (1947). *The theory of social and economic organization.* London: William Hodge.

Wilson, J. Q. (1968). *Varieties of police behavior.* Cambridge, MA: Harvard University Press.

Woodward, B., & Armstrong, S. (1979). *The brethren: Inside the Supreme Court.* New York: Simon and Schuster.

CHAPTER THREE

Law and Criminal Law

Laws regulate virtually every aspect of human social behavior in modern societies.
Eric H. Futran/Photo Researchers

A small contingent of visiting international students was visiting a local college campus. As part of their itinerary, they met with students and professors to compare the systems of law between their country and the United States. Obutu started the discussion by commenting on the volume of laws in the United States. In his country the laws could be recorded in a small book, but his visit to the legal section of the library led him to believe that it took thousands of books to record all the laws in the United States. He was confused over how we could have both state and federal law and still maintain order. He concluded that law must regulate every aspect of American life.

The discussion then moved to why law was necessary. The American contingent contended that law maintained order in their industrialized, urbanized, and complex society. The international students explained that in their country the law was changing. Historically, people were controlled by local customs, but now that their country was becoming more complex, they had to rely on formal coded laws such as the substantive law of crimes and the procedures for carrying out those laws.

Although time was running short, the discussion concluded with comparisons and contrasts on the role of precedent, the key elements of criminal law, and the difference between civil and criminal law. Both countries honored the doctrine of precedent, but foreign students were awed by the ability to file a civil action, the number and variation of crimes, and the legal requirement of proving intent. The discussion continued for several hours, and both groups of students reflected on the role of law in their countries and globally.

Key Terms

law	civil law
folkways	criminal law
mores	plaintiff
sanctions	crime
functions of law	actus reus
conflict model	mens rea
substantive law	felony murder rule
procedural law	canon law
statutory law	common law
case law	courts of equity
precedent (stare decisis)	federalization

Chapter Outline

Law
The Origins, Nature, and Functions of Law
Criminal Law

Law in the United States
Federal and State Law

We all are born and we all live, work, play, and die within the parameters of complex cultural systems. From the moment of birth, and even before birth, until death, we are affected directly and indirectly by a seemingly infinite number of rules and regulations. For example, there are rules and regulations governing the hospitals in which we are born, and the physicians and nurses who assist at birth. Other rules and regulations govern the schools we attend, the leisure-time activities in which we engage, our rights as employers and employees, and even our funeral procedures.

Among these rules and regulations are some that we come to regard as laws. These laws touch everyone—they regulate virtually every aspect of human behavior in modern societies. Try to imagine American life without laws. Something as simple as driving to the corner convenience store would be extremely risky without laws. One could drive at any speed on either side of the street (or down the middle), pass through intersections without regard for others, and park anywhere and in any fashion. Further, without laws, a company manufacturing cars could build unsafe vehicles that could result in the deaths of innocent people and have no fear of being held liable. As these examples illustrate, laws help create stability, protect private and public interests, provide for the orderly resolution of conflict, and uphold certain traditions and institutions or bring about change in these traditions and institutions.

The purpose of this chapter is to explain what law is, how it is created, the forms it takes, and the functions it serves.

LAW

What is law? Putting the question to a number of citizens might lead to such responses as "the cops are the law," "the judge is the law," and "law consists of the rules we play by." Although each of these responses is partially accurate, none will suffice to explain in meaningful form what the law is.

Law is a complex, dynamic, social phenomenon. It is more than the sum total of persons who actively participate in the administration of rules. It consists of rules administered, decisions rendered, legislation passed, and interpretations handed down by specially designated individuals who have been given the authority to impose sanctions of specified types on those who violate these rules, decisions, and interpretations. Law is a formal means of social control involving the use of rules that are created, interpreted, and enforceable by specially designated persons in a particular political community (Davis, Davis, & Foster, 1962; Hoebel, 1954).

THE ORIGINS, NATURE, AND FUNCTIONS OF LAW

Sources of law are the materials of which legal rules are fashioned once distinctively legal obligations have emerged in society. Customs based here on religions, there on secular traditions, decisions by judicial bodies or other notables, written rules, standards of justice, and, possibly, authoritative writings about law furnish these materials. Singly, or more frequently in combination, these are the sources common to all legal orders. (Ehrmann, 1976, p. 21)

How do these "distinctively legal obligations" emerge in a society? How do certain rules and regulations become recognized as less formal customs or mores, and how are they enforced in different ways?

We might speculate that the following developments occurred in the evolution of law (Durkheim, 1938; Blumer, 1969; Cox & Fitzgerald, 1996, chap. 2). Humans interacting with each other over time developed expectations concerning proper and improper (normal and abnormal) behavior of individuals in certain positions. Chiefs, priests, hunters, wives, warriors, and cooks were all expected to perform in certain ways. This role-associated behavior might vary to some extent as different individuals filled the role of chief or priest, for example, but certain expectations of the position and not the individual occupying the position remained. Behavior that met these expectations was considered normal; that which failed to meet the expectations was considered abnormal, or deviant. That is, it became customary for individuals occupying certain roles (positions) to behave in certain ways. It is not a big step from saying that chiefs behave in a particular way to saying that chiefs *should* behave in a particular way, *ought* to behave in a particular way, or *must* behave in a particular way (Malinowski, 1926; Durkheim, 1947; Wolff, 1950; Becker, 1963). Initially, those who violated the expectations of others could be sanctioned through the application of group pressure. Violations of these expectations may be considered violations of **folkways** (customs) or **mores** (religious or ethical standards), and **sanctions** (punishments) for violating folkways and mores include gossip, ostracism, and, in some cases, excommunication (Sumner, 1906).

As communities grew in numbers, specialization became necessary. The once homogeneous community became diversified. Conceptions of normal and abnormal behavior were no longer consensual. Behavior accepted as normal among warriors might be defined as deviant by farmers, yet each specialized group needed the others to survive. That is, each group had to be able to depend on the performance of certain tasks by other groups. Failure to perform needed tasks could have dire consequences. Ensuring performance (contracts) became too important to leave solely to informal or group pressure. Some tasks had to be performed. To ensure that tasks were performed, certain individuals were appointed to look for behavior that violated expectations. These specially designated individuals were given the power to use certain types of sanctions (arrest, fines, and even death) to ensure compliance with expectations or to punish those who failed to comply. The legal rights and obligations of all parties in the community had been specified, and formal institutions for ensuring that rights were protected and obligations were fulfilled emerged. Law became important as one form of social control.

Although the concept of law has probably existed in all societies, law in the sense of formal or written rules enforceable by specially designated persons has evolved over time and is particularly characteristic of complex societies. Whereas custom, tradition, and religion could once be used to handle most disputes, modern industrial societies rely more heavily on legislative and administrative law to deal with rapidly changing social conditions (Ehrmann, 1976). These laws are based, of course, to a great extent on custom, tradition, and precedent.

In the attempt to understand the origins, nature, and **functions of law,** it is important to recognize that the formulation of law does not occur in a vacuum. Law is the result of political action. One school of thought says that in a democracy, law represents the views or values of the majority of citizens and results from consensus (Dahrendorf, 1959). Another widely accepted model is the **conflict model,** which indicates that it is conflict between interest groups with varying degrees of power that leads to the formation of law (Becker, 1963; Quinney, 1975). According to proponents of this model, coalitions form among the many groups existing in society with respect to specific issues. The more powerful the coalition (in terms of money, prestige, political skills), the more likely it is to create or pass the laws it desires. Since the interests of these groups vary over time, the coalitions formed are temporary and constant change characterizes the society. There is no one stable, identifiable majority on all issues. The two approaches may both be correct: In the initial stages of the development of law, the conflict model clearly applies, but with time and practice, consensus develops (Glaser, 1978).

Law is often the consequence of conflicting interests.
AP/Wide World Photos

The discussion above indicates another important characteristic of law—its dynamic nature. The law is constantly changing as the interests of groups and individuals change, leading to the election of new political figures, the appointment of new judicial officials, the passing of new legislation, and the handing down of new court decisions. Although it is easy to talk about the law as if it were something real and concrete, numerous scholars have pointed out the difficulties in saying exactly what the law is at any given time. Thus, Ehrlich (1936) spoke of the living law, Holmes (1968) discussed law as what the courts are likely to do in a given place at a given time; and Weber (in Rheinstein, 1956, pp. 486–93) emphasized the difference between the normative aspects of a legal proposition and what actually happens in a given time as a result of these normative aspects.

Regardless of time and place, law helps perform certain functions. Law defines relationships among individuals and groups by specifying rights and obligations, and may be used to help tame the use of naked force, to assist in the orderly resolution of conflict, to dispose of problem or "trouble" cases (those that arise repeatedly) as they arise, and to help society adapt to changing conditions (Hoebel, 1954, pp. 275–76). Perhaps the way the law may be used to perform these functions will become clearer if we take a look at several different ways of classifying law.

Substantive law is the body of law that creates, discovers, and defines the rights and obligations of each person in society (Hoebel, 1954, p. 275). The two key elements of substantive law are specificity and penalty. That is, substantive law specifically defines proscribed (prohibited) behaviors and specifies the penalties that may be administered to those who commit such acts. Laws concerning sexual assault, medical malpractice, income tax evasion, and so forth are substantive in that they specifically define the acts constituting sexual assault, malpractice, and tax evasion and specify the consequences for engaging in these acts.

Procedural law is the body of law that specifies the manner in which substantive laws will be applied. If the law is to be used in the orderly resolution of conflict, specific, predictable procedural steps must be followed. Thus, we have developed rules concerning the seizure and admissibility of evidence, the circumstances under which a confession may be legally obtained and admitted in court, the use of informants, and so on.

The law may also be viewed in terms of **statutory law** versus **case law.** Statutory law consists of those laws passed by a legislative body and is typically codified and published as revised at the federal, state, and local levels. Case law is derived from court decisions that are sometimes based on statutory law and sometimes arrived at in the absence of statutes. In handing down case law, the deciding judge usually takes into account past case decisions involving similar conditions, or **precedent** (**stare decisis** is an equivalent term). The ultimate sources of formal or written law are the federal and state constitutions.

Finally, for our purposes, law may be divided into **civil** and **criminal** categories.

> The "civil law" is the portion of the law that defines and determines the rights of the individual in protecting his person and his property. The "criminal law" is that body specifically established to maintain peace and order. Its purpose is to protect society and the community from the injurious acts of individuals. The same act causing injury to person or property, a civil wrong called a "tort," may also be a breach of the peace, a "crime." The wrongdoer may then be subject to both civil and criminal proceedings. (Ross, 1967, p. 14)

This situation occurred, for example, in the O. J. Simpson case, with Simpson being convicted in civil court and acquitted in criminal court.

Differences between criminal and civil law are apparent in the manner in which cases are filed in court and cited in the legal literature. In such citations, the **plaintiff,** or person initiating the action, is always listed first. The plaintiff in all criminal cases will be a governmental entity—federal, state, or local— since the state is considered an "injured party" in such cases. In civil cases, the plaintiff will normally be a private party. It is possible for a governmental entity to be a plaintiff in a civil matter, but as a rule of thumb, the distinction outlined above holds.

Another difference between civil and criminal law concerns the nature of the sanctions involved. Sanctions in criminal cases are said to be punitive, while those in civil matters are generally compensatory (although they may also be punitive or exemplary). In criminal cases, the intent is to punish for wrongs done to society (the state); in civil cases, the intent is to award compensation for harm, damages, or suffering to the individual.

In addition to the differences listed above, there are important procedural distinctions between civil and criminal law. The most basic of these is in the standard of proof required to establish guilt. In civil proceedings, a "preponderance of evidence" must exist to support a guilty verdict, whereas in criminal proceedings, guilt must be established "beyond reasonable doubt."

Because this book deals with the criminal justice network, most of our attention is devoted to criminal law. It should be noted, however, that there are numerous, complex relationships between civil and criminal law. Thus, a finding of guilt or innocence in criminal court may be used in civil proceedings resulting from the same case.

CRIMINAL LAW

In this section we examine the characteristics of criminal law, but first we must define **crime.** According to Paul Tappan (1960), "Crime is an intentional act or omission in violation of criminal law, committed without defense or justification, and sanctioned by the state as a felony or misdemeanor" (p. 10). Included in Tappan's definition are five specific elements that, taken together, establish the criteria necessary for the violation of criminal law: (1) an unjustifiable act or omission, (2) mental state or intent, (3) a union of intent and action, (4) the existence of a statute prohibiting the act, and (5) the existence of a prescribed penalty.

The act **(actus reus)** or omission considered criminal must be defined by law. For example, under common law (still followed in some states), the crime of rape occurs only when there is penetration of the sexual organ of the victim by the alleged offender. In a battery, physical contact must occur; in criminal homicide, one person's life must be taken by another person without justification; and so on.

Notice that thoughts of committing a crime do not, in and of themselves, violate criminal law. (Many of us have probably secretly planned the "perfect crime"!) There must be some action in furtherance of these thoughts for a crime to occur. Failure to act constitutes one type of action. Therefore, failing to file an income tax report and failure to register for the draft when required to do so are criminal acts because there are legal requirements that both be performed by certain categories of individuals. In some cases, an individual may feel a moral obligation to act but not be legally required to do so. Thus, a passerby seeing a drowning person may feel morally obligated to help but will not be guilty of a crime if he or she fails to do so because there is no legal requirement that he or she act.

Criminal law recognizes that some acts, which are generally considered criminal, are justifiable under specific circumstances. In such cases, the actor must prove that she or he committed the act with justification. Thus, a police officer in the line of duty may intentionally take the life of another citizen (homicide) without committing a crime if he or she sees the person kill while committing a serious felony and has reason to believe that his or her own life, or the life of others, is in immediate danger from the felon. Such action is termed "justifiable homicide." Criminal acts committed under duress (at gun-point, for example) may also fall into this category.

The mental state of the actor, **(mens rea)**, is another important element of criminal law. An act alone is not enough for the commission of a crime. Thus, one who kills another by accident (without an accompanying culpable mental state) does not commit criminal homicide. There are four commonly recognized culpable mental states: intent, knowledge, recklessness, and negligence. These mental states are typically identified and defined in the criminal codes of various jurisdictions. There are a few circumstances under which the law does not require proof of a particular mental state. One such exception consists of strict liability offenses, such as traffic code violations. Another exception is the **felony murder rule.** Under this rule, offenders may be held responsible for the consequences of acts occurring during the commission of certain felonies even though the offenders did not intend the acts to occur or the consequences to follow. In such cases, the intent to commit the felony is regarded as sufficient to make the felon responsible for the consequences that follow. For most crimes, specific actions are required to prove mental state. For example, laws concerning shoplifting may require that shoplifters leave the store in which they have shoplifted before a charge of shoplifting can be sustained. These laws are based on the premise that as long as the shoplifters stay in the store they can argue that they intended to pay before leaving (even though they have hidden several items on their persons). For other crimes (most felonies, for example) general intent is all that is required. The intent to commit a felonious act may make the perpetrator responsible for all consequences following from the commission of the felony, even though such consequences are unforeseen.

In our society, several categories of persons cannot be convicted of crimes because they are said to be incapable of forming a culpable mental state. Among these are juveniles under a certain age, those who have been declared insane, and the severely retarded. These persons may be dealt with through legal means (commitment hearings, for example) other than criminal proceedings. Some of these categories of individuals who are exempt from criminal prosecution have caused considerable controversy, particularly following the attempted assassination of former president Ronald Reagan by John Hinckley, who was found not guilty by reason of insanity. This controversy has resulted in a series of attempts to change laws to assess greater responsibility to those who claim insanity as a defense. Some jurisdictions have created guilty but mentally ill statutes, for example, that provide for both punishment as a criminal and mental health treatment for the offender.

As we have noted, neither an act alone nor an intention alone is sufficient for the commission of a crime. Intent and act must typically coexist for a crime to be committed. Further, the act considered criminal must be prohibited by law at the time it is committed; otherwise, no crime has occurred. Finally, criminal codes must specify the punishments that may be administered for particular crimes to avoid capricious punishment.

There are many other aspects of criminal law and numerous exceptions to the general rules stated here. Some of these are discussed in later chapters. The overview presented in this chapter should help you better understand the general nature and functions of law.

LAW IN THE UNITED STATES

Although there is evidence that laws were codified as early as the twenty-fifth century B.C., the first complete surviving code, the Code of Hammurabi, originated in the eighteenth century B.C. This code deals with subjects ranging from specific punishments for specific crimes to medical malpractice. The Mosaic Code, including the Ten Commandments, was developed 500 to 1,000 years later. The impact of the Ten Commandments, prohibiting behaviors such as murder, adultery, and perjury, is well established. Roman law was codified about 450 B.C. and became the basis for **canon law,** or the law of the Roman Catholic church. These various codes were tied together in the Napoleonic Code in 1804.

In Britain, the kings traditionally dispensed law throughout the country by traveling around and establishing court at various locations. In general, the same laws were applied throughout the country; thus, the law came to be referred to as **common law.** When canon law came to England, **courts of equity** (in which decisions were based more on conscience than on strict interpretation of common law) were also established, and the two systems coexisted for a number of years. In 1215 the Magna Carta, the basis for British civil liberties, became the law, and over the following years British common law continued to develop on the basis of customs, tradition, and precedent. This common law became the most important single aspect of the legal system in the new country: America.

When the colonial period ended in 1776, a new governmental system had to be developed. The federal Constitution, written in 1787, established the executive, legislative, and judicial branches of government; it also included a system of checks and balances among the branches and between state and federal governments. The Constitution became the law of the land in 1789 and, with 27 amendments, remains so today. The 27 amendments ensure freedom of worship and speech, ensure trial by jury, abolish slavery, extend voting rights to all citizens, protect privileges and immunities of citizens, and guarantee a variety of other civil rights.

Of the 27 amendments, 5 are particularly important for the criminal justice network. These amendments establish, clarify, and regulate many elements of procedural law. The Fourth Amendment regulates arrests and searches by prohibiting unreasonable searches and seizures. The Fifth Amendment affects grand jury proceedings, self-incrimination, and double jeopardy, and provides for due process of law. The Sixth Amendment regulates interrogation and criminal prosecution by establishing the right to counsel, trial by jury, and the speedy trial doctrine. It also establishes the rules of venue, the right to confront witnesses, and the right to call one's own witnesses. The Eighth Amendment prohibits excessive bail as well as cruel and unusual punishment. The Fourteenth Amendment applies all basic constitutional privileges at the state level through due process and equal protection for all. Although many of these amendments have been interpreted and refined through court decisions, they remain the fundamental source of procedural law.

Federal and State Law

Prior to the ratification of the Bill of Rights, the Constitution said little about federal criminal law. State courts had concurrent, and often primary, jurisdiction over designated federal crimes. This made sense because crime and order maintenance on an everyday basis were principally matters of local interest. However, after the Civil War, Congress enacted federal civil rights legislation and gave federal jurisdiction to violations in the event citizens were denied their rights or when state courts refused to enforce federal law. This brought crimes such as murder and assault under federal jurisdiction in certain types of cases (Brickey, 1995). This trend continued into the twentieth century with passage of the Lindbergh Act (dealing with kidnapping across state lines), the Fugitive Felon Act (prohibiting interstate flight to avoid prosecution for certain violent crimes), the Comprehensive Crime Control Act of 1990, and the Violent Crime Control and Law Enforcement Act of 1994 (Brickey, 1995). This process of extending federal jurisdiction to civil causes of action and criminal prosecutions that could be maintained in the state courts is known as **federalization** (Young & Hindera, 1999).

The federal government's involvement in maintaining law and order at the local level is the topic of considerable debate. On the one hand, federal duplication of state criminal law strains the federal system to its limits. At the same time, federal intervention limits the discretion of states to respond to local concerns (Brickey, 1995). Additionally, both federal and state law, as we have noted elsewhere, are heavily politically motivated. As a result, under the current get-tough philosophy, crimes such as those involving drugs often result in mandatory prison time. Because they are so numerous, they clog the federal court system (which is ill equipped to deal with the large volume of these crimes), as well as the federal prison system. In addition, it appears that Congress sometimes passes legislation aimed at destroying the intent of Supreme Court decisions. In June of 2000, for example, the Supreme Court handed down a decision reaffirming the need for the police to issue a Miranda warning (see In the News, "Miranda Upheld"). This decision resulted from a case brought under the guise of a law passed by Congress in 1968 that attempted to circumvent the Miranda warning by allowing acceptance of "voluntary" confessions without Miranda. Finally, state and federal laws sometimes conflict (as in the case of the legal use of marijuana in some states although such use is prohibited under federal law). Thus individuals may be law-abiding from one perspective while criminal from the other. On the other hand, citizens who cannot receive equitable treatment in state courts may have a better chance in federal court (as in the case of Rodney King, whose police assailants were acquitted in state court but convicted in federal court). Federal laws dealing with hate crimes are another positive example, since not all states have treated such crimes seriously. Still, according to the American Bar Association's Task Force on the Federalization of Criminal Law, the amount of behavior subject to federal criminal law has dramatically increased in the past few decades. The task force notes that there seems to be no underlying principle governing the manner in which Congress criminalizes conduct and also notes that these laws are often passed without the resources required to implement them (Mountjoy, 1999; see In the News, "Making Hate a Federal Crime").

The conflict between state and federal law further illustrates the network approach to understanding criminal justice. Clearly, politics, local standards, and state and federal legislatures and courts are all involved in this conflict. Changes in policies or practices at one point in the network create repercussions throughout.

In the News

MIRANDA UPHELD; JUSTICES KEEP INTACT "RIGHT TO REMAIN SILENT"

By Joan Biskupic

WASHINGTON—Police must keep warning suspects of their right to remain silent before interrogations begin, the Supreme Court said Monday in upholding its landmark *Miranda* ruling.

The 7–2 decision was a resounding rejection of an unprecedented challenge to the opinion from 1966 that is entrenched in law and popular culture.

"You have the right to remain silent. Anything you say can be used against you in a court of law," Chief Justice William Rehnquist said as he began announcing the judgment, reciting part of the warning that has become known worldwide largely because of its use in television police dramas.

The conservative chief justice then emphatically declared that *Miranda vs. Arizona,* a ruling of the liberal Supreme Court led by Earl Warren more than three decades ago, is rooted in the Constitution and so is irreversible by Congress.

"*Miranda* has become embedded in routine police practice to the point where the warnings have become part of our national culture," Rehnquist said.

Justices Antonin Scalia and Clarence Thomas dissented. The case renewed a debate over whether the *Miranda* mandate is so rigid that the guilty often go free if police neglect to read the warning.

Many legal analysts had predicted a closer vote. The case focused on whether Congress reversed *Miranda* with a law from 1968 that allows voluntary confessions to be used at trial, even when defendants had not been read their rights. The law has never been enforced, but was thrust from obscurity last year when an appeals court ruled that it superceded *Miranda.* Rehnquist, who often has favored law enforcement over defendants, was far from an obvious vote to support *Miranda.*

The suspense was heightened when Rehnquist said he would give the majority opinion. He made it clear that he backed *Miranda,* declaring that protecting suspects from self-incrimination is integral to American law and life.

USA Today, *June 27, 2000, p. 1A.*

In the News

MAKING HATE A FEDERAL CRIME

Editorial

With an eye on the fall campaign, Senate Democrats, with some Republican help, this week passed a hate crimes bill that will do nothing to eradicate hate and bigotry, as its backers claim, but will further federalize state and local criminal laws.

One of the many drawbacks of this legislation is that no one has been able to demonstrate precisely how it will benefit existing law enforcement. The two crimes invoked to justify the bill—the dragging death of a black man in Texas and the beating death of a gay man in Wyoming, both in 1998—were fully prosecuted, and maximum penalties imposed, under existing state criminal laws. Still, it's hard to vote against fighting "hate."

Other problems with hate crimes laws are that they are selective, making crimes against one group worse than crimes against another; they are subjective in that they attempt to criminalize psychological motivation; and, at their most benign, they duplicate existing laws and jurisdictions, raising the prospect of double jeopardy prosecutions.

The backers argue their case with circular reasoning. Declaims co-sponsor Sen. Edward Kennedy, D-Mass.: "Hate crimes are rooted in hatred and bigotry, and if America is ever going to be America, we should root out hatred and bigotry." America is America, and hate and bigotry, while they are reprehensible when directed at people simply because of who they are, are not crimes unless acted on.

This hate crimes bill is presented as a simple expansion of existing laws against crimes based on race, religion or ethnicity to include gender, disabilities and sexual orientation.

But perhaps the bill's biggest drawback is that it goes much farther than that. The existing federal hate crimes law applies only to federally protected activities—voting, use of public accommodations, registering for school. The Senate-passed bill would remove that restriction and, by a further stretch of the already overstretched commerce clause, make any crime deemed by a U.S. attorney to be hate-motivated a federal crime. This is a massive expansion of federal writ into state and local law enforcement.

President Clinton lobbied hard and publicly for the hate crimes bill. Vice President Gore made a show of returning to the Senate in case of a tie vote. (It passed 57–42.) Now that they have their campaign trophy, it would be best if this bill died quietly as it has in the past.

Denver Rocky Mountain News, *June 22, 2000, p. 48A.*

Summary

1. Law is a complex phenomenon. Among the multitude of rules and regulations developed by societies over time, some come to be designated as laws. These laws help us resolve conflict in an orderly way by establishing rights and obligations of individuals and groups.

2. Law is dynamic (constantly changing) and is one form of social control that helps societies adapt to changing conditions.

3. Law is the result of political action and of conflicts of interest among individuals and groups rather than the will of the majority, at least in most cases.

4. Criminal law is only one type of law and is characterized by requiring higher standards of proof than, for example, civil law.

5. A crime is an unjustifiable act that is typically accompanied by intent. The combination of act and intent that violates a specific statute prohibiting the act in the presence of a specified punishment constitutes a violation of criminal law.

6. The body of criminal law may be analyzed in a variety of ways, using categories such as substantive versus procedural law, case versus statutory law, and so on.

7. In the past few decades, Congress has passed a number of laws at the federal level that limit states' discretion in responding to local standards. Some of these, such as the hate crimes law and civil rights legislation, provide equity across state lines. Others have led to an overloading of federal courts and crowding of federal prisons as the result of political concerns rather than a comprehensive, rational plan to address crime.

Key Terms Defined

law A complex, dynamic, social phenomenon consisting of legislative rules and court decisions as they are administered and interpreted by specifically designated individuals in a political community.

folkways Customs or traditions.

mores Ethical or religious standards.

sanctions Punishments.

functions of law Law defines relationships among individuals and groups, helps regulate the use of force, may assist in the orderly resolution of conflicts, helps dispose of "trouble cases," and may help society adapt to changing conditions.

conflict model   A model that views law as emerging from conflict between interest groups with varying degrees of power.

substantive law   Law that creates, discovers, and defines the rights and obligations of each person in a society; key elements are specificity and penalty.

procedural law   Rules specifying the manner in which substantive law is to be applied.

statutory law   Law passed by a legislative body.

case law   Law derived from court decisions.

precedent (stare decisis)   Court decisions that provide guidance as to how future similar cases might be decided.

civil law   The portion of law that defines and determines the rights of individuals in protecting person and property.

criminal law   Law established to maintain peace and order by protecting society from injurious acts of individuals.

plaintiff   Party initiating court action.

crime   An intentional act or omission in violation of criminal law.

actus reus   The act constituting a crime.

mens rea   A guilty mind; criminal intent.

felony murder rule   A rule which holds that those who commit certain kinds of felonies are responsible for all consequences of their acts, including unforeseen or unintended consequences.

canon law   Church or religious law.

common law   Law based on court decisions that become widely accepted.

courts of equity   Courts in which decisions are based more on conscience than on strict interpretation of the law.

federalization   The process of extending federal jurisdiction to civil causes of action and criminal prosecutions that are typically handled in state courts.

Critical Thinking Exercises

1. Discuss how law develops and how it differs from folkways and mores. What or who determines whether a norm will become law? What are some of the basic functions of law? What legal machinery and societal actions are necessary if these functions are to be performed successfully?
2. What are the basic requirements for a violation of criminal law? What are some of the exceptions to these requirements? Why do these exceptions exist?

Internet Exercises

The common law has played a major role in the development of the current criminal law in the United States. Access the *Encyclopedia of Common Law* at *www.factmonster.com/ce6/society/A0857484.html.*
  Read the introduction, development, and characteristics sections; then answer the following questions:

1. How did the common law obtain its name?
2. In what country did the common law originate?
3. List and explain the three courts from which the common law derives its power.
4. What role does stare decisis play in the common law?
5. Why is common law being replaced today?

References

Becker, H. S. (1963). *The outsiders: Studies in the sociology of deviance.* New York: Free Press.
Blumer, H. (1969). *Symbolic interaction: Perspective and method.* Englewood Cliffs, NJ: Prentice Hall.
Brickey, K. F. (1995). Criminal mischief: The federalization of American criminal law. *Hastings Law Journal, 46* (4), 1135.
Cox, S. M., & Fitzgerald, J. D. (1996). *Police in community relations: Critical issues* (3rd ed.). Madison, WI: Brown and Benchmark.
Dahrendorf, R. (1959). *Class and conflict in industrial society.* Stanford, CA: Stanford University Press.
Davis, F. J., Davis, E. E., & Foster, H. H., Jr. (1962). *Society and the law: New meanings for an old profession.* New York: Free Press.
Durkheim, E. (1938). *The rules of sociological method.* Chicago: University of Chicago Press.
Durkheim, E. (1947). *The division of labor in society.* New York: Free Press.
Ehrlich, E. (1936). *Fundamental principles of the sociology of law* (W. L. Moll, Trans.). Cambridge, MA: Harvard University Press.
Ehrmann, H. W. (1976). *Comparative legal cultures.* Englewood Cliffs, NJ: Prentice Hall.
Glaser, D. (1978). *Crime in our changing society.* New York: Holt, Rinehart and Winston.
Hoebel, E. A. (1954). *The law of primitive man.* Cambridge, MA: Harvard University Press.
Holmes, O. W. (1986). The path of law. In W. Murphy & C. H. Pritchett (Eds.), *Courts, judges, & politics: An introduction to the judicial process,* 4th ed. (pp. 20–23). New York: Random House.
Malinowski, B. (1926). *Crime and custom in savage society.* London: Routledge and Kegan Paul.
Mountjoy, J. J. (1999). The federalization of criminal laws. *Spectrum, 72* (3), 1–4.
Quinney, R. (1975). *Criminology: Analysis and critique of crime in America.* Boston: Little, Brown.
Rheinstein, M. (1956). *Max Weber: Law and economy in society.* Cambridge, MA: Harvard University Press.
Ross, M. J. (1967). *Handbook of everyday law.* Greenwich, CT: Fawcett.
Sumner, W. G. (1906). *Folkways.* Boston: Ginn.
Tappan, P. (1960). *Crime, justice, and correction.* New York: McGraw-Hill.
Wolff, K. H. (Trans.). 1950. *The sociology of George Simmel.* New York: Free Press.
Young, C. D., & Hindera, J. J. (1999). Judicial intergovernmentalism: The impact of federalization on the American court system. *Public Administration Quarterly, 22* (4), 407–25.

Suggested Readings

Meares, T. L., & Kahan, D. M. (1998). Laws and (norms of) order in the inner city. *Law and Society Review, 32* (4), 805–38.

Mountjoy, J. J. (1999). The federalization of criminal laws. *Spectrum, 72* (3), 1–4.

Skolnick, J. H. (1995, February). What not to do about crime: The American Society of Criminology 1994 presidential address. *Criminology, 33,* 1–15.

Umphrey, M. M. (1999). The dialogics of legal meaning: Spectacular trials, the unwritten law, and narratives of criminal responsibility. *Law and Society Review, 33* (2), 393–423.

CHAPTER FOUR

Types of Crime: I

Crimes against the person constitute one category.
Joel Rogers/Stone

*L*aura, a graduate student in criminology, was deliberating thesis topics. She had grown up in a rural community with very little serious crime and was interested in conducting her research on some form of crime. She relayed her interest to her professor, who urged her to specify the type of crime she desired to investigate. He asked her if she was interested in felonies or misdemeanors, and she chose felonies. He followed up by forcing her to choose between *mala in se* crimes versus *mala prohibita* crimes. This time she was not quite sure, and her professor then suggested a study of official versus unreported crime. That topic didn't interest Laura, and she concluded that she wanted to focus on a particular form of crime.

Her professor felt the categories of crimes against persons and crimes against property were both too broad and told Laura she would have to specify a particular subcategory within one of the larger groups. She was interested in homicides but didn't clearly understand the distinction between the degrees of murder, the types of manslaughter, and the role of suicide. She thought assaults and battery were too common to be of interest, and the changing nature of the sex crime statutes made comparisons much too difficult.

She then shifted her focus to property crimes and eliminated robbery as a thesis topic because it could arguably be placed in the other category. Thefts and burglaries occurred too frequently, and arson was difficult to determine. Her major professor suggested one of the new crimes, such as stalking or hate crimes. Laura still couldn't decide and concluded that understanding the nature and volume of crime was a major undertaking.

Key Terms

statutory law	rape
case law	sodomy
felonies	deviate sexual conduct
misdemeanors	deviate sexual assault
acts *malum in se*	statutory rape
acts *malum prohibitum*	robbery
homicide	theft (larceny)
murder	burglary
suicide	arson
malice aforethought	hate crimes
felony murder rule	stalking
manslaughter	Uniform Crime Reports (UCRs)
battery	time clocks
assault	offenses known to the police
aggravation	offenses cleared by arrest

victim survey research

National Crime Victimization Survey (NCVS)

self-report studies

Institute for Social Research

Chapter Outline

Some Important Distinctions
Crimes against the Person
   Homicide
   Assault and Battery
   Forcible Rape
   Sexual Predators or Sexually Dangerous Persons
   Other Sex Offenses
Crimes against Property
   Robbery
   Larceny/Theft
   Burglary
   Arson
Some Recent Additions to Criminal Law
Measuring Crime
   Victim Survey Research
   Self-Report Studies

In Chapter 3, we noted differences between substantive and procedural law and between civil and criminal law. In this chapter, we discuss several types of crime to familiarize the reader with some important elements of such crimes. A comprehensive examination of criminal law is well beyond the scope of an introductory text, but an overview of some types of crime should enable the reader to examine, analyze, and interpret, in general, any given criminal code. Because each state enacts its own criminal code, there is considerable variation among the states in the definitions of specific crimes. We recommend that each reader familiarize him- or herself with relevant state statutes to gain a more detailed understanding of the various offenses discussed therein. In addition, most criminal justice programs devote an entire course to the study of criminal law and will acquaint the reader with a more thorough understanding of basic concepts, special designations, and the application of the criminal code in that particular jurisdiction.

Criminal law is enacted by legislative (state and federal) bodies **(statutory law)** and interpreted and/or modified by court decisions **(case law).** Criminal law, then, represents some of society's values (that a specific behavior is wrong), and because these values are subject to change, criminal codes undergo periodic revisions. It is important, therefore, that both students and practitioners keep abreast of changes in relevant codes. This can be accomplished by periodically reviewing the revised statutes published by the various states.

The laws discussed in this chapter have been developed over time (many originate in British common law) and have undergone numerous revisions. These laws are not necessarily the ones most frequently violated, but they do cover violations that are considered serious by most, if not all, states.

SOME IMPORTANT DISTINCTIONS

The offenses discussed in this chapter are generally divided into two categories: crimes against the person and crimes against property. Crimes without complainants, organized crime, and white-collar/corporate offenses are presented in Chapter 5. Before proceeding to a more detailed discussion of these offenses, we should distinguish between certain offenses on the basis of the punishment associated with each. **Felonies** are usually offenses punishable by sentences of more than one year in state or federal prisons. **Misdemeanors** are offenses punishable by sentences up to one year, usually in a county or local jail, although some states maintain institutions specifically for misdemeanants. In addition to incarceration, both categories may be accompanied by fines. Many local ordinance violations and petty offenses are punishable by fine only.

In addition to the distinction between felonies and misdemeanors, we may categorize crimes as **malum in se,** or acts that are wrong in and of themselves, or **malum prohibitum,** or acts that are wrong merely because they are prohibited. Examples of the former include most crimes against the person (murder, rape, and battery) and some property crimes (theft, arson, and burglary). Virtually every society deems these behaviors inappropriate. Examples of the latter include the use of marijuana, underage drinking, and prostitution. Even jurisdictions that prohibit such behaviors may define them in disparate terms.

We would be remiss not to mention attempts to commit offenses. Generally, a person commits an attempt when he or she intentionally commits an act that constitutes a substantial step toward committing that offense. Thus, an individual who intentionally fires a weapon at another person, without legal justification, has attempted murder even if he or she has a bad aim.

CRIMES AGAINST THE PERSON

Homicide

Homicide is generally considered the most serious felony. In fact, it is the only crime that carries a penalty of death in the United States. The term literally refers to the killing of a human being and is often thought to be synonymous with murder, but murder is only one category of homicide.

Any time one human being kills another, a homicide occurs. However, it does not necessarily follow that a crime has been committed because the law distinguishes among justifiable homicides, a state-sanctioned execution, and the use of deadly force in self-defense that is authorized under common law; criminal homicides, murder, and manslaughter (voluntary, involuntary, and negligent); and excusable homicides, or certain self-defense killings and deaths resulting from accidents not involving negligence or illegal behavior (Perkins, 1969, p. 33).

Historically, for a homicide to occur, the death of the victim had to occur within a given time period—usually a year and a day—after the attempted killing. The time requirement has been eliminated by some states, whereas others have increased the length of the period to three years and a day (Gamage & Hemphill, 1979, p. 5). For a homicide to occur, it must also be shown that the alleged victim was alive at the time of the offense and that death was not the result of the actions of an intermediate party (e.g., medical personnel who failed to provide an available lifesaving injection) but the consequence of the offense itself.

As we focus our attention on criminal homicides, keep in mind that the types are differentiated primarily on the basis of the intent of the perpetrator. Murder and voluntary manslaughter generally require proof of a specific intent to kill or cause great bodily harm. Involuntary manslaughter and manslaughter resulting from the driving of a motor vehicle normally require only a general criminal state of mind. In either case, the key elements of criminal homicide include the killing of one human being by another without lawful justification.

Murder occurs when one human being is killed by another without lawful justification and with malice aforethought. A detailed examination of this definition explains exactly what murder is and is not. First, we note that murder involves the "killing of one human being by another." This tells us that killing oneself (commonly defined as **suicide**), killing an animal, and the killing of a human being by an animal, unless directed by a human being, are not murder. Second, we note the words "without lawful justification." These words indicate that the killing of one human being by another is not murder if the affirmative defense of lawful justification can be proved. Finally, we note that **malice aforethought** is required for murder to exist. The phrase simply means that an intention to seriously harm someone or to commit a serious crime must exist for a murder to take place and that the killing of one human by another that results from an accident is not murder because no such intention exists. It is indeed this specific phrase that distinguishes murder from other types of criminal homicide, as we will see below.

It is not our intent to analyze each definition of an offense in a step-by-step way as we have for murder. However, we encourage the reader to adopt this technique to better comprehend the nature of any given statute. Exact comprehension of any statute is difficult, even using this technique, because some of the words used to define a criminal act are unclear, ambiguous, or both. In the case of murder, the terms "killing," "human being," and "lawful justification" have empirical referents and are relatively easy to comprehend. "Malice aforethought," however, refers to a state of mind, and there is some confusion concerning what the term actually means. In common law and in the minds of many today, malice involves ill will or hatred, whereas aforethought indicates premeditation; but, as we have indicated above ill will or hatred are no longer required.

Actually, malice may be categorized as either expressed or implied. An example of expressed malice might involve a person's lying in wait, holding a pistol in another person's garage, and firing the pistol at the garage owner when he or she enters the premises. Implied malice is involved in cases in which there was no actual intent to kill. Deaths resulting from the commission of a felony other than murder and deaths occurring when the offender displays a total disregard for a substantial and foreseeable risk often involve implied malice (Kerper & Israel, 1979, p. 136). In such cases, the action (or failure to take action) of the offender is considered so serious that he or she may be held criminally accountable (culpable) for the consequences of his or her actions even though he or she did not specifically intend those consequences (see the discussion of the felony murder rule below).

Some jurisdictions distinguish between first- and second-degree murder. Generally, such a distinction is predicated on the presence of expressed malice aforethought in first-degree murder. Evidence of lying in wait, the deliberate use of poisons or intoxicants, and the brutal nature of the killing may be used to demonstrate the expressed malice aforethought and to obtain a first-degree murder conviction. The final decision usually rests with a jury, which subjectively applies the circumstances to the letter of the law.

Another form of murder, often defined as first-degree murder, involves the **felony murder rule.** This doctrine holds that deaths resulting from the attempt or commission of certain felonies are the responsibility of the perpetrator and, in some jurisdictions, his or her accomplices. Today, the felony murder rule is most frequently applied when a death results from a dangerous or forcible felony (such as robbery, rape, kidnapping, or arson), although historically it has been applied in other types of cases (Perkins, 1969, p. 45). Generally, homicides that involve malice aforethought but fail to meet the requirements of first-degree murder are defined as murder in the second degree in jurisdictions making such distinctions. Thus, second-degree murder may result from the commission of less dangerous felonies or misdemeanors, from the commission of an act intended to cause bodily harm, or from other actions that imply a significant disregard for human life (such as firing a weapon at a passing vehicle).

Manslaughter is an unlawful homicide committed without malice aforethought and is a distinct category of crime rather than a degree of murder (Perkins, 1969, p. 81). There are two categories of manslaughter: voluntary and involuntary (or negligent or reckless). Voluntary manslaughter involves an intent to kill but is distinguished from murder by the circumstances that precede the commission of the act. If great provocation exists, if the offender acted in the "heat of passion" from that provocation, or if the accused acted in a "blind rage," these factors may serve to mitigate the malice, and the offender may be charged with voluntary manslaughter rather than murder. In determining whether an act is murder or manslaughter, a jury faces the difficult tasks of determining the degree of provocation, passion, or rage involved and the extent of provocation necessary to transform murder into manslaughter. In attempting to resolve such dilemmas, the courts have developed some general guidelines. For example, it is generally agreed that mere words are not sufficient provocation to transform a murder to manslaughter (*Mullaney* v. *Wilbur*, 1974). Some action—such as a battery, mutual combat, the commission of adultery (*Dabney* v. *State*, 1897), or resistance to an unlawful arrest—is required. The courts have consistently held that the provocation must be immediately related to the killing. That is, the killing must occur while the offender is in a provoked passionate state. As the court stated in *In re Fraley*, "the law will not permit a defendant to deliberate his wrong, and avenging it by killing the wrongdoer, set up the plea that his act was committed in the heat of passion" (*In re Fraley*, 1910).

The distinguishing feature of involuntary manslaughter is its unintentional nature. (This is the reason for the frequent reference to negligent manslaughter and why deaths resulting from automobile accidents are frequently categorized as involuntary manslaughter or a similarly defined offense.) Gross negligence or recklessness is a key element of this offense. Because many of us have committed reckless or negligent acts at one time or another, a standard of gross negligence is required. The established standard requires a definite disregard for the safety of others in the conduct leading to a death. Examples include the unsafe operation of a motor vehicle (*Commonwealth* v. *Welansky*, 1944), failure to employ reasonable care in hunting game, and failure to provide proper exits in buildings. Some states have developed misdemeanor manslaughter laws that are similar to the felony murder doctrine. The basis for these laws is the belief that the commission of some misdemeanors (generally, *malum in se* offenses) implies negligence and therefore that the offender is responsible for any deaths resulting from the commission of these offenses.

Punishment of homicide varies according to the category of homicide involved. The most severe punishments, including death, are generally reserved for first-degree murder. Many states now provide for "natural life" (life without the possibility of parole) sentences for offenders convicted of first-degree murder who do not receive the death penalty. The length of sentence usually decreases, moving downward from second-degree murder to involuntary manslaughter. We advise the reader to examine the homicide statutes of his or her state to obtain a better understanding of the prescribed punishment associated with each offense.

Assault and Battery

Obviously, not all crimes against the person result in the victim's death. The unlawful application of force by one individual against another may constitute a **battery,** and the attempt or threat to commit a battery may constitute an **assault.** Some jurisdictions combine the two offenses, whereas others treat them separately. A popular misconception is that a serious injury must result for a battery to occur. It is the unlawful application of force, not the result of that application, that constitutes battery. Such actions as pushing a chair into another, pushing another, or patting another on the buttocks may constitute battery even though no serious injury has occurred (Perkins, 1969, pp. 107–8). Further, spitting on another or striking another with a thrown projectile has been deemed battery, even if the recipient was not the intended target. Batteries can also include administering poison, communicating a disease, and deliberately exposing a person to inclement weather (*Pallis* v. *State*, 1899; *State* v. *Lankford*, 1917; *Woodward* v. *State*, 1932). Of course, not all contact, or even all violent contact, constitutes battery. Contact sports, such as boxing, football, and wrestling, are generally exempt from battery rules as long as the contact is within the rules of the game. Similarly, the parent who physically disciplines his or her child does not commit a battery unless such discipline is excessive. The reasonable use of physical force against another in self-defense may also be justified and therefore not a battery.

Actions that place a person in "reasonable apprehension" of being battered (threat) or an attempt to batter may constitute assault. Thus, the unlawful attempt to strike another or otherwise cause injury constitutes an assault. If the attempt is consummated (successful), a battery has occurred. Some interpretations of assault statutes seem to require an awareness on behalf of the victim that he or she is in danger of being battered, whereas others simply require a criminal state of mind on the part of the offender. Interpretations also vary with respect to whether the offender has the ability to commit a battery or only the apparent ability. Threatening another person with a soft rubber knife might be an assault under the latter interpretations but not under the former.

The key issue in determining whether an assault has occurred is whether reasonable apprehension exists on behalf of the victim. Generally, words alone do not appear to be sufficient to generate the necessary apprehension; rather, they must be accompanied by some threatening act or behavior on behalf of the offender.

Some jurisdictions include aggravated assault and aggravated battery in their criminal codes. Factors in **aggravation** include attempts to conceal identity, brandishing or displaying a deadly weapon, and committing assaults or batteries on specially designated professionals (e.g., teachers, police officers, or firefighters) while they are officially performing their duties (*Moreland* v. *State*, 1916).

In some jurisdictions, no battery can occur without an assault (the consummated battery includes the threat or attempt to batter), and battery and assault are merged into a single statute.

Forcible Rape

Traditional definitions of **rape** generally involve the following elements: (1) sexual intercourse, (2) by a male with a female other than his wife, (3) against her will and without consent, and (4) by force or threat of force or while she is unconscious. Again, the definition may be broken down into its component parts to help us comprehend the nature of the offense.

Traditionally, sexual intercourse requires penetration of the female sex organ by the male sex organ. Lewd fondling or caressing and oral or anal sexual contact were defined as batteries, indecent liberties, or **sodomy,** but did not constitute rape. Today, many jurisdictions refer to these offenses under the headings of **deviate sexual conduct** (lewd fondling, for example) and **deviate sexual assault** (crimes involving penetration).

Historically, the courts have adhered to a principle of spousal immunity and have excepted forced intercourse by a husband with his wife from the category of forcible rape. The underlying assumption seems to have been that marriage is a permanent consent to sexual intercourse. Today, however, most states have theoretically eliminated this exemption; nonetheless, there are still few husbands convicted for the rape of their wives. Another modification being witnessed involves the gender of the offender and victim. Under the traditional definition of rape, it was virtually an all-male offense, and victims were exclusively female. Today, in some jurisdictions the word "person" has been substituted for "male" and "female," making it legally possible for a male to rape another male or for a female to rape a male (*State v. Flaherty,* 1929). Some states have also specified a minimum age for the offender.

There is considerable controversy over what constitutes consent on behalf of an alleged rape victim. In general, a victim who is incapacitated by the use of alcohol or other drugs, who is unconscious, who is mentally ill or severely retarded, or who is a victim of deception or fraud is incapable of giving a valid consent. However, some courts have held that the victim must resist to the utmost and that any form of submission, prior to forced penetration, constitutes consent. For example, an alleged offender was acquitted of rape when it was disclosed during cross-examination that the victim had a knife in her possession at the time of the incident but made no attempt to retrieve it from her purse and defend herself (Peoria *Journal Star,* 1977, p. C-14). Opinions such as this are rare today, however, and most cases hinge on factors such as the number of assailants, the presence of a weapon, and evidence of penetration. Further, there has been a continual trend toward limiting the introduction of evidence concerning the victim's previous sexual experiences in rape trials (Spohn & Homey, 1992).

The element of force or threat of force in rape is somewhat ambiguous. Cases in which a battery occurs are relatively easy to discern. It is equally clear that the presence or use of a deadly weapon is not required to prove that force was imminent. Torn clothing, cuts, bruises, or teeth marks are frequently used to indicate that force accompanied sexual intercourse. Generally speaking, courts have held that coercion sufficient to accomplish the intended result (i.e., sexual penetration) fulfills the force or threat of force requirement for rape.

Sexual Predators or Sexually Dangerous Persons

Recently, several states have passed laws that require community notification when a convicted sex offender moves into a neighborhood, as well as requiring that sex offenders register with law enforcement officials in the communities in which they live. These laws, often referred to as sexual predator laws, are variations of a New Jersey law known as Megan's Law. (See In the News, "Top Court Upholds Ruling" and "Thompson to Sign Bill.") These laws pit protection of children and victims against the offender's right to privacy and have thus been controversial. Even more controversial are laws that allow the courts to commit offenders legally declared sexual predators or sexually dangerous persons to mental health facilities subsequent to serving their prison terms (Kazak, 2000; Chicago Daily Law Bulletin, 2000).

In the News

TOP COURT UPHOLDS RULING ON PREDATORS

By Plain Dealer Bureau

The Ohio Supreme Court disposed of 81 pending sexual predator labeling cases yesterday without comment, upholding its ruling last month that the law is constitutional.

The appeals of the so-called Megan's Law came from Lake, Ashtabula and Portage counties, representing the last remaining challenges to the law before the Supreme Court.

In the earlier ruling, justices reversed an 11th District Ohio Court of Appeals determination that the predator law violated the defendant's constitutional right to privacy, right to a favorable reputation, right to acquire property and the ability to pursue an occupation.

The decision yesterday was the court's fifth favorable ruling to challenges brought against the law, which took effect in 1997. The law was modeled on a New Jersey statute enacted after 7-year-old Megan Kanka was raped and murdered in her neighborhood by a convicted sex offender living across the street.

The law requires offenders to be listed as sexually oriented, habitual or as predators. Sexual predators must register with law enforcement officials, who then notify residents, schools and other institutions that an offender lives nearby.

However, the court in its earlier ruling said convicted offenders must receive advance warning before a trial court determines how the offender will be classified.

The Plain Dealer, May 16, 2000, p. 2B.

In the News

THOMPSON TO SIGN BILL REVISING SEX OFFENDER LAWS; UPDATED RULES WILL ALLOW STATE TO KEEP $1 MILLION IN FEDERAL ANTI-CRIME GRANTS

By Steven Walters

MADISON—Wisconsin's sex offender registration and notification laws are being updated to prevent the loss of an estimated $1 million in federal funds.

Gov. Tommy G. Thompson is scheduled to sign a bill into law today that will revise the state's version of "Megan's Law." The sponsor of the bill, Rep. Scott Walker (R-Wauwatosa), said the changes will:

- Require more convicted sex offenders to register with the state. Under the change, more crimes will require registration, and anyone convicted in another state or in a federal, military or tribal court of specific crimes will have to join the state registry if they live, work or attend school in Wisconsin.
- Make a second or later failure to register as required a felony, instead of a misdemeanor.
- Authorize an Internet Web site on which victims, police and the public can learn details about individuals on Wisconsin's registry.

The bill unanimously passed the Legislature, and aides said it will be one of 17 the governor plans to sign in a morning ceremony in the Capitol.

Many of the changes were needed to bring the state law into compliance with the federal law. Wisconsin could have lost the federal funding if the changes had not been made, Walker said.

Walker said the $1 million in federal anti-crime grants the state could have lost helps pay for DNA testing of criminals, suspects and prison inmates; anti-drug programs in prisons; and literacy programs for inmates.

Chairman of the Assembly's Corrections and Courts Committee, Walker said the changes becoming law today "put teeth into state law" and the new Internet site will "facilitate the flow of necessary information" on registered sex offenders to the public.

The original law was named for Megan Kanka, a 7-year-old New Jersey girl who was killed by Jesse Timmendequas, who had been convicted of two earlier sex offenses.

Milwaukee Journal Sentinel, April 25, 2000, p. 2B.

Other Sex Offenses

Although forcible rape is usually considered the most serious of the sex offenses, a number of other offenses are worthy of mention. Some jurisdictions hold that a female under a given age (usually 15 to 18) cannot legally consent to sexual intercourse. If vaginal intercourse occurs, the male participant may be charged with **statutory rape** or a similarly defined offense. Other states have categorized sexual contact (other than intercourse) as indecent solicitation of a minor, sexual exploitation of a child, or contributing to the sexual delinquency of a minor (*Illinois Criminal Law and Procedure,* 1998, chap. 720 ILCS, sec. 5/11-6, 5/11-9.1).

As indicated above, another trend in criminal law is to reduce the overall number of sex offenses by incorporating all forms of sexual penetration (vaginal, oral, and anal, and the insertion of foreign objects) into the crime of sexual assault. In addition, cases involving weapons, minors, and family members are termed "aggravated sexual assault" and carry stiffer penalties (*Illinois Criminal Law and Procedure,* 1998, chap. 720, sec. 5/11, pp. 213–28). While historically a number of sexual acts, including oral/genital and anal/genital contact, were prohibited under the general heading of sodomy, the current trend is to accept a variety of forms of sexual penetration and/or contact if they occur privately and between consenting adults.

There are clearly numerous other sex offenses, but space does not permit a detailed examination of all such offenses. We encourage the reader to carefully examine his or her own state's criminal code under such headings as adultery, fornication, prostitution, incest, and indecent exposure.

CRIMES AGAINST PROPERTY

Robbery

Robbery is a unique crime in that it can be characterized as both a crime against property and a crime against the person. In addition, unlike homicide and aggravated assault, most robberies involve victims and offenders who have no prior personal relationship. Robbery involves taking property (theft) from another person by force or threat of force (assault, battery, or murder). The theft must occur in the presence of the victim but need not involve taking property from the person of the victim. As long as the property is within the general proximity of the victim and is under the victim's control (e.g., cash stolen from the teller at a bank) and as long as force or threat of force is used (e.g., the presence of a weapon) with the intent to permanently deprive the victim of the use of the property, a robbery has occurred. Threat of deadly force is not required—pushing, jostling, or striking with a fist are all sufficient to prove the force element in robbery. Thus, the pickpocket who is caught trying to remove the victim's wallet and who struggles with the victim to pull the wallet away has now used force and has crossed the line from theft to robbery. Similarly, threats to destroy valuable property or to inflict bodily injury have consistently been found sufficient to substantiate a robbery charge.

Graduations of robbery are fairly common. Armed or aggravated robbery (involving the use or presence of deadly weapons) is the most serious form of the offense and is subject to the most severe punishment.

The law protects the property of citizens as well as their persons. The list of crimes against property is quite extensive, and we illustrate the nature of these crimes by focusing on three in addition to robbery: theft, burglary, and arson.

Larceny/Theft

Theft occurs when one obtains unauthorized control over the property of another with the intent to permanently deprive the rightful possessor of the use of that property. Many statutes include receiving stolen property and obtaining property through deception (e.g., embezzlement) or under false pretenses under the general heading of theft. Like most crimes against property, theft is a crime against the right of possession, not necessarily ownership, and statutes usually protect both actual and constructive possession. Actual possession involves physical control over the property. For example, Jones is walking down the street carrying some packages. Smith takes one of the packages, runs away, and later sells the contents of the package. Smith has committed a theft involving actual possession. Constructive possession occurs when the property involved is outside the owner's control but the right of ownership has not been relinquished. Jones drives his car to Brown's house and leaves it there. While Brown is distracted by a fire truck, Smith steals the car. Although neither Jones nor Brown had actual possession of the auto, Jones still maintained constructive possession and was thus the victim of auto theft.

Because theft is a crime against the right of possession, it is possible for a person to be charged with stealing his or her own property. An apartment owner who signs a legally binding contract to rent an apartment complete with furnishings (stereo, refrigerator, stove, and furniture) relinquishes possession to the renter for the duration of the lease. If the apartment owner enters the apartment without the renter's knowledge and removes some of the furnishings with the intent to keep them permanently, he or she may be technically guilty of theft even though the items belonged to him or her. Thus, one does not have to own the property stolen to be the victim of a theft; he or she must simply have legal possession of the property. The property involved may be either real property (e.g., land or buildings) or personal property (all other property).

The issue of intent to permanently deprive an individual of his or her property is frequently a key element of theft cases. If you borrow a rake from a neighbor's garage to use for an afternoon, you have not committed theft because you did not intend to deprive the neighbor of the permanent use of the rake. If, however, you pick fruit from your neighbor's tree and eat it, you have unquestionably deprived the owner/possessor of the permanent use of the fruit and are subject to prosecution for theft.

The issue of intent to permanently deprive arises frequently in shoplifting cases. When a person conceals merchandise and passes the checkout lanes without paying for it or leaves the store, the intent to permanently deprive is relatively easy to demonstrate in court. If, however, an overzealous security guard confronts the person concealing the merchandise at the time the merchandise is concealed, the necessary element of intent to permanently deprive is more difficult to prove. The shoplifter can make an argument that he or she intended to pay for the items at the checkout lanes.

Automobile theft presents some of the same problems. Does the teenager who, without permission, takes an auto to go to the mall and then leaves the auto unharmed intend to permanently deprive the owner of the use of the auto? As a solution, most states have enacted "joyriding" or "unauthorized use of a vehicle" statutes. An intent to permanently deprive is not a necessary element of these statutes.

In most instances, theft is divided into two categories, depending on the dollar value of the items involved. The dividing line varies (in some states it's $300), but the lesser dollar amounts are defined as petty (or misdemeanor) theft and the more substantial sums grand (or felony) theft. As you might expect, the penalties tend to increase with the value of the property stolen.

Burglary

How many times have you heard someone cry, "I've been robbed!" when they returned to find a window or door broken and their television set or stereo removed? Actually, these individuals have been burglarized (and are also victims of theft), not robbed. Traditionally, **burglary** involves breaking into and entering the dwelling of another, at night, with the intent to commit a felony in the dwelling. The use of force to enter such a dwelling constitutes breaking into. The courts have held that the amount of force required may be exceedingly little, such as turning a doorknob (*State* v. *Perry*, 1914) or raising an unlocked window (*State* v. *McAfee*, 1957).

Most jurisdictions now hold that one who enters a building lawfully but remains inside without authorization after the building is closed commits breaking in. This type of entry may be referred to as constructive breaking and applies to acts of deception used to gain entry.

Unlawful entry must also occur for a burglary to transpire. The entry may be very slight: Reaching inside to extract some article is sufficient. Constructive entry, involving the use of a trained animal, rope, or other device, may also establish the necessary element of the offense.

Burglary statutes today cover not only the dwellings of others but also telephone booths, unoccupied buildings, automobiles, aircraft, watercraft, and other forms of transportation or conveyance. Some jurisdictions list special crimes, such as residential or aggravated burglary, which involve the burglary of a dwelling and carry stiffer penalties. Similarly, modern statutes have eliminated the requirement that the breaking and entering occur at night.

With burglary, like theft, the element of intent may be difficult to prove. The prosecution must prove both the intent to enter and the intent to commit a felony or theft once entry is gained. One who falls asleep in a library and awakens after the library is closed has not committed a burglary, nor has the individual who enters the wrong apartment while reasonably believing it to be his or her own. This sometimes happens when an intoxicated person breaks into an apartment or house near and similar to his or her own, believing that a spouse has locked him or her out. In such a case, there is no intent to enter unlawfully, and even though a physical break-in occurs, the individual has not committed a burglary, although he or she may be civilly liable for any damages that occurred.

There is some disagreement regarding the second form of intent to commit a felony or theft. Some courts have held that the intent to commit any felony will suffice, whereas other jurisdictions specify an intent to commit dangerous felonies. Most statutes state an intent to commit a felony or theft, recognizing that some thefts are not felonies. The intent is relatively easy to prove if the offender is caught with stolen property or when the burglar uses a knife or gun to threaten others at the scene. The intent to commit a felony or theft is more difficult to prove when the burglar is caught making his or her entry. The presence of a torch, burglary tools, explosives, or a weapon may be sufficient to indicate such intent. It need not be shown that the accused did, in fact, commit a felony or theft, only that he or she intended to do so.

Arson

Arson poses a serious threat to both human life and property. Arson involves the willful and unlawful burning of a building or structure. At one time, arson was limited to burning dwellings belonging to another, but contemporary statutes include all buildings and structures and many forms of personal property.

A general criminal state of mind, rather than a specific intent to commit arson, is all that is required by most arson statutes. An act intended as vandalism or an act of extortion that leads to an unlawful burning may constitute arson as well. In certain cases, gross negligence may also result in prosecution for arson.

Total destruction of the property is not required to prove arson. Similarly, the arsonist need not be physically present to ignite the fire. A bomb or explosive device may also be used to commit arson.

Arson for profit has become a major problem in the United States. Burning one's own property to defraud an insurer has become almost fashionable among some property owners experiencing financial difficulties. Ideally, the culprit hopes that the evidence of arson will be destroyed in the fire or explosion. Many insurance carriers will not issue payment when there is a suspicious origin of the fire.

A more recent development is the creation of aggravated arson statutes. Arson of an occupied building or arson that results in injury to police or fire personnel responding to the fire are deemed aggravated and often carry harsh penalties.

SOME RECENT ADDITIONS TO CRIMINAL LAW

Although many of the acts discussed in this chapter have been defined as criminal for centuries, we cannot lose sight of the fact that new laws are continually enacted in response to specific societal problems. In the past decade or so, we have seen several new crimes emerge in response to societal behavior patterns. Among these are hate crimes and stalking.

Hate crimes are offenses that target victims on the basis of race, color, creed, religion, national origin, sexual orientation, disability, or similar criteria. Hate crimes can target either groups or individuals and usually involve another offense, such as assault, battery, criminal trespass, criminal damage to property, mob action, or, in rare instances, homicide. Both the additional offense and the designation of the target are necessary elements to obtain a conviction under a hate crimes statute. On June 11, 1993, the U.S. Supreme Court issued a unanimous decision upholding the constitutionality of Wisconsin's hate crimes enhancement statute, removing any doubt that legislatures could increase the penalties for crimes in which the victim is targeted because of his or her race, religion, ethnicity, or sexual orientation. Since that decision, virtually all states have adopted some type of hate crimes statute. Such statutes typically specify stiffer penalties than the predicate offense (*Illinois Criminal Law and Procedure*, 1998, chap. 720, sec. 5/12-7.1). In spite of these statutes, research indicates there has been an increase in the number of hate crimes in recent years (see In the News, "King Claims Drugs led to Jasper Death" and "Taking Stand Against Hate"), indicating that hate is alive and well in the United States (Haider-Markel, 1998).

Society's increased focus on domestic violence has resulted in the addition of **stalking** statutes to many state criminal codes. Stalking involves the intentional or deliberate following of another person or placing that person under surveillance and either threatening that individual or placing the victim in reasonable apprehension of bodily harm. Typically, estranged spouses or lovers are perpetrators of stalking. Some jurisdictions have also created the offense of aggravated stalking when injury occurs, the victim is unlawfully restrained, or the offender violates an order of protection or a restraining order (*Illinois Criminal Law and Procedure*, 1998, chap 720, ILCS, sec. 5/12-7.3, 7.4).

In the News

KING CLAIMS DRUGS LED TO JASPER DEATH

By Richard Stewart

BEAUMONT—Awaiting execution for one of the most notorious racial murders in Texas history, Bill King claims in court documents that he did not participate in the dragging death of James Byrd Jr. and that Byrd was killed over $800 in drug money. The prosecutor in the case against King called King's claim a fabrication, noting that investigators never found any sign of drugs. King made his latest claim of innocence in a response to a wrongful death lawsuit filed by Byrd's children. Byrd's multilated body was found on a Jasper County road on June 7, 1998. King and his former prison buddy, Russell Brewer Jr., were both sentenced to die for Byrd's slaying. Prosecutors said Byrd was taken to a forest clearing, beaten and then dragged for three miles behind a pickup. Shawn Berry, a hometown friend of King's, also was convicted of capital murder, but was sentenced to life in prison. In his court brief, filed in state district court in Jasper, King repeated a claim that Berry alone drove off with Byrd that night in June. He also accused Berry of being an alcoholic with a violent temper who used steroids and illegal drugs.

"Shawn admittedly stated (Byrd) had jacked him for almost $800 a few months prior, a conclusive and verifiable motive for murder could be substantiated in an objective way," King wrote in his 17-page response filed this month. Prosecutors and lawyers representing Byrd's children in the lawsuit contend that Byrd was killed simply because he was black. Jasper County District Attorney Guy James Gray, who prosecuted all three of the white men, said, "In all our investigation we never found any indication that drugs were involved. I don't think any of the defendants ever had $800." Berry was the only defendant to give a statement to police about Byrd's slaying, and he blamed the crime on King and Brewer. The lawsuit by Byrd's children seeks unspecified damages from King, Brewer and Berry, several Ku Klux Klan organizations and a prison group King once headed called the Texas Rebel Soldiers of the Confederate Knights of America. Gray said he believes King filed his response for publicity. "He enjoys the attention," he said.

The Houston Chronicle, July 22, 2000, p. A35.

In the News

TAKING STAND AGAINST HATE; RALLY DEMANDS JUSTICE FOR GAY BLACK MAN SLAIN IN W.VA.

By Phuong Ly and Tracey A. Reeves

With the setting sun shining on the Capitol behind her, Brenda Warren choked back tears for her slain son and demanded justice in the form of stronger federal hate-crime legislation.

About 100 people gathered at Senate Park last night to mourn Arthur "J.R." Warren, a 26-year-old from Grant Town, W.Va., who many are convinced was killed because he was black, gay or both.

"Hate Kills," said Brenda Warren, raising her voice. "The injustice that my son suffered, no one—no one—should ever have to bear that. . . . If nothing else, I just want to say please, please, let it be the last time."

Earlier in the day, the Warrens had scored one victory: Deputy U.S. Attorney General Eric H. Holder Jr. announced that the Justice Department has opened a preliminary investigation into J.R. Warren's death.

Holder called the gathering, which also included representatives from the Human Rights Campaign, a gay and lesbian rights group, the NAACP and the Leadership Conference on Civil Rights, "an informative, disturbing and emotional meeting about a senseless and brutal killing."

"I am concerned about the circumstances surrounding this incident," Holder said in a statement. "We will continue to work cooperatively with local authorities in this matter to determine what, if any, additional federal action is warranted."

Warren was beaten to death early July 4. Two 17-year-old youths, now charged as juveniles with first-degree murder, allegedly threw his body into the road and drove over it several times to make the crime look like a hit-and-run accident, police said.

Warren's death had drawn national attention, with activists citing similarities to the 1998 murder of Matthew Shepard, a gay Wyoming college student, and the racially motivated dragging death the same year of James Byrd Jr. in Jasper, Tex. The slayings have spurred a movement for stronger federal hate-crime legislation.

Earlier this year, the Senate passed a hate-crime bill that extended protection to include violence based on gender, sexual orientation and disability. The proposal would drop a current restriction limiting federal intervention to cases where victims are engaged in federally protected activities, such as voting, serving on a jury or attending school. Advocates of the new measure argued that these restrictions make it difficult to prosecute the existing law and exclude many hate crimes.

Continued

The bill still awaits a vote in the House of Representatives.

The crowd at last night's rally included a broad mix of people—businessmen in suits, activists in T-shirts, gay and straight people, blacks and whites.

"Surely, action by the Congress is now morally compelled," said Del. Eleanor Holmes Norton (D–D.C.) "We are determined that this young black gay man will be remembered by more than a white cross in West Virginia. . . . We will not rest until he is remembered forever in our laws."

Sen. Gordon Smith (R–Ore.), who co-sponsored the Senate bill, called for bipartisan support of the legislation.

"When things like this happen on the Fourth of July, the federal government has a right to show up, to defend an American citizen," he said. "On this issue, we cannot be divided."

The Washington Post, July 21, 2000, p. B7.

Presence of graffiti often characterizes hate crimes.
Max Whittaker/Getty Liaison

MEASURING CRIME

Official crime statistics are available at the national level in the **Uniform Crime Reports (UCRs),** prepared annually by the Federal Bureau of Investigation. The FBI claims that the UCR covers about 99 percent of the total national population, with the most complete reporting coming from urban and suburban areas and the least reporting from more rural areas. Today, most jurisdictions participate in the UCR regardless of their size. For comparative purposes, a crime rate is calculated and standardized by multiplying the rate by 100,000. Although the FBI statistics are the most comprehensive ones available at the national level, they are subject to a number of sources of error. First, reporting is voluntary, and not all agencies report. Second, UCRs are based on reports prepared and submitted by individual police agencies, and reporting errors made by each agency are added to those made by other agencies in the final report. Such errors include mistakes in calculations and mistakes in placing offenses in the appropriate categories. Third, statistics in UCRs fail to indicate whether the alleged offender was actually apprehended and subsequently convicted for the reported offense. If we are interested in the number of offenders for certain types of crime in a certain time period, UCR data are useful, but if we want to know something about the actual extent and nature of criminal behavior, these data are considerably less valuable. Last, the UCRs also includes **time clocks** that indicate how frequently specific offenses occur accross the United States. The fact that a certain offense occurs every three seconds is unrelated to most citizens' potential to be the victim of that particular offense. It should be noted that many of the weaknesses associated with the UCRs are also noted by the FBI in its annual publication *Crime in the United States* or on its web site: *http://www.fbi.gov.ucr/faqs.htm.*

There are a variety of official statistics available at the local and state levels. Most police departments tabulate statistics on **offenses known to the police** (those offenses observed by or reported to the police) and **offenses cleared by arrest.** Of all official statistics, offenses known to the police probably provide the most complete picture of the nature and extent of certain types of illegal activities (not including white-collar, organized, corporate, or political crime). Even when we consider the Index Offenses—criminal homicide, aggravated assault, forcible rape, robbery, burglary, felony theft, arson, and auto theft—there is considerable evidence to indicate that less than 50 percent of these crimes are reported to the police (Livingston, 1996, p. 63). If estimates are reasonably accurate, the police are able to arrest a suspect in only about one out of five Index Offenses reported, which means that about 80 percent of those offenses reported to the police are not included in statistics based on crimes cleared by arrest.

Official statistics may be collected at a number of levels in the criminal justice network. However, each level includes some possible sources of error. Figure 4–1 indicates some sources of error that may affect official statistics collected at each level in the criminal justice network. Each official source of statistics has appropriate uses, but generally speaking, the sources of error increase as one moves through each level of the network. Another source of error may involve the use of slightly different definitions of certain crimes in certain jurisdictions.

Finally, there are two additional sources of error that may affect official statistics. First, in our current criminal justice network, there is a strong tendency for those who are least able to afford the luxury of private counsel and middle-class standards of living to be overrepresented at all levels. Whether

Levels at Which Data May Be Collected		Sources of Error in Official Statistics
Police	1. Offenses known to the police	All offenses not detected All offenses not reported to or recorded by the police
	2. Offenses cleared by arrest	Errors from level 1 All offenses reported that do not lead to arrest
Prosecutor	3. Offenses leading to prosecution	Errors from levels 1 and 2 All offenses that result in arrest but do not lead to prosecution
Courts	4. Offenses leading to conviction	Errors from levels 1, 2, and 3 All offenses prosecuted that do not lead to conviction
Corrections	5. Offenses leading to incarceration	Errors from levels 1, 2, 3, and 4 All offenses leading to conviction but not to incarceration

Source: Used by permission from Cox/Conrad *Juvenile Justice,* Fourth Edition, McGraw-Hill, 1996.

Figure 4.1
Some Sources of Error at Specified Levels in the Criminal Justice Network

official statistics report actual differences in the nature and extent of crime by social class or whether they reflect the inability of members of the lower social classes to avoid official labeling as readily as their middle-class counterparts is not entirely clear, although there is considerable support for the latter explanation. Second, it is important to remember that agencies collect and publish official statistics for a variety of purposes (such as justifying next year's budget request). This does not mean that all or even most agency personnel deliberately manipulate crime statistics for their own purposes, but all statistics are open to interpretation and may be presented in a variety of ways to suit the needs and purposes of the presenters.

It is apparent that using official statistics to assess the nature and extent of crime is like looking at the tip of the iceberg; that is, a substantial proportion of crime remains hidden beneath the surface. Although much crime occurs that is not reported to or recorded by officials, there is no precise method to determine just how much crime remains hidden. Attempts to assess the nature of criminal activity have involved victim survey research and self-report studies.

Victim Survey Research

Our knowledge of hidden crime has been improved considerably over the past several years by the use of **victim survey research.** The best example of victim survey research is the **National Crime Victimization Survey (NCVS)** conducted by the Department of Justice. Samples of about 100,000 citizens over age 12 are analyzed every six months on a nationwide basis, and these citizens are asked to indicate whether (and, if so, how often) they have been the victims of crime in a specified time period. Respondents who indicate they have been victimized, unlike respondents in self-report studies, are not admitting to participation in illegal behavior and may therefore be more honest than self-report respondents. Victim survey research indicates that somewhere between 50 and 66 percent of all serious crime in the United States goes unreported to the police (Livingston, 1996, p. 63). Rates for reporting vary by crime, and respondents indicate a variety of reasons for failing to report their misfortunes to criminal justice officials. The data indicate that most homicides and auto thefts are reported to the police, whereas rapes, aggravated assaults, burglaries, robberies, and thefts are not. The NCVS provides information concerning the circumstances of the crime, the characteristics of the offender (for some offenses), and the personal characteristics and actions of the victim regardless of whether or not the crime was reported to the police.

Although victim survey research has expanded our knowledge of the crime picture considerably, it too has limitations. Obviously, we cannot collect data on homicidal victimizations from victims; we generally do not ask questions about white-collar, corporate, political, or drug-related crime; and victims of some types of crime (e.g., rape) may be hesitant to report. Undoubtedly, some under- and overreporting occurs as the result of misinterpretations of the questions asked. Memory also affects the validity of victim reports.

Self-Report Studies

Recognizing that official statistics provide a false dichotomy between criminals (those officially labeled) and noncriminals (those who may engage in illegal behavior but avoid the official label), Short and Nye (1958) and others decided to use self-report studies from juveniles to compare the nature and extent of delinquent activity on the part of institutionalized (labeled) and noninstitutionalized (nonlabeled) juveniles. **Self-report studies** of delinquent behavior were obtained by distributing questionnaires to both labeled and nonlabeled juveniles. These questionnaires allowed respondents to indicate what types of crimes they had committed and the frequency with which the acts had been committed. Short and Nye concluded that delinquency among noninstitutionalized juveniles is extensive and that there is little difference in the extent and nature of delinquent acts committed by noninstitutionalized and institutionalized juveniles. In addition, Short and Nye indicated that official statistics lead us to the misbelief that delinquency is largely a lower-class phenomenon, because few differences in the self-reported incidence of delinquency exist among juveniles in lower, middle, and upper social classes. The conclusions reached in similar studies (Akers, 1964; Porterfield, 1946; Voss, 1966) generally support those of Short and Nye.

Self-report studies are subject to criticism on the grounds that those who serve as respondents may under- or overreport their illegal activities. Some researchers have included questions designed to detect deception. Clark and Tifft (1966) used follow-up interviews and polygraph examinations to assess the extent to which deception occurred in their self-report study and found that all respondents made corrections on their original questionnaires when given the opportunity. Three-fourths of all the changes increased the frequency of admitted deviancy, all respondents underreported their misconduct on at least one item, and over half overreported on at least one item. Clark and Tifft concluded that "those items most frequently used on delinquency scales were found to be rather inaccurate" (p. 523).

The **Institute for Social Research,** based at the University of Michigan, annually surveys approximately 2,500 high school seniors concerning their involvement in criminal activity. Their findings relating to drug use, violent crime, and property offenses are frequently used to measure the success of various school-based and government-sponsored prevention programs.

In conclusion, the use of self-report scales as the only means of determining the extent of crime or delinquency is risky. However, these scales provide information that can be cross-checked in a variety of ways (e.g., through police records) and allow comparisons between official and unofficial estimates of crime.

Summary

1. By analyzing the definitions of the various crimes step-by-step, we can better understand the exact nature and requirements of these crimes.

2. The general distinction between felonies and misdemeanors has been discussed, as have differences between crimes that are *malum in se* (evils in themselves) and *malum prohibitum* (evil because they are prohibited).

3. Criminal homicides, rape, and robbery are among the most serious of the crimes against the person. The elements of these offenses, as well as those of the property crimes of theft, burglary, and arson, have been briefly analyzed in this chapter.

4. In addition, several new crimes and the laws used to attempt to control them were discussed.

5. There are a variety of ways of collecting information concerning crime. The Uniform Crime Reports and the National Crime Victimization Survey are the most widely used sources of crime statistics.

Key Terms Defined

statutory   Law enacted by legislative bodies.

case law   Law based on court decisions.

felonies   Offenses punishable by a sentence of more than one year in prison.

misdemeanors   Offenses punishable by up to one year in jail.

acts *malum in se*   Acts that are wrong in and of themselves.

acts *malum prohibitum*   Acts that are wrong because they are prohibited.

homicide   The killing of another person.

murder   The premeditated and unlawful killing of another person.

suicide   Killing oneself.

malice aforethought   The intention to seriously harm someone or commit a serious crime.

felony murder rule   A rule stating that an accidental killing that occurs during the commission of a felony may be termed murder.

manslaughter   An unlawful homicide committed without malice aforethought.

battery   An intentional, unprovoked, harmful physical contact by one person (or an object controlled by that person) with another.

assault   An act that creates in one person the reasonable fear of being battered by another by reason of threat or attempt to batter.

aggravation   An act that increases the seriousness of the crime in question.

rape   Sexual intercourse by force or threat of force without lawful consent.

sodomy   Sexual contact between the sex organs of, or an object controlled by, one person with the mouth or anus of another.

deviate sexual conduct   Generally, lewd fondling or sexually "knowing" another without consent and without sexual penetration.

deviate sexual assault   Generally, sexual contact involving penetration of the mouth, anus, or sex organs of one person by another without consent.

statutory rape   Intercourse with a female under a specified age.

robbery   The illegal taking of property from another by force or threat of force.

theft (larceny)   Taking unauthorized control over the property of another with the intent to permanently deprive the rightful possessor of the property.

burglary   Generally, breaking into and entering the dwelling of another with the intent to commit a felony.

arson   The willful and unlawful burning of a building or structure.

hate crimes   Crimes that target victims on the basis of race, creed, color, national origin, sexual preference, or religion.

stalking   The intentional or deliberate following of another person or placing another person under surveillance and either threatening that person or placing the person in reasonable fear of bodily harm.

Uniform Crime Reports (UCRs)   Reports prepared by the FBI concerning reported crimes in the United States.

time clocks   Clocks showing the number of crimes occurring per minute.

offenses known to the police   Offenses reported to or observed by the police.

offenses cleared by arrest   Offenses for which one or more individuals has been made available for prosecution.

victim survey research   Research that collects reports concerning experiences as crime victims.

National Crime Victimization Survey (NCVS)   Report prepared by the Department of Justice concerning crimes occurring in the United States.

self-report studies   Studies asking respondents to report their criminal activities.

Institute for Social Research   University of Michigan-based survey research center.

Critical Thinking Exercises

1. What sources of information would you use to obtain the most accurate picture of crime in the United States? What are some of the limitations of each source of information?
2. Are there consistent threads through the various types of behavior classified as crimes? If so, what are those threads?

Internet Exercises

The crime of murder is often intriguing and fascinating to the college student. Recently, law enforcement agencies have developed an extensive literature base on serial killers. Access the serial killers website at *www.crimelibrary.com/serials/what/whatmain.htm.*

After you read this site, answer the following questions:

1. What distinguishes serial murder from other types/forms of murder?
2. What role does insanity play in the motives for serial killings and as an affirmative defense?
3. Who are the victims of serial killers, and how are they selected?
4. What effect does child abuse and the mother–son relationship have on serial killers?

References

Akers, R. L. (1964). Socioeconomic status and delinquent behavior: A retest. *Journal of Research on Crime and Delinquency, 1,* 38–46.

Chicago Daily Law Bulletin. (2000, September 29). Justice clarifies sexual predator law, p 5.

Clark, J. P., & Tifft, L. L. (1966). Polygraph and interview validation of self-reported deviant behavior. *American Sociological Review, 31* (4), 516–23.

Commonwealth v. *Welansky,* 316 Mass. 383, 53 NE 2d 902 (1944).

Dabney v. *State,* 21 So. 211, 113 Ala. 38 (1897).

Gamage, A. L., & Hemphill, C. F. (1979). *Basic criminal law.* New York: McGraw-Hill.

Haider-Markel, D. P. (1998). The politics of social regulatory policy: State and federal hate crime policy and implementation effort. *Political Research Quarterly, 51* (1), 69–88.

Illinois criminal law and procedure. (1998). St. Paul, MN: West.

In re Fraley, 109 P. 295, 3 Okla. Crim. 719 (1910).

Kerper, H. B., & Israel, J. H. (1979). *Introduction to the criminal justice system.* St. Paul, MN: West.

Livingston, J. (1996). *Crime and criminology* (2nd ed.). Upper Saddle River, NJ: Prentice Hall.

Kazak, D. R. (2000, December 20). "Sexually dangerous" man sent to prison. *Chicago Daily Herald,* p. 6.

Moreland v. *State,* 188 SWI, 125, Ark. 24 (1916).

Mullaney v. *Wilbur,* 421 U.S. 684 (1974).

Pallis v. *State,* 26 So. 339 (1899).

Peoria Journal Star. (1977, January 7). Man, 22, acquitted of rape, to face parole, pardon board, p. C14.

Perkins, R. M. (1969). *Perkins on criminal law.* Mineola, NY: Foundation Press.

Porterfield, A. L. (1946). *Youth in trouble.* Fort Worth, IN: Potisham Foundation.

Short, J. F., & Nye, F. I. (1958). Extent of unrecorded juvenile delinquency: Some tentative conclusions. *Journal of Criminal Law, Criminology, and Police Science, 49* (4), 296–302.

Spohn, C., & Homey, J. (1992). *Rape law reform: A grassroots revolution and its impact.* New York: Plenum.

State v. *Flaherty,* 146 A. 7 (1929).

State v. *Lankford,* 12 A. 13 (1917).

State v. *McAfee,* 100 S.E. 2d 249 (1957).

State v. *Perry,* 145 N.W. 56 (1914).

Voss, H. L. (1966). Socioeconomic status and reported delinquent behavior. *Social Problems, 13,* 314–24.

Woodward v. *State,* 144 So. 895 (1932).

Suggested Readings

Conklin, J. E. (1972). *Robbery and the criminal justice system.* Philadelphia: Lippincott.

Gregory, J. (1999). *Policing sexual assault.* New York: Routledge.

Lanier, M. M., & Henry, S. (1998). *Essential criminology.* Boulder, CO: Westview.

McNamara, G. M. (2000). Sexual predator identification notification. *Law and Order, 48* (4), 60–61.

Samaha, J. (1996). *Criminal law.* 5th ed. St. Paul, MN: West.

Wattendorf, G. E. (2000). Stalking-investigation strategies. *FBI Law Enforcement Bulletin, 60* (3), 10–14.

CHAPTER FIVE

Types of Crime: II

Even the wealthy commit crimes for which they may be arrested.
Tony Freeman/Photo Edit

L aura was still without a thesis topic, and time was becoming her enemy. She decided to invite some of her classmates over in hopes that they might help her find the perfect topic for her research. Laura explained her difficulty in selecting a topic from one of the traditional categories, and Steve, a former city police officer, suggested she select a crime that created its own following, a crime without a complainant.

The ensuing discussion focused on many areas of interest: why some behaviors are defined as criminal despite public demand, the relationship between crimes without complainants and corruption, and the impact of legalizing some of those behaviors. The group agreed those were all interesting topics but suggested Laura select a specific type of victimless crime for her topic.

Tami had worked in a convention hotel one summer and described the prostitution, call girl, and escort services. Steve, the former police officer, recommended doing something with one of the newer drugs—meth, GHB, or ecstasy. Larry, who had grown up in an inner-city neighborhood, encouraged Laura to research gambling. He offered to introduce her to some numbers runners, sports bookies, and a gentleman who brokered the local crap game. One of the other students claimed his girlfriend's father worked for the "Outfit," and he could arrange interviews with local mob leaders. Although these topics intrigued Laura, she was concerned about her safety if she chose one of these crimes for her thesis.

The conversation moved to a discussion of white-collar or corporate crime. Although the group couldn't agree on a specific definition, they felt that many of these crimes involved some form of fraud. Laura liked this idea and finally chose computer crime as her thesis topic. She intended to meet with the state's Consumer Fraud Division and volunteer to conduct research for them on computer-generated fraud, with the understanding that she could use the data for her thesis.

Key Terms

crimes without complainants

prostitution

white-collar crime

business world crime

fraud

organized crime

Continuing Criminal Enterprise (CCE) statute

Chapter Outline

Crimes without Complainants
  Prostitution and Related Offenses
  Drug Offenses
  Gambling

White-Collar Crime
  Fraud
Organized Crime

In this chapter, we discuss two categories of crime that have been surrounded for some time by controversy: crimes without complainants and white-collar crimes. The former, often called crimes without victims (Schur, 1965), involve the provision of goods and services that are in demand but illegal. The latter are crimes committed by persons who occupy positions of trust in business, medicine, law, and other areas (Sutherland, 1939). As we analyze these crimes, we indicate why they remain controversial, the procedures involved in dealing with individuals involved in such crimes, and the consequences of these crimes for society.

CRIMES WITHOUT COMPLAINANTS

Schur's discussion of crimes without victims, published in 1965, led to considerable controversy. His initial analysis focused on abortion, homosexuality, and drug addiction as crimes without victims in the sense that they all involve "the willing exchange, among adults, of strongly demanded, but legally proscribed, goods or services" (Schur, 1965, p. 169). In the years following the publication of Schur's book, both abortion and homosexuality have been largely decriminalized. Others, following Schur's lead, began to include in the general category of crimes without victims prostitution, gambling, and pornography/obscenity (Smith & Pollock, 1975; Walker, 1998). The debate concerning whether these activities involve victims has raged for some time. Most recently, for example, the spread of AIDS has raised questions as to the victimless nature of prostitution and drug abuse, and some contend that engaging in unlawful conduct of any kind is likely to produce victims (Bastian, 1995). We prefer to use the term **crimes without complainants** because it accurately describes the majority of such activities in the sense that the supposed victims of these acts seldom file complaints. Whether they see themselves as victims and whether society should consider them victims are issues that are indeed difficult to resolve. It is clear, however, that attempts to legislate morality and to enforce such legislation produce serious consequences for those involved in the criminal justice network (Duster, 1970; Weisheit, 1990; Walker, 1998). Among those consequences are the necessity for the police themselves to serve as complainants with respect to such activities and the tremendous costs in police resources (time and money to pay informants and to make drug buys, place bets, and so on), prosecutorial resources, court time, and rehabilitation programs. Most important, consensus exists among those who study crimes without complainants that there is seldom any payoff, or return for the investment made, in attempting to enforce laws regulating these activities (Nadelmann, 1998). It is common knowledge that the street-level drug pusher is replaced within hours (perhaps minutes) of his arrest, that the prostitute is often back working the streets before the arresting officer has finished the arrest reports, and that gamblers and addicts return to their habits more often than not, regardless of the punishment or rehabilitation programs prescribed.

Prostitution and Related Offenses

Prostitution involves agreeing to or engaging in sexual acts for compensation. Although it has traditionally been treated as an offense committed by women, today it is widely recognized that the offender may be of either sex (Weinberg, Shaver, & Williams, 1999). The offense is generally a misdemeanor, and the most common punishment on conviction is a fine. Patronizing a prostitute, allowing a house to be used for purposes of prostitution, soliciting (arranging or offering to arrange) for a prostitute, pandering (compelling or arranging for a person to commit prostitution), and pimping (making money from the prostitution of another) are also generally prohibited by law. Despite the numerous laws prohibiting prostitution and related activities, however, these activities continue to flourish more or less openly throughout the world and certainly in every major city in the United States (Vito & Holmes, 1994, p. 337). Law enforcement efforts to reduce the incidence of these activities sometimes succeed in forcing participants to move from one location to another, but the elimination of such activities seems highly unlikely. The demand and willingness to pay for sexual services virtually ensures the supply, as is characteristic of all the activities covered by the umbrella term "crimes without complainants." Recognition of this fact has led a number of countries to legalize prostitution and at least some jurisdictions in the United States (e.g., some counties in Nevada) to follow suit (Davis, 1993).

Drug Offenses

The sale, manufacture, distribution, and possession or use of all narcotic (opium-based) drugs, alcohol, most hallucinogenic drugs, cocaine, certain stimulant (amphetamine) drugs, barbiturates, and marijuana are regulated by both federal and state laws. Our society, however, can be characterized as a drug-using or -abusing society, and attempts to regulate the use and traffic of some drugs while allowing others to be used without such regulations have been highly unsuccessful. For example, we allow adults to use tobacco and alcohol (gateway drugs to controlled substances) quite freely even though tobacco has been determined by the Surgeon General of the United States to be harmful to the health of the user and alcohol to be among the most frequently abused and dangerous of all drugs (Kane & Yacoubian, 1999; Kao, Schneider & Hoffman, 2000; Golub Johnson, 2001). At the same time, we prohibit marijuana use among the general population even though test results concerning its effects are contradictory, and we prohibit the use of heroin even though there is no evidence that when taken in regulated doses under sanitary conditions, such use would be harmful (Weisheit, 1990).

Further confusion in the attempt to regulate drugs results from the fact that although the sale, use, possession, or manufacture of certain substances is illegal, addiction itself is not a crime. The addict is not a criminal unless he or she is engaged in one of the prohibited activities.

The same rules of supply and demand, and the same outcomes of enforcement attempts discussed earlier with respect to prostitution, apply to drug-related offenses. Further, the fact that many drugs of choice are illegal results in a black market that is characterized by relatively high prices for such drugs. To obtain money to purchase these drugs, users may turn to burglary, theft, robbery, or prostitution. The incidence of these crimes then increases, placing further demands on the resources of the criminal justice network. This cycle is perpetuated when attempts to rehabilitate users fail and they return to society unemployed to take up their old habits.

Recently, the criminal justice network has responded to the "grow your own" and "make your own" trends associated with marijuana, methamphetamine, and gamma hydroxybutyrate (GHB). Although large amounts of marijuana are grown and distributed through established criminal syndicates, the proliferation of decentralized smaller networks with concealed growing fields, which market their product on the local level, places greater demand on limited law enforcement resources. Similarly, crank, a form of methamphetamine, can be manufactured with over-the-counter ingredients in a relatively short time span. Law enforcement officials in the Southwest and Midwest devote valuable hours to locating and dismantling these illegal, clandestine labs. GHB, the main ingredient in ecstasy, can also be manufactured in clandestine laboratories by amateur chemists. Some of these drugs pose considerable health risks involving fire, explosion, and the use of ingredients with unknown properties.

The criminal justice network has been actively involved in the so-called war on drugs for a large part of the twentieth century (Vito & Holmes, 1994, p. 352; Walker, 1998; Nademann, 1998). The prohibition of alcohol in the early part of the century placed law enforcement in a difficult dilemma. Although the use of alcohol was prohibited and the police were responsible for enforcing the law, many Americans objected to Prohibition and flaunted their use of alcohol. Thus, the criminal justice network was ineffective in enforcing an unpopular law. Today, society has taken a more reasonable approach to curbing alcohol abuse. Many citizen support groups advocate "sensible drinking" and work with criminal justice practitioners to educate the public rather than simply trying to enforce an unpopular moral code.

Public support for drug interdiction has been consistently strong. Drug Awareness Resistance Education (D.A.R.E.) is available in many school districts, and the criminal justice network enjoys cooperative relationships with many community groups. Attempts to reduce drug use focus on alcohol, marijuana, cocaine and its derivative products, and more recently, the resurgence of LSD and other hallucinogens. Most evidence indicates that our efforts to curb drug abuse have not been highly effective, and some argue that legalization of at least some currently proscribed drugs is an option that ought to be explored (Walker, 1998, pp. 261–66).

Gambling

Another common, though often illegal, practice in our society involves placing a bet or wager on the outcome of some event. As Gardiner (1967) noted some time ago, public attitudes toward gambling are often more permissive than the statutes that are common to the United States: "Gambling is either positively desired or else not regarded as particularly reprehensible by a substantial proportion of the population" (p. 134). The Commission on the Review of the National Policy toward Gambling (1976) made the following observation: "Gambling is inevitable. No matter what is said or done by advocates or opponents of gambling in all its various forms, it is an activity that is practiced, or tacitly endorsed, by a substantial majority of Americans. That is the simple, overriding premise behind all the work of this Commission" (p. 1). That this remains true is illustrated by the fact that in some states and counties, gambling is legal (e.g., in Atlantic City, New Jersey, and in some counties in Nevada), although presumably it is subject to licensing and regulation by the state. Also, some types of gambling are legal in many states (e.g., state-operated lotteries, on- and offtrack horse race betting, bingo games, Indian reservation casinos, and riverboat casinos) (Walker, 1998, p. 235).

The major objection to gambling appears to be its perceived relationship to organized crime. The commission mentioned above (1976) determined that "there is no uniformity of organized crime control of gambling throughout the country; in some cities such control exists; in others, not. The Commission regrets the notion that organized crime controls all illegal gambling or that all illegal gambling provides revenues for other illegal activities" (p. 4). The commission's report, however, indicates that some proceeds of some illegal gambling do go to organized crime, and many law enforcement officials continue to believe that gambling is a major source of income for organized crime and therefore should be eliminated or strictly controlled. The commission's report is reinforced by Kenney and Finckenauer (1995, pp. 272–73), whose discussion of organized crime concludes that many ethnic/international organized crime groups are involved in gambling. Other research has concluded that legalized gambling does not lead to higher crime rates (Walker, 1998, p. 236). In any case, the enforcement of gambling laws is extremely difficult because of the many forms that exist and the demand for gambling activities. Although most local law enforcement officials are willing to concede that control of social gambling (e.g., a card game at an individual's home or the weekend office football, basketball, or baseball pools) is impossible, these same officials may, from time to time, make serious attempts to curtail more organized forms of gambling (e.g., bookmaking or punchboards). State and federal officials are also concerned about illegal gambling because winners are not inclined to declare their winnings at income tax time. At the same time, however, revenues from legalized gambling play an important part in the economic picture of municipalities and states where they are licensed.

Despite selective local, state, and federal law enforcement attempts to control organized gambling, it is unlikely that such attempts will be successful as long as there is a public demand for such activities. In fact, the rise in riverboat casino gambling, the increased number of government-operated lotteries, and the adoption of pari-mutuel betting by some states may indicate the government's concession that gambling is inevitable and can serve as a viable source of revenue. These changes, however, do not relieve the criminal justice network of all gambling-related responsibilities. Legalized gambling requires regulation, and even where state-controlled gambling exists, illegal gambling has not been totally eliminated. As is often the case with the other crimes without complainants, the payoff for criminal justice personnel is often minimal in terms of the resources expended.

WHITE-COLLAR CRIME

The term **white-collar crime** was coined in 1939 by Edwin H. Sutherland, although the concept itself was not new at that time. The term, as used by Sutherland, referred to crimes committed by persons of respectability and high social status in the course of their occupations. There have been many attempts to refine and particularize this definition, and it is probably safe to conclude that today the term "white-collar crime" is used as an umbrella to cover most crimes committed by guile, deceit, and concealment, whether or not they are committed by persons of "respectability and high social status" (Clinard & Quinney, 1973, pp. 206–23; Shapiro, 1990). Commonly referred to as **business world crime** (Reed, 1997), the term now includes such offenses as computer crimes, product liability, embezzlement, conspiracy, insider trading, violations of workplace safety, false advertising, income tax evasion, environmental crime, credit card fraud, medical/health fraud, insurance fraud, false weights and measures, and tax fraud (Conklin, 1998, p. 92).

The overall costs of white-collar crime are difficult to measure accurately, but in strictly economic terms, the annual cost to Americans is probably over $200 billion and may be as high as $500 billion (Donziger, 1996, p. 66). More difficult to measure are costs that result from loss of public confidence in business and the professions. For example, unnecessary surgery, ghost surgery, reports issued by nonexistent or nonfunctioning medical laboratories, occupational diseases and injuries, fraud committed by computer over the Internet, and the intentional release of hazardous waste materials erode public trust in the professions and industries involved and cause health-related problems and deaths, the costs of which are tremendous (Kappeler, Blumberg, & Potter, 1996, pp. 144–45; see In the News, "Sheriff's Dispatcher Suspected of Internet Fraud"). Penalties assessed often appear trivial in comparison with the profits realized by white-collar offenders.

Although white-collar crime is clearly widespread, the frequency with which it occurs cannot be determined by looking at police records or the Uniform Crime Reports. The extent of white-collar crime remains largely

In the News

SHERIFF'S DISPATCHER SUSPECTED OF INTERNET FRAUD; ONLINE AUCTION USERS CLAIM WOMAN NEVER SENT BEANIE BABIES OR POKEMON CARDS

By Linda Spice and Lisa Sink

Internet auction customers across the United States and as far away as England have accused a Waukesha County Sheriff's Department dispatcher of taking their money for Beanie Babies and Pokemon card bids but not delivering the goods, according to court documents.

After receiving phone calls and email complaints from victims, Waukesha police said Wednesday they will be seeking eight counts of theft by fraud from the Waukesha County district attorney's office against the woman.

The dispatcher, who is not being identified because she has not been charged, is suspected of using her son's name and her work identification number to set up an e-mail account used in auction transactions.

She then used her daughter's name as the person to whom buyers should send their cash, according to an affidavit filed in Waukesha County Circuit Court this week.

"I was just saying, 'Well, thank God it wasn't more' money," said Vivian Veard of Columbus, Ohio, who sent the Waukesha woman $45 for Pokemon cards. "Had I spent more on it, I would be really sick."

Veard thought she was getting a rare deal on a Pokemon Charizard card that the seller offered for $27.50, a buy Veard couldn't find for any less than $250 from other sellers. When she made her bid, she was offered a second Pokemon card, and the seller offered to knock off the cost of shipping for the dual buy.

Veard had hoped to surprise her 8-year-old nephew with her find on the day it arrived in the mail. That day never came, though.

When she went back to the auction site to check the seller's feedback, other buyers had started complaining that they were not receiving their items.

A Huntsville, N.C., woman said she lost the $53.50 she mailed for the last remaining Beanie Buddie she needed to complete her collection—Twigs the giraffe. After buying 20 to 25 dolls on auction sites without problems, the Twigs fraud has scared her away from all Internet auctions and prompted her to box up her Beanies.

She said the seller was "clever—she really took several of us for a ride."

Veard said, "We all e-mailed each other back to see what recourse we could take."

Continued

The case came to the attention of Waukesha police when they received a phone call from a De Pere man in March complaining that the seller, believed to be living in Waukesha, was offering items, taking payment and failing to deliver the purchases, according to police Lt. William H. Graham Jr.

Others started e-mailing police shortly thereafter, he said.

Negative responses by irritated customers who posted their feedback on the woman's account referred to her as a "rip off artist" and a "scam artist," according to Waukesha County court documents.

Assistant District Attorney Kevin Osborne said this was his first case of Internet auction fraud.

Misdemeanor charges of theft by fraud are most likely to fit the case, Osborne said. Felony charges could be filed only if the total value was more than $1,000, which does not appear to be the case, he said.

He said it was disappointing that the woman under investigation is a dispatcher. "In a perfect world, people who work in law enforcement would . . . never break the law, but that's not the world we live in," he said.

Graham said the woman was picked up at her job July 3 and later arrested. She was booked and released.

Waukesha County Sheriff's Department Deputy Inspector Dan Trawicki said the agency's administrative staff sat down with the woman and a union representative to talk with her about the case and potential discipline, after which time she voluntarily resigned, he said.

Milwaukee Journal Sentinel, *August 3, 2000, p. 1B.*

unknown, and, perhaps partly because of the nebulous nature of these offenses, public reaction to the offenders remains largely unorganized. Traditionally, legislators have remained relatively unconcerned about passing statutes designed to reduce the incidence of white-collar crime. Recently, however, Congress has been playing close attention to "cyberspace" crime, passing legislation such as the Computer Fraud and Abuse Act, the Digital Millennium Act, and the No Electronic Theft Act (Andreano, 1999). Still, municipal police continue to have few if any personnel who are properly trained to investigate such crimes, prosecutions remain few, and criminal court action is infrequent (Kappeler et al., 1996, pp. 153–60).

Because those who commit white-collar offenses are not particularly likely to be treated as criminals, they often do not view themselves as criminals, and, except for periods of anger and frustration, the public does not view these offenders with the same distaste as they do other criminals. Coupled with the fact that white-collar crimes are often undetected and difficult to prosecute because of their complexity, these attitudes do little to help reduce the likelihood of such offenses. Perhaps looking at fraud as an example of white-collar crime will illustrate some of the difficulties associated with prosecution.

Fraud committed by administrators of lending institutions has cost Americans millions of dollars.

UPI/Bettmann-Corbis

Fraud

Fraud involves obtaining the property of another by misrepresenting a material fact. The accused must also intend to permanently deprive the owner of the use of that property. In this offense, the property is relinquished willfully by the owner, and the illegal act centers on the misrepresentation that induces the relinquishing. Although fraud is often predicated on deceit, some frauds go unreported, and others are not prosecuted because the victim was a willing participant in the fraud.

The misrepresentation must be of a material fact and not an opinion or a prediction. For example, if a car salesman claims that a car will be the "fastest, hottest car in town," he is not misrepresenting a material fact; he is simply giving an opinion or possibly a prediction. On the other hand, if he alleges that the car has accumulated only 10,000 miles but the odometer was turned back and the car actually has been driven 50,000 miles, he has misrepresented a material fact.

The misrepresentation must be known by the offender and must be one that a "reasonable person" would not be aware of. In the previous example, if a second party purchases the auto, thinking it to have been driven only 10,000 miles, and without detecting the misrepresentation sells it to a third party, then no fraud has occurred. A person who purchases the Brooklyn Bridge or the Eiffel Tower has gone beyond the standards of reasonableness to claim fraud.

As with theft and embezzlement, the accused must intend to permanently deprive the owner of the use of the property. Courts generally hold that once ownership has passed, the fraud has transpired.

Some of the more commonly known frauds involve the work of con men who play on people's greed or willingness to get rich quick. Credit card fraud has become a crime of major proportions in the United States (Vito & Holmes, 1994, pp. 321–22).

Fraud among retailers and wholesalers is common as well. Such practices as false advertising, violations of truth in labeling, and use of false weights and measures are detected frequently enough to suggest that they commonly occur. Like other types of white-collar crime, these offenses are often difficult to detect but are very rewarding to their perpetrators. Consider, for example, a supermarket chain that has 100 stores. If the chain were to misrepresent the weight of every package of steak sold by adding only 1 ounce to the real weight of the meat, if the cost per ounce for steak was 20 cents, and if each store in the chain sold 100 packages of steak in a day, the additional profit to the chain would be 20 cents times 100 times 100, or $2,000 per day, or $14,000 per week, or over $700,000 per year! Still, each customer would be paying only an additional 20 cents. In addition, the risk involved is minimal compared with the potential return because few customers take their steak home and weigh it, and even those who did so might believe their own scales to be in error; those who were suspicious would be unlikely to take much definite action to recoup only 20 cents; and even if the violation were somehow detected, most customers would not become overly irate at the loss of a few dollars over the period of a year or so.

Not all frauds are targeted toward consumers. Friedrichs (1996) has noted that several frauds are perpetrated with the government as the intended victim. Tax cheating or evasion, welfare scams, false Medicare claims, and inflated expenses on government-funded projects result in huge losses for the government and its taxpayers.

Insurance companies are also frequent victims of frauds. Clients exaggerate losses and have been known to stage automobile accidents and fake falls or spills. Forty to fifty percent of all auto theft claims may be false, at an annual cost of more than $6 billion (Friedrichs, 1996, pp. 208–9).

There are some organized attempts to prevent or reduce the incidence of white-collar crime. More than 20 years ago, the National District Attorneys' Association, in conjunction with the Chamber of Commerce of the United States, distributed a handbook that includes sections on combating bribery, kickbacks, and payoffs; countering computer-related crime; combating fraud; and preventing embezzlement; as well as a section on collective action as a means of combating white-collar crime. Specific tactics for dealing with white-collar crime are discussed, and available sources of assistance listed (Chamber of Commerce of the United States, 1974). In addition, there are now numerous community-based groups across the country oriented toward publicizing and confronting a variety of white-collar offenses and offenders through the use of civil suits (Coleman, 1994, p. 158).

No consideration of white-collar crime would be complete without reference to the work of Ralph Nader and his associates. Nader is convinced that illegitimate practices are widespread in corporate America and that there ought to be more, and more severe, criminal penalties for white-collar criminals. Nader and his associates combat white-collar crime through both publicity and recourse to legal processes, and they have been identified, to some extent at least, with the establishment of the Environmental Protection Agency and the Occupational Safety and Health Administration (Friedrichs, 1996, p. 32). Nader appears to remain convinced that the American public will rise up and take action against white-collar offenders if they are made aware of the extent and seriousness of the problem and if they can be organized. There is, however, a great deal of evidence to indicate that although some segments of the public do become concerned about some types of white-collar crime, the concern is short-lived. Most citizens, in fact, appear to be apathetic about this type of crime most of the time.

ORGANIZED CRIME

The long-standing prevalence of prostitution, gambling, drug use, and other crimes without complainants has made them attractive "business" ventures for criminal syndicates. **Organized crime** involves a self-perpetuating criminal conspiracy that exists to profit from providing illicit goods and services through the corruption of public officials and the use or threat of force (Kenney & Finckenauer, 1995, pp. 25, 28). Although there is a wide variation of definitions, law enforcement and criminological researchers are consistent in associating the following attributes with organized crime (Abadinsky, 1997, p. 5):

1. Nonideological.
2. Hierarchical.
3. Limited or exclusive membership.
4. Self-perpetuating.
5. Willingness to use illegal violence and bribery.
6. Specialized division of labor.
7. Monopolistic.
8. Governed by explicit rules and regulations.

Although they may employ illegal means, organized criminal syndicates often operate under rational business principles. Maximum profit is predicated on public demand for illicit goods and services and efficient delivery of "products" through a formally organized system. In addition, payments for political protection are not uncommon (Kenney & Finckenauer, 1995).

Although the most celebrated organized crime unit has been the Mafia, or La Cosa Nostra, organized crime as defined here includes street gang activities, drug distribution networks, and racially or ethnically based criminal syndicates (*Economist*, 1998). Organized crime now includes many globally recognizable criminal syndicates that have emerged on the scene, including Chinese triads, the Japanese yakuza, Colombian and Mexican drug cartels,

In the News
_____

INDICTMENT TARGETS 18TH STREET GANG IN RACKETEERING CASE

By David Rosenzweig

Federal prosecutors Tuesday unsealed a racketeering indictment against 26 suspected members of an 18th Street gang clique who are accused of controlling drug trafficking in the MacArthur Park area near downtown Los Angeles.

The Columbia Li'l Cycos were described by law enforcement officials as one of the most violent and financially successful gang contingents in the city.

By wholesaling drugs to street dealers and then charging them for the right to operate, the group generated hundreds of thousands of dollars in profits, which it plowed into homes in Burbank and El Monte, a restaurant in South Gate and an auto business in Los Angeles, officials said.

Stephen Wiley, a senior FBI official in Los Angeles, said Columbia Li'l Cycos, also known as CLCs, "were held up in the gang community as examples of how to do business."

The gang reigns through intimidation and violence, he said.

The indictment accuses various gang members of carrying out three executions, several attempted murders and many beatings.

Eight suspects were arrested in predawn raids Tuesday. Ten others were already in custody from previous arrests, three are expected to surrender and five are fugitives.

Investigators said they seized about $500,000 in cash from gang members' hangouts.

"This wealth was accumulated one cocaine rock at a time," U.S. Atty. Alejandro N. Mayorkas told reporters.

He said the arrests will cripple the gang's grip on the MacArthur Park area, which has been a hotbed of drug dealing for many years.

"We think it will be very difficult for them to bounce back," Mayorkas said, "but if they do, we will cripple them again."

The indictment grew out of a 2½-year probe by a task force of investigators from the FBI, the Los Angeles Police Department and the state Department of Justice.

It is the first use of the federal Racketeer Influenced and Corrupt Organizations (RICO) statute against members of the 18th Street gang, which has about 15,000 members, according to FBI estimates.

The 18th Street gang was a major target of LAPD's discredited and now-disbanded Rampart Division CRASH unit.

Some of the nearly 100 people whose criminal convictions have been overturned because of evidence planting and other alleged misconduct by Rampart CRASH officers were 18th Street gang members.

Continued

One victim of Rampart police abuse was among the 26 defendants named in the federal indictment Tuesday.

Ismael Jimenez, 34, also known as "Loner," is accused of racketeering, drug trafficking and conspiring to commit two murders in 1999.

Earlier this year, the City Council agreed to pay him a $231,000 settlement for a beating he received in 1998 inside the Rampart Division station house.

He said in his civil rights lawsuit that he was standing outside a tattoo parlor when Rampart Officer Brian Hewitt approached him with a drawn gun, slapped handcuffs on him and drove him to the station.

Inside an interrogation room, he said, Hewitt grabbed him by the neck, shoved him into a wall and punched him repeatedly in the chest and stomach until he began to vomit blood.

Hewitt was fired because of the incident.

Jimenez's lawyer in the civil rights case did not return a call seeking comment Tuesday.

While the gang exacted "taxes" or "rent" from independent drug dealers in the MacArthur Park area, it, too, was obliged to pay a "tax" on its profits—to the prison-based Mexican Mafia, according to the indictment.

The Columbia Li'l Cycos' indicted leader, Francisco Ruiz Martinez, 36, is a Mexican Mafia member, prosecutors said. Martinez, also known as "Puppet" or "Pancho," allegedly controlled nearly all aspects of the group's business. He has been in federal custody since last year.

Also indicted was Martinez's wife, Janie Maria Garcia, 49, of Monterey Park. Prosecutors said she acted as his proxy on the street, issuing orders on his behalf and collecting money for the organization.

The indictment cited three homicides allegedly carried out by members of the gang: the Sept. 4, 1994, slayings of Carlos "Truco" Lopez and Donatilla Contreras, and the July 14, 1995, killing of Javier "Lefty" Cazales.

Los Angeles Times, *July 19, 2000, p. B1.*

Nigerians, the Russian Mafiya, and the Jamaican posses. One can argue that conventional street gangs (e.g., the Blood, Crips, Vice Lords, and Gangster Disciples) now constitute organized crime syndicates with their attempts to generate huge profits in the drug and weapons markets. We should note that not all organized crime activities are criminal. In an attempt to fend off the Internal Revenue Service (one common prosecutor of organized criminals), many criminal syndicates engage in legal business activities, often entered through illegal means, in an attempt to launder their illegally obtained profits.

One attempt to help control the spread of organized crime was the passage of the Racketeer Influenced Corrupt Organizations (RICO) Act of 1970. RICO, actually Title IX of the Organized Crime Control Act of 1970, was intended to combat the infiltration of organized crime into legitimate business. RICO focuses on the conspiratorial nature of most organized criminal syndicates and on a series of illegal activities related to the investment of funds in legitimate enterprises that may constitute racketeering. Convictions for RICO carry lengthy prison sentences and heavy fines and provide for forfeiture of all assets associated with the conspiracy (Kenney & Finckenauer, 1995). Although RICO was constructed to attack fully developed criminal syndicates, it has been extended to a number of organizations and to crimes of violence, corruption, and fraud (see In the News, "Indictment Targets 18th Street Gang"). Some drug syndicates are prosecuted under the **Continuing Criminal Enterprise (CCE) statute** (21 U.S.C. 848). Similar to RICO, the statute makes it illegal to commit or to conspire to commit a continuing series of violations (three or more) of the 1970 Drug Abuse Prevention and Control Act when the offenses are committed in concert with five or more persons. This statute permits the prosecution and conviction of drug lords, who obtain substantial income from drug transactions without direct participation.

Summary

1. Crimes without complainants involve the provision of goods and services that are in demand but illegal. These offenses include illegal drug manufacture, sales, and distribution; prostitution; gambling; and obscenity/pornography.

2. Because complainants rarely come forth voluntarily with respect to these offenses, the police themselves often serve as complainants.

3. The costs involved in developing these cases are high, and the payoff is minimal. Attempts to legislate morality generally lead to such results.

4. Nonetheless, a considerable proportion of the resources of various components of the criminal justice network is expended on crimes without complainants.

5. White-collar crime involves offenses committed by people in the course of their occupations or professions. Tax evasion, embezzlement, consumer fraud, and medical malpractice are examples of white-collar crime.

6. The costs of white-collar crime are high in terms of both economic considerations and loss of confidence and trust in government, industry, and the professions. Still, despite numerous crusades to arouse the public, white-collar offenders are seldom treated or thought of as criminals.

7. Only organized, sustained action on behalf of a concerned public is likely to reduce the incidence of white-collar crime, and such action appears unlikely at this time.

Key Terms Defined

crimes without complainants Crimes that provide goods and/or services that are in demand but illegal and in which the police themselves typically serve as complainants because citizens are usually not willing to accept this role.

prostitution Engaging in or agreeing to engage in sexual acts for compensation.

white-collar crime Crime committed by guile, deceit, or concealment, typically by people in positions of trust.

business world crime Offenses such as computer crimes, product liability, embezzlement, insider trading, and credit card fraud.

fraud An act that involves obtaining the property of another, with the intent to permanently deprive the owner of the use of that property, by misrepresenting a material fact.

organized crime Criminal conspiracies providing illicit goods or services through the corruption of public officials and the use or threat of force.

Continuing Criminal Enterprise (CCE) statute Statute used to prosecute drug syndicates.

Critical Thinking Exercises

1. What is the importance of the distinction between crimes without complainants and crimes without victims? In your opinion, are crimes without complainants crimes without victims? What similarities and differences do you see between crimes without complainants and white-collar crimes?
2. What would you consider an effective means for attempting to combat white-collar crime and crimes without complainants? What is the likelihood that your suggestions would be effective in our current society?

Internet Exercises

The use of club/rave drugs is becoming an epidemic in many regions of the United States. Access the Lake County, Illinois, website on club/rave drugs at *www.lakecountymeg.org*
   Read the PowerPoint presentation; then answer the following questions:

1. What are the five basic drugs used at rave parties?
2. Compare and contrast the effects of GHB (liquid ecstasy) with ecstasy (MDMA).
3. Develop a list of warning signs (indicators of use) to help parents and teachers identify club drug use.

References

Abadinsky, H. (1997). *Organized crime* (5th ed.). Chicago: Nelson-Hall.

Andreano, F. P. (1999). The evolution of federal computer crime policy: The ad hoc approach to an ever-changing problem. *American Journal of Criminal Law, 27* (1), 81–103.

Bastian, L. (1995). *Criminal victimization 1993.* Washington, DC: U.S. Department of Justice.

Chamber of Commerce of the United States. 1974. *A handbook on white collar crime: Everyone's problem, everyone's loss.* Washington, DC: Author.

Clinard, M. B., & Quinney, R. (Eds.). (1973). *Criminal behavior systems: A typology* (2nd ed.). New York: Holt, Rinehart and Winston.

Coleman, J. W. (1994). *The criminal elite: The sociology of white-collar crime.* New York: St. Martin's Press.

Commission on the Review of the National Policy toward Gambling. (1976). *Gambling in America.* Washington, DC: U.S. Government Printing Office.

Conklin, J. E. (1998). *Criminology* (6th ed.). Boston: Allyn and Bacon.

Davis, N. J. (1993). *Prostitution: An international handbook on trends, problems, and policies.* Westport, CT: Greenwood Press.

Donziger, S. R. (1996). *The real war on crime: The report of the National Criminal Justice Commission.* New York: Harper and Row.

Duster, T. (1970). *The legislation of morality: Law, drugs, and moral judgment.* New York: Free Press.

Economist. (1998). Out of jail and on to the street, *349* (8097), 29–30.

Friedrichs, D. O. (1996). *Trusted criminals.* Belmont, CA: Wadsworth.

Gardiner, J. A. (1967). Public attitudes toward gambling and corruption. *Annals of the American Academy of Political and Social Science, 374,* 123–34.

Golub, A. & Johnson, B. D. (2001). Variation in youthful risks of progression from alcohol and tobacco to marijuana and to hard drugs across generations. *American Journal of Public Health,* 91 (2), 225–232.

Kane, R. J., & Yacoubian, G. S., Jr. (1999). Patterns of drug escalation among Philadelphia arrestees: An assessment of the Gateway theory. *Journal of Drug Issues,* 29 (1), 107–120.

Kao, T., Schneider, S. J. & Hoffman, K. J. (2000). Co-occurence of alcohol, smokeless tobacco, cigarette, and illicit drug use by lower ranking military personnel. *Addictive Behaviors,* 25 (2), 253–262.

Kappeler, V. E., Blumberg, M., & Potter G. W. (1996). *The mythology of crime and criminal justice* (2nd ed.). Prospect Heights, IL: Waveland Press.

Kenney, D. J., & Finckenauer, J. O. (1995). *Organized crime in America.* Belmont, CA: Wadsworth.

Nadelmann, E. A. (1998). Commonsense drug policy. *Foreign Affairs, 77* (5), 111–126.

Reed, S. (1997). *Crime and criminology* (8th ed.). Madison, WI: Brown and Benchmark.

Schur, E. M. (1965). *Crimes without victims: Deviant behavior and public policy.* Englewood Cliffs, NJ: Prentice Hall.

Shapiro, S. P. (1990). Collaring the crime, not the criminal: Reconsidering the concept of white collar crime. *American Sociological Review, 55* (3), 346–65.

Smith, A. B., & Pollock, H. (1975). *Some sins are not crimes: A plea for reform of the criminal law.* New York: New Viewpoints.

Sutherland, E. H. (1939). *White collar crime.* New York: Holt, Rinehart and Winston.

Vito, G. F., & Holmes, R. M. (1994). *Criminology: Theory, research, and policy.* Belmont, CA: Wadsworth.

Walker, S. (1998). *Sense and nonsense about crime and drugs: A policy guide* (4th ed.). Belmont, CA: West/Wadsworth.

Weinberg, M. S., Shaver, F. M., & Williams, C. J. (1999). Gendered sex work in the San Francisco Tenderloin. *Archives of Sexual Behavior, 28* (6), 503–21.

Weisheit, R. (1990). Challenging the criminalizers. *The Criminologist, 15* (4), 1–5.

Suggested Readings

Abadinsky, H. (1997). *Organized crime* (5th ed.). Chicago: Nelson-Hall.

Albonetti, C. A. (1999). The avoidance of punishment: A legal-bureaucratic model of suspended sentences in federal white-collar cases. *Social Forces, 78* (1), 303–29.

Chicago Crime Commission. (1997). *The new faces of organized crime.* Chicago: Author.

Duke, S. B., Bandow, D., & Jonas, S. (1995). Drug prohibition: An unnatural disaster. *Connecticut Law Review, 27* (2), 569–697.

Friedrichs, D. 0. (1996). *Trusted criminals.* Belmont, CA: Wadsworth.

Gregory, J. (1999). *Policing sexual assault.* New York: Routledge.

John, A. (1994). On the backs of working prostitutes: Feminist theory and prostitution policy. *Crime and Delinquency, 40* (1), 69–83.

Potterat, J. J., Rothenberg, R. B., & Muth, S. Q. (1998). Pathways to prostitution: The chronology of sexual and drug abuse milestones. *Journal of Sex Research, 35* (4), 333–40.

Schur, E. (1965). *Crimes without victims.* Englewood Cliffs, NJ: Prentice Hall.

Sherrill, R. (1997, April). A year in corporate crime. *The Nation,* 11–12, 14, 16–20.

Stoil, M. J. (1994, July/August). Gambling addiction: The nation's dirty little secret. *Behavioral Health Management, 14,* 35–37.

Sutherland, E. H. (1939). *White collar crime.* New York: Holt, Rinehart and Winston.

Wattendorf, G. E. (2000). Stalking-investigation strategies. *FBI Law Enforcement Bulletin, 60* (3), 10–14.

CHAPTER SIX

The Police

Police have historically been called upon to deal with protests and demonstrations.
AP/Wide World Photos

D avid, a senior criminal justice major, was one semester away from graduation and still hadn't finalized his career choice. In an attempt to narrow his options, David attended a local career fair and talked with many of the participants. After the fair had concluded, he was looking over all the materials he had gathered and realized that most of the agencies he had met with were law enforcement–oriented. He had taken a Survey of Policing course and was familiar with many of the police processes, such as booking and patrol investigation. Before making his final decision, he decided to go back and skim some of the texts to ensure policing was the right choice for him.

He easily found the sections describing the historical development of the police both here and in England. He marveled at how he remembered his professor discussing the relationship between developments and politics, social trends and technology. He still hadn't grasped what he thought was the true meaning of the police role but remembered it was complex and involved more mediation and negotiation than actual law enforcement. The readings and discussion on police misconduct and the need for ethics quickly came to memory, and he vowed not to succumb to the many temptations associated with the job.

He concluded that municipal policing was the career for him and scanned the web pages of agencies he was interested in joining. David paid close attention to the job requirements and the qualifying stages of the selection process. With his goal established, he wanted to prepare himself for each stage. Last, he called up former employers, his professors, and some family friends to ask if they would serve as personal references in support of his applications. David was committed and prepared for the career that awaited him.

Key Terms

social control

community policing

SARA process

due process

crime control

arrest

booking

chain of evidence

mediation and negotiation

dual career system

directed patrol

split-force policing

accreditation

Peace Officer Standards and Training (POST) boards

assessment centers

probationary officer

corruption

perjury

emotional abuse

physical abuse

Chapter Outline

The Role of the Police in Social Control

From Watchmen to Crime Fighters to Community Organizers

Community- and Problem-Oriented Policing

As the official agency most accessible to and most frequently used by the public, the police play a crucial role in the criminal justice network. As gatekeepers for the other official criminal justice agencies, some 650,000 police officers in more than 17,000 police agencies are a vital link between the public (who are also gatekeepers in terms of reporting or not reporting crimes) and the remainder of the network.

THE ROLE OF THE POLICE IN SOCIAL CONTROL

There are at least two distinct means of attempting to persuade people to adhere to group expectations or norms. The first involves the use of informal or group pressure. The second involves the use of formal pressure or legal coercion. Both are clearly important to **social control,** which may be defined as the process of attempting to persuade persons or groups to conform to group expectations. Police activities in the form of legal coercion are likely to be unsuccessful in preventing violations of legal norms (laws) unless they are supplemented by informal, group, or social pressure to conform. This is so because successful legal coercion depends on reasonable rates of detection and apprehension. The ratio of police officers to other citizens in the United States (roughly 650,000 to 260,000,000, or 1 to 400) should be enough to convince us that the likelihood of detection and apprehension for those who violate laws is quite low if we rely totally on the police for such detection and apprehension. The various groups that constitute the public (families, peers, religious groups, for example) must also take an active part in social control if conformity to norms is to occur and if those who violate norms are to be detected and apprehended. It is important, therefore, to realize that the police are only one of many groups involved in the social control process and that their efforts are sure to fail unless they receive cooperation from these other groups.

FROM WATCHMEN TO CRIME FIGHTERS TO COMMUNITY ORGANIZERS

Perhaps nowhere is the importance of the public to the criminal justice network clearer than in a historical discussion of the development of the police. In the Western world, citizens have been formally responsible for assisting in the maintenance of public order and the enforcement of law for centuries. In both England and colonial America, male citizens were called on to serve terms as watchmen who were responsible for protecting their cities and towns from invasion from the outside, and fire and criminals from the inside. In addition, these watchmen were given the responsibilities of containing those afflicted with plague, preventing commercial fraud, and enforcing licensing regulations (Rubinstein, 1973). These watchmen were paid little, held in low esteem by the public, and subject to considerable manipulation by the wealthy, who wished to use the law for their own benefit (Barlow, 2000, p. 163; Conser & Russell, 2000, p. 40).

Over time, as crime became an increasingly complex problem, watchmen were recognized as inadequate for the protection of other citizens from criminals. The watchmen were unorganized, untrained, and undependable. In addition, they were operating under a system of laws that many people considered barbaric, so citizen support was often lacking. Reformers such as Jeremy Bentham, Edward Chadwick, and Patrick Colquhoun, who recognized the importance of public support for successful law policing and believed prevention to be an important part of policing, called for drastic changes in the law (Uchida, 2001). Along with others, they called for the development of a centralized, organized, mobile, preventive force to deal with the crime problem. As towns became larger and citizens continued to refuse to perform police duties voluntarily, some cities began to pay their watchmen, but seldom enough to allow them to make a living (Johnson, 1981, p. 7). In America, there were strong objections to the creation of an organized police force because many citizens were afraid it might be used as an instrument of government oppression. However, in the late eighteenth and early nineteenth centuries, an increasing demand for public order led to a growing consensus about the need for an organized police force (Richardson, 1974).

Although there were several localized police forces operating in England in the early 1800s, the first municipal force was the London police force, organized in 1829 under the direction of Sir Robert Peel. This force, referred to as the Metropolitan Police, was organized to help allay public fears arising from an increasing number of crimes being committed with impunity in and about the city of London. Peel believed that the police could be effective only if they were centrally organized, had the support of the public (i.e., enforced laws that received wide public support), exhibited a restrained demeanor, and understood the norms of the community in which they policed.

The London police were organized according to territories, or beats, which they patrolled in such fashion that they could be fairly easily located by those desiring their assistance. The beat patrol concept was soon adopted in cities and towns throughout Europe and the United States. With the advent of community policing in the United States during the 1980s, policing had come full circle. The concepts on which Peel based the first municipal police force (public support, human relations, and community norms) were once again front and center on the police stage.

Between 1830 and 1860, most large municipalities in the United States created police departments based on the British model. In the 1830s and 1840s, Philadelphia, New York, and Boston established full-time, centralized police departments (Conser & Russell, 2000, p. 54). As other cities followed suit, policing began to take on different forms. Vigilance committees were organized in areas unprotected by police departments, and private police forces (Pinkertons in 1855, Wells Fargo in 1852, Brinks in 1859, and Burns in 1909) were established by the railroads and other industries (Fischer & Green 1992, p. 10). These forms of policing developed to protect life and property in areas where municipal or county authorities were few and far between. Their counterparts, often with the same names, continue to provide services today.

While Peel's principles of organization solved many of the problems of the watch and ward system, other problems remained unsolved. In the United States, the police were in frequent conflict with some segments of the public as a result of their attempt to enforce vice laws, which did not have widespread public support (Richardson, 1974, pp. 29–30). In addition, hiring and promotion were based on political patronage systems in many American cities, which made the impartial administration of justice by competent police officers highly suspect. Despite attempts beginning in the 1870s to introduce reforms to reduce direct political influence, the political image remained (Walker, 1999, p. 26). In the first part of the twentieth century, the introduction of the automobile led to further police community relations problems since many middle- and upper-class citizens who had previously supported crime control efforts by the police were now, themselves, subject to the actions of traffic officers.

Another early police problem involved communication, and this problem, to a great extent, negated the advantages of an organized, mobile police force, since the police could not be summoned, and could not summon other police assistance themselves, without the use of messengers or face-to-face contact. The invention and use of the telegraph, telephone, two-way radio, and patrol car made rapid, relatively certain communication possible by the 1930s in many police departments. Now many police administrators felt that crime (in the urban areas, at least) could be greatly reduced, if not eliminated. Public expectations concerning police performance were raised, and the public responded by dramatically increasing requests for services to the police, who were the only public service agency (other than the fire department) available 24 hours a day, every day. The police soon found themselves unable to respond adequately to all these service requests, found little time available for crime-related activities, and found public dissatisfaction growing. At the same time, police administrators began to realize that they had underestimated the ingenuity of law violators, who rapidly achieved the same level of communication and mobility attained by the police. In short, by the middle of the twentieth century, the police (particularly those in large urban centers) were having difficulty living up to their image as crime fighters, and the public knew it. In attempting to be all things to all people, the police found themselves unable to perform all the services requested, capable of solving only about one in five reported major crimes, and unable to find ways out of these dilemmas. The issues of political corruption, lack of professionalism, and public distrust, which shaped police public relations historically, had been complicated by increasing demands for services based on unrealistic expectations. Today these dilemmas remain unsolved, and the police are attempting to improve their image, along with the quality of life of those they serve, by returning to some of the principles originally espoused by Sir Robert Peel over 150 years ago (under the guise of community policing).

There have, of course, been numerous attempts to deal with the dilemmas outlined above and to develop a more professional image for the police. In the early 1900s, August Vollmer, chief of police in Berkeley, California, was a strong advocate for police professionalism. Working with the Wickersham Commission appointed by President Hoover in 1929, Vollmer surveyed police in America. On the basis of his findings, Vollmer believed the police should be removed from the direct influence of politics and should be college-educated and well trained. He became a trainer, an educator, and an author of numerous works on the police. He was also an innovator in police technology and a strong supporter of police ethics. He established foundations for hiring and training police officers that remain the model today. One of Vollmer's followers, O. W. Wilson, authored several still popular police administration texts (the first in 1950) and later became the superintendent of the Chicago Police Department. Wilson, William Parker (chief of the Los Angeles Police Department from 1950 to 1966), V. A. Leonard (author of several police texts in the 1950s), Richard Sylvester (chief of District of Columbia Police from 1898 to 1915), and J. Edgar Hoover (director of the FBI from 1924 to 1972) were among others who called for increasing professionalism and initiated major changes in American policing (Conser & Russell, 2000). These calls for reform and change continued in the 1970s, 1980s, and 1990s, and still echo as we enter the twenty-first century.

The professional image of the American police suffered major setbacks in the 1960s and 1970s. Although the police were better trained, better educated, and better equipped than ever before, police–community relations, particularly with minority communities, became increasingly problematic. Major riots occurred in cities across the United States between 1964 and 1968, almost all of which began with police encounters with minority citizens. In the aftermath of the riots, the Kerner Commission (*Report of the National Advisory Commission on Civil Disorders*, 1968) pointed to several apparent shortcomings of the professional model of policing. Officers had become alienated from the people they were to serve, partly as a result of aggressive police tactics, partly as a result of increasing awareness of civil rights on behalf of minority Americans, and partly because the police did not, in terms of race, gender, and ethnicity, represent the public. These difficulties continued throughout the 1970s, compounded by studies that indicated routine patrol, long considered the backbone of traditional policing, was probably not the best way to employ police resources (Kelling, 1974). By the end of the decade, the police reform movement was stagnant and the future of the professional policing model was in question. It was apparent that traditional, law enforcement–oriented, policing had not achieved the lofty goals established earlier in the twentieth century. As the 1980s began, problem-oriented and community-oriented policing appeared to be ways to revive the reform movement and solve at least some of the problems that historically have plagued American police.

COMMUNITY- AND PROBLEM-ORIENTED POLICING

Nowhere is the network concept better illustrated than in the development and implementation of community-oriented policing (now typically referred to as community policing). Defining exactly what **community policing** means is difficult because it refers to a variety of initiatives tailored to different communities. In general terms, however, community policing refers to a philosophy of policing that emphasizes a cooperative approach between the police and other citizens focusing on alleviating community problems with the intent of improving the quality of life in the community (Eck & Rosenbaum, 1994; Cox, 1996; Rosenbaum, 2000). It is important to note that community policing is *not* a program, but a new and different approach to policing. Whereas traditional policing deals with treating the symptoms of crime by handling calls or incidents, community policing attempts to identify and attack the underlying problems that lead to calls (Goldstein, 1990). Often this is accomplished by going through four steps— *scanning,* or detailing the nature of the problem; *analysis,* or obtaining answers to the questions who, what, why, when, and how; *response,* or identifying possible solutions and selecting those most likely to work; and *assessment,* or evaluating the chosen solution to determine whether or not it worked. These four steps are commonly referred to as the **SARA process** (Goldstein, 1990).

To adequately address underlying problems, community police officers are encouraged to attempt to form partnerships with residents of the areas they police, with other public service agencies, and with private service providers. Officers are empowered to attempt nontraditional approaches to dealing with the problems addressed and are rewarded for innovative and creative programs and solutions. This approach represents almost the exact opposite of traditional policing, which has typically rewarded officers for following in the footsteps of generations of officers. In fact, officers who innovate in traditional departments are viewed as troublemakers. Officer discretion is at a premium in community policing, as are the abilities to develop proactive programs and new solutions to old problems. Accountability, openness to public observation and input, community organization skills, and customer-oriented or personalized police service are encouraged.

Organizational changes are required so that the philosophy of community policing can be implemented. Officers should be assigned to permanent beats so that they can develop the ties necessary to implement the philosophy. Control should be decentralized because the officers must be free to deal innovatively with problems encountered and in creating solutions that may differ from one neighborhood or beat to another. And the police must be willing to admit that they are not the only persons who can contribute to order maintenance, law enforcement, and crime prevention.

Community and problem-solving policing strategies are now generally accepted by police practitioners in the United States (and elsewhere too, for that matter). Still, the implementation of these strategies has proved difficult in many areas, the result of resistance by police personnel and lack of long-term commitment by community participants (Glensor, Correia, & Peak, 2000, p. 3). Is community policing a panacea for law enforcement and order maintenance? Probably not. But it is clear that traditional policing has failed to deal effectively with problems in these areas, and community policing is an alternative strategy that is certainly worth a try. Only careful evaluation of ongoing programs will allow us to determine the success of community policing. The few evaluations that have been conducted have shown either positive (Lurigo & Rosenbaum, 1994) or ambiguous (Lurigo & Skogan, 2000) results. In a review of community policing efforts in six American cities ranging in size from 38,000 to 1,500,000, Weisel and Eck (2000) found that "regardless of the type and longevity of community policing effort, and the variety and intensity of implementation activity, a solid core of personnel (about 75 percent) believe community policing is here to stay and their behaviors are likely to reflect that perception" (p. 270). If the network perspective of criminal justice is accepted, community policing would appear to be a step in the right direction because it recognizes the interrelationships among the police, other service agencies, and the public.

CURRENT POLICE FUNCTIONS

Before discussing specific police functions, we should note that although the police may be technically responsible for the full enforcement of a variety of statutes, in reality, they selectively enforce the law (as we indicated in Chapter 1). To be sure, they make every attempt to enforce laws prohibiting predatory crimes, but even these are subject to selective enforcement on the basis of whether violations are observed and reported, whether the victim is willing to serve as a witness/complainant, the seriousness of the offense, and numerous other factors. With respect to less serious but more common offenses, the police often tailor their efforts to specific geographic locations and/or times. For example, the police cannot fully enforce traffic laws prohibiting speeding. While an officer is writing a citation to one offender, several other speeders may escape his or her attention. Further, as members of the criminal justice network, police officers often tailor their activities on the basis of decisions of prosecutors and judges. The police officers who see violations relating to the use of marijuana, for example, may initially arrest violators, but if the prosecutor or judge routinely dismisses such cases, the officers will in all likelihood alter their enforcement patterns so that their behavior conforms to the expectations of others (including the public) in the network.

The police are visible representatives of authority whose decisions, to a great extent, determine whether or not other components of the official criminal justice network will take official action. They are largely a reactive agency, dependent on public cooperation and information. The police are "members of the public who are paid to give full-time attention to duties which are incumbent on every citizen, in the interests of community welfare and existence" (Davis, 1978, p. 7). This makes apparent the importance of the point that we have repeatedly emphasized: Public cooperation is necessary if the police are to perform their functions effectively, as community policing fully recognizes. Yet there is little doubt that public cooperation with the police leaves a great deal to be desired. Many segments of the public are uncooperative with the police, and some are openly hostile a good deal of the time. Other segments criticize the police for being unable to do anything about the crime problem or appear largely apathetic regardless of police action or inaction. The police are equally critical of and hostile toward some segments of the public. What are the major functions that the public expects the police to perform? Why are the police often judged ineffective? What do the police expect from the public?

The police in the United States are primarily providers of services. Among the services they provide are law enforcement, order maintenance, and crime prevention. In community policing departments, these services are provided largely through the use of problem-solving techniques and police–community partnerships. In more traditional departments, the police have attempted to provide the services with little input from or attention to the public. Traditional agencies have often been unsuccessful in satisfying public demands for these services because successful performance requires public cooperation. When members of the public take their responsibilities seriously, a high level of police performance is possible. When members of the public fail to accept their responsibilities, or when the police fail to participate in partnerships with the public, the police are not likely to be highly effective. For much of the twentieth century, large segments of the American public have appeared to be willing to leave law enforcement largely to the police. Failure to report crimes, failure to assist victims of crimes in progress, a desire not to get involved, and failure to assist police officers upon request have been commonplace. The prevailing attitude seems to have been "it's not my job" or "it's none of my business." Thus, the police have been left to handle the tasks of law enforcement themselves. While the vast majority of police work involves providing services that have little to do with criminal conduct, the ability to detect crime and apprehend criminals remains a critical part of policing. These tasks are particularly difficult, perhaps impossible, to accomplish without public support.

Most police officers in metropolitan areas spend their working hours responding to one service request after another. Normally, some time is spent on routine patrol, even though, as we have seen, the value of such patrol is seriously in doubt. Only a small percentage of the police officer's time is spent handling criminal matters, contrary to the image presented by the media in the United States. Other services commonly provided by the police include the following:

Checking security of buildings.
Regulating traffic.
Investigating accidents.
Transporting prisoners and the emotionally disturbed.
Providing information.
Escorting funeral processions and parades.
Finding lost children.
Providing first aid.
Making public speeches.
Handling calls about animals.
Handling domestic disputes.
Enforcing licensing regulations.
Fingerprinting.
Administering breathalyzer tests.
Staffing and managing jails.
Using the computer to file reports and to collect information.
Engaging in problem-solving activities.
Seeking to improve quality of life in the community.

POLICE LAW ENFORCEMENT PROCEDURES

There are certain crime-related tasks that the police are expected to perform, although, as we have seen, they perform numerous additional tasks as well. Generally speaking, the police are held responsible for the following crime-related tasks:

1. Prevention.
2. Recording.
3. Investigation.
4. Apprehension.
5. Arrest.
6. Interviewing and interrogation.
7. Booking.
8. Acceptance of certain types of bail or temporary detention.
9. Collection and preservation of evidence.
10. Recovery of stolen property.
11. Transmission of reports to the prosecutor in usable form.
12. Testifying in court.

As we discuss each of these areas, recall our previous discussions of the exercise of discretion and the influence of politics at all levels in the criminal justice network.

With respect to crime prevention, the police are generally expected to provide programs to educate the public, to provide deterrent patrol, to make house and building checks, and to use informants and intelligence sources to stop criminal acts from occurring. In some societies, the task of prevention is made easier by legislation that allows the police to stop, search, inventory, and detain any suspicious person. In our society, such tactics are severely limited in the interest of preserving **due process** and individual rights. To maintain a relatively free society, we, the citizens, have decided that due process is at least as important as **crime control.** Although this may hamper police efforts to prevent and solve crimes, few of us would be willing to sacrifice the right to due process to make the work of the police easier. Although crime prevention programs developed by the police may deter some crimes, it is clear that prevention is one area in which public cooperation is critical (in terms of following police guidelines for security, reporting suspicious persons, and other activities). Prevention is made even more difficult by the fact that there is no visible end product to prevention programs, so it is difficult to justify resources to support such programs.

A second crime-related duty of the police is to record crimes reported by the public or observed by police officers. Such recording is important, since both our local and national official statistics on the incidence of different types of crime depend on accurate recording. Further, information recorded and shared with other agencies may be useful in solving crimes, arresting offenders, or preventing additional offenses. Once a citizen exercises his or her discretion to report an offense to the police, the police exercise their discretion as to whether the report should become part of the official record. When the report is accepted as worthy of attention, it becomes a crime known to the police.

Having accepted and recorded a crime report, the police are expected to investigate the crime. A great deal of discretion is used by the police in deciding whether or not to expend police resources on an investigation, and if an investigation is to be conducted, how extensive it should be. Investigations range from simply making a preliminary report describing stolen property (used largely for insurance purposes) with little or no follow-up, to investigations of homicide requiring that the crime scene be sealed off, that complete inventories of evidence be made, and that many persons be located and interviewed. Investigations such as the former are often conducted over the phone in a matter of minutes, while the latter may take months or years.

The use of informants to help solve or prevent crimes is common in police departments. Informants can often provide information that cannot be obtained in any other way, and where they have been shown to be reliable, informants may be important in helping prevent crime and/or in apprehending offenders. Perhaps nowhere is the use of discretion by the police more clearly illustrated than in dealing with informants. To obtain valuable information, the police frequently overlook minor (and occasionally, even fairly serious) violations by informants. It is not uncommon, for example, for the police to be aware of the fact that an informant is in possession of illegal drugs and, in fact, to provide the informant with funds that they know will be used to purchase such drugs. The discretion not to arrest is exercised in the hopes of obtaining information about more serious offenses committed by others.

When an investigation turns up a likely suspect, the police are expected to apprehend that suspect and, where appropriate, to make an **arrest.** Here, at the point of arrest, the police officer possesses considerable discretionary power. It is true that she or he is influenced by the law, departmental policy, and other network constraints. Still, there is often no one physically present to supervise the officer's actions, and she or he may respond to a variety of cues other than legal ones. The age, gender, race, dress, prior history, or location of a suspect may all influence the officer's decision, which is crucial because if the police officer decides not to arrest, the matter is, practically speaking, closed. It is the exercise of discretion by individual police officers in thousands of police–citizen encounters every day that helps shape public attitudes toward the police (and, we might add, the exercise of discretion by members of the various publics that help shape police attitudes toward them) as In the News, "Legislators Hear Testimony about Racial Profiling," indicates.

If the officer arrests one person for a particular offense but allows another who has committed the same offense to go free, the arrested party (when he or she knows about the discrepancy) can hardly be expected to feel the criminal justice network is just. When one officer ignores a particular offense, but another arrests everyone who commits that offense, the public is confused. The way police officers exercise discretion, therefore, plays an important part in shaping relations between the police and the public.

The process of arrest itself is quite complicated. Generally speaking, however, a police officer is empowered to make an arrest when he or she has a warrant or signed complaint, sees someone commit a felony or misdemeanor, or has reason to suspect that someone has committed a felony. The actual point at which an arrest occurs depends on the officer's intent to arrest and the citizen's understanding that intent. When the officer says, "You are under arrest!" the intent is quite clear provided the officer is speaking the same language as the arrestee. It is less clear when the officer says, "You, stay here. I want to talk to you." Further, a police officer exercising discretion may try to use this ambiguity to gain time to decide whether or not to make an arrest. For the most part, arrests based solely on suspicion are illegal. But, at what point does suspicion become probable cause or a reasonable belief? It is at this stage, during or just after the arrest, that the suspect is informed of his or her Miranda rights (to remain silent, that anything said may be used in a court of law, and to contact a lawyer) (*Miranda* v. *Arizona*, 1966). Depending on the suspect's desires or the suspect's lawyer's advice, interviewing and/or interrogation may occur. You can see, then, that even arrest, a function that all of us would agree is important to the police, is not as simple as it first appears.

When a suspect has been arrested and made available for prosecution, the police say the crime has been cleared by arrest. Note that a crime listed as cleared by arrest may involve a police suspect who is never prosecuted for the crime or who is eventually determined to be not guilty. With respect to the crimes classified by the FBI as Index Offenses (criminal homicide, forcible

In the News

LEGISLATORS HEAR TESTIMONY ABOUT RACIAL PROFILING ON STATE'S ROADS; CONFIDENCE IN POLICE AND COURTS IS AT STAKE, SPEAKERS SAY

By James Walsh

They sat down Wednesday, one by one, to tell Minnesota lawmakers how law enforcers stopped them, searched them and often humiliated them for no other obvious reason than the color of their skin.

Ramsey County District Judge Salvador Rosas told of the embarrassment of being frisked after supposedly failing to signal a turn.

Jerry Patterson, a Hennepin County assistant public defender, told of police stopping him 14 times in 1997 and 1998 for reasons including that he fit the description of a crime suspect and, once, because he allegedly drove past a crack house.

And John Solomon, a Hennepin County child protection worker and a former Washington, D.C., cop, recalled the time an officer pulled him over because he looked "suspicious."

Their message to the state Senate's crime prevention and judiciary committees: Racial profiling happens. Do something about it now, before the public's trust in the police and the courts erodes to the point that effective law enforcement becomes impossible.

Sens. Jane Ranum and Allan Spear, Minneapolis DFLers, said they called the three-hour hearing because the issue of racial profiling has become

the top concern facing law enforcement across the country. Recent studies showing that Minnesota ranks among the worst states in the disparities between blacks and whites in arrest and incarceration rates only highlight the need for study and action, they said.

They heard that faith in law enforcement is rare among blacks in the Twin Cities.

Samuel Payne was pulled over shortly after midnight in January 1999 near the intersection of 42nd St. and Girard Av. N. in Minneapolis. The police ordered him to show his hands. Then they ordered him out of the car, searched him, put him in their squad car and refused to say why they had stopped him.

They ordered his girlfriend out of the car, searched her and put her into the squad car. They finally told him his crime: His license plate didn't match up with his car, according to a records search. They paid attention to his license plate, they said, because he'd failed to dim his high beams.

His car was impounded. At 3 a.m., a police sergeant called to say they'd made a mistake. Police gave him a ride to the impound lot to get his car.

Continued

"I was asked if I had gold teeth. I was asked if I had tattoos," said Payne, a social worker. "This was wrong. And something needs to be done about it."

David Harris, a University of Toledo law professor who has studied racial profiling, told the committee that the criminal justice system risks more than the continued alienation of minorities if profiling continues. It risks losing whites as well.

A Gallup poll shows that a majority of white Americans also believe that minority motorists are more likely than whites to be stopped by police. Once that perception of unequal justice becomes pervasive, he said, try finding people willing to serve on juries. He also said stops of black motorists are less likely to turn up evidence of crime than stops of whites.

Harris and others urged the legislators to begin collecting statewide race data on stops, as Minneapolis and St. Paul have begun doing. It's a start, he said, to restoring trust in police.

Star Tribune (Minneapolis, MN), June 15, 2000, p. 2B.

rape, aggravated assault, robbery, burglary, grand theft, arson, and auto theft), the police are successful in clearing by arrest about 20 to 25 percent. In other words, about four out of five Index Offenses are not cleared by arrest. This inability of the police to clear crimes by arrest is both caused by and causes public belief that the police are ineffective.

Once an arrest is made, the police are responsible for informing the suspect of the charges against him or her, for **booking**, and for interviewing or interrogating the suspect. The booking process involves taking an inventory of the suspect's property, fingerprinting, and photographing. Also at this stage, the police may inform the suspect that he or she is eligible for bail and, under certain circumstances (generally in the case of misdemeanors), may accept bail and release the suspect from custody. If bail is not allowable or if the suspect cannot make bail, the police may detain him or her in a holding cell or, in the case of a county sheriff, in a jail until the suspect makes bail or goes to trial.

From the time of the initial investigation through arrest, interviews, and interrogations, the police are responsible for collecting evidence (physical and testimonial) concerning the crime in question. The collection of evidence depends on the skill of the investigator and available clues. The preservation of evidence to be presented in court requires that a **chain of evidence** begin when the evidence is first collected and continue until the evidence is presented in court or determined to be of no value. The chain of evidence must be fashioned in such a way that location and control of the evidence can be documented at every point from discovery to presentation and often involves the investigative division of the department. Investigators handle most of the serious criminal cases and are specially trained in crime scene investigation and preservation.

In larger departments, there may also be criminalists or crime scene technicians, fingerprinting experts, polygraph operators, and juvenile officers in the investigative division. The chain of evidence typically begins when a patrol officer or investigator finds what he or she considers evidence, and collects and tags or clearly identifies the evidence. He or she then turns it over to an evidence custodian or technician, who gives the officer or investigator receipts for the evidence. The chain of evidence typically concludes with the presentation of the evidence in court by the officer or investigator who originally collected the evidence. This officer signs a receipt for the evidence custodian when he or she removes the evidence from the evidence locker or room.

During the investigation and collection of evidence, the police officers involved are also interested in recovering stolen property that will eventually be returned to its rightful owner. Similarly, the officers involved in the arrest and investigation are aware that they must proceed in such a way that they can establish both a factual and legal (following due process) case against the suspect that the prosecutor can use in court. Police reports form the starting point for the prosecutor's case, and inadequate performance in any of the areas we have just discussed may make prosecution either impossible or unsuccessful. The same is true of the last requirement of the police—testifying in court. Inaccurate or perjured testimony can lead not only to the release of guilty persons or the conviction of innocent persons, but also to serious repercussions for the officer personally and the police image in general (Cunningham, 1999). It is important, therefore, that police officers take and retain complete, accurate notes during the investigation; that they be honest; and that they be unafraid to admit they don't know when, in fact, they don't know. Only when police testimony meets these standards can we expect public cooperation with, and support of, the police.

Community support is essential to successful policing.
Michael Newman/Photo Edit

POLICE ORDER MAINTENANCE ACTIVITIES

As we have repeatedly indicated, law enforcement activities are a small, though critical, part of policing. The police spend far more time attempting to maintain order. To accomplish this goal, they engage in **mediation and nego-tiation.** That is, they mediate disputes between parties and attempt to negoti-ate settlements that will restore order. Typically, these techniques involve compromises suggested by the police officer. For example, an officer receives a complaint of loud music. She may talk to the person responsible for the music, indicate that it is bothering others, and ask that the volume be turned down. The officer may then talk to the complaining party, indicating that the respon-sible party has agreed to turn down the volume, but also noting that there needs to be some give-and-take between neighbors and that the partygoers are just trying to have a good time without injuring others. Or a police officer may try to mediate a dispute between a youth who frequently runs away from home and his parents. He may ask the parents to try to be more understand-ing of the youth's needs and desires and vice versa. He may point out to both parties that taking official action will only drive the parties further apart and suggest that they try to strike a compromise.

Negotiating and mediating are among the most frequent activities in which the police engage. Officers frequently attempt to negotiate settlements to avoid official action (law enforcement). As is the case with law enforcement, negotiation and mediation require reciprocity on behalf of the other citizens with whom the police are involved. This need for reciprocity was originally recognized by Sir Robert Peel more than 150 years ago but seems to have gone unrecognized in American policing for much of the time. In the past 20 years, however, police administrators, politicians, and civic groups have begun to focus on the need for a police partnership with those they serve. The efforts have been summarized in the section on community policing.

POLICE ORGANIZATIONS

To achieve the goals of providing service by maintaining order and enforcing the law, many police agencies have developed organizational structures simi-lar to the one depicted in Figure 6.1. Note that there are many variations on this formal organizational structure (for example, the use of an assistant chief). Also note that this chart concerns the police department only and does not show that the department is accountable to a mayor, city manager, or commis-sioner, and the public.

The operations division is normally the largest division in terms of per-sonnel and other resources, and the duties of patrol officers and investigators have been outlined previously. The other division commonly found in police departments may be referred to as the administrative division or staff services division. Primary functions of this division are record keeping, communica-tions, research and planning, training and education, and sometimes logistics.

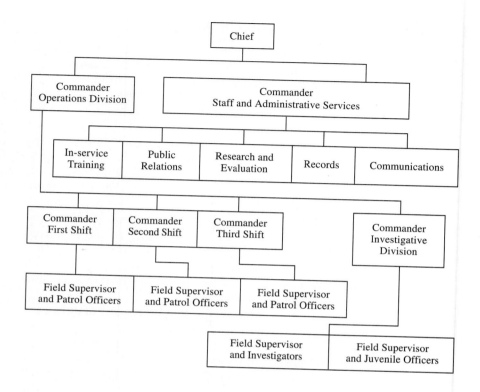

Figure 6.1
Typical Police Organizational Chart

In some departments, most of these functions are performed by sworn officers, but there is a clear-cut trend toward hiring civilian employees to perform the majority of these tasks.

Although some departments have divided the tasks mentioned above differently, most follow this division of activity. Normally, a division commander in charge of each division reports to the chief of police or a deputy chief of police. These division commanders have shift commanders, field supervisors, and staff personnel under their control as well as line officers and/or civilians. In metropolitan departments, several precinct headquarters are established throughout the city, and each precinct may be organized as indicated above, or various types of services may remain centralized, to be called in when the need arises.

In most instances, police departments have maintained a paramilitary structure that stresses use of the chain of command in issuing orders and directives and solving problems. Although this structure has some advantages in terms of discipline and control, it is resistant to change. In addition, it fails to promote communication and interaction among members of different divisions and, in fact, often promotes a sense of competition among departmental personnel, which may not always have beneficial consequences. In some departments, patrol officers and investigators seldom interact because of rivalry between division commanders, physical separation of facilities, and aloof attitudes on the part of the investigators. In addition, patrol officers tend to view investigators as glory seekers. As a consequence, investigators who are actively looking for a wanted felon are not always provided with available information as to his or her whereabouts. Several patrol officers might see the individual in question but be unaware that investigators are looking for him or her because of the lack of communication.

Many students of the police believe that the paramilitary structure typical of many police agencies is one reason the police have not kept pace with private industry in adapting to changing conditions. When followed to the letter, such formal organizational structure is often quite cumbersome. Partially as a response to the inflexibility of the formal organizational structure, informal arrangements often arise among various divisions and individuals, which may speed up organizational procedures or impede such procedures. Thus, a police lieutenant who wants to change the activities of his or her shift personnel may not go to the patrol commander, who would then have to go to the assistant chief, who would then have to seek the chief's approval. Instead, the lieutenant may see the chief after hours or may discuss the idea with an alderman or the mayor over drinks to gain support. Similarly, individual patrol officers and investigators may meet informally to discuss a case and share information that their immediate supervisors may not wish to share as a result of divisional rivalries. In organizational structures, then, it is important to consider both the formal and informal arrangements that characterize the agency in question.

As a result of some of these problems with traditional police organizations and as a result of ongoing research, some police departments have started to make changes in their organizational structures. Let us now turn our attention to some of these changes.

SOME VARIATIONS ON THE TRADITIONAL POLICE ORGANIZATION

A number of attempts have been made in recent years to make police departments more flexible and responsive to the needs of both the public and other criminal justice agencies. Many of these attempts are still in the experimental stage, but let us take a brief look at some of the more promising innovations.

As noted earlier, one strategy employed by some departments to improve services and efficiency is community policing (variations of which have been referred to as neighborhood policing, team policing, or neighborhood service teams). As originally conceived, a number of police officers, each having some special training, are assigned as a team to serve a particular geographic area. The team is responsible for providing services to area residents 24 hours a day and operates under the direction of a field supervisor who coordinates the team's efforts with those of the larger department. The rationale for this style of policing is that such teams will be more familiar with area problems and more familiar to area residents. Further, decentralized control should result in greater flexibility and responsiveness to the varying needs and desires of different neighborhoods (Eck & Rosenbaum, 1994). In contemporary community policing, most city agencies are involved in an attempt to build partnerships between agency personnel and neighborhood residents. The police–community partnership proceeds by trying to restore pride to the neighborhood through organizing general cleanup projects, closing crack houses, improving conditions in neighborhood schools, and helping rediscover a sense of community. The effectiveness of such programs remains to be determined, but at least some seem to be enjoying moderate success (Barber, 1996; Weisel & Eck, 2000).

Another attempt to change traditional police structure involves instituting a career system that provides more than one promotional channel for officers. In most police departments, chances for promotion are tied to a military rank supervisory structure (patrol officer to corporal, to sergeant, to lieutenant, and so on). Promotional opportunities depend, then, on vacancies at each supervisory level and on the ability and desire to supervise personnel. Obviously, in any given department there is only one chief and a limited number of deputy chiefs or division commanders, so possibilities for upward mobility are rather limited. In addition, many patrol officers and investigators who possess high levels of skills in the field have little desire or ability to supervise others. Traditionally, these individuals have remained in a single status with pay increases based on longevity and cost of living. A **dual career system** allows those patrol officers who are highly skilled but who wish to remain on the streets to demonstrate their proficiency with attendant pay increases and recognition (Bratcher, 1999). The outcome of such a program is higher morale among patrol officers and better services for the public. Traditional promotional opportunities through supervisory positions, of course, remain open.

In an attempt to improve community relations and provide better services (to say nothing of complying with affirmative action guidelines), many police departments now employ women and minorities. This invasion of a predominantly white male world has come about slowly and with considerable resistance. Nonetheless, the evidence is quite clear: Women and minorities perform police duties as well as white males (Cox, 1996, pp. 141–60; Walker 1999, pp. 230–32). As time passes, these newcomers to police operations will gain supervisory positions and, if they can avoid being co-opted by the police hierarchy, further structural changes in police departments may be expected. These changes may not come easily, as In the News, "Women Confront Police Challenge" and "White Blasts Police Union," indicate.

In the News

WOMEN CONFRONT POLICE CHALLENGE

By Amelia Robinson

DAYTON—Leatha Savage and Jeri Maupins know that being black female police officers won't always be easy.

But the pair welcomed the challenges of wearing blue for the Dayton Police Department on Thursday night as the Dayton Police Academy graduated its 91st recruit class.

Savage, Maupins and 19 others, standing before family and friends, took the oath to service the Constitution of the United States and state of Ohio.

The class ranged in age from 21 to 42.

Maupins, 35, and Savage, 29, were the only blacks in the class, which also included four white women.

The next recruit class, which will also have 21 members, begins in July.

The Dayton Police Department has long been criticized for the lack of minority representation on the force.

The department has struggled with its racial mix. About 88 percent of its police is white; about 40 percent of Dayton's population is black.

Although there are black females in administrative positions within the department, Savage and Maupins will be two of only three black female officers walking beats.

Because of the rarity of black females on the force, the women said they feel as though they have been forced to be in the forefront.

They said they hope more females and minorities will be interested in law enforcement.

"I don't think a lot of black people consider law enforcement as a career," said Maupins, a Dayton native. "Hopefully they will see us and this is something they can do."

Maupins, a graduate of Stebbins High School, said she has always wanted to be a police officer but personal commitment prevented her from doing so earlier in life.

She said she is looking forward to patrolling her hometown.

Savage, who moved to Dayton from Rubonia, Fla., with her husband four years ago, said she had positive experiences with police officers as a child and thought they had interesting jobs.

The desire to be a police officer "is not something you can explain," she said. "You either want to do it or you don't."

Dayton Daily News, *April 14, 2000, p. 3B.*

In the News

WHITE BLASTS POLICE UNION FOR FILING SUIT; MAYOR CLAIMS FOP WANTS TO BLOCK MINORITY HIRING

By Alison Grant

Mayor Michael R. White said yesterday that a police union lawsuit filed this week is intended to undermine his efforts to hire more minority police officers.

The mayor charged the Fraternal Order of Police filed the suit because it wants to keep members of minority groups off the Cleveland police force.

White had planned to appoint 30 cadets to the next police academy class from a 1996 eligibility list and the rest from a list based on a 1998 test. Of the 30, 21 are minority group members, of whom eight are women, he said.

"I can find no other reason to understand their reasoning," White said of the FOP suit. "At every class, at every promotion, they have threatened, they have blamed, they have offered every reason under the sun to resist making the Police Department as diverse as our city."

White's comments came during a hastily called news conference outside the offices of the FOP, which sued the city Monday, contending the 1996 eligibility list has expired. FOP officials stood behind reporters taking notes on the mayor's comments.

"I believe the mayor has obscured the real issue, and the issue is the law," FOP President Roy J. Rich said afterward.

"For him to play the race card is irresponsible and inflammatory."

Cuyahoga County Common Pleas Judge Frank Celebrezze yesterday issued an order preventing the city from appointing cadets to its 120th police academy from the 1996 list until a court hearing on the validity of the list. A new class was supposed to start Monday, but administration officials have said they would delay it a month.

Civil Service rules state that eligibility lists have a two-year life span. White argues the city had the right to pull candidates from the list before it expired, certify them as eligible to enter the academy and use them at a later date.

Rich said Civil Service rules make it clear that is not allowed.

"If the city is trying to violate the law to manipulate the list, then that's racism and discrimination, and it's wrong," he said.

White noted that candidates from the 1996 list scored 86 percent on the exam.

"The last time I checked at Ohio State, where I went, that's a pretty damn good B+," he said. "They're not getting an affirmative action pass. They belong here."

Continued

Councilman Roosevelt Coats also spoke, saying of the lawsuit, "I think the motivation is racism. What else?

"We are a sea of diversity. And, my friends, that's not going to change."

The eligibility list made up of people who took the police exam in 1998 also is under scrutiny.

Bob Beck, president of the Cleveland Police Patrolman's Association, wants the Cuyahoga County prosecutor's office to investigate how almost 600 of 2,150 tests given in October 1998 did not get graded for a year.

First Assistant Prosecutor Robert Coury said he is meeting with Beck tomorrow to discuss what Beck alleges is evidence of criminality in the tests' mishandling.

The Plain Dealer *(Cleveland, OH), March 16, 2000, p. 1A.*

No discussion of changes in police organization and practices would be complete without a brief mention of technological changes. Computers, including personal, notebook, and on-board computers, have made possible virtually instant analysis of crime and accident trends, recall of information on suspects, and analysis of the frequency, duration, and type of activities engaged in by departmental personnel. Computers and cameras mounted in patrol vehicles provide not only instant access to information concerning vehicle registrations, licenses, and wants or warrants, but also instantaneous communications with both other police vehicles and headquarters. This rapid communication capability, coupled with greater willingness to experiment on behalf of many police administrators, has enabled the police to become more responsive to changing conditions (Couret, 1999). A good example of the impact of technology is the National Crime Information Center (NCIC) which, in addition to allowing rapid checks of criminal backgrounds, supports the transmission of photographs and fingerprint data. The new NCIC 2000 can process almost 250,000 inquiries per day and provides access to some 80,000 criminal justice users (FBI National Press Office, 1999).

As a result of research conducted in Kansas City and elsewhere, the effectiveness of patrol officers on routine patrol has been questioned. This cornerstone of police work is defended by many police administrators, but evidence indicates, in some cities at least, that routine patrol does not prevent crime, improve citizen satisfaction, or cut down response time. These findings suggest that valuable police resources have been, and are currently being, wasted. If this is so, a thorough rethinking of police operations is required. Such rethinking has already occurred in many police departments that now employ various types of **directed patrol** strategies to improve efficiency. **Split-force policing** involves designating certain areas high-risk, assigning certain officers to those areas, and saturating the areas with patrols (saturation patrols), both overt and covert. In the meantime, other designated officers are responsible for handling service requests and routine patrol in the area. Suspect-oriented policing techniques involve assigning officers to concentrate on known offenders or suspects (Gaines, Kappeler, & Vaughn, 1994, pp. 166–71). In addition to identifying and using special types of patrol strategies, many departments have broadened their patrol approach by adding bicycle patrols, aircraft patrols, boat patrols, and foot or mounted patrols (Reaves & Goldberg, 1999).

Another change in policing involves the **accreditation** of police departments. The objectives of accreditation include developing standards against which agency performance may be measured and developing accreditation procedures that facilitate objective assessment of police performance. Given the strong American tradition that police power should be decentralized, it has been nearly impossible to establish generally accepted standards of quality in law enforcement. There are almost as many points of view concerning how different police functions ought to be performed as there are police departments. Nonetheless, a number of state and national police organizations are involved in attempting to develop standards for police departments. **Peace Officer Standards and Training (POST) boards** in 48 states set requirements for becoming certified as a police officer. These boards certify police officers who meet predetermined standards of training and education, and who pass standardized written examinations. The certification process is intended to ensure a minimum level of knowledge among police officers throughout the state and is an important step toward professionalization. Some states, such as Illinois, also have voluntary certification for the chiefs of police with the same goals in mind.

The Commission on Accreditation for Law Enforcement Agencies (CALEA) was established in 1979 and administers a voluntary accreditation program aimed at achieving excellence, efficiency, and professionalism among police agencies. The commission has established 439 standards by which to evaluate police agencies. These standards are tailored to fit agencies of various sizes and to help police agencies evaluate themselves. If an agency desires to be evaluated by a team of assessors working for the commission, it submits an application. The agency is then sent a questionnaire that is used to determine the standards that apply to that particular agency. A self-assessment is then conducted by agency personnel, and if the agency desires, an on-site assessment by a team of assessors follows. The on-site assessment is then reviewed by the commission to determine whether the agency will be accredited. Currently, more than 500 agencies have been accredited, a number have been reaccredited, and some 500 others are involved in the process (Commission on Accreditation for Law Enforcement Agencies [CALEA], 1999). Some 21 percent of full-time local and state police officers in the United States are officially in the accreditation process (CALEA, 2000, p. 1)

The implications of police certification and accreditation are far-reaching. Transfer between departments and lateral entry would be facilitated among certified officers. The overall level of training among law enforcement personnel should improve. Finally, the overall level of service provided to the public should improve. Yet accreditation, in particular, has not been unopposed. Some states have decided to develop their own standards for accreditation as opposed to accepting the national standards of CALEA. Costs related to accreditation have also been subject to criticism.

These and numerous other adaptations being made in police agencies throughout the United States indicate that the organizational structure of police departments can take a variety of forms and still permit the police to play their roles in the criminal justice network. Let us now turn our attention to a discussion of the procedures used to fill those roles.

SELECTION, TRAINING, AND EDUCATION OF THE POLICE

It is clear that adequate police performance in all the areas mentioned above requires specially selected, specially trained, and perhaps specially educated personnel. How are such personnel selected? What type of education and how much training do these personnel require?

Standards for police officers vary across the United States, but certain considerations appear to be important in most jurisdictions. Generally speaking, potential police officers must meet some or all of the following

Physical fitness is important to all police officers.
Michael Newman/Photo Edit

criteria, which are governed by the Civil Rights Act of 1964, the Equal Employment Opportunity Act of 1972 (EEOA), the Americans with Disabilities Act (ADA) of 1990, and the Civil Rights Act of 1991, as well as by numerous court decisions:

1. Age: minimum age is typically 19 to 21 at time of first employment.
2. Height and weight are in proportion to each other; to test for body fat composition.
3. Education: generally, a high school diploma or GED, but more departments now require some college credits.
4. Agility test: to evaluate physical capabilities required by the job.
5. Written test: to measure aptitude and/or intelligence.
6. Psychological exam: to determine mental fitness for the job; may be required only after an offer of a job has been made.
7. Medical exam: to ensure that no disabilities that might prevent the applicant from performing the essential functions of the job exist at the time of initial employment; may be required only after an offer of a job has been made.
8. Polygraph exam: to determine honesty.
9. Background investigation: to ensure character of applicant.
10. Oral interview: to determine applicant's reactions to job-related issues (Cox, 1996; Walker, 1999).

Many of the traditional requirements for becoming a police officer have come under attack in the last quarter of the twentieth century. Realistically, a number of these requirements have been applied subjectively with the effect (if not the intent) of excluding females and minorities from police work. We know of several division commanders in different police departments who have advanced through the ranks from patrol officer to lieutenant or captain but who could not have met existing height requirements at the time of their initial employment. Yet they were hired, and others who met these requirements were not. One police captain told us that he was measured with his boots on, while others were measured in bare feet. In short, height might exclude certain applicants, but if those responsible for hiring felt a certain individual would make a good police officer, the height requirement could be manipulated. As another example of subjectivity, agility tests at one time were set up in such fashion as to routinely exclude women. But these tests have since been shown to have little or no relationship to activities performed by police officers. Today, tests of physical agility must be based on job task analyses.

Psychological exams are generally considered unreliable (scores for the same individual are subject to considerable variation over time). In addition, analyzing scores of potential police officers often involves comparing the scores they obtain with an "ideal" profile. Because no one knows what the characteristics of an ideal police officer are, such testing seems highly questionable. Still, liability issues related to negligent hiring lead most police agencies to continue to require psychological exams.

Written tests vary tremendously in content and form. Some are job-related or situation-specific; others are general aptitude or intelligence tests. The validity of most of these tests in terms of predicting successful performance as a police officer is yet to be established.

Similarly, the oral board interview is extremely subjective. Although race, gender, dress, and the like are formally excluded from the criteria to be considered by the board in most jurisdictions, one of the authors who has repeatedly served on such boards notes that these variables are frequently subjects of discussion among board members and undoubtedly influence the ratings received by applicants. Affirmative action programs have, in many locales, improved the chances that applicants will be selected without regard to race or gender, although informal pressures clearly counteract such programs in some areas.

As Gray (1975) and Falkenberg, Gaines, and Cox (1990) aptly point out, all these selection procedures may be used for covert as well as overt purposes. Overtly, the procedures are designed to fulfill the requirements of the formal police organization. Covertly, they may be used to satisfy the requirements of the police subculture. This subculture, or police fraternity, has developed over the years as the police and other citizens have increasingly come to view each other as "we" and "they." To the police, "we" consists of other police officers (members of the fraternity). These members are expected to be loyal to the police subculture, trustworthy, willing and able to use force, authoritarian, and so forth. "They" consists of everyone who is not a police officer, who cannot be regarded as loyal to the subculture, trustworthy, and so on. As one police officer recently put it, "We work in our little world that those outside don't understand." To some other citizens (members of racial minorities, for example), the police constitute the "they" group. This relationship between the police and other citizens is both caused by, and helps maintain, a gap in communication.

At any rate, the requirements of the police subculture are often made known to police selection boards. As a result, most new recruits, though certainly not all, meet both formal and informal requirements for the job. Using the network approach, let us examine how these informal or subcultural requirements can influence hiring procedures even though the law may prohibit their consideration.

The authors are aware of several cases in which police chiefs, mayors, city managers, or council members have contacted selection board members informally to express their feelings concerning who should be hired to fill a police vacancy. In one case, a police chief indicated to the president of a selection board that he wanted no more college graduates hired because they were too intellectual and very likely to move to another department in a short time. In another, a chief of police informed two of the three board members that the department really needed a minority officer.

Informal suggestions or pressures such as these may, of course, be ignored by board members. Theoretically, they must be ignored because the
applicant is to be rated on the formal qualifications discussed above, and,
short of a consent decree agreement, there is no formal mechanism for
adding or detracting rating points for reasons involving race, gender, or
creed. Practically speaking, however, members of selection boards are often
political appointees, appointed precisely because they are willing to listen to
the desires of.the police chief or police commissioner. We know of a case in
which a college professor was appointed to a board of fire and police com-
missioners. His idea of the selection process was that applicants should be
rated strictly on the basis of their qualifications, regardless of race, gender,
or creed. He felt informal pressures should be prohibited or ignored, and refused to listen to those not on the board who tried to influence him. He was
a rather persuasive fellow and was able to persuade one or both of the two
more conservative board members to support him on some occasions. When
he resigned from the board, several police officials confided they were not
disappointed. Now, they said, someone who "understood the requirements
of real police work" would be appointed and things would run more
smoothly.

In some instances, particularly in the selection for upper ranks in police
agencies, **assessment centers** are being employed as a solution to some of the
difficulties mentioned above. Assessment center personnel work on the basis
of job task analyses to create job-related exercises. A team of independent assessors evaluates candidate performance on those exercises. The team facilita-
tor then typically recommends one or more candidates to the mayor, city manager, and/or chief of police. The value of assessment centers rests on the
accuracy of the job task analyses and the training of the assessors. There is
some evidence that assessment centers, though quite costly, are better at predicting future on-the-job success for police officers than are paper-and-pencil
tests (Pynes & Bernardin, 1992; Swanson et al., 1998).

Applicants who successfully meet the requirements outlined above and
are selected for police work generally go to a training institute or academy
where they receive training in a variety of police subjects, ranging from self-
defense and weapons through first aid to criminal law and human relations
(see Table 6.1). Successful completion of a training program leads to the status
of **probationary officer,** a status that normally lasts from 6 to 18 months. During the probationary period, the new officer receives on-the-job training from
senior officers and supervisors. If the recruit successfully completes the probationary period, he or she becomes a full-fledged police officer.

As we indicated above, many of the criteria involved in the selection of
police officers have been questioned. One area of controversy worthy of mention here is that of education. Do college-educated people make better police
officers than non-college-educated individuals? Are certain types of college
programs preferable to other types? Is level of education an important vari-

able to consider when selecting police officers? If so, why do 79 percent of local police agencies still require a high school diploma or GED rather than some college as a condition of employment?

In the past 100 years, there has been a hue and cry for professional police. While training may help make the police more technically proficient, many believe the real hope for professionalization rests with education, since educational requirements are a basis for most highly regarded professions in our society (e.g., medicine, law, teaching). The issue of education is complicated by financial considerations. In an era of increasing concern over cost effectiveness, are the higher salaries required to hire and retain college-educated police officers justifiable? Currently, there is some evidence to indicate that college-educated officers are likely to have fewer citizen complaints filed against them than are non-college-educated officers (Kappeler, Sapp, & Carter, 1992), and the emphasis on community policing would also seem to dictate the need for better-educated officers (Varricchio, 1998). Whether or not these differences are worth higher salaries and whether or not other differences, which have not yet been detected, exist are still areas of controversy. In addition, the issue of whether criminal justice or law enforcement college programs are more or less desirable than liberal arts programs remains unresolved. These ambiguities were reflected by changes in federal programming, which originally gave financial aid to police officers interested in furthering their education, but which later placed less emphasis on this area. The debate continues, with an emphasis on empirical research to help provide answers to questions concerning the necessity or desirability of advanced education for police officers. Recent legislation signed by President Clinton created a Police Corps that provides financial assistance to college students who desire to become community police officers for a period of at least four years.

POLICE MISCONDUCT

No discussion of the police would be complete without considering police misconduct. In recent years, newspaper headlines dealing with alleged police misconduct have become all too common. Police performance has been subject to a good deal of moral controversy, partly because the police deal with moral issues on a regular basis, partly because their behavior has sometimes offended the moral sensitivities of others. The police engage in discretionary behavior regularly, and other citizens must place a good deal of trust in their conduct with little in the way of assurances that their conduct is subject to adequate control (Cox, 1996; Palmiotto, 2001, p. vii).

Police misconduct may be broadly divided into two categories: corruption and physical and emotional abuse, and may be either organizational or individual in nature. Both categories include numerous subcategories, the categories often overlap, and both are violations of the ethical standards of police officers

Table 6.1

Length of State Police Basic Training Programs (by course content and state, 1990)

State	Total Hours	Total Weeks	Introduction to the Criminal Justice System[a] Hours	Introduction to the Criminal Justice System[a] Percent of Total Training	Law[b] Hours	Law[b] Percent of Total Training	Human Values and Problems[c] Hours	Human Values and Problems[c] Percent of Total Training	Patrol/Investigation Procedures[d] Hours	Patrol/Investigation Procedures[d] Percent of Total Training	Police Proficiency[e] Hours	Police Proficiency[e] Percent of Total Training	Administration[f] Hours	Administration[f] Percent of Total Training
National Average	804.8	17.9	9.2	1.0%	110.1	13.5%	44.9	5.3%	279.1	33.8%	289.3	36.7%	72.4	8.9%
Alabama	985	26	2	0.2	97	10.1	29	2.9	323	32.8	408	41.4	126	12.0
Alaska	690	13	7	1.0	122	17.7	34	4.9	201	29.1	265	38.4	61	8.8
Arizona	559	13	2	0.4	96	17.2	45	8.1	164	29.3	190	34.0	62	11.1
Arkansas	436	10	8	1.8	76	17.4	15	3.4	123	28.2	194	44.5	20	4.6
California	1,034	21	5	0.5	168	16.2	29	2.8	315	30.0	444	42.9	73	7.0
Colorado	798	19	23	2.9	109	13.7	25	3.1	331	41.5	219	27.4	91	11.4
Connecticut	1,029	26	16	1.5	181	17.6	34	3.3	374	36.3	399	38.8	25	2.4
Delaware	593	14	2	0.3	97	16.4	33	5.5	236	39.8	210	35.4	15	2.5
Florida	744	16	10	1.3	124	16.7	43	5.8	281	37.8	224	30.1	62	8.3
Georgia	761	16	5	0.7	63	8.3	39	5.1	221	29.0	347	45.6	86	11.3
Idaho	691	12	0	X	40	5.8	69	10.0	284	41.1	272	39.4	26	3.8
Illinois	980	18	2	0.2	187	19.1	22	2.2	143	14.6	478	48.8	148	15.1
Indiana	649	18	2	0.3	111	17.1	63	9.7	201	31.0	241	37.1	31	4.8
Iowa	698	13	10	1.4	103	14.8	55	7.8	270	38.7	207	29.7	53	7.6
Kansas	687	15	6	0.9	68	9.9	39	5.7	266	38.7	214	31.1	94	13.7
Kentucky	1,032	22	12	1.2	114	11.0	31	3.0	393	38.1	392	38.0	90	8.7
Louisiana	430	12	4	0.9	31	7.2	16	3.7	142	33.0	207	48.1	30	7.0
Maine	773	18	3	0.4	88	11.4	47	6.1	229	29.6	336	43.5	70	9.1
Maryland	1,187	24	33	2.7	179	15.1	75	6.3	252	21.2	490	41.3	158	13.3
Michigan	878	18	2	0.2	108	12.3	23	2.6	250	28.5	408	46.5	87	9.9
Minnesota	558	12	1	0.2	37	6.6	9	1.6	287	51.4	171	30.6	53	9.5
Mississippi	778	16	4	0.5	71	9.1	23	2.9	216	27.8	238	30.6	226	29.0
Missouri	1,071	23	12	0.1	204	19.0	45	4.2	371	34.6	386	36.0	53	4.9
Montana	698	14	19	2.7	92	13.2	31	4.4	291	41.7	232	33.2	33	5.7
Nebraska	860	24	8	0.9	111	12.9	82	9.5	303	35.2	252	29.3	104	12.0
Nevada	859	19	17	2.0	118	13.7	26	3.0	332	38.6	279	32.5	87	10.1
New Hampshire	432	10	2	0.5	81	18.8	27	6.2	125	28.9	178	41.2	19	4.4
New Jersey	1,032	21	6	0.6	84	8.1	100	9.7	289	28.0	358	34.7	195	18.9
New Mexico	873	16	4	0.5	53	6.1	22	2.5	484	55.4	273	31.3	37	4.2

State													
New York	1,030	24	17	1.6	208	20.2	111	10.8	301	29.2	319	31.0	74	7.2
North Carolina	1,008	24	15	1.5	140	13.9	73	7.2	295	29.3	402	39.9	83	8.2
North Dakota	751	17	5	0.7	129	17.2	45	6.0	342	45.5	180	24.0	50	6.7
Ohio	847	22	25	3.0	124	14.6	57	6.7	185	21.8	350	41.3	106	12.5
Oklahoma	861	16	13	1.5	79	9.2	42	4.9	308	35.7	322	37.4	98	11.4
Oregon	611	13	12	2.0	85	13.9	27	4.4	189	30.9	292	47.8	6	0.9
Pennsylvania	996	23	2	0.2	266	26.7	35	3.5	148	14.9	435	43.7	110	11.0
Rhode Island	745	16	18	2.4	105	14.1	24	3.2	209	28.1	343	46.0	46	6.2
South Carolina	642	12	9	1.4	80	12.5	24	3.7	211	32.9	295	46.0	23	3.5
South Dakota	627	15	2	0.3	45	6.0	141	18.7	330	43.8	166	22.0	70	9.3
Tennessee	576	12	2	0.3	65	11.3	21	3.6	202	35.1	197	34.2	89	15.5
Texas	947	22	10	1.1	162	17.1	48	5.1	332	35.1	351	37.1	44	4.6
Utah	437	12	6	1.4	54	12.3	23	5.3	165	37.7	121	27.7	69	15.8
Vermont	942	19	4	0.4	120	12.7	86	9.1	355	37.7	284	30.1	93	9.9
Virginia	1,098	25	11	1.0	156	14.2	64	5.8	389	35.2	383	34.9	95	8.7
Washington	893	21	3	0.3	65	7.3	12	1.3	383	42.9	289	32.4	141	15.8
West Virginia	1,381	32	56	4.1	180	13.0	252	18.2	619	44.8	264	19.1	10	0.7
Wisconsin	699	20	2	0.3	132	17.2	35	4.6	397	51.6	126	16.4	7	0.9
Wyoming	749	15	21	2.7	74	9.6	32	4.2	341	44.4	252	32.8	48	6.3

Note: These data are from a mail survey of 49 state police organizations conducted in May 1990. Hawaii was not included because it does not have a statewide law enforcement agency comparable to those in other states. The Massachusetts state police was revising its basic training program at the time of the survey and therefore was excluded. Agencies included here are of two types: "state police," defined as a uniformed field patrol responsible for general police services, and "highway patrol," defined as a state law enforcement agency with a uniformed field patrol, and police services restricted to or concentrated on traffic-, vehicle-, and highway-related activities. Alaska, Arkansas, Connecticut, Delaware, Idaho, Illinois, Indiana, Kentucky, Louisiana, Maine, Maryland, Massachusetts, Michigan, New Hampshire, New Jersey, New Mexico, New York, Oregon, Pennsylvania, Rhode Island, Vermont, Virginia, and West Virginia are "state police" states. Alabama, Arizona, California, Colorado, Florida, Georgia, Iowa, Kansas, Minnesota, Mississippi, Missouri, Montana, Nebraska, Nevada, North Carolina, North Dakota, Ohio, Oklahoma, South Carolina, South Dakota, Tennessee, Texas, Utah, Washington, Wisconsin, and Wyoming are "highway patrol" states.

[a] An examination of the foundation and functions of the criminal justice system with specific attention to the role of the police in the system and government.

[b] An introduction to the development, philosophy, and types of law; criminal law; criminal procedure and rules of evidence; discretionary justice; application of the U.S. Constitution; court systems and procedures; and related civil law.

[c] Public service and noncriminal policing; cultural awareness; changing role of the police; human behavior and conflict management; psychology as it relates to the police function; causes of crime and delinquency; and police-public relations.

[d] The fundamentals of the patrol function including traffic, juvenile, and preliminary investigation; reporting and communication; arrest and detention procedures; interviewing; criminal investigation and case preparation; equipment and facility use; and other day-to-day responsibilities.

[e] The philosophy of when to use force and the appropriate determination of the degree necessary; armed and unarmed defense; crowd, riot, and prisoner control; physical conditioning; emergency medical services; and driver training.

[f] Evaluation, examination, and counseling processes; department policies, rules, regulations, organization, and personnel procedures.

Source: Terry D. Edwards, "State Police Basic Training Programs: An Assessment of Course Content and Instructional Methodology," *American Journal of Police*, Vol. 12, No. 4 (1993): 30–34. Table adapted by SOURCEBOOK staff. Reprinted by permission.

(Hyatt, 2001, p. 75). Applied specifically to police officers, ethical conduct is especially important because of the authority granted officers and because of the difficulty of overseeing the daily behavior of police officers on the street.

Police Corruption

In 1894 the Lexow Commission reported that corruption was systematic and pervasive in the New York City Police Department. The next 15 years found similar investigations and similar findings in almost every major American city (Bracey, 1989, p. 175). Bribes from bootleggers made the 1920s a golden era for crooked police, and gambling syndicates in the 1950s were protected by a payoff system more elaborate than the Internal Revenue Service (Lacayo, 1993, p. 43). In 1971, Frank Serpico brought to light police corruption in New York City, and the Knapp Commission investigation which followed uncovered widespread corruption among officers of all ranks. In the 1980s more than 30 officers in Philadelphia were convicted of taking part in a scheme to extort money from drug dealers. In Miami in the mid-1980s, about 10 percent of the city's police were either jailed, fired, or disciplined in connection with a scheme in which officers robbed and sometimes killed cocaine smugglers on the Miami River, then resold the drugs. In 1993, 22 years after Serpico's disclosures in the same department, Michael Dowd and 15 to 20 other New York City police officers led "a parade of dirty cops who dealt drugs and beat innocent people [which] has shocked the city during seven days of corruption hearings" (Frankel, 1993, p. 3A).

Police **corruption** occurs when a police officer acts in a manner that places his or her personal gain ahead of duty, resulting in the violation of police procedures, criminal law, or both (Lynch, 1989). "Corrupt acts contain three elements: (1) they are forbidden by some law, rule, regulation, or ethical standard; (2) they involve the misuse of the officer's position; and (3) they involve some actual or expected material reward or gain" (Barker & Carter, 1986, pp. 3–4).

Types of Police Corruption

Barker and Carter (1986) identified a number of types of police corruption. *Corruption of authority* involves officially unauthorized gains by police officers that do not violate the law. Included here are things such as taking free liquor or meals, free entertainment admissions, police "discounts," free sex, and other free services. The difficulty with accepting such gratuities is that the officer never knows when the corruptor may expect or request special services or favors in return. This, of course, may never happen, but if it does, it places the officer who has accepted the gratuities in a difficult position, though he or she may certainly refuse to grant the requests. In addition, it becomes difficult to draw a line between such gratuities and other types of corrupt activities in terms of monetary value and violation of ethical standards.

Kickbacks constitute a second type of police corruption. Here, tow truck operators, lawyers, bondspeople, and others reward police officers who refer customers to them. The difficulties inherent in such referrals are obvious, but in some departments they, too, are condoned unless a public issue arises as a result.

A third type of corruption involves *opportunistic theft* from victims, crime scenes, and unprotected property. *Shakedowns* involve police officers who accept bribes for not making an arrest or writing a citation. While the officer may not actively seek such bribes, he or she may indicate a willingness to consider "other alternatives" offered by guilty parties.

Some police officers engage in *protection of illegal activities* for profit. They accept payments and/or services from those engaged in gambling, prostitution, drug sales, pornography, code violations, and other activities in return for doing nothing about such activities and sometimes for creating obstacles to investigations of these activities. Protecting the illegal behaviors often requires a good deal of organization. It does little good for one officer to look the other way when gambling occurs if his or her replacement for days off and vacations, or officers on other shifts, fails to protect the parties involved.

The fix involves quashing prosecution following arrest or taking care of tickets for profit. Police actions here may range from failure to show up in court when testimony is required to losing tickets, to perjury. *Direct criminal activities* include burglary, robbery, battery, intimidation, and other clearly criminal actions committed by officers. Finally, *internal payoffs* involve one police officer paying another (typically a superior officer) fees for assignments of particular types, promotions, days off, and so on. Although one type of corruption does not necessarily lead to another, where one finds more serious types of corruption, one is also likely to find most of the less serious types.

It is difficult to estimate the proportion of police officers directly involved in corruption, but it is probably small. Still, the actual number of police officers involved nationwide is quite large, and these officers attract a good deal of negative attention when their corruption is made public. Although most police officers are not directly involved in corrupt activities, large numbers do appear to condone such activities by their failure to speak out or take action against corruption (Cox, 1996).

Police corruption has been recognized as a problem in this country for at least 100 years, and various reform movements and departmental programs to reduce or eliminate corruption have been attempted. Why, then, does police corruption remain problematic? The answer seems to lie, in part at least, in the relationship between the police and the larger society. It has been said that the police are a reflection of the society or community they serve, and this is nowhere more true than with respect to police corruption. If other citizens stopped offering bribes, free services, and other gratuities, and started reporting all police attempts to benefit in unauthorized fashion from their positions, it would be very difficult for corrupt police officers to survive.

Physical and Emotional Abuse

In 1991, the world watched as a home videotape of Los Angeles police officers beating Rodney King was repeated dozens of times on major news networks. In 1993, two Detroit police officers were sentenced to prison for beating to death motorist Malice Green (Ferguson, 1993). Similar incidents occurred during the same time period in New York City, Atlanta, Washington, DC, and Denver. In 1997, Abner Louima was brutally tortured by a New York City police officer who was later sentenced to 30 years in prison for the act (Frey, 2001, p. 232).

Police misconduct is not limited to corrupt activities, but includes **perjury** (lying under oath), **emotional abuse** (psychological harassment), and **physical abuse** (the use of unnecessary or excessive force), including murder, as well. To some extent, perjury and other forms of unauthorized deception serve as links between corruption and other forms of misconduct. What is the difference, for example, between a police officer who commits perjury to fix a ticket in return for payment from the defendant and one who commits perjury to cover up having used physical force unnecessarily against a defendant? How does one draw the line between lying to informants and drug dealers and deceiving one's superiors? Once perjury and deception gain a foothold, they tend to spread to other officers and to other types of situations until, in some cases, the entire justice system becomes a sham. This is the case, for instance, when police officers perjure themselves in criminal cases in which the defendant is also committing perjury, where the respective attorneys know that perjury is occurring, and where the judge knows that none of the parties is being completely honest. The outcomes of such cases seems to ride on who told the most believable lie, or the last lie. The overall impact is to increase the amount of suspicion and distrust of the justice system among all parties, which is certainly not the desired end product if we wish citizens to participate in and believe in the system. It is difficult for citizens to believe in the system in cases where police misconduct has occurred and the officers involved are trying to cover up the misconduct.

Police officers who stop other citizens without probable cause and/or harass them, and police officers who use force unnecessarily, must attempt to justify their actions or face relatively severe sanctions. As indicated previously, police officers, like those in other occupational groups, sometimes employ stereotypes and divide the world into "we" and "they," or insiders versus outsiders. Those who are perceived as outsiders are often labeled, and occasionally these labels are used openly to refer to the members of groups so designated. The use of racial slurs is but one example of the kind of harassment under consideration. Other special categories and labels are created for particular types of deviants, for example, drug dealers, homosexuals, prostitutes, and protestors. The police, of course, are supposed to represent all other citizens, regardless of race, creed, nationality, gender, or political beliefs. When they use dehumanizing terms or harass others, the impression may be that since they represent government, they are expressing the attitudes of those who govern, though in fact they may simply be expressing personal dislikes, contempt, or hostility.

Members of minority groups, particularly in high-crime areas, report that psychological and emotional abuse are routine parts of encounters with the police. Although his study is now dated, Reiss (1968) provides information concerning the incidence of police psychological mistreatment of other citizens:

> What citizens object to and call "police brutality" is really the judgment that they have not been treated with the full rights and dignity owing citizens in a democratic society. Any practice that degrades their status, that restricts their freedom, that annoys or harasses them, or that uses physical force is frequently seen as unnecessary and unwarranted. More often than not, they are probably right. (pp. 59–60)

It is clear, then, that what constitutes police brutality is, at least in part, a matter of definition, and that police definitions and those of other citizens may not always be the same. What some segments of the public see as police harassment or brutality, the police are likely to view as aggressive policing, necessary for their survival on the streets as well as for maintaining some degree of order and crime control. Is a police officer in a high-crime area where many residents are known to carry deadly weapons harassing a citizen when he or she approaches cautiously, pats the citizen down for weapons, appears suspicious, and calls another officer for backup?

What is clear is that the perception that such incidents occur is widespread, especially in minority communities in cities of all sizes across the country (Lersch, 1999). This perception becomes the reality for those involved, whether or not the perception is grounded in reality. The perception creates hostility and resentment on behalf of some citizens, who view themselves as particularly likely to be victims of harassment and brutality, and on behalf of the police, who view themselves as particularly likely to be harassed, challenged, and criticized by certain segments of the population.

In spite of these misgivings on both sides, the vast majority of police encounters with other citizens continue to be carried off without physical brutality on the part of either party. This observation holds true with respect to police misconduct in general. Although there have been improvements, the police are not, and likely never will be, perfect, as the incidents described above clearly indicate. Still, through recruitment and retention of police officers who understand the importance of ethics and personal integrity, and by providing them with appropriate laws, training, resources, public support, and role models, we can minimize the likelihood of their misconduct.

Summary

1. The evolution from the watch and ward system to the notion of protect and serve occurred over several centuries in both England and America.

2. Increasing public concern over crime, rapidly growing population, urbanization, and industrialization led to the development of the Metropolitan Police in London in 1829.

3. The territorial strategy of the London police was adopted by most American cities by the end of the nineteenth century.

4. By the mid-twentieth century, technological advances (telephone, radio, automobile) led to the belief that crime would soon be controllable. However, increasing numbers of calls for service and the adaptability of offenders placed serious strains on police resources. Additionally, the tremendous variety of services demanded by the public (and often promised by the police) made it difficult for the police to meet public expectations.

5. The role of the police has become increasingly multifaceted, including provision of a variety of services in order maintenance and law enforcement. The police have attempted to provide these services by offering better training to officers and by encouraging officers to seek advanced education.

6. Still, in the 1960s the professional image of the police suffered serious setbacks as the result of racial disturbances in urban areas, almost all of which were triggered by police encounters with minority citizens.

7. The emphases on fighting crime, handling incidents, and providing a plethora of other services eventually led the police to recognize that they could not meet all expectations by themselves. The result was a movement toward problem-oriented and community-oriented policing (actually representing a return to many of the principles of the original London Metropolitan Police Act).

8. Community policing represents an attempt to formalize relationships among the police, the public, and other social and public service agencies in the pursuit of improved quality of life in the community. These approaches require both philosophical and organizational changes in policing to consistently address the problems underlying the symptoms the police have traditionally attempted to treat. The success of these approaches is yet to be determined, but they clearly illustrate the importance of the network concept in criminal justice.

9. In an attempt to meet public expectations and legal requirements, police selection and training procedures are constantly being modified. Although selection procedures leave much to be desired, innovations such as the use

of assessment centers show promise as better predictors of successful job performance than more traditional paper-and-pencil tests. Recruits selected are expected to be mentally and physically fit, of reasonably good character, and able to fit into the police subculture.

10. Formal basic training is required for virtually all full-time law enforcement officers, and the training is becoming increasingly comprehensive in nature. Once training at an academy or institute has been completed, the new officer goes through a probationary period and she or he is regularly evaluated during this period by senior and supervisory officers.

11. The need for education, once assumed to be a prerequisite for professionalization, is currently being reevaluated; further research is needed in this area, especially as community policing becomes more widespread. In the meantime, an increasing number of police departments require at least some college education as a condition of initial employment.

12. In this chapter, we have discussed both traditional, paramilitary police organizations and some of the more recent changes in these organizations. Attempts are being made to solve problems caused by centralization—rigidity, single promotional channels, and the chain of command—by decentralizing, offering dual career programs, and placing less emphasis on authoritarianism. Additionally, strategies such as community policing to improve cooperation and communication between the police and the public are being implemented.

13. The effectiveness of routine patrol has been rethought, and more realistic alternatives (such as split patrol and targeted or directed patrol) are being tried. Many of the traditional requirements for entry-level police officers have been revised to meet legal (EEOA, ADA) guidelines, and increasing numbers of women and minorities are being employed as police officers.

14. Police misconduct, including corruption and emotional and physical abuse, have been and remain problematic for the police. From acceptance of gratuities through participation in criminal activities, an unknown number of police officers attempt to gain unauthorized rewards while compromising the integrity of their positions. Other officers feel compelled to harass either psychologically or physically those with whom they come in contact.

15. Although most officers refrain from engaging in either type of activity, many fail to take the necessary steps to bring corruption and brutality to a halt. These activities often involve other components of the criminal justice network when they result in perjury.

16. Both the public and police administrators could greatly reduce the incidence of police misconduct by taking it seriously and removing those involved from the ranks of the police.

Key Terms Defined

social control   The process of persuading persons or groups to conform to group expectations.

community policing   A philosophy of policing in which police officers are assigned to specific geographic areas to form partnerships with neighborhood residents to solve problems and improve the quality of life for all concerned.

SARA process   A model in problem-oriented policing that uses scanning, analysis, response, and assessment to address problems.

due process   A concept of justice designed to ensure the rights of individuals as guaranteed by the Constitution and that various court decisions are enforced.

crime control   A concept of justice emphasizing the importance of factual guilt and minimizing the importance of legal guilt or due process.

arrest   The process of taking an individual into official custody.

booking   The recording of facts about a person's arrest, including fingerprinting, inventorying personal property, and photographing.

chain of evidence   A method of preserving evidence in such a way that it can be accurately accounted for from the time it is seized until the time its usefulness has been determined (generally, in court).

mediation and negotiation   Processes used by police officers in the interest of order maintenance in their attempts to settle disputes between parties.

dual career system   A system for recognizing and promoting through a number of patrol ranks those officers who do not wish to be supervisors, but who are able to meet certain objective performance standards.

directed patrol   Patrol that focuses on specific areas, as opposed to routine, nonspecific patrol.

split-force policing   Patrol strategy based on the use of saturation patrols, both overt calls and covert, in high-risk areas as well as designating other officers for routine patrol in those areas.

accreditation   Acknowledgement of compliance by a police agency with a set of nationally recognized standards established and evaluated by professional police organizations.

Peace Officer Standards and Training (POST) boards   Licensing boards for police officers.

assessment centers   Selection process based on job task analyses and conducted by independent assessors who are specially trained to evaluate performance.

probationary officer   A person who has successfully completed all the requirements for being a police officer and is obtaining on-the-job training (generally, for 6 to 18 months) while being evaluated in terms of potential for becoming a full-fledged police officer.

corruption   Acting in a manner that places unauthorized personal gain ahead of duty, resulting in violation, of police procedures and/or criminal law.

perjury   Lying under oath.

emotional abuse   Psychological harassment.

physical abuse   The use of unnecessary or excessive force.

Critical Thinking Exercises

1. It has been said that the police and the public are, or should be, one. What historical basis for this statement can you find? What contemporary basis? Can the police successfully perform their functions without the support of the public?
2. Are the terms "law enforcement" and "policing" synonymous? If not, in what ways are they different?
3. Discuss the concept of community policing. How is it related to problem-oriented policing? How does it illustrate the concept of the network approach to criminal justice?

Internet Exercises

A number of organizations provide support for law enforcement. Among these are the International Association of Chiefs of Police (IACP) and the Commission on Accreditation for Law Enforcement Agencies (CALEA).

1. Locate the website for CALEA. What are some of the recent developments with accreditation discussed on the website?
2. Go to *www.theiacp.org/*
   a. What are some of the types of training offered through the IACP? (*Association of Chiefs of Police*)
   b. Would you be able to search for a job in law enforcement using this site?
   c. Could you learn about some of the latest law enforcement technology by using a link from this source? How?

References

Barber, R. R. (1996). Neighborhood service team. *FBI Law Enforcement Bulletin, 65* (1), 17–22.

Barker, T. & Carter, D. L. (1986). *Police deviance.* Cincinnati. Pilgrimage.

Barlow, H. D. (2000). *Criminal justice in America.* Upper Saddle River, NJ: Prentice Hall.

Bracey, D. H. (1989). Proactive measures against police corruption: Yesterday's solutions, today's problems. *Police Studies, 12* (24), 175–179.

Bratcher, J. (1999). Personal interview with retired chief of the Palatine, Illinois, Police Department.

Campbell, L. P. (1991 March 24). Police brutality triggers many complaints, little data. *Chicago Tribune,* p. 10.

Commission on Accreditation for Law Enforcement Agencies. (1999). *Standards for law enforcement agencies* (4th ed.). Fairfax, VA: Author.

Commission on Accreditation for Law Enforcement Agencies. (2000, June). It's a fact. *Update.* Fairfax, VA: Author.

Conser, J. A., & Russell, G. D. (2000). *Law enforcement in the United States.* Gaithersburg, MD: Aspen.

Couret, C. (1999). Police and technology: The silent partnership. *American City & County, 114* (9), 31–32.

Cox, S. M. (1996). *Police: Practices, perspectives, problems.* Boston: Allyn & Bacon.

Cunningham, L. (1999). Taking on testilying: The prosecutor's response to in-court police deception. *Criminal Justice Ethics, 18* (1), 26–40.

Davis, E. M. (1978). *Staff one: A perspective on effective police management.* Englewood Cliffs, NJ: Prentice Hall.

Eck, J. E., & Rosenbaum, D. P. (1994). The new police order: Effectiveness, equity, and efficiency in community policing. In D. P. Rosenbaum (Ed.), *The challenge of community policing: Testing the promises,* pp. 3–23. Thousand Oaks, CA: Sage.

Falkenberg, S., Gaines, L. K., & Cox, T. C. (1990). The oral interview board: What does it measure? *Journal of Police Science and Administration, 17* (1), 32–39.

FBI National Press Office. (1999, July 15). NCIC 2000 begins operation. Washington, DC: Federal Bureau of Investigation: *http://www.Fbi.gov/pressrm/pressrel/ncic2000.htm*

Ferguson, C. (1993, October 13). Cops get long terms for beating. *USA Today,* p. 1A.

Fischer, R. J, & Green, G. (1992). *Introduction to security* (5th ed.) Boston: Butterworth-Heineman.

Frankel, B. (1993, September 30). You'll be in the fold by breaking the law. *USA Today,* p. 1A.

Frankel, B. (1993, October 7) For NYC Cops, license for crime. *USA Today,* p. 3A.

Frey, R. G. (2001). The Abner Louima case: Idiosyncratic personal crime or symptomatic police brutality? In M. J. Palmiotto (Ed.), *Police misconduct: A reader for the 21st century,* pp. 232–41. Upper Saddle River, NJ: Prentice Hall.

Gaines, L. K., Kappeler, V. E., & Vaughn, J. B. (1994). *Policing in America.* Cincinnati: Anderson.

Glensor, R. W., Correia, M. E., & Peak, K. J. (Eds.). (2000). Policing communities: Understanding crime and solving problems. Los Angeles: Roxbury.

Goldstein, H. (1990). *Problem-oriented policing.* New York: McGraw-Hill.

Gray, T. C. (1975). Selecting for a police subculture. In J. H. Skolnick & T. C. Gray (Eds.), *Police in America.* Boston: Little Brown.

Hyatt, W. D. (2001). Parameters of police misconduct: In M. J. Palmiotto (Ed.) *Police misconduct: A reader for the 21st century.* (pp. 75–99). Upper Saddle River, NJ: Prentice Hall.

Johnson, D. R. (1981). *American law enforcement: A history.* St. Louis: Forum Press.

Kelling, G. L., et al. (1974). *The Kansas City preventive patrol experiment: A summary report.* Washington, DC: Police Foundation.

Lacayo, R. (1993, October 11). Cops and robbers. *Time,* 43–44.

Lersch, K. M. (1999). Police misconduct and minority citizens: Exploring key issues. *Justice Professional, 12* (1), 65–82.

Lurigo, A. J., & Rosenbaum, D. P. (1994). The impact of community policing on police personnel. In D. P. Rosenbaum (Ed.), *The challenge of community policing: Testing the promises,* pp. 147–63). Thousand Oaks, CA: Sage.

Lurigo, A. J., & Skogan, W. G. (2000). Winning the hearts and minds of police officers: An assessment of perceptions of community policing in Chicago. In R. W. Glensor, M. E. Correia, & K. J. Peak (Eds.), *Policing communities: Understanding crime and solving problems*, pp. 246–56. Los Angeles: Roxbury.

Lynch, G. W. (1989). Police corruption from the United States perspective. *Police Studies, 12* (4), 165–170.

Kappeler, V. E., Sapp, A. D., & Carter, D. L. (1992). Police officer higher education, citizen complaints, and departmental rule violations. *American Journal of the Police, 11* (2), 37–54.

Miranda v. Arizona, 384 U.S. 436 (1966).

Palmiotto, M. J. (2001). *Police misconduct: A reader for the 21st century.* Upper Saddle River, NJ: Prentice Hall.

Pynes, J., & Bernardin, H. J. (1992). Entry-level police selection: The assessment center as an alternative. *Journal of Criminal Justice, 20* (1), 41–52.

Reaves, B., & Goldberg, A. L. (1999). *Law enforcement management and administrative statistics, 1997: Data for individual state and local agencies with 100 or more officers.* Washington, DC: U.S. Department of Justice.

Reiss, A. J. (1968). Police brutality . . . Answers to key questions. In M. Lipsky (Ed.) *Police encounters.* (pp. 57–83) Chicago: Aldine.

Report of the National Advisory Commission on Civil Disorders. (1968). New York: Bantam Books.

Richardson, J. F. (1974). *Urban police in the United States.* Port Washington, NY: Kennikat Press.

Rosenbaum, D. P. (2000). The changing role of the police. In R. W. Glensor, M. E. Correia, & K. J. Peak (Eds.), *Policing communities: Understanding crime and solving problems*, pp. 46–66. Los Angeles: Roxbury.

Rubinstein, J. (1973). *City police.* New York: Farrar, Straus and Giroux.

Swanson, C. R., Territo, L. & Taylor, R. W. (1998). *Police administration: Structures, processes, and behavior.* Upper Saddle River: Prentice Hall.

Uchida, C. D. (2001). The development of the American police: An historical overview. In R. G. Dunham & G. P. Alpert (Eds.) *Critical issues in policing: Contemporary readings* (pp. 18–35), Prospect Heights, The Waveland Press.

Varricchio, D. (1998). Continuing education: Expanding opportunities for officers. *FBI Law Enforcement Bulletin, 67* (4), 10–14.

Walker, S. (1999). *The police in America: An introduction* (3rd ed.). Boston: McGraw-Hill.

Weisel, D. L., & Eck, J. E. (2000). Toward a practical approach to organizational change. In R. W. Glensor, M. E. Corriea, & K. J. Peak (Eds.), *Policing communities: Understanding and solving problems*, pp. 257–71). Los Angeles: Roxbury.

Selected Readings

Cox, S. M. (1996). *Police: Practices, perspectives, problems.* Boston: Allyn & Bacon.

Glensor, R. W., Correia, M. E., & Peak, K. J. (Eds.). (2000). *Policing communities: Understanding crime and solving problems.* Los Angeles: Roxbury.

Palmiotto, M. J. (2001). *Police misconduct: A reader for the 21st century.* Upper Saddle River, NJ: Prentice Hall.

Skolnick, J. H. (1994). *Justice without trial: Law enforcement in democratic society* (3rd ed.). New York: Macmillan.

Stevens, D. J. (2001). *Case studies in community policing.* Upper Saddle River, NJ: Prentice Hall.

Walker, S. (1999). *The police in America: An introduction* (3rd ed.). Boston: McGraw-Hill.

CHAPTER SEVEN

The Courts

An Overview

Innocence and guilt are determined in the state and federal courts.
Mark Burnett/Stock Boston

K aren was arrested for embezzling several thousand dollars from the bank where she had been employed for many years. She knew she was innocent of the charge, but probable cause was found to bind her over for trial. After being denied a change of venue, which was requested as a result of considerable publicity in the local newspaper, Karen was convicted of the offense in a trial court exercising appropriate jurisdiction. Knowing that she was innocent and believing she was the victim of an incompetent defense attorney, she appealed the verdict.

The appellate court found numerous errors in the trial record of the lower court and overturned her conviction. No one else was ever convicted of the crime. Karen is free today but has never been able to land another job in the banking industry.

Key Terms

jurisdiction

venue

stare decisis

precedent

lower courts

magistrates

trial courts

de novo

circuit courts

appellate courts

state supreme court

magistrate judges

district courts

en banc

U.S. Supreme Court

writ of certiorari

speedy trials

dispute resolution programs

Chapter Outline

Basic Concepts
The Court Systems
    State Court Systems
    The Federal Court System
The Sixth Amendment and Speedy Trials

In the previous chapter, we discussed the front line of the criminal justice network: the police. In this chapter, we focus our attention on another component, namely, the court system. The basic function of the court is to determine the legal outcome of a dispute. In the criminal justice network, this process usually involves the determination of guilt or innocence of one accused of a criminal violation. Disputes in civil matters often concern the determination of monetary damages, custody of children, and injunctions against certain business practices, to name only a few.

Although the determination of guilt or innocence is central to the function of the criminal court, it is by no means the only function. The court is also responsible for determining bail, conducting preliminary hearings, ruling on the admissibility of evidence, and determining the appropriate sentence when a finding of guilty has been reached.

One of the major responsibilities of the court is to provide impartiality to the criminal justice network. This goal is to be achieved by using neutral bodies as decision makers (judges and juries) and by allowing both parties—the prosecution and the defense—to present their arguments in open court. The court operates under formal rules of procedure to guarantee objectivity. For example, there are limitations as to how evidence may be introduced, what types of evidence may be admitted, and what types of questions may be asked. Questions that are clearly leading are generally not allowed, evidence that was obtained illegally is inadmissible, and evidence admitted must be material (i.e., it must relate to a relevant issue in the case in terms of the charges against the accused). The procedures often evolve from interpretations and are subject to be challenged in the future.

The court system is not a new phenomenon, although the method of trial has varied greatly throughout history. Some techniques that have been used are trial by ordeal (in which the accused had to withstand some physical ordeal, such as walking through heated plowshares blindfolded) and trial by battle (in which the defendant challenged his or her accuser to combat, the outcome of which determined the outcome of the case).

Today, we employ a more formalized system of presenting evidence, both physical and testimonial, in a court, following a strict procedural format. Although historically, the courts and court personnel have been held in high esteem, criticism and scrutiny of this branch of the criminal justice network have increased considerably in recent years. Many blame the courts for allowing too many defendants to go free or for issuing sentences that appear exceptionally lenient. Others blame the courts for overcrowding the prisons by sentencing too many defendants to incarceration. One of the major complaints is that the court process is very slow, frequently delaying trials for long periods of time for various reasons. More recently, critics have charged that cases have been tried in the media by allowing television crews in the courtroom. In this chapter, we provide a general overview of the court systems, both federal and state, in the United States. We begin by looking at some basic concepts.

BASIC CONCEPTS

One of the most fundamental concepts concerning the court system is that of **jurisdiction,** or the authority or power to hear a case. No court in the land has unlimited jurisdiction. Even the U.S. Supreme Court is restricted to hearing specific kinds of cases (discussed later in this chapter).

As a general rule, a distinction is made between courts possessing general jurisdiction and those with specific, or limited, jurisdiction. A court of general jurisdiction has the power to hear a variety of cases. For example, many county or district courts hear both criminal and civil cases involving such issues as murder, probate, divorce, and suits for monetary damages. Courts with specific, or limited, jurisdiction can hear only a narrow range of cases. The juvenile court can hear only cases involving youth in a specific age group; thus, it has a fairly limited jurisdiction. Also, some states maintain magistrate and/or police courts that are restricted to hearing cases carrying a narrowly defined punishment, usually petty offenses and some misdemeanors.

A distinction is also made between courts of original jurisdiction and those with appellate jurisdiction. Original jurisdiction means the court is empowered to hear the case initially. Appellate jurisdiction means that a specific court can hear a defendant's appeal of conviction from the court of original jurisdiction. The power to hear cases is defined through statute, the Constitution, or previous court decisions.

A key related concept is that of **venue,** which is commonly referred to as the place of trial. Under normal conditions the trial will take place within the legally defined geographical area in which the alleged offense was committed. This may be on a municipal, county, or regional basis. Obviously, if you were charged with committing an offense in Los Angeles, California, you would be tried in that vicinity rather than in Dallas, Texas. It should be noted that the possibility to have a change of venue, or location of the trial, does exist. If the defendant can show that he or she cannot obtain a fair trial in the geographical jurisdiction of trial, a petition may be filed with the court to have the venue changed to a neutral jurisdiction. This is a matter not of right but of privilege. Generally, reasonable grounds for the requested change must accompany the petition. One of the more common grounds is that pretrial publicity has biased potential jurors.

There are situations in which more than one court has jurisdiction. For example, when a federally insured bank is robbed, both the state in which the bank is located and the federal court system would have jurisdiction. These situations are often referred to as cases involving concurrent jurisdiction. An excellent example of concurrent jurisdiction is the Rodney King case. In that case, officers who used force to arrest Mr. King were first tried in California state court and found not guilty. The same defendants were later tried in federal court under civil rights statutes. As a practical matter, usually one court will waive (give up) jurisdiction, and the defendant will be tried in only one court. Cases in which only one court has jurisdiction are referred to as involving exclusive jurisdiction.

The terms **stare decisis** and **precedent** are also important in the understanding of the court system. Stare decisis means "let the decision stand." When a court issues a ruling on a matter of law, future cases should abide by or adhere to the precedent or legal rule set forth by the earlier case. For example, if a court rules that a defendant charged with a capital offense must be represented by counsel, then, as a rule of law, all future defendants in capital cases must also be represented by counsel. Such decisions may be applied prospectively (only in subsequent cases) or retrospectively (to past cases as well). Most decisions are applied prospectively.

As you can see, the concepts defined here are important in determining how and where the law will be enforced. A system without such formalized concepts and subsequent rules enforcing them would be chaotic and inconsistent.

THE COURT SYSTEMS

The United States has what is commonly called a dual court system. This system employs approximately 375,000 judges, court administrators, clerks, bailiffs, and other court personnel with an estimated budget in the billions of dollars (Maguire & Pastore, 1998, p. 18). There is a federal court system that hears cases involving violations of acts of Congress with separate court systems in the District of Columbia, Puerto Rico, the Virgin Islands, Guam, American Samoa, and the Northern Mariana Islands. In addition, state court systems hear cases concerning violations of state statutes. This dual system is a product of the Tenth Amendment to the U.S. Constitution. As we previously stated, there are circumstances in which a single act can violate both an act of Congress and a state statute (concurrent jurisdiction). In general, the role of the federal government in the criminal justice system is limited. It is estimated that 80 to 90 percent of all criminal cases will be heard in the state courts. However, the recent trend to federalize criminal law by expanding federal criminal jurisdiction beyond concerns with federal property and interstate commerce is having an impact on the number of criminal cases now heard in federal court.

State Court Systems

If one were asked to describe the state court system of the United States, the most definitive term used would have to be "variation." The states have considerable latitude in the organization of their court systems. Because no single state adequately depicts the 50 systems, we encourage each student to examine his or her own state's statutes to obtain a better understanding of how the state court system is structured. What follows is a general overview of state court systems.

State court systems are divided into three levels: appellate courts, trial courts of general jurisdiction, and trial courts of lower jurisdiction (lower courts). These levels are arranged hierarchically.

Lower courts are usually courts of limited jurisdiction. They are empowered to hear only cases of a minor nature (e.g., traffic cases and misdemeanors) with lower levels of punishment. The lower court system is probably one of the most neglected areas of study in the criminal justice network even though most of the public's experience with the court system is at this level. There are about 14,000 such courts in the United States, and these courts hear over 61 million cases annually (Neubauer, 1999). Attitudes about the courts and the criminal justice network in general are often based on experiences and impressions gained from lower courts.

The lower court system has been severely criticized for the way it processes cases. Most lower courts are characterized by an emphasis on speed and routinization. They are basically courts of assembly-line justice where one can answer a charge with a guilty plea and pay a standardized fine within a matter of minutes or even seconds. Some critics argue that lower courts serve as a system of sentencing rather than seeking truth. The lower courts have also been criticized for neglecting constitutional procedures. Most defendants enter the court without counsel and may or may not be made aware of this and other constitutional rights (Neubauer, 1999, p. 465). In addition, lower courts are not courts of record; that is, they do not keep written records of proceedings unless requested by, and paid for by, defendants. Despite these criticisms, the lower court system fulfills an important function. Most court cases are heard in lower courts (perhaps up to 90 percent). If they were abolished, other courts would have to handle the cases now heard by the lower courts. Presently, many of the other courts have such overloaded dockets that there is a backlog of cases, and a considerable time gap exists between the act in question and the decision of the court. If we did not have a lower court system, the lag would increase, defendants would spend more time in jail, other criminal justice personnel would be overworked, and important cases might be overlooked or slighted in an effort to lessen the backlog. Despite the many criticisms of the lower system, it fulfills a necessary function, and its abolition without provisions for some alternative would result in grave consequences for the entire criminal justice network.

There have been many attempts to upgrade the lower court systems. Historically, the lower court system was often staffed by justices of the peace. These justices were often laypersons possessing little or no legal training and who were almost totally ignorant of proper judicial decorum and procedures (Abraham, 1998). Records were often ill kept, if they were kept at all, and facilities depended on whatever the justice could afford. Justice of the peace courts have been held in living rooms, on front porches, and in the backs of stores. The trend has been to abolish justice of the peace courts and replace them with other, more formalized courts, although they still exist in some jurisdictions. Attempts at reform short of abolition include elimination of the fee system (in which justices of the peace are paid only if the defendant is found guilty) and upgrading the quality of court personnel (Neubauer, 1999, pp. 467–69).

Currently, one of the more common lower-level court systems is the magistrate system. **Magistrates** are members of the bar who are either elected or appointed (depending on the jurisdiction). They are limited to hearing specific types of cases but are generally better qualified than their predecessors; they are familiar with constitutional guarantees and court procedures; and they can, and in some states are empowered to, perform other functions, such as issuing warrants and conducting bail hearings.

Some jurisdictions also have police courts and traffic courts, which are also known as municipal courts. These too are considered lower courts and are limited in their jurisdiction. Some of the problems commonly associated with justice of the peace courts continue to plague these lower courts.

The second level of the state court system consists of the **trial courts,** also known as district, superior, circuit, or county courts. These courts have general jurisdiction and hear both civil and criminal cases as well as appeals from lower courts in some jurisdictions. These courts number more than 2,500, and more than 9,000 judges preside over them (Ostrom & Kauder, 1996).

The stereotyped image of the court often produced by the media, characterized by proper decorum, flowing orations, and extreme formality, is based primarily on the trial courts. Unlike cases in the limited courts where trials generally last a few minutes, cases heard in trial courts may run for days or, in some instances, weeks and months. Unlike the lower courts, trial courts are characterized by full-time court personnel, sophisticated methods of record keeping, the use of juries, more emphasis on formality, and the protection of constitutional guarantees. There is also a lesser degree of routinization in sentencing in the trial courts than in the lower courts.

Although the trial courts are courts of general jurisdiction, most of their cases are civil rather than criminal. Some jurisdictions maintain separate specialized trial courts to hear each type of case. Trial courts hear some 33 million civil and criminal cases annually (Neubauer, 1999, p. 90). In some jurisdictions, trial courts hear appeals from the lower courts, but as a practical matter, this occurs infrequently (less than 10 percent of the time) and does not generally tax the resources of the trial courts. If an appeal is heard from a lower court, it may be heard **de novo** (over again; anew) because many lower courts do not keep adequate records of their proceedings.

Trial courts are often organized on a county or a regional (multicounty) basis. Historically, trial courts were county courts. The county court system was to some extent impractical because many small counties could not afford to maintain their own courts and, before transportation was modernized, county inhabitants often encountered difficulty in traveling to the county seat. As a result of these and other factors (including greater emphasis on governmental efficiency), **circuit** (or regional) **courts** appeared. These courts may cover considerable geographical area and are characterized by the use of judges who move from courthouse to courthouse on either a scheduled or an as-needed basis.

The third level of the state court system consists of **appellate courts,** including the state supreme court and intermediate appellate courts. The presence of intermediate appellate courts is characteristic of the more largely populated states as a method of relieving the caseload of the state supreme court. It should be noted that 39 states maintain intermediate appellate courts (Neubauer, 1999, p. 90). Where such courts exist, they typically consist of three-judge panels and are usually organized on a regional, statewide, or multi-county, basis (one intermediate appellate court for a specific number of county or district courts). These courts are normally restricted to appellate jurisdiction; that is, they can only review cases based on trial records. In some jurisdictions, they are limited by law to hearing cases arising from specific lower courts or cases involving less than a specified dollar value. Again, as with cases in courts of general jurisdiction, most cases heard at this level are civil rather than criminal. In states that employ intermediate appellate courts, decisions are largely finalized at this level because very few cases are heard by the highest court.

At the top of the state court hierarchy we find the **state supreme court,** or, as it is referred to in some jurisdictions, the state judicial court or the supreme court of appeals. Like the United States Supreme Court, the state supreme court frequently exercises its discretion over the types of cases it chooses to hear. In some states, death penalty cases are automatically reviewed by the state supreme court.

In cases requiring an interpretation of state statutes or the state constitution, the state supreme court has the final decision unless that statute or portion of the state constitution is inconsistent with the U.S. Constitution. State supreme courts are composed of three to nine judges who primarily hear civil cases and review cases on their record (by reviewing the transcripts). Additional powers they may possess include issuing judicial assignments, confirming the nomination of judges, and reviewing cases of alleged judicial misconduct.

There have been some attempts to simplify the administration of state courts by establishing a unified court system, which would shift local control to a centralized management structure. Such a shift would lead to centralized administration, rule making, and judicial budgeting as well as to statewide financing for the courts. This reform would limit the ability of lawyers to choose the court in which their cases are heard and would largely destroy local control of the courts.

The Federal Court System

The other branch of the dual court system is made up of the federal courts. These courts are empowered to hear both civil and criminal cases. The federal system consists of U.S. magistrate courts, U.S. district courts, U.S. courts of appeal, and the U.S. Supreme Court.

Congress created the position of U.S. **magistrate judge** in 1968. These judges are the equivalent of state trial court judges of limited jurisdiction and a subcomponent of the federal district courts. They are selected by district court judges and appointed for eight-year terms if full-time. Some part-time magistrate judges are appointed for four years. These judges perform a multitude of tasks, ranging from holding initial appearances in felony cases to setting bail to issuing warrants. They also handle a variety of civil matters and in general reduce the caseload of district court judges (Abraham, 1998, p. 173; Neubauer, 1999, pp. 63–65).

The U.S. **district courts** were created by Congress in the Judicial Act of 1789. These 94 courts are the trial courts of the federal system. Each state has at least one, and some of the larger states have as many as four federal district courts, with the number of judges ranging from 2 to 28. The District of Columbia and U.S. territories maintain federal district courts as well. Judges in federal district courts are appointed by the president of the United States, with Senate confirmation, for life terms.

The federal district courts were created to lessen the demands on the U.S. Supreme Court. As we will see, the Supreme Court hears only a small portion of the cases it is asked to hear. By establishing the district courts to hear the actual cases, Congress has provided an alternative to the Supreme Court. In fact, the district courts hear about 300,000 civil and criminal cases annually, excluding misdemeanor and bankruptcy cases (Neubauer, 1999, p. 66).

The criminal jurisdiction of the U.S. district courts includes all cases where a federal criminal statute has been violated. Examples include kidnapping, the assassination or attempted assassination of the president, postal violations, violations of federal fish and game laws, and cases involving interstate transportation of stolen goods as well as interstate flight to avoid prosecution. The federal courts also maintain jurisdiction over cases where a constitutional question, such as search and seizure, is involved. Again, we should note that in some instances, concurrent jurisdiction might exist with a state court. The civil jurisdiction of the district courts is limited to suits in which (1) a federal question is raised, (2) the suit involves citizens of two or more separate states and the amount in controversy exceeds $75,000, (3) a citizen of one state sues another state, or (4) a prisoner petitions the court claiming that his or her rights under federal law are being violated.

Within the federal court system are intermediate appellate courts: the U.S. courts of appeals. Created in 1891, these courts were established to reduce the number of appeals made to the Supreme Court. Defendants have a right to appeal the decision from the federal district courts. Most, but not all, appeals from the federal trial courts will be heard at this level, and for most, the final decision will be rendered here.

Prior to 1949, these intermediate appellate courts were referred to as circuit courts of appeals. Today, the geographical division of circuits is maintained, but judges are not required to travel to various locations to hear cases as they did in the past. There are 13 courts of appeals: 11 are composed of three or more states, one is for the District of Columbia, and one is for the federal circuit. Generally, each circuit is identified by a number. Circuit courts are generally located in the larger metropolitan areas, and the appellant must travel to the location of the court to have his or her case heard.

Each court of appeals has at least 6 permanent judgeships; larger circuits have as many as 28. Judges are appointed by the president for life or good behavior. The most experienced judge who has not reached his or her seventieth birthday will serve as chief judge of the circuit. In most instances, cases will be heard by three-judge panels, with two considered a quorum. In certain circumstances all judges will hear a case—a process called sitting **en banc.**

The courts of appeals maintain appellate jurisdiction and only review records of lower courts rather than retrying cases. These appellate courts review the records for interpretation and application of law (both statutory and constitutional) but do not generally decide issues of fact (i.e., whether a defendant was provided with counsel at required times or whether there was an error in admitting evidence or instructing the jury). The courts of appeals also review and enforce the decisions of 19 quasi-judicial tribunals, including the Food and Drug Administration and the National Labor Relations Board. Currently, over 50,000 cases are heard annually in U.S. courts of appeal.

We should also mention briefly a number of specialized federal courts created by Congress. These courts hear only a limited range of cases and deal primarily with civil cases. Among the types of cases heard by these courts are tax disputes, patent disputes, and cases relating to the Uniform Code of Military Justice.

The court of last resort for both the federal and the state systems is the **U.S. Supreme Court,** which is composed of nine judges appointed by the president and confirmed by the Senate, who sit for life or good behavior. They may be removed by impeachment or voluntary retirement. The president also appoints one of the judges as chief justice. The chief justice assumes administrative duties (e.g., assigning one of the judges to write the Court's decision) but has no greater authority than the other judges in the determination of each case.

By statutory provision the Court convenes the first Monday each October and sits until mid-June, unless all cases have been decided prior to that time. Many of us have heard someone proclaim, "I will take this case all the way to the Supreme Court." Realistically, this is very unlikely. In most instances, an appellant must petition the Court to hear his or her case. The Court hears approximately 100 cases per year. If the Court decides to hear the case, it issues a **writ of certiorari,** or a demand for the transcripts of the proceedings to be sent to the Court for review. In special circumstances, arguments may be presented, as in the decision of the constitutionality of the death penalty, but they are limited to a specific time frame. The Court operates on the basis of majority opinion, with six members constituting a quorum. One judge who voted with the majority is assigned by the chief justice to write the Court's opinion, or the chief justice personally writes it. In addition, any other member may write a concurring opinion (if in the majority) or a dissenting opinion (if in the minority). Neither opinion has an impact on the case, but in the future it may be a basis for changing the precedent set in the present case.

The Court was established by the U.S. Constitution; however, its status as the supreme determinant of legal issues was not conferred at its inception. One of the important factors in the development of the Supreme Court's authority was the case of *Marbury* v. *Madison* (1803). This decision gave the Court the power of judicial review. In essence, it held that the authority of the U.S. Constitution shall supercede acts of Congress and that the Constitution should be interpreted by the Court.

The Supreme Court is somewhat unique in that it maintains both original and appellate jurisdiction. The Court has limited original jurisdiction in cases involving treaties made by the federal government, controversies in which the U.S. government is a party, and disputes between two states, to name only a few areas.

The Court also has been granted appellate jurisdiction by Congress, and most of its work involves this responsibility (cases of original jurisdiction account for less than 1 percent of the Court's activities). We previously noted that the Court has considerable discretion in determining which cases it hears. Although this is basically true, the Court is required to grant review when (1) a federal court holds an act of Congress to be unconstitutional, (2) a court of appeals finds a state statute unconstitutional, (3) a state's highest court holds a federal law to be invalid, and (4) an individual's challenge to a state statute is upheld by a state supreme court.

We should note the different decisions the Court can reach. If it affirms the decision, the lower court decision is held to be correct, and the case is finalized. It may also reverse the lower court decision in part or in total. Frequently, a petition will raise several issues and the Court may find that some issues were handled properly while others constitute errors and will remand the case (send it back to be retried with modifications) to the court of original jurisdiction. In some instances, there are such serious constitutional errors that the original decision is completely overturned.

THE SIXTH AMENDMENT AND SPEEDY TRIALS

As guaranteed by the Sixth Amendment, "In all criminal prosecutions, the accused shall enjoy the right to a public and speedy trial." In this area, courts are the targets of considerable criticism. Failure to provide **speedy trials** is one of the leading areas of concern. In reality, most of the people who obtain speedy trials do so only by pleading guilty in a lower court. At the trial level, it is not uncommon for the trial to commence at least a year after arrest in felony cases, although many times the delays are at the request of the defendant. Delays in civil cases are often much greater, exceeding three or more years in some cases. Delays also plague the appellate courts, and appeals are often not finalized until years after a decision was reached at the trial level. In recent years, appellate courts have instituted procedural changes, such as limiting oral arguments and minimizing the number of published opinions, in an effort to reduce their caseloads.

A major question surrounding this problem is the definition of "speedy trial." The President's Crime Commission recommended a maximum of 81 days between arrest and trial for those defendants not detained in jail and 71 days for those who are detained (President's Commission on Law Enforcement and Administration of Justice, 1967). This was only a recommendation, and no jurisdiction is bound by it. In fact, few cases at the trial court level are processed within this time frame. At the federal level, Congress has applied the Speedy Trial Act of 1974 (1975) to the federal system. The act holds that only 70 days may elapse between the filing date or the defendant's initial appearance in court and the trial. In 1972, the U.S. Supreme Court established a Constitutional threshold for determining whether a defendant has been denied a speedy trial (*Barker v. Wingo*). All 50 states have crafted speedy trial statutes that apply within their court systems as well. These statutes typically set specific times in which the defendant must be brought to trial depending on whether the accused is in custody or not. Although such efforts are commendable, few defendants, at either the trial or the appellate level, actually receive speedy trials, again, due in part to their own actions. For example, defense attorneys may ask for continuances to avoid appearing before certain judges or to maximize their fees.

Why the concern over court delay or backlog? First, it has tainted the image of the justice network in the eyes of the public, who have little respect for a network that moves so slowly. Second, and closely related, it has necessitated the practice of plea bargaining or pleading guilty for consideration. Roughly 90 percent of all felony convictions are processed by negotiation rather than by trial (Brown & Langan, 1998, p. 3). Victims, the public, and the police are frequently unhappy about this practice, but if it were to be discontinued now, the delays would be unconscionable. Third, delay can cause undue financial and/or emotional hardship both on those defendants who remain in jail and on their families, particularly if the defendants are eventually found innocent. Guilty defendants who are released on bail may commit additional illegal acts while awaiting trial. Repeated delays also cause hardships for victims and witnesses who must appear in court on numerous occasions.

Why, with such negative effects, does the problem persist? The most common reasons for court delay are a shortage of judges and courtrooms, the use or abuse of continuances by attorneys, the filing of too many petty cases, and inefficient methods of court administration (see In the News, "U.S. Law Enforcement Is Surging"). It has been noted that the increase in the number of criminal prosecutions under federal law has resulted in a greater backlog of civil cases in federal court. This is because the court must give priority to the criminal cases because of the criminal defendant's right to a speedy trial. Prisoner lawsuits have also dramatically added to the federal court dockets. However, efforts such as the Prison Litigation Reform Act have resulted in a reduction in these cases. Neither the number of courtrooms nor the number of judges has kept pace with population increases or with increases in criminal prosecutions on civil cases. Legislatures have been hesitant or unwilling to appropriate adequate funds for judicial budgets.

The crowded and chaotic court system adversely affects everyone connected with it.
Florent Flipper/Unicorn Stock Photos

In the News

U.S. LAW ENFORCEMENT IS SURGING; FEDERAL ARRESTS, PRISON TERMS RISING, STATISTICS SHOW

By Michael Hedges

Federal law enforcement is on the rise, the first comprehensive gathering of federal arrest figures shows.

Fueled by drug-law enforcement and greater efforts to curtail illegal immigration, the number of federal criminal court cases rose nearly 13 percent from 1997 to 1998.

Federal agents arrested 106,139 people in 1998, according to Justice Department statistics.

Almost half of those apprehended were for drug law or immigration violations.

More than 43,000 people were sent to federal prisons that year, for an average sentence of almost five years.

The figures were released Wednesday by the Bureau of Justice Statistics.

There were 83,000 federal law-enforcement officers in 1998, including 33,000 in four Justice Department agencies that conduct nearly three out of four federal criminal investigations: the FBI, the Drug Enforcement Administration, the Immigration and Naturalization Service and the U.S. Marshals Service.

That number has risen steadily since 1993, when there were 69,000 federal agents, with about 24,000 of them in the DEA, FBI and immigration and marshals services.

In one year, from 1997 to 1998, the number of people brought to trial in

Continued

federal court rose from 69,351 to 78,172, a 12.7 percent increase.

Of those, 87 percent were convicted, usually as a result of a guilty plea.

The last decade has seen a steady rise in the percentage of those convicted in federal court who go to prison.

In 1998, 71 percent of those found guilty were incarcerated, compared with just 60 percent in 1990.

The average sentence for the 43,041 convicted in federal court was four years, 11 months.

Some analysts and legal experts see in the statistics a confirmation of the "federalization" of law enforcement in America.

"Under our constitutional system, the federal government is supposed to have a very limited crime-fighting role," said Tim Lynch, an analyst with the Cato Institute, a libertarian foundation in Washington. "But for the past 20 years, it seems every session of Congress has escalated the drug war, and that has led to an increase in federal agents, and federal prisons and the federal court system."

Edward Mallett, a Houston lawyer and the incoming president of the National Association of Criminal Defense Lawyers, said, "What is being reported here is pretty much what one would expect. . . . The federalization of some formerly state offenses accounts for some of this."

Mallett said that in Texas, as the number of federal law-enforcement agents involved in anti-drug and anti-immigration activities has grown, the threshold for triggering a federal crime has fallen.

"Cases federal prosecutors would have declined a year ago they are prosecuting now," he said. "They used to turn down drug prosecutions under five kilos; now they'll prosecute for an ounce and a half. They're looking for work."

Since 1990, the number of people being held in federal jails awaiting trial or deportation has grown rapidly from just over 140,000 to more than 200,000.

The number of inmates in federal prison is up more than 90 percent for the same period, from 57,000 to 109,000.

Chicago Sun-Times, *June 1, 2000, p. 26.*

Additionally, a lawyer sometimes waives a defendant's right to a speedy trial by asking for a continuance. Undeniably, the continuance may be necessary to uncover evidence or to aid in the development of the case for the defense (see In the News, "Commentary"). But, as Blumberg (1967) and Neubauer (1999, p. 124), among others, have argued, it is also used as a method to collect fees. The continuance may be part of the defense strategy. Banfield and Anderson (1968) found that the longer a case was continued, the more likely it was that the defendant would not be found guilty. As the time between the crime and the trial increases, witnesses are more difficult to locate and cannot always testify accurately to what has transpired months or years ago.

In the News

COMMENTARY; RAMPART HASN'T CHANGED HOW CRIMINAL COURTS DO BUSINESS

By Tamar Toister

I am the defense lawyer who tried the case of People vs. Javier Ovando in 1997. In the year since Ovando's conviction was overturned, I have had an opportunity to reflect on what went wrong with that trial and to see whether the justice system learned any lessons from the injustice done to him. Sadly, I see that it hasn't.

For those unfamiliar with the case, Javier Ovando was shot three times in the chest and head by former LAPD officers Rafael Perez and Nino Durden. He was left a paraplegic for life. The officers then testified falsely in Ovando's criminal trial, where he was convicted of assault on police officers and given the maximum sentence of more than 23 years in prison. Two and a half years later, Perez, plea bargaining to lessen his own sentence after being caught for stealing cocaine from the LAPD evidence room, confessed to framing Ovando as well as routine thefts, shootings, planting of evidence and framing of other innocent men conducted by himself and other members of the Rampart anti-gang CRASH unit.

In the Ovando case, the prosecuting deputy district attorney disclosed to me on the day we started trial that the police officers were claiming that they left their observation post in a vacant apartment, moved their police vehicle and then jumped over a fence to get back into the building and their post shortly before Ovando burst in with a machine gun. This was crucial information because it closed a large gap in the prosecution's case, namely how could Ovando have known the cops were hiding in the dark in apartment 407? It was also information that was not contained in the detailed interviews with the LAPD officer-involved-shooting team, not mentioned in any police report or given in testimony at the preliminary hearing.

According to the rules of evidence, this new information should have been given to me 30 days before trial. I objected to the evidence coming in. My motion was denied. I asked the judge for a few days continuance to investigate these new revelations. The deputy district attorney objected, and my motion was denied. At trial, the D.A. objected to my attempts to impeach the officers with this new information. His objections were sustained, and I was not even allowed to cross-examine Perez about the discrepancies between his preliminary hearing testimony and the trial testimony.

Even though the law requires the deputy district attorney to prove his case beyond a reasonable doubt—even if the defense doesn't put on any witnesses—he was allowed to argue that he should prevail because he put on witnesses and there was no defense. I may have lost the trial under

Continued

the best of circumstances: Perez and Durden were polished, smooth liars. Nonetheless, it is appalling that despite having no prior convictions, Ovando was sentenced to the maximum by the judge because he "showed no remorse." It was equally appalling that the sham of a trial withstood appellate review and the conviction was allowed to stand.

Has anything changed in the last year since we've become aware that innocent men and women have been convicted of crimes they did not commit? Has the attitude of the courts or the district attorney's office become more concerned that defendants receive fair trials? I have seen that it hasn't.

I have seen defense lawyers reveal the name of a newly discovered witness on the eve of trial, only to be reprimanded and have sanctions declared against them. On the other hand, I have seen prosecutors given leeway with information supplied tardily. A recent example is a murder case where the prosecutor turned over the name and statement of a new witness on the eve of trial. Not only was this allowed, but the defense lawyers were not allowed a continuance to investigate the reliability and veracity of the new witness.

An excuse frequently given for denying defense continuances is the "fast track" system for trying felony cases within 60 to 120 days. Each judge has a computerized list of the older cases on his calendar and forces those older cases to trial, whether or not defense attorney is ready. Attorneys making earnest attempts to find necessary defense witnesses are frequently told that it is unlikely they would find the witness even if a continuance were granted. The judge usually will make these rulings without knowing the case, the defense or the missing witness. Defense lawyers are then "deemed" ready and sent to trial with their objections overruled by irate judges.

One of the problems for the defense is that our clients don't always tell us everything right away, either because they don't trust us or because they don't realize the importance of certain information. Prosecutors, loath to have any complications to an easy conviction, frequently object to any such continuances. And the judges, who tend to defer to the prosecutors, frequently comply.

Last week I attended Loyola Law School's symposium on the Rampart scandal. Two judges on my panel objected to a portion of law professor Erwin Chemerinsky's review of the LAPD report on Rampart. This was the part that suggested that judges might be less prone to show a bias toward the prosecution if they were further removed from political pressure by longer terms. These judges strongly denied that judges feel any political pressure to be pro-prosecution or that police officer witnesses are any more likely to be believed, when lying, than a civilian witness.

One of the judges added that the only troubling issue he saw in Rampart was the fact that so many innocent

Continued

people pled guilty to crimes they did not commit. That judge suggested re-examining so-called West pleas, in which defendants take a plea bargain in order to serve less time but continue to deny actual guilt. What that judge failed to see was that the problem is not the use of West pleas by innocent defendants to crimes they did not commit. The problem is that truly innocent people are afraid to go to trial because they know they don't have a chance with cops who lie, prosecutors who defer to the cops and judges who defer to the prosecutors. The problem is that innocent people are afraid to go to trial because they know they will be punished with the maximum sentence if they lose.

The real answer, I suggest, is to give defense lawyers adequate time to properly prepare their cases and to stop punishing defendants for going to trial. Ovando was offered 13 years to plead to something he didn't do. When he lost at trial, he was sentenced to 23 years, four months. Why? Because he showed no remorse for a crime that he did not commit and that did not happen.

Los Angeles Times, *September 21, 2000, p. B11.*

As previously noted, most court cases are civil rather than criminal. Citizens are quite willing to file suit with respect to almost any issue. The result is court congestion. One recommendation to remedy this situation is to use quasi-judicial tribunals to arbitrate claims involving less than a specified dollar amount, thus allowing judges to handle more trials. Some jurisdictions have adopted **dispute resolution programs** in an attempt to resolve in the community matters that would otherwise be heard in court. However, the problem of court delay is very complex and will not be resolved simply. An effort involving the court system, the government, and the public is needed if change is to occur.

Inefficient court administration is a contributing factor to court delay. Traditionally, the chief judge is primarily responsible for the administrative duties of the court as well as for hearing cases. These duties include (1) preparing the budget, (2) scheduling cases, (3) assigning and overseeing personnel, and (4) maintaining records. Unfortunately, many justices are not qualified to handle all these responsibilities. Law schools do not traditionally offer courses in court administration, so, unless the judge has prior experience in this area, these tasks are often not effectively or efficiently performed (Jacob, 1997).

There has been a movement over the past two decades to employ professional managers to perform the administrative functions of the courts. The assumption is that a trained and/or experienced administrator can more effectively perform these duties, allowing the judge more time to hear cases. The federal counts, and some larger jurisdictions in the state courts, have employed court administrators with considerable success. Experimentation with court administrators and computerization have led some to believe that these changes will help decrease the court backlog at both the trial and the appellate level because witnesses are better notified and records better kept. Despite the commonsense appeal and the success enjoyed by courts using these techniques, there have been criticisms. Some argue that the practice diminishes the authority of the chief judge in that he or she becomes only another judge. It is also contended that the practice is too impersonal (too businesslike) and that the court is supposed to process cases individually not like freight (Reinkensmeyer, 1991; Hoffman, 1991). Finally, there is the problem of expense. Federal funding has supported the hiring of many court administrators and the use of computer systems. Whether or not these positions can be maintained when funding expires remains to be seen, as many states find it difficult to allocate enough funds to increase the size of the judiciary, let alone hire other personnel or enter the computer age.

Summary

1. A number of concepts are common to all types of courts in the United States: jurisdiction (general, limited, exclusive, concurrent, original, and appellate); venue; stare decisis; and precedent (on which courts generally rely).

2. The court system of the United States consists of two more or less distinct systems: state and federal.

3. There is considerable variation among the states systems, but most states employ a three- or four-tiered hierarchy, whereas the federal system is three-tiered.

4. Lower courts typically hear minor cases and are the most numerous of the courts.

5. Trial courts hear both civil and criminal cases and are known as courts of general jurisdiction.

6. Appellate courts normally review cases based on trial records from the lower courts.

7. Most cases heard in trial and appellate courts are civil rather than criminal.

8. The supreme courts at state and federal levels are the courts of last resort and hear a relatively small number of cases.

9. There are serious problems of court delay at all levels. There are many identifiable causes and proposed solutions to court delay, but the problem is complex and difficult to solve satisfactorily.

Key Terms Defined

jurisdiction   The authority to hear a particular case.

venue   The place of trial.

stare decisis   Let the decision stand; a policy of following principles laid down in previous decisions.

precedent   Decision handed down previously in a similar case.

lower courts   Courts of limited jurisdiction, empowered to hear only cases of a minor nature.

magistrates   Judges limited to hearing only specific types of cases, usually in lower courts.

trial courts   Courts with general jurisdiction (usually over both civil and criminal matters) to hear cases.

de novo   Over again; anew.

circuit courts   Trial courts serving a particular geographic region or circuit.

appellate courts   Courts hearing appeals from lower courts.

state supreme court   Court of last resort in a state.

magistrate judges   Federal equivalents of state trial court judges of limited jurisdiction.

district courts   Trial courts of the federal system.

en banc   With all judges sitting together.

U.S. Supreme Court   Court of last resort (highest appellate court) in the nation.

writ of certiorari   An order from a higher court asking a lower court for the record of a case.

speedy trials   Trials for which the time period between arrest and trial is reasonable.

dispute resolution programs   Community programs designed to help relieve court congestion by resolving issues through negotiations.

Critical Thinking Exercises

1. Why is our court system called a dual court system? Explain, in general terms, the organization and functions of each component. How do we deal with cases that might be tried in both state and federal courts?

2. Discuss the role of the U.S. Supreme Court. What factors play a role in determining whether a case is heard by the Supreme Court? Is it true that anyone can take a case all the way to the Supreme Court? What obstacles, if any, make this difficult to accomplish?

Internet Exercises

Most citizens experience the court system at the lower-court levels of their state. Click on Arizona's Courts of Limited Jurisdiction at *www.supreme.state.az.us/info/guide/gtc3.htm*
After reading the materials, answer the following questions:

1. Discuss the magistrate court system in Arizona in terms of court personnel, geographic jurisdiction, and subject matter jurisdiction.
2. What are the geographic boundaries of the justice of the peace courts, and how do they differ from the magistrate courts in the types of cases they hear?
3. List and explain the qualifications for becoming a justice of the peace. Is this the type of individual you want hearing your case?

References

Abraham, H. J. (1998). *The judicial process* (7th ed.). New York: Oxford University Press.
Banfield, L., & Anderson, C. D. (1968). Continuances in the Cook County criminal courts. *University of Chicago Law Review, 35,* 279–280.
Barker v. Wingo, 407 U.S. 514 (1972).
Blumberg, A. (1967). *Criminal justice.* Chicago: Quadrangle.
Brown, J. M., & Langan, P. A. (1998). *State court sentencing of convicted felons, 1994.* Washington, DC: U.S. Department of Justice.
Hoffman, R. (1991). Beyond the team: Renegotiating the judge–administrator partnership. *Justice System Journal, 15,* 211–33.
Jacob, H. (1997). Governance by trial court judges. *Law and Science Review, 31,* 3–37.
Maguire, K., & Pastore, A. L. (1998). *Bureau of justice statistics sourcebook of criminal justice statistics—1997.* Albany, NY: Hindelang Criminal Justice Research Center.
Marbury v. Madison, 1 Cir. 137 (1803).
Neubauer, D. W. (1999). *American courts and the criminal justice system* (6th ed.). Belmont, CA: West/Wadsworth.
Ostrom, B., & Kauder, N. (1996). *Examining the work of state courts, 1995.* Williamsburg, VA: National Center for State Courts.
President's Commission on Law Enforcement and Administration of Justice. (1967). *Task force report: The courts.* Washington, DC: U.S. Government Printing Office.
Reinkensmeyer, M. (1991). Compensation of court managers: Current salaries and related factors. *Judicature, 75,* 154–62.

Suggested Readings

Abraham, H. J. (1998). *The judicial process* (7th ed.). New York: Oxford University Press.
Blumberg, A. S. (1967). *Criminal justice.* Chicago: Quadrangle.
McWilliams, M. (1997). *The American court system.* New York: Garland.
Neubauer, D. W. (1999). *American courts and the criminal justice system* (6th ed.). Belmont, CA: West/Wadsworth.

CHAPTER EIGHT

Court Personnel

Judges exercise discretion in interpreting the law and sentencing defendants.
David Young-Wolff/Stone

A fter graduating from law school, Sharon went to work as an assistant public defender in a major metropolitan area. She had been interested in criminal law and the adversary system even before entering law school and wanted to put into practice the skills she had learned by defending the indigent.

Within a year, Sharon learned that many of her clients were guilty of the offenses charged, that she lacked the time and resources to adequately defend even those who maintained their innocence, and that there was little future in continuing as a public defender. The road out and up seemed to go through the prosecutor's office, although Sharon briefly considered going into private defense practice.

The prosecutor was impressed with Sharon's legal skills and hired her as an assistant in her office. Sharon proved to be an asset to the office and, as it turned out, had political party connections in common with the prosecutor and the chief judge. She also had good interpersonal skills and got along well with other court personnel. In a short time, Sharon was appointed associate judge. She served well in that position and is now being considered for a judge's position.

Key Terms

prosecutor (state's attorney, district attorney, prosecuting attorney)

independent counsels

defense counsel

public defenders

adversary system

judge

probation officer

Chapter Outline

The Prosecutor
The Defense Counsel
The Relationship between the Prosecutor and Defense Counsel
The Judge
The Probation Officer
Managing the Courts
    Chief Judges
    Court Clerks
    Court Administrators

In this chapter, we focus on the roles and functions of personnel who staff the courts. In the typical course of events, an alleged offender first encounters the police and then either a public or private defense counsel, or the prosecutor. Because the **prosecutor** is the person to whom the police present their case with respect to an alleged offender, let us turn our attention first to that officer.

THE PROSECUTOR

Called by a variety of names—state's attorney, district attorney, prosecuting attorney—prosecutors are found at federal, state, and local levels in the United States. There are also prosecutors known as **independent counsels**—private attorneys appointed because public prosecutors are too closely tied to government officials being investigated—who conduct investigations and bring charges when warranted. A good example is the case of President Bill Clinton, who was investigated by Kenneth Starr, an independent counsel. Because President Clinton appointed Attorney General Reno, cries of partisanship would surely have been raised had she taken on the investigation herself. Appointing Starr as an independent counsel basically removed the attorney general from the fray. As you can see, the activities of a prosecutor involve him or her in all aspects of the criminal justice network.

Typically, the cases processed by the prosecutor originate with a law enforcement agency, and smooth working relationships between these agencies and the prosecutor's office are essential if the criminal justice network is to be effective and efficient. Grand juries work under the supervision of the prosecutor and rely on the prosecutor for information, evidence, and advice. The role of the prosecutor in plea bargaining is detailed elsewhere in this chapter, as is his or her role in establishing court dockets and recommending sentences to the judge. Parole boards and probation officers also rely on the prosecutor to provide information relevant to their functions. In many instances, prosecutors are also involved in a variety of pretrial diversion programs (such as unofficial probation). Their willingness to use alternatives to incarceration determines to some extent whether such programs will survive.

There are about 2,400 state prosecutors' offices and 93 federal prosecutors' offices in the United States. These agencies employ about 70,000 support staff and cost taxpayers about $16 billion per year to operate (DeFrancis & Steadman, 1998). The basic function of these prosecutors is to represent the people (the state) in criminal proceedings. This function is accomplished through the charging process and the trial process. Charging is a two-step process. In step one, the prosecutor decides whether or not to file criminal charges against an individual. In step two, the prosecutor decides the nature of such charges. Any charges filed must be based on the facts of a particular case and on the law as it relates to that case.

To make a charging decision, the prosecutor reviews case records, presents the case to a grand jury, or files an information (a formal accusation).

The prosecutor may go through a preliminary hearing and a series of negotiations with defense counsel in determining whether to file charges and, if so, what charges are to be filed.

When a prosecutor decides to proceed to criminal trial, she or he becomes the state's champion, who engages in courtroom combat (generally verbal) with the defense. The final decision about whether an alleged offender will be brought into court rests with the prosecutor. If the prosecutor decides not to take the case into court, no further official action is likely to be taken on the case in question. The prosecutor, then, exercises an enormous amount of discretion in the criminal justice network. Whereas the police officer may open the gate to the official justice system, the prosecutor may close that gate. The prosecutor may do this without accounting for his or her reasons to anyone else in the network (except, of course, to the voters who elect the prosecutor to office, and the elections often take place long after the case has been decided). The decision not to prosecute (*nollee prosequi*) in addition to the discretion in determining the number and severity of charges renders the prosecutor a very powerful figure in the court process (see In the News, "We Targeted Minorities").

Clearly, under some circumstances, the prosecutor would be foolish to proceed with court action. For example, lack of evidence, lack of probable cause, or lack of due process may make it virtually impossible to prosecute a case successfully. However, a number of somewhat less legitimate reasons exist for failure to prosecute. Evidence indicates that the prosecutor may fail to take cases to court for political reasons (e.g., when the person in question is a powerful, local political figure) or because the caseload of the prosecutor includes an "important" or "serious" case (i.e., one in which successful prosecution will result in favorable publicity). As a result, the prosecutor may screen out or dismiss a number of "less serious" cases, such as burglary and assault. In short, the prosecutor is the key figure in the justice system and is recognized as such by both defendants and defense counsel (Misner, 1996).

As Pollock (1994) indicates:

> Whether to charge or not is one of the most important decisions of the criminal justice process. The decision should be fair, neutral, and guided by due process, but this is an ideal; often many other considerations enter into the decision . . . despite the ideal of prosecutorial duty, an individual factor in prosecutorial discretion is that the prosecutors want to and must win; therefore their choice of cases is influenced by this value, whether it is ethically acceptable or not. . . . To give one person who participated in a brutal crime immunity to gain testimony against others is efficient, but is it consistent with justice? To not charge businesspeople with blue law violations because they are good citizens is questionable if other businesses are prosecuted for other ordinances. (p. 153)

Of course, not all prosecutors employ the tactics and techniques discussed above, but abuses do happen. Sometimes prosecutorial abuse occurs as the result of a desire for revenge, but perhaps more often it results from lack of adequate training on behalf of the prosecutor or his or her staff.

In the News

N.J. ATT'Y GENERAL; WE TARGETED MINORITIES

By Owen Moritz

New Jersey's attorney general admitted yesterday that the state's acclaimed war on drugs unfairly targeted minority drivers—and that hundreds of drug charges may be scuttled.

At the same time, the state could be forced to settle dozens of lawsuits from black and Hispanic state troopers who charge they were forced to practice racial profiling.

Attorney General John Farmer's stunning admission came after his department made public 100,000 pages of documents that showed state troopers on the New Jersey Turnpike and other main roads pulled over disproportionate numbers of minorities in drug searches.

Farmer said his office would examine each criminal case in which bias allegedly tainted drug seizures—and that this could lead to a dismissal of charges.

Civil lawsuits also will be reviewed.

"Where they are reasonable, we're going to settle these cases," Farmer said. "We'll certainly look at it a lot more closely, based on what we've discovered."

Lawyers for the motorists and troopers returned to Trenton yesterday to resume searching the documents, many marked confidential and never before made public.

Besides showing that troopers systematically selected minority drivers in searches for drugs, the records demonstrate that the state's top law enforcement officials knew about racial profiling as far back as 1989.

The state, however, didn't admit that such profiling was widespread until April 1999.

That report came a year after two troopers fired 11 shots at a van they had pulled over for speeding on the Turnpike. Three of the four men inside were wounded. Criminal charges against the two troopers have been dropped.

The four young men, three black and one Hispanic, were heading south to Durham, N.C., for a basketball tryout that they hoped could win them college scholarships. Troopers said they pulled the van over for speeding in Cranbury.

"The constitutional violations are so egregious, and they've been sitting on these documents for years," public defender Kevin Walker said.

Walker, who represents several defendants stopped on the Turnpike, said the state's only option is to dismiss the charges. His office is considering a motion to ask a judge to do that.

"If they're talking about settlement, if they're taking that approach with the civil cases, it's certainly more important with the criminal ones because of the constitutional violations," Walker said.

Lawyers predicted that courts would be overwhelmed with pleas to overturn drug convictions.

Daily News *(New York), November 29, 2000, p. 29.*

A brief look at the reasons for becoming a prosecutor and the process through which this occurs will help us understand how and why such abuses occur.

The position of prosecutor may be attractive for a variety of reasons. For those attorneys who wish to become judges or state or federal legislators, it is an excellent starting point. It is, then, attractive to some individuals interested primarily in political careers rather than in prosecution.

For young attorneys just out of law school, the position of assistant prosecutor ensures a steady income while it provides opportunities to make contacts on which to build a private practice. Some of these assistants eventually become prosecutors to further their political ambitions or to gain notoriety as criminal lawyers, or because the tremendous power and discretion accompanying the position attract them. Finally, some attorneys become (and some remain) prosecutors because they are committed to the practice of criminal law and to representing the state in criminal cases.

A variety of other functions are performed by most prosecutors. These include representing the state in court, administering the office, providing legal advice to governmental bodies (especially law enforcement agencies), providing training for police on criminal law and legal processes, preparing drafts of search warrants and wiretapping applications, participating in decisions regarding court administration, and engaging in a wide variety of public information and community relations programs (Holten & Jones, 1982, p. 185; Neubauer, 1999). The chief prosecutor must also administer his or her own office and engage in the political activities essential to remain in office. Increasingly, prosecutors are also becoming involved in the development and operation of teen courts and community conflict resolution groups of one type or another.

We should note that the prosecutor, although he or she is the state's champion, is obligated to protect the rights of the defendant as well. On taking office, prosecutors take an oath, which requires them to seek justice. He or she must, for example, present evidence to show that a defendant is not guilty when it comes to his or her attention.

Because we have previously discussed the political process by which the prosecutor is selected, we will simply point out once again the importance of understanding political affiliations and considerations when considering the prosecutor's role.

THE DEFENSE COUNSEL

There are two major categories of **defense counsel:** private and public. According to one report, nearly 75 percent of prison inmates were represented by **public defenders.** In urban areas, nearly 80 percent of felony defendants are too poor to hire private attorneys (Smith & DeFrances, 1996). Generally financed by some governmental body (state, county, or a combination), public defenders represent indigent clients, who cannot afford to retain private counsel. The total cost of this representation in 1990 was over $1.3 billion. For many young lawyers interested in criminal law, the position of public defender represents a stepping-stone. In most jurisdictions the public defender is paid a relatively low salary, but the position guarantees a minimal income, which can be supplemented by private practice. As a rule, caseloads are heavy; investigative resources are limited; and many clients are, by their own admission, guilty (see In the News, "More Public Defenders Requested"). The public defender, therefore, spends a great deal of time negotiating pleas and may spend very little time with his or her clients. As Estrich (1998) indicates:

> The right to counsel guaranteed by the Constitution only guarantees the defendant a warm body. The issue for a poor defendant is not whether his attorney will lie for him, create reasonable doubt where there isn't any, or undermine truth-telling witnesses but, quite literally, whether he'll even get to meet his lawyer for an interview to give his side of the story before they face the state in court. (p. 97)

As a result, public defenders often enjoy a less than favorable image among their clients.

Some public defenders seem to have little interest in using every possible strategy to defend their clients. On numerous occasions, prosecutors and judges make legal errors to which the public defender raises no objection. In addition, appeals are sometimes not initiated by public defenders even when chances of successful appeal seem good. There are also public defenders who do pursue their clients' interests with all possible vigor, even to the point of alienating the judges who initially appointed them (see In the News, "Teen's Lawyer Fights Trial in Adult Court"). On the whole, however, defendants who can afford to retain private counsel often believe they fare better than those who are represented by public defenders, and there is some evidence to support this belief. Given the amount of evidence against him, for example, many observers believe that O. J. Simpson would almost certainly have been convicted had he not been able to afford the team of lawyers who represented him. Many poor defendants are induced in brief consultations with overworked public defenders to plead guilty (Editorial, 1998). As Barlow (2000, p. 377) notes "Public defenders cannot forget that they are paid by the government. This fact puts them in an odd situation, considering that their job is to defend clients whom their employer prosecutes. They are sworn to do their best for their clients, but they are paid by their judicial adversary." Still, a study by Hanson and Ostrom (1998, p. 283) found that public defenders fare reasonably well in court in comparison to private attorneys. "How frequently do indigent defenders gain favorable outcomes for their clients? Are they more successful than, less successful than, or equally as successful as privately retained counsel in gaining favorable outcomes? The evidence gained from an examination of felony dispositions in the nine courts [studied] is that indigent defenders generally are as successful as privately retained counsel."

More recent research has led to the following conclusions concerning public defenders: They tend to resolve their cases more expeditiously than private attorneys; such resolution did not compromise the rights of defendants; public

In the News

MORE PUBLIC DEFENDERS REQUESTED

By Abdon M. Pallasch

Public interest lawyers asked the Cook County Board last week to let Public Defender Rita Fry hire 10 more lawyers to handle what they called a massive backlog of 800 prisoners waiting for their convictions to be appealed.

But Fry said she does not need any more staff. Board President John Stroger lifted a hiring freeze long enough for Fry to fill 10 vacancies on her staff in September. Fry said those new attorneys are helping tackle the backlog, which she said the public interest lawyers overstate.

"I think for now, things are under control," she said. Fry still has 15 vacant attorney positions and 25 vacant clerical and investigator slots.

The American Civil Liberties Union and the McArthur Justice Center disagree. The county needs to hire 10 more lawyers immediately, said Lauren Raphael of the ACLU. The groups hope the county will amend its budget before Tuesday's scheduled final vote.

"That does not clear up the backlog," Raphael said of the September hires. Referring to Fry's insistence that her office needs no more help, Raphael said, "It's a mystery to me—there's no logical explanation why someone who had an office whose own clients were in jeopardy of having their rights denied would not go along with additional funding."

The presiding judge of the appellate court called Fry in this summer to tell her he was tired of granting her office continuances.

The last time a huge backlog created 18-month delays before cases got appealed by the state appellate defender, the McArthur Justice Center persuaded a federal judge to order more lawyers hired to handle the backlog.

Fry is caught in a turf war between state and county officials.

Stroger insists the state appellate defender's office, not the Cook County public defender, should handle the appeals the way it does for every other county in the state. He questions why Cook County taxpayers should have to fund criminal appeals when other counties get a free ride from the state.

"Unless we impose some new taxes right now, we can't do it," he said.

Stroger asked Raphael and McArthur legal director Locke Bowman to accompany him to Springfield to argue for more state money so the state appellate defender can handle a larger share of appeals in Cook County.

They said they'd be happy to go but that the county had to act on its own in the meantime.

Stroger faces an uphill battle persuading state legislators to find more money for defending convicted criminals on appeal. Elected officials at the state and county level historically have

Continued

been far more generous with public agencies that prosecute criminals than with those that defend them.

The state appellate defender's office was created in the 1960s because few counties' public defenders could handle appeals for their clients. The Cook County public defender's office already had an appellate division.

The state appellate defender's office handles about a third of the appeals here, while Fry's office handles two-thirds. Fry would prefer that her office handle about 20 percent of appeals and the state appellate defender handle the rest.

Chicago Sun-Times, *November 20, 2000, p. 21.*

In the News

Teen's Lawyer Fights Trial in Adult Court

By Tracy Wilson

A defense lawyer for a 17-year-old Oxnard boy facing murder charges in the fatal shooting of a Santa Paula woman says he will fight a decision by prosecutors to try his client as an adult.

Isaac Daniel Lara is the first teenage murder defendant in Ventura County to be charged as an adult under Proposition 21.

The measure, approved by voters in March, allows prosecutors to avoid juvenile court proceedings and directly file charges in Superior Court against teenagers accused of certain felony offenses.

Lara, who is charged with murder, attempted murder, shooting at an occupied vehicle and using a firearm, appeared for an arraignment in Superior Court on Tuesday. He did not enter a plea.

During the hearing, Deputy Public Defender William Markov told the judge he plans to file a motion in opposition to the district attorney's decision—a challenge that lawyers say may be among the first to test the new law.

"We definitely have to look at the issues with it being such a new piece of legislation," Markov said after the hearing.

Those issues are expected to be taken up at a Dec. 19 hearing.

So far, prosecutors have filed five juvenile cases in adult court, including Lara's, since the passage of Proposition 21, said Senior Deputy Dist. Atty. Richard Holmes.

Lara is accused of shooting Joanna Maria Orozco, 21, and her friend, Shane Joseph Longoria, 22, during a dispute Nov. 7 at a house in Santa Paula.

According to authorities, Lara asked Longoria if he was a gang member and then briefly argued with Orozco before killing her and shooting Longoria in the arm.

Lara was arrested after a brief standoff with police at his relatives' home in Santa Paula.

Los Angeles Times, *November 22, 2000, p. B2.*

defenders and prosecutors tend to be equally experienced; and the outcomes of criminal appeals are not significantly different for the two groups (Hanson, Hewitt, & Ostrom, 1992; Williams, 1995).

It is, perhaps, most interesting that while differences between private and public counsel do exist with respect to dismissals and not-guilty verdicts, these do not indicate an overwhelming superiority of private attorneys over public defenders. There are relatively few private attorneys making good money from the private practice of criminal law. In fact, most good law schools offer few courses in criminal law, and most graduates of these schools have little or no interest in practicing criminal law. This is so, among other reasons, because of the type of clientele involved, difficulties in collecting fees, and the reputation generated by legal practitioners who openly solicit cases in the halls and courtrooms of courthouses and practice law out of their briefcases (Estrich, 1998).

Whether defense counsel is private or public, his or her duties remain essentially the same. The duties are to see that the client is properly represented at all stages of the system, that the client's rights are not violated, and that the client's case is presented in the most favorable light possible, regardless of the client's involvement in criminal activity. And these duties are to be fulfilled while adhering to the Code of Professional Conduct, which requires that lawyers neither lie in court nor suborn perjury. To accomplish these goals, the defense counsel is expected to battle, at least in theory, the prosecutor in adversary proceedings. Here again, the difference between theory and practice is considerable.

THE RELATIONSHIP BETWEEN THE PROSECUTOR AND DEFENSE COUNSEL

In theory, adversary proceedings result when the champion of the defendant (defense counsel) and the champion of the state (prosecutor) do battle in open court where the truth is determined and justice is the result. In practice, the situation is quite often different because of considerations of time and money on behalf of both the state and the defendant.

The ideal of adversary proceedings is perhaps most closely realized when a well-known private defense attorney does battle with the prosecutor, as in the O. J. Simpson case. Prominent defense attorneys often have competent investigative staffs and considerable resources in terms of time and money to devote to a case. Thus, the balance of power between the state and the defendant may be almost even. "As the lawyers and law professors lined up to help O. J. Simpson, it was striking to see how quickly the usually dominant prosecutors were outsmarted" (Estrich, 1998, p. 109). This balance of power is generally not the case when defense counsel is a public defender who may be less experienced than the prosecutor and generally has more limited access to an investigative staff than the prosecutor. For a variety of reasons then, both defense counsel and the prosecutor may find it easier to negotiate a particular case rather than to fight it out in court, since court cases are costly in both time and money.

Lawyers in court—adversaries or part of a cooperative work group?
Jim L. Shaffer

Most adult criminal cases in the United States are settled by plea bargaining. In fact, it has been suggested that justice in the United States is not the result of the **adversary system,** but is the result of a cooperative network of routine interactions between defense counsel, the prosecutor, the defendant, and, in many instances, the judge (Blumberg, 1967, pp. 255–76; Neubauer, 1999, p. 164).

In plea bargaining, both prosecutor and defense counsel hope to gain through compromise. The prosecutor wants the defendant to plead guilty, if not to the original charges then to some less serious offense. Defense counsel seeks to get the best deal possible for his or her client, which may range from an outright dismissal to a plea of guilty to some less serious offense than the original charge. The nature of the compromise depends on conditions such as the strength of the prosecutor's case and the seriousness of the offense. Most often, the two counselors arrive at what both consider a just compromise, which is then presented to the defendant to accept or reject. As a rule, the punishment to be recommended by the prosecutor is also negotiated; thus, the nature of the charges, the plea, and the punishment are negotiated and agreed on before the defendant actually enters the courtroom. The adversary system, in its ideal form at least, has been circumvented (see In the News, "No Jail for Son Who Beat Mother").

To the prosecutor, defense counsel, and the court, the benefits of plea bargaining are clear. The prosecutor is successful in prosecuting a case (she or he obtains a conviction), defense counsel has reduced the charges and/or penalty against his or her client, and all parties have saved time and money by not contesting the case in court. The dangers in plea bargaining, however, should not be overlooked. First, the defendant might have been found not guilty even

In the News

NO JAIL FOR SON WHO BEAT MOTHER

By Jamie Malernee

A Clearwater man faces two years of house arrest instead of prison for last year's attack in Spring Hill on his mother, who wouldn't testify against him.

BROOKSVILLE—A man accused of beating his mother nearly to death will not go to prison after she refused to testify against him in court.

Mark Higgins, 40, of Clearwater will instead spend the next two years on house arrest as part of a plea bargain that reduced the charges he faced Monday from attempted murder to battery on a senior citizen, of which he was found guilty.

Assistant State Attorney Bill Catto said prosecutors were forced into lowering the charges because Higgins' 73-year-old mother, Adele, begged them not to prosecute her son and said if she was put on the stand she would change her testimony as to what occurred Sept. 10, 1999.

According to authorities, Higgins, who was unemployed and lived with his mother in Spring Hill at the time of his arrest, beat her with his fists in the face and head, then kicked her arms, legs and back. He also threw her head into a bedroom door and knocked her semiconscious with a wooden table frame, a report said. He told her that he was going to kill her, the mother initially told investigators.

Now Mrs. Higgins says her son was angry but he never meant to hurt her. "Mark did call me two days after this last incident and said he was sorry and (he) loves me and (I) didn't deserve what he did to me," wrote Mrs. Higgins to Circuit Judge Richard Tombrink, who handled the case before it was transferred to Circuit Judge Jack Springstead. "I still love him and miss him. Mark really is a good person, but (he) was born with this temper. I want him to get help, not jail."

Catto said the mother's refusal to help left him with little choice.

"The Sheriff's Office would like him to go to prison (but) we are making this offer, anyway, given the victim's wishes," he said. "That's the best I can do for the victim and the state, given the circumstances."

As part of the agreement, Higgins will no longer be allowed to live with his mother and must obtain written permission from her to contact her, Springstead said Monday. Mrs. Higgins has already told officials she plans to give her immediate consent.

Higgins also must undergo mental health counseling.

Higgins has previously stated in court that he and his mother have always had a violent relationship and

Continued

that she beat him viciously and repeatedly while he grew up. He claims that he was angry with his mother because of this treatment and that it contributed to the violence of his September attack.

In a letter Higgins wrote to the *St. Petersburg Times,* Higgins blamed deputies for "harassing" his mother and said officers were pursuing his case "so they can put another notch in their 'win' column and puff out their chests at other people's expenses."

But the attack was not his first, records show. Higgins pleaded no contest in 1993 to battery after hitting his mother and threatening her with a knife.

St. Petersburg Times, *November 29, 2000, p. 5.*

if he or she had been tried in court. Second, because negotiations occur most often in secret, there is a danger that the constitutional rights of the defendant may not be stringently upheld. For example, the defendant does not have the chance to confront and cross-examine his or her accusers. Finally, the judge is often little more than a figurehead in cases settled by plea bargaining. In a court case, the judge has the responsibility to see that the trial is conducted in the best interests of both the offender and society as well as the responsibility to ensure due process. Neither of these can be guaranteed in most cases involving plea bargaining.

Because of some of the difficulties characteristic of plea bargaining, some jurisdictions have taken action to greatly reduce or eliminate the practice. A ban on plea bargaining in Alaska led to a decline in charge bargaining, an increase in the workloads of both defense attorneys and prosecutors, a decrease in the time required to process felonies, an increase in trial convictions, and more severe sentences for certain types of offenses (Rubenstein & White, 1979). A more recent study of a ban on plea bargaining in El Paso, Texas, found evidence that the ban did have an adverse affect on the ability of the courts to process felony cases (Holmes, Daudistel, & Taggart, 1992).

The future of plea bargaining remains uncertain, with some recommending retention with modifications, whereas others recommend abolition. Presently, there is a national trend toward greater use of plea bargaining, especially in felony cases (Champion, 1998, p. 223). Regardless of the outcome of such recommendations, plea bargaining currently illustrates quite clearly the value of the network approach in understanding criminal justice. Plea bargaining occurs because of a variety of factors relevant to different components of the criminal justice network. Among these are (1) a desire for convictions on behalf of prosecutors; (2) a desire for acquittals or charge reductions on behalf of defendants and defense counsel; (3) a desire on behalf of all practitioners and the public to conserve valuable resources (time and money); and, (4) overcrowding of prison facilities. These and other factors impinge on prosecutors, judges, and defense attorneys when they consider plea bargaining as an alternative.

THE JUDGE

At the state trial court level, more than 8,000 judges hear cases. Another 1,200 judges hear cases at the level of the state appellate and supreme courts (Maguire & Pastore, 1998, p. 63). As of 1996, there were 603 federal district court (trial court) judges in the various circuits.

Theoretically, the **judge** is the most powerful figure in the justice network, although he or she often allows the prosecutor to usurp most of this power. The judge decides matters of law (is certain evidence admissible?), supervises the selection of juries, instructs jurors, presides over the trial, often does the sentencing, ensures that defendants understand the consequences of different pleas and that any plea entered is voluntary, and, in bench cases, also decides matters of fact. He or she is supposed to perform these duties impartially, attending only to facts that are legally relevant to each individual case. However, political and/or financial considerations sometimes outweigh the requirement for neutrality or impartiality. In the 2000 presidential election, for example, observers noted that almost all the judges sitting on the Florida Supreme Court were Democrats and therefore, perhaps, more inclined to decide cases in favor of Vice President Gore than Governor Bush.

Most research indicates that the power and discretion of the judge are demonstrated most clearly in the area of sentencing. Sentencing disparity may be due to the judge's perceptions of the dangerousness of certain types of offenders, age, gender, race/ethnicity, social class, or other factors. Some judges may be more lenient than others in imposing sentences on older offenders or with female offenders, for example (Daly & Bordt, 1995; Lopez, 1995; Tonry, 1995). Attorneys for both the prosecution and defense learn over time which judges are more likely to be lenient in which types of cases and often attempt to schedule cases accordingly.

The judge, prosecutor, and defense counsel are (in the vast majority of cases) members of the legal profession who have graduated from law school and who have become licensed to practice law by passing a bar (law) examination. A great deal of on-the-job training characterizes individuals filling all three positions because unlike some other countries, we do not require extensive training after graduation from law school and prior to employment for lawyers who occupy these positions. Individuals filling these three roles form their own more or less cooperative network as they work with one another on a regular basis. In addition, each has ties with other components in the criminal justice network.

THE PROBATION OFFICER

Another officer of the court is the **probation officer.** Unlike the judge, prosecutor, and defense counsel, the probation officer is not likely to be a lawyer. Nonetheless, evidence suggests that probation officers have considerable impact on judges and prosecutors, particularly with respect to sentencing. Probation officers are generally civil service employees at the state level and appointees of the courts at the county level. Although training and educational requirements vary considerably among the states, there is a definite trend toward hiring college graduates as probation officers. In some states (Illinois, for example), the tendency is to appoint those with some graduate work or a master's degree. By 1990, the majority of states required college degrees for entry-level probation positions.

The rationale for requiring a college education is clear when the duties of the position are analyzed. In addition to being an officer of the court and, therefore, an authority figure to probationers, the probation officer is expected to be a caseworker/therapist and, in many instances, a community liaison officer (working with local industries and businesses as well as with social agencies). Among the tasks typically performed by probation officers in the more than 2,000 probation offices in the United States are (1) conducting a presentence investigation, (2) making recommendations to the trial court judge on sentencing, (3) supervising probationers, including electronic monitoring and intensive supervision, (4) recommending revocation of probation when necessary, and (5) serving as a role model for probationers (Petersilia, 1999). As the probation officer accomplishes these tasks, he or she must attempt to maintain a reasonably close and friendly relationship with probationers to help change the behaviors that resulted in conflict with the criminal justice network, but the probation officer must maintain sufficient distance to take authoritative action when appropriate. Like other officials in the criminal justice network, the probation officer exercises considerable discretion in the performance of duties. The extent to which conditions of probation are enforced and the extent to which technical violations of probation (as opposed to the commission of a new crime) lead to official action are largely determined by the probation officer, who is often required to fulfill the duties outlined here while managing a relatively heavy caseload.

Given the scope and nature of probation work, it is easy to understand the trend toward hiring better-educated individuals to fill probation positions. Unfortunately, salaries in the probation field have often lagged behind those of other criminal justice employees, making it difficult to recruit and retain probation officers with such educational backgrounds.

MANAGING THE COURTS

Traditionally, American courts have been independent and self-governing because of their role as a check and balance on the other two branches of government. At the federal level, many support functions, such as budgeting, docket control, and statistical analysis, are performed by the Administrative Office of the United States Courts. Historically, the concept of a judicial system has not been completely adopted in most states. Although there has been a trend toward unified state court systems, there is so much variation that most state judiciaries should still be classified as nonsystems because of local jurisdictional autonomy, complexity, and lack of centralized control.

In most states, there are three distinct sets of court managers: chief judges, court clerks, and court administrators.

Chief Judges

Judges have always been responsible for the administration of their courts. Individual judicial autonomy has resulted in a variety of uncoordinated and inconsistent administrative practices. Judges are often as involved with the many aspects of management as with adjudication. Unfortunately, most judges are not trained in management. The result is that most lawyers who become judges are not adept at analyzing patterns of dispositions or at managing large dockets.

The chief judge faces the same problems. The chief judge has general administrative responsibilities in his or her jurisdiction. Since most chief judges assume their position by virtue of seniority, there is no guarantee of effective management. Election of the chief judge (by other judges) may produce a strong and effective manager or a middle-of-the-road candidate.

Court Clerks

Clerks of the court play an important role in the administration of local judiciaries. They are responsible for docketing cases, collecting court fees, arranging for jury selection, and maintaining court records. Historically, they have competed with judges for control over judicial administration. Since they are elected officials in most states, they can function somewhat independently from the judge. As with judges, most clerks are not trained to manage the local courts (Neubauer, 1999, p. 112).

Court Administrators

One solution to some of the court problems addressed above has been the creation of a professional group of trained administrators to assist judges in administrative and nonjudicial functions (as discussed in Chapter 7). Nonjudicial functions are those associated with the business management of the courts. These may include record keeping, data gathering and analysis, research and planning, budget preparation, management of physical space and supplies, management of support personnel, docketing of court cases, and dispensing of information to the public. Business management plays a support role to the judicial function of the courts and is essential for more effective and efficient court operations.

In 1937, Connecticut established the first centralized office of court administrator, with a number of other states following after World War II. By the 1980s, every state had established a statewide court administrator (Neubauer, 1999, p. 112). Because the position is relatively new, several aspects of the court administrator's role are still being debated. Most arguments center on qualifications and administrative relations with other agencies.

Since the creation of the Institute for Court Management in Denver, Colorado, in 1970, an increasing number of colleges and universities have been offering programs in court administration at the undergraduate and graduate levels. However, there is still no agreement as to the skills and qualifications a court administrator should possess. Many believe managerial expertise is needed and a law degree is unnecessary. Conversely, many judges believe a law degree is essential. Some contend, for example, that court administrators hired for their business background have been ineffective because they know too little about the courts and the law.

A second area of concern centers on the relationship between the court administrator and other judicial agencies. Often clerks view this position as a threat and resent the intrusion, yet to be effective, the court administrator requires the type of data on cases that only the clerk can provide. Court clerks have played an important role in resisting the creation of court administrator positions. If the position is created, court clerks can significantly reduce the administrators' effectiveness by not cooperating.

There can also be friction between judges and administrators. Some judges are reluctant to delegate responsibility over important aspects of the court's work, for example, case scheduling. The distinction between administration and adjudication is not entirely clear. A court administrator's proposal to streamline court procedures may be seen by judges as intruding on how they decide cases (Neubauer, 1999, p. 113). Despite their potential for improving the efficiency of the court, court administrators have encountered opposition from both clerks and judges. Most have not been given full responsibility over the court's nonjudicial functions. If the issues concerning qualifications, authority, and accountability can be resolved, court administrators could significantly increase the efficiency of the courts.

Other persons routinely involved in court operations include court reporters and bailiffs. Their roles tend to be more specific and less controversial than those of the court managers.

Summary

1. The extent to which criminal justice practitioners are involved in a network in their daily operations is clearly illustrated by court personnel.

2. The prosecutor, perhaps the most powerful individual in the network in terms of discretion, takes into consideration a variety of factors in deciding whether and how to prosecute cases. Among these factors are community norms, political party affiliation, his or her relationships with the police, defense counsel, and judges, prior court decisions, and so on.

3. Defense counselors, judges, and probation officers also take into account these factors as well as the recommendations and desires of the prosecutor and one another in processing cases.

4. The extent to which plea bargaining occurs and the nature of the bargains depend upon these factors and on the extent of overcrowding in jails and prisons.

5. Local public defenders and probation officers are often appointed to their positions by judges who consider the prosecutor's recommendations in making such appointments. And, of course, judges and prosecutors are either elected by the public or appointed by other politicians who are elected by the public.

6. Judges, prosecutors, public defenders, and probation officers are assisted in their functions by individuals appointed or elected to help run the courts in an orderly way.

7. Controversy about the proper functions of court administrators, court managers, and court clerks characterizes the current court scene.

Key Terms Defined

prosecutor (state's attorney, district attorney)   An attorney representing the people (the state); also called the state's attorney, district attorney, prosecuting attorney.

independent counsels   Private attornies appointed because public prosecutors are too closely tied to government officials being investigated.

defense counsel   An attorney representing the defendant.

public defenders   Defense counsels paid from public funds.

adversary system   The system of law in the United States, involving the opportunity of both prosecution and defense to present their cases at a trial presided over by a neutral judge.

judge   An attorney (generally) elected or appointed to preside over court cases.

probation officer   An individual appointed to serve as an officer of the court who supervises probationers and provides certain other services to the court.

Critical Thinking Exercises

1. Why is the prosecutor such an influential and important figure in our criminal justice network? To whom is the prosecutor ultimately accountable for his or her actions? What is the role of politics in prosecution? Are you comfortable with the considerable power of the prosecutor?

2. Discuss the courtroom work group in terms of its potential impact on defendants and victims. From your perspective, do we have an adversarial system of justice? Why or why not?

Internet Exercises

After monumental decisions in *Gideon* v. *Wainwright* and *Argersinger* v. *Hamlin*, the role of the public defender has become very important for the court process. You can find Iowa's State Public Defender website at *www.spd.state.ia.us*.
   Read the materials presented; then answer the following questions:

1. What types of individuals does the public defender represent? Explain the types of cases he or she can become involved with.
2. What advantages does the public defender system offer to criminal defendants?
3. What is the state appellate defender, and what types of clients does he or she represent?

References

Barlow, H. D. (2000). *Criminal justice in America.* Upper Saddle River, NJ: Prentice Hall.

Blumberg, A. S. (1967). *Criminal justice.* Chicago: Quadrangle.

Champion, D. J. (1998). *Criminal justice in the United States* (2nd ed.). Chicago: Nelson-Hall.

Daly, K. & Bordt, R. L. (1995). Sex effects and sentencing: An analysis of the statistical literature. *Justice Quarterly, 12,* 141–145.

DeFrances, C. J. & Steadman, G. W. (1998, July). Prosecutors in state courts, 1996. *BJS Bulletin.* Washington, DC: U.S. Government Printing Office.

Editorial. (1998). Too poor to be defended. *Economist, 347* (8063), 21–22.

Estrich, S. (1998). *Getting away with murder: How politics is destroying the criminal justice system.* Cambridge, MA: Harvard University Press.

Hanson, R. A., Hewitt, W., & Ostrom, B. J. (1992, Summer). Are the critics of indigent defense counsel correct? *State Court Journal,* 20–29.

Hanson, R. A. & Ostrom, B. J. (1998). Indigent defenders get the job done and done well. In G. F. Cole & M. G. Gertz (Eds.). *The criminal justice system: Politics and policies* (pp. 264–288). Belmont, CA: Wadsworth.

Holmes, M. D., Daudistel, H. C., & Taggart, W. A. (1992). Plea bargaining policy and state district court caseloads: An interrupted time series analysis. *Law and Society Review, 26,* 139–59.

Holten, G., & Jones, M. E. (1982). *The system of criminal justice* (2nd ed.). Boston: Little, Brown.

Lopez, A. S. (Ed.). (1995). *Latinos in the United States: History, law, and perspective.* New York: Garland Press.

Maguire, K., & Pastore, A. L. (1998). *Bureau of Justice Statistics sourcebook of criminal justice statistics—1997.* Washington, DC: U.S. Department of Justice, Hindelang Criminal Justice Research Center.

Misner, R. (1996). Recasting prosecutorial discretion. *Journal of Criminal Law and Criminology, 86,* 717–58.

Neubauer, D. W. (1999). *America's courts and the criminal justice system* (6th ed.). Belmont, CA: West/Wadsworth.

Petersilia, J. (1999). Probation in the United States: Practices and challenges. In J. L. Victor (Ed.), *Annual editions: Criminal justice 99/00,* pp. 160–65. Sluice Dock, Guilford, CT: Dushkin/McGraw-Hill.

Pollock, J. M. (1994). *Ethics in crime and justice: Dilemmas and decisions* (2nd ed.). Belmont, CA: Wadsworth.

Rubenstein, M. L., & White, T. J. (1979). Plea bargaining: Can Alaska live without it? *Judicature, 62,* 266–79.

Smith, S., & DeFrances, C. (1996). *Indigent defense.* Washington, DC: Bureau of Justice Statistics.

Tonry, M. (1995). *Malign neglect: Race, crime and punishment in America.* New York: Oxford University Press.

Williams, J. (1995). Type of counsel and the outcome of criminal appeals: A research note. *American Journal of Criminal Justice, 19,* 275–85.

Selected Readings

Berlow, A. (2000). Requiem for a public defender. *American Prospect, 11* (14), 28–32.

Burke, E. J. (1998). Don't expect the expert. *Trial, 34* (12), 76–77.

Harriger, K. J. (1994). Separation of powers and the politics of independent counsel. *Political Science Quarterly, 109*, 261–86.

Ogletree, C. J. (1995). An essay on the new public defender for the 21st century. *Law and Contemporary Problems, 58*, 81–93.

Strier, F. (1999). Adversarial justice. In J. L. Victor (Ed.), *Annual editions: Criminal justice 99/00*, pp. 96–103. Sluice Dock, Guilford, CT: Dushkin/McGraw-Hill.

CHAPTER NINE

Pretrial Procedures

Arrest is the first step leading to trial.
Stephen Osman/911 Pictures

*H*erman was arrested for illegal possession and sale of narcotics. Twenty-four hours later, at his initial appearance, the prosecutor built a prima facie case and the judge determined that probable cause existed to bind him over for trial. Because this was his sixth arrest for similar charges, and because he had attempted to flee the jurisdiction on two other occasions, bail was denied and Herman was placed in preventive detention in the county jail.

Following a grand jury hearing, a true bill was returned and Herman was indicted. He was arraigned, and his attorney filed motions for discovery and disclosure. On seeing the prosecutor's evidence, Herman's attorney encouraged him to plead guilty to the possession charge. In a plea bargain agreement, Herman was convicted of illegal possession, the charges relating to sale of narcotics were dropped, and Herman was sentenced to six months in the county jail.

Key Terms

48-hour rule

probable cause

initial appearance

bail

nulla poena sine crimine

bail bondsperson

preventive detention

released on recognizance

supervised release

grand jury

ex parte proceeding

bill of indictment

prima facie case

information

preliminary hearing

arraignment

nolo contendere

motion for discovery

motion for disclosure

Chapter Outline

Initial Appearances

The Administration of Bail

Consequences of Bail

Protecting Society

The Determination of Bail

The Effects of Monetary Bail

Formal Charging or Accusation

The Grand Jury

Information and Preliminary Hearings

Arraignment

Pretrial Motions and Hearings

Motion for Change of Venue

Motion for Continuance

Motions for Suppression and Exclusion of Evidence

Motion for Discovery

Motion for Disclosure

Motion for Dismissal

In this chapter, we focus our attention on the various stages of the criminal justice process prior to an actual criminal trial. Although the stages in the pretrial process have not received the same attention as the trial, they are of considerable importance. We must keep in mind that our criminal justice network is supposed to be based on the principles of innocent until proven guilty and due process of law for all those accused of criminal wrongdoing. Inherent within these principles are attempts to ensure that only those rightfully accused will proceed to the trial stage. Many of the pretrial processes, then, act as a sieve to filter out cases lacking necessary levels of proof for a finding of guilt. These stages are beneficial to the citizenry in that they prohibit the state from administering arbitrary punishment.

The pretrial stages are also beneficial to the government and the taxpayer because they help eliminate expensive and time-consuming trials when there is little probability of conviction. Because of our emphasis on due process, these stages also protect the rights of the accused specified in the U.S. Constitution and the Bill of Rights (the first 10 amendments to the Constitution). We must keep in mind that our criminal justice network includes an adversary system consisting of two opponents: the state (prosecution) and the defense (the accused). As we have indicated, the balance of power rests with the state. Due process is an attempt to keep the scales of justice balanced despite this imbalance of power.

In this chapter, we closely examine the six stages in the pretrial process: the initial appearance, the administration of bail, the formal charging of the accused, the preliminary hearing, the arraignment, and the concepts of discovery and disclosure. Most of our attention focuses on the pretrial stages as they apply to felony cases. We identify differences as they apply to lesser offenses. In addition, we indicate and discuss some of the more controversial stages and practices. There is, for example, considerable debate over bail, the use of grand juries, and the plea of not guilty by reason of insanity. We examine proposed changes in these areas and address their ramifications.

INITIAL APPEARANCES

After an accused has been taken into custody by the police, he or she is to be taken without unnecessary delay before the nearest and most accessible magistrate (judge), and a charge should be filed (Ferdico, 1999, p. 139). The definition as to what constitutes "unnecessary delay" has been constantly reinterpreted in a series of cases: *McNabb* v. *United States* (1943), *Mallory* v. *United States* (1957), and *Gerstein* v. *Pugh* (1975). The current standard, the **48-hour rule,** decided in *Riverside County, California* v. *McLaughlin* (1991), holds that delays of up to 48 hours may be constitutional. Delays caused by police procedures such as lineups, fingerprinting, and booking are usually considered reasonable. In addition, delays caused by the unavailability of the magistrate and by weekends and holidays are generally considered justifiable.

There are many responsibilities of the presiding magistrate at this stage. First, the judge is responsible for determining if **probable cause** existed for the arrest. If it is determined that probable cause did exist, the accused will be held for further criminal processing. If not, the defendant is released, and no formal charges are filed. This is the first stage of the filtering effect of pretrial procedures. Prior to this, both the public and the police have exercised discretion in reporting offenses or suspicious circumstances and effecting the arrest. Ideally, as the result of the **initial appearance,** only those cases in which there is a reasonable belief that a crime did occur and that the accused is the perpetrator of the act, will be processed for further court action.

If probable cause is found, the accused is informed of the charges against him or her and is generally given a written copy of those charges. The magistrate will also inform the defendant of his or her right to counsel as guaranteed by the Sixth Amendment to the Constitution and interpreted by the Supreme Court. Initially, the right to counsel was applied at the federal level, with some controversy as to whether the doctrine applied to state proceedings. In *Gideon* v. *Wainwright* (1963), the court held that counsel must be provided in state felony proceedings. In *Argersinger* v. *Hamlin* (1972), the court extended the right to counsel to all cases where the penalty was imprisonment. If the accused is indigent (without funds), the magistrate will appoint counsel.

If the charge is a misdemeanor, the case is often heard at this time. In many instances the defendant will plead guilty and the judge will impose a standardized fine as sentence, although there may be circumstances that warrant incarceration. In felony cases, the judge may also inform the accused of the next stage in the process, usually setting a date for a preliminary hearing. Another function of the judge at the initial appearance is the administration of bail.

THE ADMINISTRATION OF BAIL

One of the most controversial pretrial procedures involves setting bail. Simply stated, **bail** is the practice of releasing a defendant prior to trial with the promise that he or she will appear before the court as directed. As we will see, the issue of bail is extremely complex.

The practice of bail is traceable to England, as are many other facets of the American criminal justice network. Because judges often rode circuits and court was not held for months at a time, the English would release defendants prior to trial on the oath of responsible individuals who would ensure that the accused would be present when the trial commenced. This practice was maintained by American settlers but was altered by requiring the posting of a bond by the accused or by someone on his or her behalf. The practice was formalized by the Judiciary Act of 1789, through which the practices of admitting defendants to bail (except in capital cases) and permitting considerable discretion in the determination of bail became routinized in the American criminal justice network.

Constitutionally, there are few guidelines regarding bail. The Eighth Amendment provides that bail shall not be excessive. There is no federal constitutional right to bail, but if bail is provided by state legislation, it cannot be excessive. This ambiguous mandate has generated conflict in several areas; for example, does "excessive" pertain to the financial capabilities of the accused, the nature of the charge, or some other criterion?

Before addressing these specific questions, let us first examine the practice of bail. Bail involves the posting of cash, property, or securities by the defendant or someone on his or her behalf. Originally, the manifest function of bail was to ensure that the accused would be present for trial or other pretrial procedures. In most jurisdictions, bail is set by the court as a monetary sum. The defendant or another party (legally, the surety) usually posts 10 percent of that sum in cash, property, or securities and pledges to pay the remaining 90 percent if the defendant is not present for trial (called skipping or jumping bail). The amount posted and the pledge for the remainder is commonly referred to as the bail bond, and the party other than the defendant, who posts the amount and pledges for the bond, is referred to as the bail bondsperson. (See In the News, "Bondsman Knows Human Condition.") If the accused is present for trial, the amount posted (or a portion of it) may be returned or, on conviction, may be used to pay a fine or attorneys' fees, or it may serve as an appeal bond. In some jurisdictions, the amount posted is not returned.

Consequences of Bail

At least in theory, then, bail is intended to ensure that a defendant appears before the court and answers charges. Suffet (1966) referred to this as the manifest function of bail. Earlier we raised several questions concerning the administration of bail. We must add to this list the question of how successfully bail realizes its intended purpose.

Under our judicial system, we adhere to a policy of **nulla poena sine crimine** (no punishment without a crime). Although bail may not have been intended to alter this legal doctrine, in practice it has, and sometimes dramatically. Some defendants spend months in jail awaiting trial simply because they cannot afford to post 10 percent of the bail bond. Bail is often attacked as discriminating against the poor. Although defendants from the upper classes or those engaged in lucrative criminal ventures can make bail more readily, is their financial status indicative of the likelihood of appearing before the court? As a result of the inability of many accused to obtain bail money, the professional **bail bondsperson** has become a central figure in the bail controversy. It is not uncommon for bondspeople to be as much (or more) of a determining factor than is the offense in deciding who will or will not be held in confinement prior to trial. In theory, the bondsperson posts the required 10 percent and pledges to pay the remainder if the accused fails to appear. In return he or she charges the accused a percentage of the bond. Thus, in theory, the bondsperson is risking considerable financial loss and must exercise caution in

In the News

BONDSMAN KNOWS HUMAN CONDITION

By Thom Marshall

People and their problems caught Johnny Nelms' attention many years ago and still hold a firm grip on it.

His work, his interest, his passion, focused upon the human condition when he was a country singer and songwriter, during the term he served as state representative three decades ago, and for the many years he has been a bail bondsman.

As I left after visiting his tiny, cramped office in a small portable building on the corner of the parking lot at 1301 Franklin, across the street from the county jail, Nelms gave me a CD of songs by Sonny Claghorn, which Nelms said is his stage name.

One number has the classic plot: A fellow is lowdown and blue because "she left" and he turns to booze whenever "the memory of her kiss starts to hurt and just won't stop." And you can tell by the chorus it happens far too often: "Just please don't call me wino, 'cause I'll drink anything."

A man who can write such woeful lyrics, and then stand in front of a crowded dance hall singing them, obviously is a scholar on the subjects of pain, regret, heartache, guilt, bad choices, bad luck. . . .

Trusts parents, grandparents

"If there's one thing I know, it's people," Nelms said.

As a bail bondsman located so conveniently near the courthouse and jail, Nelms said he's seen all kinds of people come in and go out. Said he deals mostly with "moms and dads, grandmas and grandpas."

These parents or grandparents come to him, willing to risk their savings or other assets to allow their grown children or grandchildren to stay out of jail while waiting for the slow wheels of justice to turn.

His decision about whether to make the deal to bail someone out of jail is based more on the parents or grandparents than on the one who is in trouble.

"I'm on some now," Nelms said, "where I don't trust the boy at all. It's the mom and dad. I can tell if they're from the old school."

He recalled being disappointed after a friend came to him for help in getting a daughter out of jail. Nelms did, but when they were in his office after the release, the daughter behaved in a most ungrateful manner, telling her dad: "You didn't need to come and get me, I've got a lot of friends."

Nelms responded: "Where were they? You've been in there two weeks," and he asked his friend to remove the young woman from his office.

Continued

If the person on bond doesn't show up in court when he is supposed to, the first action Nelms takes is to call the parents. He said if they can't produce the fugitive, they usually know where he can be located.

Nelms estimated that 99 percent of the people who are the subjects of visits to his office are in trouble for nonviolent offenses. He said they go to work every day and have other qualities appreciated by their families.

"They just got on a bad road," he said, using a phrase that sounds like one Claghorn might sing.

New approach to probation

Nelms sees many who get hooked on illegal drugs and get busted. Some straighten up, but "some people's minds aren't big enough to quit," he said.

However, he has been wondering more and more lately how far society can go in punishing nonviolent crimes.

"I can't see how we can keep building prisons," he said. "How long can they keep hiring probation people?"

His suggestion is that use of the bail-bonding system be expanded and available after a person is found guilty of a nonviolent crime in about the same way it is now before a case gets to court. He said there are about 80 state-licensed bonding companies operating in Harris County, and estimates they could handle an average of 200 cases each.

He said a bail-bonding company could keep up with a client to see that he fulfills the judge's orders regarding community service and any restrictions, with failure to result in bond forfeiture.

"We have to do something," Nelms said, "and that's the best I can think of."

He said such a system for dealing with the many nonviolent offenders would cost taxpayers nothing and allow prisons to do a better job dealing with people convicted of violent crimes.

The Houston Chronicle, January 28, 2001, p. A27.

selecting clients. In practice, some bondspeople simply adjust their fee according to the risk they are taking. It is sometimes argued that bondspeople generate additional crime by charging such high fees that the accused must commit another crime to pay off the bondsperson. Bondspeople have also been known to engage in illegal relationships with other criminal justice personnel. Investigations have shown that bondspeople pay referral fees to police officers, and it has been alleged that judges and bondspeople split fees in some instances (Galliher & McCartney, 1977). It is also argued that bondspeople occasionally employ unethical practices in retrieving clients who fail to appear. Unlike the police, who are regulated by the Fourth Amendment, bondspeople have often literally kidnapped defendants to ensure their appearance. Chamberlin (1999), on the basis of his analysis of bail-enforcement agents, found that despite their rather shady reputation, they are better at what they do than are traditional law enforcement officers. It is clear that without much regulation bail bonds-people often exercise considerable power over other citizens.

Protecting Society

Another alleged consequence of bail has been to protect society from danger-ous offenders. Jurisdictions commonly designate specific offenses as nonbail-able in an attempt to protect society, or bail may be set in an amount high enough to ordinarily preclude the release of particular defendants. The rise in both crime and the fear of crime in the 1970s and early 1980s led to the Bail Re-form Act of 1984. This act, passed by Congress, provided for the **preventive detention** of defendants charged with violent crimes or perceived as a high risk to commit additional crimes prior to trial (Corrado, 1996). Although some scholars criticized Congress, the Supreme Court later upheld the practice in *United States* v. *Salerno* (1987). In practice, the high bail seldom protects society (Fagan & Guggenheim, 1996). As we have indicated, bail may actually gener-ate more crime under certain circumstances. In addition, criminals involved with syndicates can meet bail even when it is set high. Again, we see that fi-nancial advantage can easily overcome the intent of bail.

Bail bondspersons are often able to find and return those who flee the court's jurisdiction.

Jim L. Shaffer

The Determination of Bail

What factors should the court consider in setting bail? Historically, the nature of the charge and the defendant's criminal record have been important criteria in setting bail. Some judges recognize that factors extraneous to the offense are also relevant in determining the defendant's probability of appearance. Such factors as residence in the community, employment, and the presence or absence of relatives and friends in the community are now being considered in the administration of bail. This practice stems from an experiment sponsored by the Vera Foundation, entitled the Manhattan Bail Project (Vera Institute of Justice, 1972). The New York City project began in 1961 and involved the use of law students who interviewed defendants to determine present or recent residence at the same address for six months or more, current or recent employment for six months or more, relatives in New York City with whom the defendant was in contact, prior criminal record, and residence in New York City for 10 years or more. It was assumed that these factors would be relevant to pretrial release.

After this information was obtained, the staff commenced to determine whether to recommend that the defendant be **released on recognizance,** that is, released without posting bond. If the staff recommended release on recognizance (ROR), the recommendation was forwarded to the arraignment court, where defendants were randomly assigned to experimental and control groups. Those in the experimental groups had their recommendation given to the judge, prosecutor, and defense attorney; those in the control group did not. The findings were interesting, to say the least: 60 percent of those in the experimental group were granted ROR, whereas only 14 percent of the control group were released. Thus, the presence or absence of the recommendation is of great importance in releasing defendants. In general, those who were released did in fact appear. Those who failed to appear generally did so because of illness, confusion over the legal process, or family emergencies. This project was the forerunner of numerous other projects designed to circumvent the often discriminatory nature of bail (O'Rourke & Salem, 1968). Today, the use of ROR is common at all levels and in all jurisdictions.

In a later and more sophisticated experiment, Des Moines, Iowa, implemented a **supervised release** program that attempts to expand the ROR concept and serves to prepare some clients for probation (Boorkman et al., 1976). Defendants who may not meet ROR criteria are counseled and supervised prior to trial. Attempts to secure employment, reunite or maintain family ties, and otherwise become a viable member of the community serve to ensure appearance at trial. More recently, pretrial intensive supervision has been used to conserve jail resources and prevent pretrial offending (Barlow, 2000, pp. 395–97).

The use of recognizance bail recognizes that the nature of the charge is not the only factor relevant to a defendant's pretrial release. Factors that tie the accused to the community should also be considered in determining bail. The practice of releasing defendants on their own recognizance has several advantages:

1. It maintains or upholds the principle of no punishment without crime (many defendants can avoid being detained in jail because of lack of money).
2. It limits the negative impact of pretrial detention in terms of costs to the taxpayer.
3. It makes bail more equitable (those without financial advantage have the same opportunity to be released as the financially advantaged).

The Effects of Monetary Bail

We previously stated that recognizance bails reduce the negative impacts of bail on defendants. In this section, we identify negative impacts that may result from the practice of setting monetary bail.

First, bail may encourage plea bargaining. Some innocent defendants may agree to plead guilty and receive probation or a fine rather than be detained in jail prior to trial. Thus, the principles of justice are subverted. Second, those who cannot make bail may suffer from being detained in jail. It is estimated that over 50 percent of America's jail population are there awaiting trial. Although there has been considerable jail reform, conditions in many of these jails are bad at best. Inmates are subjected to prolonged boredom, assault, homosexuality, poor physical conditions, substandard medical care, and exposure to convicted criminals. Those who will later be found innocent, as well as those who will be found guilty, are faced with these conditions before a determination of guilt. Third, as a result of being confined, the accused may encounter current or future employment problems. His or her family may be forced to request government assistance, and his or her absence alone may be disruptive. Additionally, the stigma of spending time in jail may follow the individual regardless of the outcome of the case. Finally, pretrial confinement may affect the outcome of the case. An accused who undergoes pretrial confinement may lack the ability to assist in his or her own defense. Research by Rankin (1964) found significant differences in receiving or not receiving prison sentences between defendants making bail and those being jailed continuously. This may be due to the fact that those defendants most likely to be denied bail are also those convicted of prior offenses, charged with violent offenses, or on probation or parole at the time of their arrest (Reaves, 1998).

In conclusion, we have found bail to be a highly discretionary practice with numerous, complex side effects. In its present form, bail cannot ensure that defendants will appear, that the public will be protected, or that justice will be done. The use of recognizance bonds may help alleviate some of the discrimination in setting bail, but the issue of monetary bail remains controversial.

FORMAL CHARGING OR ACCUSATION

Before an actual criminal trial commences, there must be a formal accusation of the accused. The process of accusation is basically a review of the evidence to ensure that the evidence is substantial enough to warrant further processing of the defendant. Here again we see the criminal justice network employing a filter. Those cases that appear to be lacking in evidence are rejected or filtered out, thereby saving the taxpayers money, limiting the stigma facing the accused, and reducing congestion in the courts. The process of formal accusation is usually reserved for felonies and some serious misdemeanor cases. Traffic cases, petty offenses, and minor misdemeanors are usually handled routinely and do not involve a detailed review of the evidence. In many of these cases, the defendants answer to charges by pleading guilty at the initial appearance. The American network of criminal justice uses two basic means of accusation: grand jury indictments and prosecutorial informations. The next two sections examine these two procedures and discuss the strengths and weaknesses of each.

The Grand Jury

The Fifth Amendment holds that "No person shall be held to answer for a capital or otherwise infamous crime, unless on a presentment or indictment of a Grand Jury." The **grand jury** was created in England to ensure that arbitrary charges were not brought against the citizenry by the government. We must remember that, in that era, the judicial and executive branches of government in England were not totally separate.

The Crown could, and did, have charges brought against those who spoke out or otherwise opposed the government. In theory, if not in practice, grand jury members were charged with reviewing the facts of a particular case and determining the validity of the charges. Like many other aspects of the English criminal justice system, the concept of the grand jury was adopted as part of the American legal system during the colonial period.

The grand jury is an accusatory jury only and should not be confused with the petit (or trial) jury, which determines innocence or guilt. The two juries differ in size, purpose, level of proof required. and other areas. Still, as one component of the justice network, both give members of the public an opportunity for input into the network. Table 9.1 highlights the major differences between grand and petit juries.

Although the Fifth Amendment provides for the use of grand juries, they are not used in all felony cases. Federal courts employ grand juries as mandated by the Fifth Amendment. State courts, not obligated to follow this mandate, vary in their use of grand juries. Some states require grand jury review in all felony cases, whereas others require it only in cases involving the possibility of a death sentence or life imprisonment; still others permit proceedings to commence on a prosecutorial information without grand jury review. It should also be noted that, in those jurisdictions requiring grand jury review, the defendant can waive the proceedings.

Table 9.1

Distinctions between Grand and Petit Juries

	Grand Jury	Petit Jury
Purpose	Formal accusation	Determination of guilt or innocence
Size	16–23 members	6–12 members
Level of proof required	Probable cause	Beyond reasonable doubt
Secrecy	Secret proceedings	Public proceedings
Rules of evidence	Can use illegally obtained evidence	Strict rules of evidence
Presiding authority	Prosecutor	Judge

The grand jury normally has two functions. The first, the presentment, permits the grand jury to act as an investigative unit. The grand jury has the power to investigate possible criminal activity of a general nature, meaning such activities as police and political corruption, organized crime activities, and offenses against the public at large. It does not investigate specific crimes. The final report and recommendations of the investigation are called the presentment. If the investigation is productive, charges will be sought.

The second and more common function is the accusatory role. In jurisdictions where the grand jury is employed, grand jury members review evidence and determine if it is substantial enough to warrant prosecution. In this role, they represent the community conscience. It should be remembered that grand juries simply weigh the strength of the evidence. They do not decide guilt or innocence.

Grand jury procedures are nonadversarial. Witnesses are called and answer questions from the prosecutor. A grand jury proceeding is an **ex parte proceeding;** that is, it is for only one party: the prosecution. The accused's counsel is not present in the courtroom, nor is the accused, unless he or she is testifying. There is no right to cross-examination during grand jury hearings. The only parties present at the technically secret proceedings are the judge, prosecutor, grand jury, and witnesses, who are called individually. If the evidence is sufficient for a prima facie case, the grand jury will issue a **bill of indictment** charging the accused with a specific crime or set of crimes. A **prima facie case** is one in which "on the face of it," the evidence without any objections or contradictions is of such a nature that probable cause exists to charge the individual with a crime.

Because the grand jury hearing is nonadversarial, it is subject to rules and regulations that differ from those governing the trial process. The grand jury hearing is similar to the trial in that witnesses must take an oath and are subject to charges of perjury if they give false testimony. Witnesses also have the right against self-incrimination. A grand jury may rely on evidence that would be inadmissible at a trial. The Supreme Court held in *Castella* v. *United States* (1953) that hearsay evidence and in *United States* v. *Calandra* (1974) that evidence obtained illegally can be admitted during grand jury proceedings. The basis for these decisions is that the proceedings are nonadversarial. The grand jury is only a fact-finding body, not a determiner of guilt; thus, evidence that cannot be admitted at the trial may still be heard by the grand jury.

Occasionally, prosecutors will use the grand jury as a method of screening politically sensitive cases. For example, a prosecutor wanting to test the community's reaction to a controversial case may proceed before the grand jury. If no bill of indictment is issued, the prosecutor may opt to drop the charges and not proceed with the case. This practice benefits the state financially and protects the prosecutor politically, but it also opens the possibility of abuse on behalf of the prosecutor (Gibeaut, 2001).

Grand juries usually consist of 16 to 23 members, with each jurisdiction deciding on the number of members by statute. Selection is usually from those age 18 and over who are residents of the jurisdiction and who possess U.S. citizenship. Usually, grand juries are selected randomly from voting lists or other such means of registration. According to Kalmanoff (1976), grand juries are not proportionately representative by race, age, or income. The grand jury has also been criticized as being costly and subject to easy manipulation by the prosecution (Frankel & Naftalis, 1977). Although such criticisms may be sound, the grand jury remains one of the methods of involving the citizenry in the criminal justice process. In fact, in Virginia, a law was recently passed giving grand juries the authority to conduct investigations and require witnesses to testify rather than depending solely on evidence gathered by the police and prosecutors ("Legislature toughens," 2001).

Information and Preliminary Hearings

Most felony cases today proceed on the basis of an information rather than an indictment. An **information** is a written charge issued by the prosecutor rather than the grand jury. When an information is issued, a **preliminary hearing** will be scheduled. The preliminary hearing serves the same purpose as the grand jury: to establish probable cause. If probable cause is established, the accused will stand trial; if not, the charges are dismissed and the accused is given his or her freedom. However, the prosecution is not prohibited from refiling charges later.

Although the functions of the grand jury and the preliminary hearing are similar, the procedures involved differ significantly to ensure that only those rightfully accused stand trial. As we noted previously, grand jury proceedings are not open to the public, are conducted ex parte, and are not subject to some of the rigid rules of evidence. In contrast, the preliminary hearing is usually conducted before the judge or magistrate in open court, the accused is represented by counsel and is permitted to cross-examine prosecutorial witnesses as well as to call his or her own witnesses, and the defense can challenge the legality of the prosecution's evidence. Even in jurisdictions that require grand jury hearings, many defendants waive the hearing and go forward on an information because they gain the opportunity to challenge the evidence at a preliminary hearing, which they could not do if they were accused by the grand jury. It is often argued that the preliminary hearing is closer to the concept of due process.

In addition to waiving the grand jury, the accused can also waive the preliminary hearing. Reasons for such a waiver may include speeding up the process, gaining some compensation in the process of plea bargaining, and avoiding negative publicity that may result from the hearing (e.g., sex crimes and other crimes that invoke strong social response). The advantages of proceeding with the preliminary hearing include the possibility of having the case dismissed and avoiding the stigma of trial and having the opportunity to examine the prosecution's evidence so that the defense can better calculate trial strategy.

As we have seen, there are two distinct methods of formal accusation. Both are designed to determine probable cause; however, they differ as to rules, decision makers (prosecutor or judge), and the openness of the proceedings. Although the information affords the opportunity to confront witnesses and challenge evidence, the grand jury permits the decision to be made by the citizenry. As a practical matter, most cases proceed on the basis of an information, and grand juries are not routinely impaneled in many jurisdictions.

ARRAIGNMENT

The **arraignment** in felony cases usually occurs shortly after the return of an indictment or the issuance of an information. In minor cases, the arraignment occurs at the time of the initial appearance. At the arraignment the judge reads and explains the charges to the defendant in open court. The defendant, who has a right to be represented by counsel, is then asked to plead, or answer, to the charges. Although jurisdictions vary in the pleas they will accept, the most common are not guilty, guilty, not guilty by reason of insanity, and nolo contendere. A plea of once in jeopardy is also possible, though it is used infrequently.

If the accused pleads not guilty, the plea will be recorded and a date set for trial. If the accused fails to enter a plea, he or she will be considered as standing mute, and the court will enter a plea of not guilty on the defendant's behalf. Usually, any conditions of bail will be continued at this time. It is possible, however, to have the present conditions reconsidered on request.

Most defendants enter a plea of guilty. As previously mentioned, the process of plea bargaining accounts for a substantial majority of guilty pleas. Estimates concerning the frequency of guilty pleas range from 60 to 90 percent of all felony cases. On the surface it may appear that a plea of guilty negates some of the formalities of the proceedings. Obviously, it saves both the court and the defendant time and money, but because it constitutes a waiver of due process, there is a formal requirement to question the defendant concerning his or her guilty plea. By pleading guilty, the accused is relinquishing the Fifth Amendment right against self-incrimination and the Sixth Amendment rights to trial by jury, to a public trial, and to confront witnesses against him- or herself. The Supreme Court requires judges to question defendants who plead guilty. Through various decisions, the Court has required the right to counsel during plea negotiations (*Brady* v. *United States,* 1969), the need for a public record showing that the defendant voluntarily pled guilty (*Boykin* v. *Alabama,* 1968), and the necessity that a prosecutor's promise be kept (*Santabello* v. *New York,* 1971). The judge must ascertain, by questioning the defendant, that he or she is aware of waiving the constitutional rights and that the plea is being entered voluntarily. In addition, the judge must inform the accused of the statutory provisions for sentencing someone convicted of that particular offense. In many cases, the accused will enter the guilty plea and the prosecutor will recommend a specific sentence in accordance with a bargain they have reached, often with the knowledge of the judge. The judge will then pass sentence. In other cases, a separate sentencing hearing will be set at a later date. This is more likely if the accused pleads guilty without engaging in plea bargaining.

As we have indicated earlier, the plea of not guilty by reason of insanity is one of the most controversial aspects of the criminal justice process. Jurisdictions vary in the labels used and the terms for accepting this plea, which in essence holds that the accused did in fact engage in the criminal conduct but lacked the ability to form the necessary mental element of intent and/or is incapable, because of a mental condition, of aiding counsel in his or her defense.

To the public, the finding of not guilty by reason of insanity is tantamount to an acquittal. In reality, those defendants who are so adjudicated may be subjected to longer confinement than if they had pled guilty. In many cases, a defendant found not guilty by reason of insanity is committed to a state mental hospital until he or she is found mentally healthy. Technically, this could be a few months, but it could also mean until death. In some jurisdictions defendants are placed in mental hospitals and may be tried if they are later declared sane. The frequency of the plea of not guilty by reason of insanity is greatly exaggerated. It usually occurs during the course of murder or serious assault cases, which seems to heighten public attention. Estimates of its successful use range from 2 to 5 percent. The actual decision of sanity is left to the court. In most jurisdictions, once the plea is entered, the accused must undergo psychiatric examination. Evidence resulting from this examination is presented in court, and the jury must then reach a decision.

The insanity plea is fraught with problems. First, the term is strictly a legal one. Psychologists and psychiatrists are concerned with mental disorders that are extremely difficult to define and diagnose, yet we expect them to make pinpoint decisions in court. Second, conflicting psychiatric testimony in court often confuses and baffles jury members who are not familiar with the terminology used or conditions discussed. Finally, it is very time consuming. Usually, both the prosecutor and the defense provide one to three expert witnesses to testify to the accused's mental status. Such testimony consumes valuable time, is often contradictory, and serves to further confuse the jury.

In the early 1980s, a number of politicians called for the abolition of the insanity defense. While it has not been abolished, several changes in the law have occurred. Several jurisdictions have established an assumption of sanity and placed the burden of proving insanity on the defense. This approach lessens the likelihood of a successful insanity defense. Some jurisdictions have also developed a "middle ground" defense of guilty but mentally ill. Under such laws, a defendant may be found guilty and sentenced like any other defendant but is also ensured of receiving treatment for her or his mental illness. Although the defense is plagued by serious problems and is in need of reform, to abolish it goes against one of the long-held foundations of law: Criminals must have the mental capacity to know that they are acting wrongfully. This is the same principle that protects infants and the severely retarded from criminal charges.

The plea of **nolo contendere** is essentially a plea of guilty. Its literal translation is "no contest." The consequence of a plea of nolo contendere is that it cannot be entered into the record of a subsequent civil proceeding. For example, A is driving a vehicle while under the influence of alcohol and runs into B's house. If A enters a plea of nolo contendere to the criminal charge of driving under the influence, B cannot use the plea as evidence of responsibility in a civil proceeding to hold A responsible for damages to the house. It does not mean that A cannot be held civilly responsible, only that his plea cannot be used in this regard. Other evidence (e.g., a breath or blood test or eyewitness accounts) may be used to find A liable. Courts vary widely on the acceptance of nolo contendere pleas. Only about half the states allow such a plea, and most limit the plea to specific offenses.

The plea of once in jeopardy is fairly infrequent. As the Fifth Amendment states, "nor shall any person be subject for the same offense to be twice put in jeopardy of life or limb." By pleading once in jeopardy, the defendant is contending that the current charge violates the Fifth Amendment. Usually, through counsel, the defendant will supply evidence contending that the accused has already been held accountable for this act. The court may review such a plea at that time or postpone the arraignment until it has had time to review the evidence.

PRETRIAL MOTIONS AND HEARINGS

In cases where the defendant pleads not guilty at the arraignment, there are usually several motions and hearings on those motions prior to the actual criminal trial. Most of these motions will be filed by the defense attorney. We must remember that these, in effect, are requests to the court, and usually the judge must issue a ruling on such requests. Some of the more common motions follow.

Motion for Change of Venue

Under the principles of due process, the defendant has the right to a trial in the jurisdiction in which the alleged crime occurred. This principle is called venue, meaning "place of trial." The rationale is that local norms, values, and attitudes should be reflected in jury composition.

The motion for a change of venue is usually reserved for the defense. The defense is asking to have the trial moved to another venue—county, district, or circuit. Usually, the motion is based on the contention that the defendant cannot obtain a fair trial in the court of original jurisdiction because of prejudice against him or her. For example, X, who has a prior criminal record, is accused of murdering Y, the only doctor in the county. X was formerly an employee of a local granary that went bankrupt and left many farmers in the community with heavy financial losses. Some factors, such as prior record, occupation, and nature of the crime and victim, may bear heavily on X's right to a fair trial. If X files for a change of venue, he or she must provide evidence or testimony to establish that prejudice and hostility exist. The judge makes the decision, and even if the request is denied initially, it may be honored later, particularly if there is difficulty selecting and impaneling the jury.

Motion for Continuance

Although the defendant's right to a speedy trial is guaranteed by the Sixth Amendment, it is quite common for trials to take place months and even years after the act for which the accused is being tried. Although there are many reasons for this delay, one of the most common is simply that there has been a request for a continuance.

Either party may ask for a continuance. These motions are usually made shortly after arraignment, but they can be made at any time. Motions for continuance must be accompanied by an explanation of the reasons additional time is needed. Some of the more common reasons are illness, unavailability of witnesses, defense counsel's workload being in conflict with the trial date, or defense counsel's inability to be prepared. In addition, the court may arrange for a continuance if it finds it is in the interest of justice, usually meaning that the docket is overcrowded and space and/or court personnel will not be available on the stated date of trial.

Motions for Suppression and Exclusion of Evidence

In 1961 in *Mapp* v. *Ohio* (see Appendix), the Supreme Court held that evidence obtained or seized illegally was inadmissible in criminal trials at the state level. From that time forward, defense attorneys have made motions to exclude evidence on the grounds that it has been obtained in violation of the Fourth Amendment. These motions are usually filed prior to the trial, and the judge conducts a hearing to determine the legality of the search that produced the evidence in question. These hearings are very important because the evidence in question is often the tie between the defendant and the crime, and without this evidence, the prosecutor may have only a circumstantial case. In addition, confessions made by the defendant may be subject to suppression motions if the confessions were made involuntarily, without counsel, or without the defendant's being informed of his or her rights pursuant to the *Miranda* decision (*Miranda* v. *Arizona*, 1965; see Appendix). Again, even if the judge suppresses the confession, this is not tantamount to an acquittal. Only the confession is suppressed. Other evidence, such as fingerprints, eyewitness identification, and possession of stolen property, may still be introduced to increase the likelihood of obtaining a conviction.

Motion for Discovery

In most states, the defense has the right to discovery, that is, to examine the prosecutor's evidence, including a list of proposed witnesses, prior to trial. The rationale for a **motion for discovery** is to ensure fairness in the trial (see In the News, "Prosecutors Undermine Cases"). Motions to exclude and suppress evidence often occur after the granting of a motion for discovery. The United States Supreme Court has held that due process requires disclosure of certain information prior to the trial (*Brady* v. *Maryland*, 1963). States vary in how broadly they apply discovery. Some allow full or complete discovery, whereas others are not as liberal. There is also the possibility of reciprocal discovery, in which both parties examine their opponent's evidence, but very few jurisdictions have adopted this practice.

Motion for Disclosure

The **motion for disclosure** is usually filed by the defense. If granted, the prosecution must produce a list of witnesses they intend to call with each witness's last known address. This list does not preclude the prosecution from calling additional witnesses if there is good cause for those witnesses' not having been included on the original list. Like discovery, the purpose of disclosure is to provide the defense with the opportunity to plan a strategy and to investigate the witnesses concerning their credibility. Like many other pretrial procedures, these motions are designed to balance the scales of justice (see In the News, "Prosecutors Undermine Cases by Failure to Heed the Rules of Law").

Motion for Dismissal

The defense will also frequently make a motion for judicial dismissal of the charges. If previous motions (e.g., exclusion and suppression) have been granted, the case may be weakened to the point that there is insufficient evidence on which to proceed. Motions to dismiss during pretrial stages do not bar prosecution at a later date if new evidence is uncovered.

PROSECUTORS UNDERMINE CASES BY FAILURE TO HEED RULES OF LAW

Outraged Judges Find City's Attorneys Still Withholding Evidence

By Caitlin Francke

The rules seem clear: Prosecutors must tell a defendant about any evidence that could help prove his innocence or reduce the extent of his guilt.

They must also show him all material they plan to use against him in a trial, a right that dates to the American Revolution and is incorporated as a guarantee in the U.S. Constitution.

But in Baltimore, city prosecutors continue to run afoul of these rules, enraging judges and defense attorneys and placing viable criminal cases at risk of being dismissed.

In just the past month, three criminal cases have highlighted how prosecutors' failure to turn evidence over to defense attorneys, a process known as discovery, can undercut cases and lead to delays.

The latest problems come two years after federal consultants concluded that slipshod discovery practices impeded justice in the city courts and 18 months after the disclosure of serious evidence violations prompted legislative hearings and the creation of a court to resolve discovery disputes.

"It is difficult to comprehend that this remains an issue," said Circuit Judge David B. Mitchell, who oversees the criminal docket. "You've got two years' worth of notice. You've got no-tice upon notice upon notice . . . that discovery is taken very seriously by this court.

"Prosecutors are sometimes not turning over information because they may not believe the information should be disclosed or the folder has gone through so many hands that the assistant state's attorney standing in court is not aware of what did or not did happen in the case," the judge said.

In the recent cases:

Four defendants found with $50,000 worth of cocaine and a loaded .22-caliber handgun received a light sentence because prosecutors did not disclose any basic evidence, including the search warrant for the house, until the day of trial, six months after the arrests.

The trial of four men accused in one of the worst mass killings in city history was postponed eight months—risking its dismissal—because prosecutors did not disclose statements given to police that indicate people in addition to the defendants may have been responsible for the crime.

In a police brutality case, the prosecutor did not disclose to defense attorneys a statement by the alleged victim that supports the officer's defense—prompting a city judge to chastise the prosecutor.

Continued

Asked to respond to the recent problems, Baltimore State's Attorney Patricia C. Jessamy's spokeswoman sent a copy of an order by the judge in the police brutality case. It says the prosecutor did not act in "bad faith" when she didn't turn over the evidence.

She did not respond further.

In the past, Jessamy has said she needs more law clerks to help handle the crush of paperwork owed to defense attorneys.

That reasoning does not apply in two of the recent cases. In those, prosecutors said in court they did not turn over evidence because it was not, in their view, "exculpatory," meaning that it did not prove a defendant's innocence or lessen his guilt.

The judges disagreed.

Part of the problem is that what constitutes exculpatory evidence can boil down to a matter of opinion. Prosecutors are allowed to choose which evidence in a case they believe should be turned over.

Judges are so frustrated by the discovery violations and trial delays that they are suggesting they intervene in the discovery process, handing over evidence or providing guidance to prosecutors.

Circuit Judge John N. Prevas was appointed in 1999 to resolve evidence disputes as part of a reform effort. Last year he handled about 50 cases, according to a local criminal justice think tank.

Two weeks ago, Prevas told prosecutor Elizabeth A. Ritter that she and other lawyers in her office "had better get better training" after he found that she did not disclose exculpatory evidence.

"If there continues to be a pattern of the state routinely concealing exculpatory evidence because they don't know what exculpatory means," then judges may have to take over the discovery process, Prevas said Jan. 29. "We may have to consider that if the state doesn't begin to get a more realistic picture of what exculpatory means."

Mitchell said defense attorneys who receive no evidence at all because of prosecutor sloppiness—such as that in the four-defendant drug case—should take the issue up with Prevas.

"If the defendants don't press, then the state is not going to give," Mitchell said.

But defense attorneys contend that it is the prosecutors' duty to provide information. Discovery rules require prosecutors to disclose certain evidence within 25 days of a suspect's arraignment, especially if it is exculpatory.

Exculpatory evidence is "any material or information tending to negate or mitigate the guilt or punishment of the defendant as to the offense charged," the rules say.

If evidence is not disclosed, it can be barred from trials, witnesses can be excluded from testifying and charges can be dismissed.

In the police brutality case, Prevas ruled that a police report that recounted an interview with the alleged victim was exculpatory for the defendant, Officer Clyde Rawlins Jr. In the interview,

Continued

the alleged victim acknowledged that he slapped the officer and recounted a scuffle with Rawlins that backs up the officer's version—information that suggests Rawlins was acting within the scope of his duties.

In addition, the victim, Larry Nathaniel, never mentioned that he was beaten, though his family members said he was.

Ritter, the prosecutor, never turned the report over to the defense. Rawlins' attorneys discovered it when it was anonymously placed in Rawlins' mailbox.

Prevas decided not to dismiss the case because the defense "fortuitously" got the information. He said the "embarrassment" of the hearing was Ritter's punishment.

In the mass killing case, prosecutor Lawrence C. Doan did not disclose to defense attorneys two statements that suggest that at least five other men were responsible for the slayings of five women in a Northeast Baltimore rowhouse until a few days before trial on Jan. 23.

Judge David Ross ruled that the statements did not exonerate the defendants but recommended that the case be postponed to allow the defense more time to investigate the information.

In one statement, a friend of the main eyewitness to the killings, Ronald McNeil, told police that McNeil named four men who McNeil believed were responsible for the killing of the women, in addition to those arrested.

Judge Mitchell, who must approve every postponement, told the lawyers that Ross felt it was "marginally exculpatory." He was furious that the information had not been disclosed earlier.

"If the state chose to do so, they could qualify this case for a death penalty," Mitchell thundered in a hearing Jan. 24. "This is not yesterday's simple homicide. These folks are defending these individuals who have a right to a defense. . . . You play it close to the vest, this is the consequence."

He set the case for September because one of the defense attorneys had a long federal death penalty case. His action could have led to the case's being dismissed.

On Friday, prosecutors salvaged the case when Mitchell agreed to have three defendants tried June 11. The fourth will be tried in September.

Also last month, punishment for four drug defendants evaporated because prosecutors failed to turn over basic evidence.

Two men and two women were arrested July 27 after police—armed with a search warrant—raided their house in the 6100 block of MacBeth Drive. Police found $50,000 worth of cocaine, a loaded .22-caliber handgun, two scales and $1,410 in cash.

The four were indicted on possession with intent to distribute drugs and use of a firearm during a drug trafficking offense, among other charges. Their trial was scheduled for Jan. 31.

In the six months between the arrest and the trial, prosecutors did not turn over any evidence, such as a copy of the search warrant. When the case came to trial, prosecutors asked for a

Continued

postponement to comply with discovery. Circuit Judge M. Brooke Murdock refused, calling the state's failure "inexcusable" and "outrageous."

She referred the case to Judge Wanda K. Heard, who that day was overseeing postponement court. When the defense attorneys told Heard they had not gotten any discovery, she was shocked.

"Nothing?" she asked incredulously. "Not a single solitary piece of discovery?"

Heard said the state's errors did not amount to reason for a postponement. She sent the case to Judge David Ross for trial that day.

Prosecutors quickly assembled the evidence and gave it to defense attorneys. When Ross asked why the evidence had not been turned over earlier, prosecutors said the case had changed hands and gotten lost in the shuffle.

Prosecutor Catherine C. Hester said she reviewed the file nine days before and did not realize that no discovery had been filed.

"I guess I will accept responsibility, Your Honor," Hester said.

Prosecutors and defense attorneys hastily agreed on plea agreements. At first prosecutors demanded five years in prison without parole, according to the defense. By the end, prosecutors agreed to shelve the cases against the women and give five-year suspended prison terms to the men.

This is how Ross explained the sentence in court records: "State prosecution in jeopardy because of failure to provide discovery."

"Virtually every judge on this court that sits in criminal cases is at the point of total frustation, and I expect to see outrage in the future. I've reached it. I'm past the point of outrage," Ross said. "Someone has got to tell Mrs. Jessamy that the state's attorney's office has got to figure out some way to learn how to comply with the discovery rules."

This is not a new problem for Jessamy's office.

In December 1998, a study paid for by the Department of Justice found that evidence was turned over in a "piecemeal fashion," creating a "substantial impediment" to the resolution of cases.

In 1999, *The Sun* chronicled serious evidence violations that led to the wrongful first-degree murder conviction of a man in a case the judge called an "injustice." The series also detailed how several cases had been dismissed by judges because police or prosecutors had bungled the evidence.

Legislative hearings were called, and Jessamy pledged to have all her division chiefs counsel lawyers on discovery procedures.

Mitchell said requests for postponements because of discovery problems have decreased since then. But it remains a problem.

"It should only be an exception when either side on the eve of trial discovers that information that should have been exchanged wasn't," the judge said. "The superior burden is on the state."

The Baltimore Sun, *February 11, 2001, p. 1A.*

Summary

1. The period from arrest to actual trial may be a very active one. Many activities are designed to ensure that the defendant will be afforded due process of law. Some of these procedures are brief and relatively uncomplicated, whereas others are very demanding in both time and energy. Many of the proceedings, such as bail and the use of grand juries, have been subject to controversy.

2. At the initial hearing, usually held within 48 hours of arrest, a probable cause determination is made.

3. Bail is the process of releasing a defendant prior to trial based on the promise that he or she will appear for the trial.

4. Presently, there are several proposals in various states to modify pretrial procedures. Most are attempts to shore up the insanity defense and to ensure that dangerous criminals are not released on bail.

5. Although pretrial procedures are beset with problems and may require re-examination, we must not lose sight of the fact that they also aid an already overcrowded court docket, save tax dollars by filtering out cases in which evidence is lacking, and afford constitutional protections to the accused.

Key Terms Defined

48-hour rule   The current standard for unnecessary delay, which is that an accused must be taken before a magistrate within 48 hours of arrest to determine whether probable cause exists to detain him or her further.

probable cause   The presence of sufficient facts to convince a reasonable person that some official action (arrest or charging) should be taken.

initial appearance   The first appearance of a person taken into custody before a judge (magistrate), at which time a decision is made as to whether probable cause to proceed exists and the person is notified of the charges against him or her and informed of his or her constitutional rights.

bail   The practice of releasing a defendant prior to trial with the promise that he or she will appear before the court as directed or will forfeit money or property (or some portion of it) accepted by the court as a guarantee of such appearance.

nulla poena sine crimine   No punishment without a crime.

bail bondsperson   A person who puts up bail money for others for profit.

preventive detention   Detention in jail between arrest and trial to prevent further injury or damage.

released on recognizance   Released on the promise to appear before the court at the appointed time without posting bail.

supervised release   Release of a defendant prior to trial without bail under the supervision of an assigned counselor.

grand jury   An investigative body whose duty is to determine whether to indict an accused.

ex parte proceeding   A proceeding at which only one party is represented (as in the case of the grand jury, where only the prosecution is allowed to present a case).

bill of indictment   Formal accusation issued by a grand jury.

prima facie case   Case in which "on the face of it" or "at first sight," the evidence is such that probable cause exists to charge the individual with a crime.

information   A formal, written accusation made by the prosecutor.

preliminary hearing   a probable-cause hearing in a criminal case.

arraignment   A court hearing at which the defendant is formally charged and asked to enter a plea.

nolo contendere   No contest (essentially, a plea of guilty).

motion for discovery   A motion to be allowed to examine the evidence of the other side prior to trial.

motion for disclosure   A motion to be provided with a list of the witnesses to be called at a trial.

Critical Thinking Exercises

1. What are some of the problems associated with the use of bail? Can you think of any ways to solve these problems so that bail might be effectively and fairly administered?
2. Compare and contrast the two methods of formal accusation. What are the advantages of an indictment over an information, or are there no advantages? Are there any dangers inherent in the use of informations? If so, what are they?

Internet Exercises

Pretrial procedures may seem rather complicated for those never having been arrested and arraigned. There are some organizations dedicated to helping defendants and the curious to understand these procedures.

1. What is the mission of the National Association of Pretrial Services Agencies (*www.napsa.org/pretrial.htm*)?
2. What other websites can you find that deal with pretrial issues? What sorts of information do they contain?

References

Argersinger v. *Hamlin*, 407 U.S. 25, 37 (1972).

Barlow, H. D. (2000). *Criminal justice in America.* Upper Saddle River, NJ: Prentice Hall.

Boorkman, D., Fazio, E. J., Jr., Day, N., & Weinstein, D. (1976). *Community-based corrections in Des Moines.* Washington, DC: U.S. Government Printing Office.

Boykin v. *Alabama*, 395 U.S. 238 (1968)

Brady v. *Maryland*, 373 U.S. 83 (1963).

Brady v. *United States*, 397 U.S. 742 (1969).

Castella v. *United States*, 350 U.S. 359 (1953).

Chamberlin, J. (1999). Private-sector enterprise (bounty hunters). *Economist, 351* (8124), 26–27.

Corrado, M. L. (1996). Punishment, quarantine, and preventive detention. *Criminal Justice Ethics, 15,* 3–13.

Fagan, J., & Guggenhiem, M. (1996). Preventive detention and the judicial prediction of dangerousness for juveniles: A natural experiment. *Journal of Criminal Law and Criminology, 86,* 415–48.

Ferdico, J. N. (1999). *Criminal procedure for the criminal justice professional.* Belmont, CA: West/Wadsworth.

Frankel, M., & Naftalis, G. (1977). *The grand jury: An institution on trial.* New York: Hill and Wang.

Galliher, J. F., & McCartney, J. L. (1977). *Criminology: Power, crime and criminal law.* Homewood, IL: Dorsey Press.

Gerstein v. *Pugh*, 420 U.S. 103 (1975).

Gibeaut, J. (2001, January). Indictment of a system. *ABA Journal, 87,* 34–40.

Gideon v. *Wainwright*, 372 U.S. 335 (1963).

Kalmanoff, A. (1976). Criminal justice enforcement and administration. Boston: Little, Brown.

Mallory v. *United States*, 354 U.S. 449 (1957).

Mapp v. *Ohio*, 367 U.S. 543 (1961).

McNabb v. *United States*, 318 U.S. 332 (1943).

Miranda v. *Arizona*, 384 U.S. 348 (1965).

Organized Crime Digest, 22, Legislature toughens grand jury system. (2001, January 31). 11.

O'Rourke, T. P., & Salem, R. G. (1968). A comparative analysis of pretrial procedures. *Crime and Delinquency, 14* (4), 367–73.

Rankin, A. (1964). The effect of pretrial detention. *New York University Law Review, 39,* 641.

Reaves, B. A. (1998). *Felony defendants in large urban counties 1994.* Washington, DC: U.S. Department of Justice.

Riverside County, California v. *McLaughlin*, 500 U.S. 144 (1991).

Santabello v. *New York*, 404 U.S. 257 (1971).

Suffet, F. (1966). Bail setting: A study of courtroom interaction. *Crime and Delinquency, 12* (4), 318–31.

United States v. *Calandra*, 414 U.S. 358 (1974).

United States v. *Salerno*, 481 U.S. 789 (1987).

Vera Institute of Justice. (1972). *1961–1971: Programs in criminal justice.* New York: Author.

Suggested Readings

Corrado, M. L. (1996). Punishment and the wild beast of prey: The problem of preventive detention. *Journal of Criminal Law and Criminology, 86,* 778–814.

Ferdico, J. N. (1999). *Criminal procedure for the criminal justice professional.* Belmont, CA: West/Wadsworth.

Goldkamp, J. S. (1995). *Personal liberty and community safety: Pretrial release in the criminal court.* New York: Plenum Press.

Richman, D. C. (1999). Grand jury secrecy: Plugging the leaks in an empty bucket. *American Criminal Law Review, 36* (3), 339–56.

CHAPTER TEN

Criminal Trial

Trial by jury remains the ideal of the American criminal justice network.
David R. Frazier/Stone

S even months later, Herman, who had been released from jail the previous month, was again arrested, this time for selling a large amount of narcotics to an undercover police officer. The prosecutor would not agree to a plea bargain this time, and Herman's attorney decided to go to jury trial rather than a bench trial before the judge.

A pool of jurors was selected from the list for the county, and potential jurors were questioned during voir dire. Both sides excluded jurors using challenges for cause (the prosecution excluding those who saw little wrong with legalizing drugs, the defense excluding those who indicated they thought people who sold drugs should be shot). Peremptory challenges (not for cause) were used by both sides to exclude people whose answers troubled the respective attorneys.

During the trial both real (physical) and testimonial evidence was introduced by the prosecutor during direct questioning. Cross-examination by Herman's attorney failed to discredit the evidence presented, and evidence presented on Herman's behalf was less than convincing. The judge occasionally excluded evidence objected to as hearsay and cautioned both attorneys not to use leading questions. Closing argument by the prosecutor was persuasive, and Herman was convicted.

A presentence investigation was conducted on Herman. The results were disastrous because they included information on all of Herman's previous convictions. At his sentencing hearing, Herman was given a lengthy prison sentence as mandated by law for his offense.

Key Terms

speedy trial
plea bargain
bench trial
summary trials
jury pool
venire
voir dire
challenges for cause
peremptory challenges
real evidence
testimonial evidence
direct questioning

cross-examination
redirect examination
recross-examination
expert witnesses
hearsay evidence
leading questions
presentation of the defense's case
closing argument
hung jury
sequester
presentence investigation

In Chapters 7, 8 and 9, we discussed the organization of the court systems, the roles of the various participants in those systems, and pretrial procedures. In this chapter, we describe and analyze the actual trial process by emphasizing legal requirements, some consequences of those requirements, and societal reaction to them.

THE RIGHT TO A SPEEDY TRIAL

The Sixth Amendment to the U.S. Constitution guarantees defendants in federal criminal cases the right to a **speedy trial,** and the court's decision in *Klopfer* v. *North Carolina* (1967) extended the doctrine to the state courts. In practice, however, many criminal trials still commence months and sometimes years after the filing of formal charges or arrest.

The speedy-trial doctrine is often criticized as being vague and ambiguous despite the fact that the Supreme Court has attempted to clarify the meaning of the doctrine through various decisions. In *Klopfer* v. *North Carolina* (1967), the court applied the speedy-trial doctrine to the states, recognizing it as a fundamental right of those accused of crimes. In applying this doctrine, the justices were attempting to protect the defendant from public scorn, protect the defendant's employment status, and limit the anxiety of those awaiting trial. In short, the Court clearly recognized the numerous hardships the accused may suffer if not afforded the right to a speedy trial.

In contrast, it is not uncommon for a defendant to benefit from judicial delay. The credibility and availability of witnesses diminishes with time. As a result, many defense attorneys waive their clients' rights to a speedy trial as a strategy. Can an accused use the speedy-trial doctrine as a defense if his or her attorney's actions have caused or contributed to the delay? In *Barker* v. *Wingo* (1972), the Court held that such cases must be decided after balancing four factors: (1) the length of the delay, (2) the reason for the delay, (3) the defendant's responsibility to assert his or her right to a speedy trial, and (4) the prejudice resulting from the delay. Although these tests are far from objective, they do represent attempts to clarify the issue and perhaps make it more difficult for a defendant to ask for continuances or fail to object to a prosecutor's motion for continuance and still challenge the proceedings on the basis of the violation of the right to a speedy trial.

Yet another major legal issue concerning speedy trial involves the determination of when the right commences. For example, Jones burglarizes Smith's house while Smith is vacationing. Five months later, when Smith returns home, he discovers that his stereo and some money are missing. Smith reports the crime to the police, but the perpetrator is not identified. Four months later, Jones is arrested on another charge, and a subsequent search of his premises uncovers Smith's stolen property. Obviously, the time lapse between the offense and the arrest is considerable, and it may be another four or five months before the case is brought to trial. Can Jones successfully claim that his right to a speedy trial has been violated?

In *United States* v. *Monroe* (1971), the Court held that the time period involved does not commence until an indictment or information has been issued or the accused has been arrested for a criminal charge. Most jurisdictions employ statutes of limitations that state the maximum allowable time period between the offense and formal accusation (after which time the offender can no longer be charged with the offense). This is not to be confused with the time period for a speedy trial. Most jurisdictions also have statutes specifying the time period involved in the speedy-trial doctrine. For instance, in Illinois, a defendant held in custody must be tried within 120 days, and one out on bail has the right to have his or her case heard within 160 days (*Illinois Criminal Law and Procedure,* 1995, chap. 725, sec. 5/103–5). At the federal level, the Speedy Trial Act of 1974 states that a defendant in a federal criminal case must be brought to trial within 100 days of arrest. Defendants can still, of course, waive their right to a speedy trial by filing motions for continuances. Only the prosecution is prohibited from prolonging the delay without good cause.

JURY TRIALS: A GREAT AMERICAN MYTH

One of the basic elements of the American criminal justice process is the right to a trial by jury. Like the right to a speedy trial, the right to trial by a jury of one's peers is guaranteed by the Sixth Amendment. This right was extended to defendants in state court proceedings through the Supreme Court's decision in *Duncan* v. *Louisiana* (1968). In a later decision, *Baldwin* v. *New York* (1970), the Court qualified the doctrine by holding that the right to trial by jury applies only in cases in which the defendant faces the possibility of a prison term of six months or more.

How frequently do jury trials actually occur? The vast majority of cases, about 90 percent, are actually settled by a plea of guilty that may occur at any time between the arraignment and the commencement of trial proceedings. The two major sources of guilty pleas are plea bargains and summary trials.

Plea Bargains

Although we have previously discussed plea bargaining (see Chapter 9), a closer look at the way it affects criminal trials is in order. You will recall that a **plea bargain** involves pleading guilty for some consideration. In his classic study of plea bargaining, Newman (1956) indicated that the considerations involved fall into four categories: considerations concerning charge, considerations concerning sentence, concurrent sentences, and dropped charges. In bargaining charges, the accused agrees to plead guilty to a charge less serious than the original charge to obtain less severe punishment. In bargaining for sentence, the accused pleads guilty to the original charge with the understanding that a lenient sentence will be recommended. In bargaining for concurrent sentences, the accused pleads guilty to more than one charge in return for receiving sentences that run concurrently. For example, a defendant may be arrested for one burglary, and during a legal search of his house, the police may find evidence that he also committed five other burglaries. If burglary is punishable by 5 years of imprisonment, the burglar, if found guilty of all six burglaries, could be sentenced to 30 years in prison. In a bargain for concurrent sentences, the burglar might agree to plead guilty to all six burglaries if the prosecutor agreed to sentence him to six concurrent terms of 5 years, in which case the defendant would actually serve a maximum of 5 years. In bargaining to drop charges, the defendant may agree to plead guilty to the most serious charge if all other charges against him are dropped. For example, Green is charged with aggravated battery, disorderly conduct, and resisting arrest. Green might plead guilty to the aggravated battery charge if the prosecutor agreed to drop the disorderly conduct and resisting arrest charges.

On several occasions, the courts have attempted to regulate plea bargaining. In *Boykin* v. *Alabama* (1969), the Supreme Court held that when a defendant enters a plea of guilty, it must be made in open court, and the defendant must be informed of the nature of the charge, the potential sentence, and the consequences of his or her plea. The Court noted that the accused is waiving the protections of both the Fifth (against self-incrimination) and the Sixth (of trial by jury and a right to confront one's accusers) Amendments and therefore that serious attempts must be made to ensure the voluntariness of the plea. As a result of the *Boykin* decision and a later decision in *Brady* v. *United States* (1970), most judges now question the defendant concerning the waiver of his or her rights, inform the defendant of the possible penalties on conviction, and ask if the plea is being entered voluntarily. In *Santobello* v. *New York* (1971), the Court held that the prosecutor must honor promises made during negotiations or the guilty plea may be withdrawn. In a later decision, *Bordenkircher* v. *Hayes* (1978), the Court determined that a prosecutor's threat to seek reindictment under a habitual criminal statute, if the defendant refuses to plead guilty to a lesser charge, does not violate due process. A more recent decision, *Ricketts* v. *Adamson* (1987), ruled that defendants must also live up to their terms of a plea bargain to receive leniency.

Plea bargaining is controversial for a variety of reasons. It is largely unobservable, and it eliminates citizen participation as jurors. Frequently, victims and witnesses appear at court only to find that their testimony and participation are not required because the case has been bargained. In some cases, plea bargaining makes a mockery of the justice network in that offenders may be convicted of charges quite different from those leading to their arrests and/or may receive punishments that are regarded as extremely lenient by victims and witnesses. Finally, some innocent parties may plead guilty to offenses they did not commit because they fear being convicted on more serious charges if they maintain their innocence to the point of trial (Gorr, 2000). Although the actual incidence of such cases is probably very low, all these criticisms combined led Alaska to prohibit the practice of plea bargaining, with few if any unpleasant side effects (Rubenstein & White, 1979). Other proposals to restrict plea bargaining involve increasing court resources and requiring preplea conferences in which the judge, victim, defendant, prosecutor, police, and defense counsel all meet and discuss the issues involved in resolving the case. Palermo, White, and Wasserman (1998) conclude that in spite of its critics, and in view of the overburdened legal system, plea bargaining is here to stay.

Summary and Bench Trials

The Sixth Amendment and the Supreme Court's decision in *Duncan* v. *Louisiana* (1968) have defined the right to trial by jury in serious cases. In *Baldwin* v. *New York* (1970), the Court went on to define a serious case as one in which the possible penalty is more than six months of imprisonment. In *Patton* v. *United States* (1930), the Court ruled that a defendant can waive his or her right to trial by jury. In a later decision, *Singer* v. *United States* (1965), the Court upheld a federal statute requiring that the waiver of trial by jury be contingent on approval of the prosecutor. But why would a defendant waive his or her right to a jury trial? Some defendants may feel that they will receive some consideration if they save the court's time by not invoking their right to a jury trial. Others may fear a jury because they are charged with an emotion-laden crime such as child molesting. Still others may seek the perceived dispassion of a neutral judge in deciding their fate. Whatever the reason, the federal court and most state systems permit waiver of the right to trial by jury. About 40 percent of those found guilty at trial are convicted by a judge in what is commonly referred to as a **bench trial** (Cole, 1995, p. 403).

Most criminal defendants are charged with misdemeanors or petty offenses rather than felonies and are not guaranteed the right to jury trial. Justice is dispensed for these individuals at **summary trials,** which are expedient for both the court and the defendant. A large number of cases can be dealt with in a short time period during which charges are read, guilty pleas accepted, and fines levied. If we add those dealt with in summary courts to defendants who waive their right to jury trial and those pleading guilty for considerations, it is apparent that only a small number of criminal defendants are tried by a jury of their peers.

The Jury Trial

Jury trials probably occur in between 2 and 8 percent of all criminal cases (King, 1999). The jury trial, nonetheless, remains important because it is one of the few areas in criminal justice in which members of the public are directly involved (as jurors, witnesses, and victims). Theoretically, the basic advantage of the jury trial is the assurance that the accused will be judged by a fair and impartial group. Specific procedures for selecting jurors have been developed to ensure that this occurs.

The selection of the jury involves a multistage process, the final result being a group of 12 (sometimes fewer) citizens chosen to decide the criminal case. First, a **jury pool** is randomly selected from the host community. So that a random cross-section of the community is maintained, a variety of lists, including tax rolls, voter registration lists, and utility lists, are used to ensure that no specific group of individuals (e.g., members of a racial or ethnic minority or gender) are systematically excluded. Recently, some jurisdictions have used licensed drivers as a source of jurors. This method is currently being used on an experimental basis in some federal courts. An individual listed in the jury pool is subject to service for a specified time period, generally three months.

Second, for each jury trial, a group of potential jurors are randomly selected, constituting the **venire,** the size of which varies according to the population of the jurisdiction. Members of the venire are legally summoned to appear in court on a specific date and will undergo yet another stage in the process to determine if they are to sit on a particular jury.

In the third and final stage of the process, both the prosecuting and the defense attorney question members of this panel in open court in the process of **voir dire** (literally, "look-speak," or to tell the truth). This process is intended to further guarantee a fair trial by allowing interested parties the opportunity to question jurors and discharge those who may be biased. For example, 30 people might be directed by the court to appear and be able to serve as jurors on a given date. In court, 12 members of this panel will be summoned to the jury box, where they must take an oath of honesty before answering questions under voir dire examination. Both attorneys will question prospective jurors concerning their knowledge about the case, their relationships with any of the participants, any opinions they may have formed about the case, and other pertinent issues. In some jurisdictions, including the federal courts, the trial judge questions the potential jurors using his or her own questions as well as those submitted by the prosecutor and the defense attorney. This method is used to promote efficiency and to avoid the attorneys' conditioning the jurors to their side of the case before the trial begins.

In determining the actual jurors, both attorneys may challenge (excuse) potential jurors by using challenges for cause and peremptory challenges. **Challenges for cause** are unlimited in number. In challenges of this type, the attorney asks the court to excuse a prospective juror because his or her responses to voir dire questions show an inability to view the case objectively. The judge makes the final decision on the basis of evidence heard during voir dire. Because challenges for cause are unlimited, most attorneys extensively question potentially hostile jurors in an attempt to prove bias and excuse such jurors.

Peremptory challenges are usually limited in number by statute. In some jurisdictions, an attorney is limited to 3 challenges, whereas in capital cases the number may range as high as 20. No reason has to be offered for a peremptory challenge, but because they are limited, most attorneys will try to save them and will challenge jurors for cause if possible. Both the state's attorney and the defense attorney have specific types of people they want to excuse, depending on the charge, and will often use peremptory challenges to exclude members of those groups. For example, in drunk driving cases prosecutors may want to exclude younger jurors because they are more likely to have recently engaged in similar behavior and will be less likely to return a conviction. In comparison, some defense attorneys will try to exclude females and deeply religious people from serving as jurors in rape cases. If the challenge for cause is not honored, the attorney may use one of his or her peremptory challenges to ensure that jurors with certain characteristics do not serve on a particular case.

Let us return to our example. Of the first 12 potential jurors, the prosecutor challenged 2 jurors, and the defense attorney challenged 3, which left 7. If both attorneys approve these 7, they will not be questioned further and will remain in the jury box until 5 more jurors have been accepted by the attorneys. Next, 5 new prospective jurors will replace those excused, and the voir dire examination will continue until 12 members have been chosen. The 12 selected will be sworn in, and the remaining members of the jury panel will be excused but are eligible to be called for future trials.

To many, the process of jury selection is one of the most important stages in the criminal process. Some attorneys attempt to stack the jury rather than to obtain a fair jury. It is common for both attorneys to employ investigators to conduct background investigations on prospective jurors so that they can conduct an extensive and complete voir dire and select a jury that is more open to their case. Additionally, in some high-profile cases, defendants will employ jury consultants. These consultants are experts who claim to be able to identify who will make the best jurors for the defendant's case.

In addition to the trial jury, many jurisdictions also select alternate jurors during voir dire. Alternate jurors remain in the courtroom and are able to replace an original juror who has to be excused during the trial. They do not participate in the deliberations unless there is a need to replace one of the 12 original jurors. This practice saves the court time and the defendant time and money because, without it, if a juror has to be excused during the trial, a mistrial would be declared and the entire process repeated.

Traditionally, juries have consisted of 12 individuals, as in our example above. The Supreme Court, however, has held that juries of 6 members do not violate constitutional guarantees (*Williams* v. *Florida*, 1970). The Court upheld a Florida statute permitting 6-person juries in noncapital cases. The Court contended that the 12-person jury was a historical accident and that the right to trial by jury did not specify the number of jurors. This decision does not, of course, require the use of 6-person juries, but it does permit the states to engage in the practice of using fewer than 12 jurors in noncapital cases if they so desire. Most states still employ 12-member juries, and those permitting juries of fewer than 12 often limit their use to misdemeanor cases or those in which both parties stipulate. Later, in *Ballew* v. *Georgia* (1978) and *Burch* v. *Louisiana* (1979), the Court deemed unconstitutional 5-member juries and nonunanimous verdicts from 6-person juries. The number of jurors and the issue of whether a unanimous decision is required are important; according to Dino (2000), when unanimous verdicts are required from large (12-member) juries, they seldom convict the defendant.

Another legal issue involved in jury trials centers on the composition of the jury. In *Glasser* v. *United States* (1942), the Court stated that a jury of one's peers means a random cross-section of the community. Thus, a white female is not entitled to be tried by a jury of all white females, but by a jury that is randomly drawn with all community members having an equal chance of being selected. In *Taylor* v. *Louisiana* (1975), the Court declared Louisiana's system of excluding females from jury service unconstitutional. Applying the *Glasser* ruling, we can see that this practice would not provide a cross-section of the community.

Although the Court has been explicit in demanding that jury lists not be drawn in a discriminatory manner, the use of peremptory challenges to exclude specific types of jurors remains controversial. Historically, there were no limits placed on the use of peremptory challenges, and in some instances, attorneys used peremptory challenges to fashion juries along social and racial lines. In 1986, the Supreme Court put an end to such practices in *Batson* v. *Kentucky*. The Court held in *Batson* that using peremptory challenges to eliminate jurors based on race violates the Fourteenth Amendment. Under certain circumstances, the prosecutor must now explain to the court his "race-neutral" reason for challenging a juror who is of the same race as the defendant. This procedure has received some criticism because it prolongs jury selection and interferes with the unfettered use of peremptory challenges. It has, however, become an entrenched part of the jury selection process. Recalling our discussion of voir dire, we can see why the use of peremptory challenges is limited and why attorneys consider their use important in courtroom strategy.

Those who support the practice of trial by jury argue that juries reflect community values, reduce the potential for bias, and are politically free. Those who oppose the jury system argue, for the most part, against the way the principle is applied rather than against the principle. One of their arguments focuses on jury composition. In most jurisdictions, citizens in certain professions are systematically excluded from jury duty (e.g., doctors, lawyers, teachers, and other professionals). Other qualified jurors can ask to be excused because jury duty will cause a hardship on them or their families. Who is left to serve? Some critics claim that juries are generally composed of the elderly, the uneducated, and bored homemakers. A further àrgument against juries centers on the decision-making process. Jurors receive no formal training; thus, if the charge that they are educationally unrepresentative is valid, their ability to reach a just decision is questionable. Juries have been accused of relying on characteristics of the parties involved rather than on the evidence presented to determine the outcome of cases (see In the News, "Juries, Their Powers under Seige".) Also, some challenge the ability of jurors to interpret the law, arguing that judges and attorneys who have studied and practiced for years have difficulty making legal applications. Recently, there has also been much concern about the issues of jury nullification. Nullification occurs when jurors, who are instructed to follow the applicable law, ignore the law to reach what they perceive a correct result. There is a dispute among legal scholars as to whether jury nullification is a legitimate exercise of power by a jury. Some analysts have suggested the verdict in O. J. Simpson's criminal trial was a product of jury nullification.

Once again we are faced with the dilemma of considering the cost of democratic involvement. Given that juries have made mistakes and have decided outcomes on the basis of nonlegal factors, is it worth the sacrifice to exclude the public from court involvement and to relinquish all power to criminal justice officials?

In the News

JURIES, THEIR POWERS UNDER SIEGE, FIND THEIR ROLE IS BEING ERODED

By William Glaberson

The role of the American jury, the central vehicle for citizen participation in the legal system, is being sharply limited by new laws, court rulings and a legal culture that is moving away from trials as a method of resolving disputes.

At the heart of the trend, some experts say, are fundamental questions about whether jurors who return huge awards and sometimes clear people who seem to be guilty are up to the task that has been assigned to them for centuries.

"We as a society have to decide: Do we want to have our justice system essentially run by experts—lawyers and judges—or do we want to retain a role for the jury?" said Valerie P. Hans, an expert on juries who is a professor at the University of Delaware.

Increased plea bargaining, tort-reform laws limiting jury awards, and Supreme Court rulings giving judges new power to screen the evidence presented to jurors are among many forces

Continued

marginalizing the role of the jury, some lawyers and judges argue.

Court statistics show, for example, that jury trials are a rapidly shrinking part of federal court caseloads, with only 4.3 percent of federal criminal charges now ending in jury verdicts, down from 10.4 percent in 1988. The number of federal civil cases resolved by juries has also dropped, to 1.5 percent from 5.4 percent in 1962.

And those awards that civil juries do make are being overturned with greater frequency. Federal appeals courts are reversing certain types of civil jury awards twice as often as they did a few years ago.

Meanwhile, the explosive growth of private arbitration as an alternative to the courts for consumer, workplace and business disputes is channeling tens of thousands of cases away from jury trials annually.

This trend is likely to continue. Because George W. Bush made what proponents call "reform" of the civil justice system a priority when he was governor of Texas, some legal experts predict that his new administration will accelerate efforts to limit jury power.

Although jury trials in modern times have long accounted for a small part of the legal caseload, judges and court experts say the diminishing role of the jury in state and federal courts reflects rapidly changing attitudes about how much power jurors ought to have. The judicial system's commitment to the jury as an institution, they argue, is being tested as never before.

"Why have a jury at all?" one former juror, Michael McCarthy asked bitterly in an interview.

Mr. McCarthy said he and his fellow jurors were outraged in December when a Houston judge told them that Texas' tort-reform law would require a reduction of more than $100 million in an award they had given the family of a pipefitter killed in an industrial accident at a Phillips Petroleum plastics plant in 1999.

The worker, Juan Martinez Jr., died when highly volatile chemicals exploded in a 500-degree fireball. The jury concluded that the accident had resulted from lax safety measures at the complex, which had experienced three explosions over 12 years, including one that killed 23 workers and injured 132 others in 1989.

Not everyone is critical of the trend limiting the role of juries. Some legal scholars, judges and business lawyers say that reining in juries is a necessity in an overloaded legal system. Others argue that juries must be controlled to limit excesses, and curb prejudices like hostility to big corporations.

"Not every legal rule that constrains a jury's discretion is an attack on the jury system," said David F. Levi, a federal district judge in Sacramento. "It may be a limit on raw power, but that may be what we need to have a fair system."

Among appeals judges, the growing skepticism of juries is reflected by their increasing willingness to overturn verdicts. In an analysis prepared for this article, Kevin M. Clermont and

Continued

Theodore Eisenberg, law professors at Cornell University, found that federal appeals courts reversed civil jury awards in injury and contract cases less than 20 percent of the time in 1987. Over the next decade, reversals rose to nearly 40 percent.

For those jurors who do decide cases, the experience can be mystifying. It can also be embittering.

Last spring, Tyrone N. Neal, a retired government printing worker, served on a case in which a young man had lost a leg because, he claimed, of improper care in a Maryland hospital. The jury Mr. Neal was on awarded the man $5.4 million.

When he learned during an interview that a judge had reduced the award to $515,000, Mr. Neal was disturbed. "It's like a slap in the face," he said. " 'We get your opinion and then we just go decide it our way.' "

Mr. McCarthy, the Houston juror, said his panel had concluded that only a big verdict would protect workers by showing the managers at Phillips Petroleum that there was a large cost associated with the repeated worker deaths. The award was $117 million, including $110 million in punitive damages, which Phillips' lawyers argued was excessive. They also said the complex was making strenuous efforts to improve safety for its workers.

The judge told the jurors it would almost certainly be cut to $11 million under Texas laws that sharply limit punitive damages.

"I felt betrayed," Mr. McCarthy said. "You think you've done a good service to the community and then you find out all your work has come to nothing."

Because the jury occupies a near mythical spot as the centerpiece of the justice system, its denigration has been discouraged by lawyers and judges in the past. Americans imported the vehicle from English common law, and it has long allowed for the expression of community values in the legal system.

But in recent years, events like the jury acquittal of O. J. Simpson on murder charges in 1995 have helped broaden the debate over the proper role of the jury.

In many states, advocates of tort reform have turned their cause into a populist political rallying cry, with billboards and radio advertising attacking "runaway juries." Some judges have spoken publicly about their skepticism of the jury system.

Last spring, John E. Babiarz Jr., a Superior Court judge in Delaware who headed a state jury study, made a speech proposing that the use of civil juries be sharply curtailed.

"It is simply impossible," Judge Babiarz said, "to achieve fairness when each case is decided by a different group of 12 people who are called to serve on a civil jury perhaps only once in their lives."

In a new survey of 594 federal trial judges nationally, 27.4 percent said juries should decide fewer types of cases. The survey, conducted by *The Dallas Morning News* and the Southern

Continued

Methodist University School of Law, is to be published this spring in the school's law review.

Some scholars argue that appeals judges are now substituting their own opinions for those of jurors.

In an age-discrimination case last spring, the Supreme Court reinstated a jury verdict in favor of a man who said he had been dismissed from his job after being told he was "too damn old." A federal appeals court had overturned the verdict. The Supreme Court, in turn, overruled the appeals court, saying it had "impermissibly substituted its judgment concerning the weight of the evidence for the jury's."

But the Supreme Court itself has done as much as any court in the country to accelerate the trend. In two major rulings in 1993 and 1999, the justices directed trial judges to screen technical and scientific testimony before it gets to jurors.

The limits on juries are being instituted not only by courts but also by Congress and state legislatures. In a series of articles last spring, *The Dallas Morning News* found that, often through legislation, 41 states imposed some limits on the types of cases juries could hear. Included are rules banning jury trials dealing with issues like consumer fraud.

Some judges say jury trials are a shrinking part of the legal system because lawyers distrust them. They ask for jury trials less often and, in turn, lose their ability to argue before ordinary people.

"You have a bar that is increasingly lacking in jury skills, and they distrust juries so they stay away from them," said Judge Patrick E. Higgenbotham of the United States Court of Appeals for the Fifth Circuit, which hears cases from Louisiana, Mississippi and Texas.

In the Maryland hospital case, two of the jurors said in interviews, the jury spent considerable time trying to find an amount that would compensate Gilford V. Tyler Jr., the man who had lost his leg as a result, the jury found, of the hospital's negligence. A spokeswoman for the hospital, Prince George's Hospital Center, said Mr. Tyler had appropriate care.

The judge, Thomas P. Smith of Circuit Court in Prince George's County, agreed that the jury's verdict had been fairer than the reduction to the $515,000 the hospital's lawyers demanded.

"The thought that the injuries sustained by plaintiff are in any way compensated by $515,000," the judge said in a hearing, was "abhorrent."

But in January he ruled that Maryland law required him to reduce the jury award to the lower amount. Mr. Tyler's lawyers are appealing to Maryland's highest court, claiming the law is unconstitutional.

In the meantime, the jurors who heard Mr. Tyler's case are wondering whether the legal system values the work they did.

"In one sense," said Elizabeth Pearson, a retired postal worker who was on the jury, "it does seem like a waste of time."

The New York Times, *March 2, 2001, p. A1.*

Order of Trial

There are well-established procedures in jury trials. As we have discussed, the voir dire examination is the first step in the process. Additional steps include opening statements, presentation of evidence, closing arguments, jury instructions, deliberation, return of the verdict, sentencing, and appeal.

Once the jury has been selected, charges will be read in open court, and the judge will ask both parties if they wish to make opening statements. Because the burden of proof rests with the state, the prosecutor makes his or her opening statement first. The defense attorney may make his or her opening remarks immediately after the prosecutor or in some jurisdictions may wait until later in the proceedings. Opening statements can be waived, but this is rare in major felony trials. There are at least two good reasons for making opening remarks. First, they can provide the jury with a general overview of what the attorney intends to prove and how he or she intends to prove it. Second, the opening statement can help the attorney establish rapport with the jury if he or she maintains good eye contact, talks to the jurors in a personal manner, and explains to the jurors how important their role is in the criminal justice process. Opening statements are not to be argumentative, and lawyers are generally required to prove later, with evidence, any claims they made in opening statements.

The state has the burden of proving (1) that a crime was committed and (2) that the accused was the offender. The prosecutor (state's attorney or district attorney) always presents the state's case first. The prosecutor will rely on real evidence and testimony to present his or her case. **Real evidence** consists of objects that can be seen by the judge and/or jury. **Testimonial evidence** is simply evidence entered by a witness. When the prosecutor calls and questions a particular witness, he or she is engaging in **direct questioning.** The term is also applied to witnesses called and questioned by the defense attorney. Because the Sixth Amendment guarantees the accused the right to confront his or her accusers, the opposing attorney (in this case, the defense attorney) is provided an opportunity to cross-examine each witness. During **cross-examination,** attempts may be made to discredit the witness or to lessen the impact of the witness's testimony. For example, a witness testifies under direct examination that he or she saw the accused engaging in criminal activity. Under cross-examination, the defense attorney may ask questions concerning the distances involved, the witness's eyesight, or any other factor that might refute the witness's testimony. Cross-examination is limited in scope. The attorney administering cross-examination can ask only questions related to testimony given under direct examination; questions of untouched areas cannot be asked. Once cross-examination is completed, the party calling the witness will be provided the opportunity for redirect examination, again being limited to testimony challenged during cross-examination. **Redirect examination** is usually an attempt to clarify points challenged in cross-examination. The opposing party is also provided with a second line of questioning in **recross-examination** and is limited to evidence discussed during redirect examination. As you can see, the rules governing testimony are specific and act as a filter in terms of the quantity of testimony covered.

The prosecutor will proceed by calling all the witnesses named in disclosure and will provide the defense counsel with the opportunity to cross-examine each witness. When the prosecution has concluded calling all his or her witnesses, the state will rest its case.

Once the prosecution has rested its case, the defense attorney will usually move to dismiss the charges because the state has failed to reasonably prove that the accused committed the offense. In ruling on such a motion, the trial judge is required to view the state's evidence in a light most favorable to the prosecution. Although the motion is generally denied, the judge retains the authority to halt the proceedings if he or she believes that the state has failed to prove the charges. By moving to dismiss the charges at this time, the defense attorney is attempting to have the case dismissed, to lay foundation for possible postadjudicatory appeals, or both.

Before we continue with our discussion of the stages in the trial process, we need to analyze some of the rules of evidence. Real evidence includes such objects as weapons, fingerprints, shell casings, blood samples, and any other physical objects relevant to the proceedings. Before real evidence can be introduced, proper foundation must be provided. For example, in a murder case, the prosecutor must establish that a homicide has occurred and the type of weapon used before the weapon can be entered into evidence. The process of laying proper foundation may be quite lengthy and involve several witnesses, including doctors, victims, witnesses, and laboratory technicians.

Closely related to the rule of laying foundation is the requirement to certify expert witnesses. **Expert witnesses** can answer hypothetical questions and render opinions, whereas lay witnesses can only testify to facts. Certifying an expert witness includes questioning the witness as to his or her education, experience, record of publication, and participation in other cases to prove that the witness possesses a special skill or ability enabling him or her to give an opinion. Qualifying a witness as an expert may provide greater credibility for the witness's testimony and, consequently, affect the judge's or jury's decision (Foot, Stolberg, & Shepherd, 2000). It is this concern that justifies strict controls in qualifying a witness as an expert.

In television and movie trials, one often observes the attorneys objecting to the introduction of direct evidence. Normally, these issues would have been decided during pretrial suppression hearings, but the attorney may enter an objection to make that objection a part of the court record, which is generally required to preserve the issue for an appeal.

One of the more well-known rules of evidence is the hearsay rule. Generally, **hearsay evidence** is inadmissible. A witness may testify that she saw the accused rob a liquor store but cannot testify that a third party told her that he saw the accused commit the robbery. There is a growing list of exceptions to the hearsay rule, and time and space do not permit a detailed analysis of all these exceptions. For instance, there are 24 exceptions to the rule against hearsay in the federal rules of evidence. Common exceptions might include excited utterances and dying declarations. Generally, the rule still applies, but we suggest that the reader consult his or her jurisdiction's criminal code to learn the exceptions.

The last rule we will cover is that of leading the witness. An attorney is prohibited from asking **leading questions.** From a practical viewpoint, this problem is rare under current practices. Most attorneys meet with their witnesses prior to the trial and coach them as to what questions will be asked and how to present their testimony. Because of the familiarity with the questions, the witness can anticipate upcoming questions and the attorney can easily avoid charges of leading the witness. Leading questions are acceptable when inquiring into background information from a witness.

Another issue that has received much discussion in recent years is whether to allow jurors to ask questions during the trial. The recent trend in some courts is to allow jurors to question witnesses on a limited basis. Additionally, judges have always had the authority to question witnesses.

The rules presented here represent only a portion of the many rules governing the trial and the presentation of evidence, but they are among the most frequently used.

The next stage in the proceedings is the **presentation of the defense's case.** If defense counsel did not make opening statements at the commencement of the proceedings, he or she will make them here. The defense attorney will then present his or her case in much the same manner and by the same rules of evidence as the prosecution presented its case. The defense is not required to present a case, but it normally does so to refute the state's evidence. Common strategies include offering an alibi, casting doubt on the motive, introducing contradictory testimony, or employing an affirmative defense. Once the defense has called and questioned all its witnesses, it will rest its case.

The next stage in the proceedings is the closing arguments. In some jurisdictions, the order of presentation is reversed at this stage: The defense will present closing arguments first, and the prosecution will follow. During a **closing argument,** the parties summarize their arguments and attempt to conclusively prove their version of the case. Some lawyers also employ dramatic and emotional pleas in an attempt to affect the trial's outcome. The closing arguments are the attorneys' last chance to reach the jury before deliberation, and it is often felt that the impact of closing arguments outweighs the evidence presented. There are few limitations on closing arguments, but lawyers are not allowed to do such things as make inflammatory or highly prejudicial comments or refer to a defendant's refusal to testify.

When closing arguments have concluded, the judge will charge the jury to render a true and just verdict and will provide them with legal instructions. The instructions stage requires the judge to explain the laws that apply to the case. For example, in homicide cases the judge may have to explain differences between varying degrees of murder or between murder and manslaughter. In many cases the judge also instructs the jury as to what constitutes reasonable doubt. Oftentimes the parties may disagree as to the proper instructions. An instructions conference is usually held in which the lawyers submit their version of the instructions to the judge and the judge, after listening to arguments from both parties, decides what instructions to give to the jury. Jury instructions are a common source of appeals in criminal cases. Those who argue against the jury system often contend that most jurors are incapable of understanding such instructions, which may vary in length from a few minutes to hours. In an attempt to alleviate this problem, jurors are sometimes permitted to take sets of written instructions with them into deliberations.

After they have received their instructions, the jurors retire to a private area in which they deliberate the outcome of the case. The bailiff generally serves as a link between the jury and the judge. A first step in most deliberations is the selection of a jury foreperson, who will preside over the deliberations. The jurors then discuss the case, examine the evidence presented, and may refer to transcripts to clear up disagreements or settle disputes. Some court rules limit or prohibit the use of transcripts in the jury room. Eventually, the jurors take a vote on the guilt or innocence of the defendant, Traditionally, votes had to be unanimous before a guilty verdict could be returned, but in *Johnson* v. *Louisiana* (1972) and *Apodaca* v. *Oregon* (1972), the Supreme Court upheld verdicts of 10 to 2 as constitutional in felony and capital cases. However, most jurisdictions still require unanimous decisions and if the first vote is not unanimous, require that the jury return to deliberation and attempt to produce a unanimous decision concerning guilt. If the jurors cannot reach such a decision, the jury is referred to as a **hung jury,** and a decision concerning retrial must be made.

During some trials, publicity concerning the trial becomes an issue. When publicity is extensive, the judge may feel that it is difficult to maintain an impartial jury and may choose to **sequester** the jurors, that is, to isolate them physically from news and other sources of information that might affect their decisions. Because sequestering is a costly operation, it is normally reserved for very highly publicized or sensitive cases.

Once the jurors have reached a decision, the foreperson notifies the judge, and court is called back into session. The defendant is asked to stand, and the verdict is read aloud. The return of the verdict is a brief but important part of the trial procedure. If the verdict is not guilty, charges are dismissed, and the defendant is released. If the verdict is guilty, the judge usually sets a date for sentencing and then recesses.

SENTENCING

Sentencing in most cases poses no particular problem for the judge. In cases involving plea bargaining, the judge generally accepts the recommendation of the prosecutor as to the sentence. In summary trials, penalties are often standardized by specific fines for specific offenses. In those cases resolved by criminal trial, however, sentencing is often considerably more problematic.

Sentencing by the judge follows the verdict.
Bob Daemmrich/The Image Works

By and large, sentencing is the exclusive province of the judiciary. A few states provide for jury sentencing, but such sentencing is normally limited to cases involving the possibility of the death penalty. The defendant has a right to be represented by counsel at the sentencing hearing. The major complaint against current sentencing practices has to do with sentence disparities. Although some disparities are bound to occur, critics argue that sentencing disparities in many cases represent discriminatory practices, generally based on race, social class, gender, or some combination of those factors. There is little doubt that some judges do engage in discriminatory sentencing, but the judiciary is certainly not the sole body responsible for the overrepresentation of minorities and lower-social-class inmates in prison. As we have indicated before, discrimination based on these factors occurs at all levels of the criminal justice network: in reporting crimes, in making arrests, in deciding to prosecute, and so on. Differential treatment at each of these levels determines the characteristics of those individuals who proceed to the trial and sentencing stages.

Judges have considerable discretion in imposing sentences, as we have previously noted. Several factors appear to affect sentencing decisions, including the judge's view of the defendant (e.g., tough or remorseful), the ethnicity or race of the defendant (Steffensmeier & Demuth, 2000), the political ramifications of the case, the nature of the offense, the availability of prison space, and, perhaps, the gender of the judge. Songer and Crews-Meyer (2000) studied the impact of state supreme court judges' gender over a 10-year period on decisions involving obscenity and death penalty cases. They conclude that women judges tend to vote more liberally on both issues than their male counterparts and that the presence of women judges tends to increase the probability that male judges will support a more liberal position.

Although sentencing is a complex process, few law schools provide much training in sentencing, and few lawyers who become judges have much prior experience with sentencing. As a result of these shortcomings and the fact that social scientists have very little good information on the effects of various types of sentences, most judges sentence on a trial-and-error basis. There is, however, a national trend to send judges to sentencing institutes and workshops such as those provided by the National Judicial College in Reno, Nevada. Such workshops are intended to help judges better understand sentencing options and their consequences and perhaps to reduce sentencing disparities.

Another attempt to reduce the problem of disparate sentencing has been a shift from indeterminate to determinate sentencing. In indeterminate sentencing, the judge would sentence a convicted party to an indefinite period in prison (e.g., two to five years). Prison officials and parole boards actually determine the length of the sentence as a result of their involvement in granting good time and early release. In determinate sentencing, the legislature provides a range of possible sentences, and the judge must impose a specific sentence within these parameters. For example, the penalty for robbery might be 5 to 25 years, and a judge sentencing a guilty party would have to determine the specific number of years to be served (e.g., 11 years). At this point, whatever its other positive contributions, determinate sentencing does not appear to have had much impact on sentencing disparity. In much the same way as the federal government, Minnesota and Kansas have implemented sentencing guidelines. These guidelines limit judicial discretion by creating sentencing grids that are based on the seriousness of the offense, the defendant's criminal history, and other relevant factors (see In the News, "Ex-D.C. Detective Gets One Year for Contempt"). The grids are to be strictly followed and allow little range in which to sentence each particular defendant. In another attempt to reduce sentencing disparity, some jurisdictions allow a judge to depart from the normal sentencing range, whether upward or downward, if certain exceptional circumstances exist. The sentencing guidelines approach remains controversial. Some experts believe it strips the judge of too much sentencing discretion and dehumanizes the sentencing process. Other critics charge that disparities are built in to the scheme and result in inequitable impacts on certain classes of defendants.

One of the decisions made by the judge with respect to sentencing concerns the issue of sentences for multiple offenses. The judge must decide whether such sentences will be concurrent or consecutive and in some cases whether to invoke habitual criminal statutes. Suppose, for example, that a defendant has been convicted of rape and kidnapping and is sentenced to concurrent terms of 30 years for rape and 10 years for kidnapping. The maximum time that could be served would be 30 years. If the sentences were imposed consecutively, the maximum time to be served would be 40 years. Under habitual criminal statutes, persons convicted of committing three or more felonies in a given time period may be sentenced to life imprisonment. Judges' decisions concerning whether to sentence under these statutes contribute to the controversy surrounding sentencing.

In the News

Ex-D.C. Detective Gets One Year for Contempt; Judge Received Phony Reference Letters

By Bill Miller

Johnny St. Valentine Brown Jr., the former D.C. police detective convicted last year of perjury, got an additional one-year prison term yesterday for submitting a batch of phony letters to the court that attested to his "redeeming" character.

The sentencing concluded another chapter in the strange saga of Brown, who for more than 20 years won acclaim—and helped secure convictions—as the D.C. police department's top narcotics expert at criminal trials.

Brown's career ended in 1999 when it turned out that he had been lying under oath about his educational background. He later pleaded guilty to eight perjury counts resulting from testimony in drug cases. Then came the bogus letters.

Last month, Brown admitted in court that he wrote and sent four letters in hopes of getting a break at his sentencing in the perjury case. The letters, purportedly signed by community leaders and friends, were full of tributes to Brown and condemnations of the U.S. attorney's office.

At Brown's sentencing in June, U.S. District Judge Henry H. Kennedy Jr. made reference to the correspondence and said he found that Brown was a "good man." Kennedy gave Brown a two-year term for perjury, instead of the maximum 2½ years.

The ruse fell apart when Kennedy contacted the supposed letter writers after the sentencing to thank them for their interest. They included the Rev. Walter E. Fauntroy Jr., pastor of New Bethel Baptist Church and a former D.C. delegate to Congress, who told the judge that he didn't know Brown and that he had written nothing on Brown's behalf.

After an FBI investigation turned up copies of the letters on Brown's home computer, Brown, 58, pleaded guilty last month to contempt of court. Yesterday, he appeared before U.S. District Judge Thomas F. Hogan, who gave him the one-year term.

In conversations with the FBI, the purported letter writers denied any part in the letters, but Brown said he believed that he had authorization to write them. Although Brown said writing the letters himself was much extra work, he explained the logic behind it: "Certainly, no one can write a better letter about me than me."

Assistant U.S. Attorney Randall D. Eliason said Brown was nothing but a con man.

Continued

Hogan said he believed that Brown intentionally deceived Kennedy. Brown's lies were no different from those of a police officer who manufactures evidence in a case in hopes of sealing a conviction, and his conduct harmed the entire police force, Hogan said.

Brown's initial troubles stemmed from his testimony at trials that he was a registered pharmacist and had a doctorate in pharmacology from Howard University. Hogan said yesterday that he does not understand why Brown began lying about himself many years ago—something prosecutors said he did in hundreds, if not thousands, of cases.

The Washington Post, March 2, 2001, p. B4.

More recently, there has been a movement to enact truth-in-sentencing legislation, which requires a convicted person to serve a specified portion of his or her sentence (generally 80 to 85 percent) before he or she is eligible to be released from prison.

Prior to passing sentence, the judge will normally require a **presentence investigation.** This investigation is the responsibility of the probation officer and is used to provide the judge with information on which to base a sentencing decision. The probation officer prepares a report that is made available to the judge, the prosecutor, and the defense counsel. Information contained in the report includes prior criminal record, employment, family, military history, length of residence in the community, and in some cases a recommendation from the probation officer concerning sentence. When properly conducted, the presentence investigation can be very valuable to the judge. However, two major problems characterize such investigations. First, because of heavy caseloads, some probation officers do not conduct in-depth investigations and/or fail to verify all the information contained in the report. Second, presentence reports are often highly subjective, and the biases of the probation officer simply replace those of the judge. Carter and Wilkins (1967) found that in California, judges follow the recommendations of probation officers as much as 96 percent of the time. If this is the case nationally, a great deal of sentencing power has been relinquished by judges.

The network approach to criminal justice makes clear the impact of the sentencing decision on various components of the network. To the extent that the judge makes an appropriate sentencing decision, the public is protected for at least some period of time from further crimes by the offender, and the police will not be involved with rearrest or the prosecutor with preparing for another trial. Further, caseloads of probation officers, prison personnel, and parole boards are largely determined by the judges' decisions at sentencing hearings. In some hearings, political ties clearly affect the judge's decision and, for that matter, may affect whether the case is heard on appeal by the higher courts. Inappropriate decisions at this stage also have obvious (and often less desirable) consequences for the various segments of the criminal justice network.

APPEALS

Even after the sentence has been imposed, there is no guarantee that a criminal case is over. Convicted parties generally enjoy the right to appeal. Appellate courts review trial transcripts for legal errors, such as improper jury instructions or improperly admitted evidence, because the appellate court is limited to consideration of the trial record only. Such review does not constitute a new trial. Appellate courts overturn approximately 13 percent of the cases they review (Tanaford & Penrod, 1986).

Summary

1. The process of adjudication in criminal cases is complex and often controversial.

2. Most criminal cases are resolved through plea bargaining or summary trials, which involve guilty pleas.

3. In the small percentage of cases decided by a jury, both legal and nonlegal factors play a major role, as can be seen in the selection of jurors, the presentation of cases by opposing counsel, and sentencing disparities.

4. During the actual criminal trial, the order of presentation and the types of evidence admitted are governed by a set of procedural regulations.

5. The determination of sentence for those individuals found guilty is one of the most difficult duties of the judge.

6. The judge typically requires a probation officer to conduct a presentence investigation and frequently follows the recommendation of the probation officer in sentencing.

Key Terms Defined

speedy trial   Trial without unreasonable delay.

plea bargain   An agreement between the prosecution and defense (and sometimes the judge) concerning charges, plea, and often, sentence.

bench trial A trial in which evidence is heard and a decision rendered by a judge without a jury.

summary trials Trials in which there is no need to resolve factual issues (as when a defendant pleads guilty to a misdemeanor).

jury pool A group of citizens formed by using a number of lists in an attempt to attain a representative cross-section of potential jurors in the jurisdiction.

venire The pool of citizens from which jurors are selected for a particular trial.

voir dire Look-speak; the process of examining potential jurors to determine whether they are acceptable as actual jurors.

challenges for cause Objections to a prospective juror generally based on demonstrated (usually during voir dire) inability to view a case objectively.

peremptory challenges Objections to a prospective juror for which no cause need be stated.

real evidence Demonstrative evidence consisting of objects seen by the jury.

testimonial evidence Evidence given verbally by a witness.

direct questioning The initial questioning of a witness in a trial by the attorney who called the witness.

cross-examination The initial questioning of a witness called by an opposing attorney during a trial.

redirect examination Additional questioning of a witness during a trial by the attorney who called the witness.

recross-examination Additional questioning of a witness during a trial by an opposing attorney.

expert witnesses Persons possessing special knowledge or skills who (following proper certification) are allowed to testify at a trial concerning both facts and conclusions that may be drawn from those facts.

hearsay evidence Secondhand evidence; information provided to the witness by another party that has not been substantiated by the personal observations of the witness.

leading questions Questions that lead the witness to answer in a particular way.

presentation of the defense's case The stage in a trial when defense counsel presents the case for the defendant.

closing argument A summary of the evidence presented in a trial, generally intended to indicate that the evidence presented by the attorney presenting the argument has supported his or her version of the facts in a case.

hung jury A jury that cannot reach a decision as to innocence or guilt.

- arrest -
initial appearance
administration of bail
formal charging of the accused
preliminary hearing
arraignment
concepts of discovery / disclosure

___

initial appearance -
:g. to determine if
bable cause existed for
_ arrest

if yes - informed of
arges, written copy

formal charging of accused
review evidence to ensure
solid case to go forward
) grand jury - accusatory
only: probable cause
→ billy indictment

3) information - written
charge issued by Prosec.

④ Prelim. hearing
same purpose as grand jury

⑤ arraignment
reads /explains charges in open
court : Def. pleads
not guilty → date for trial

⑥ pretrial motions:

sequester To isolate (as in isolating a jury from media presentations while the jury is deliberating a case).

presentence investigation An investigation conducted by a probation officer to help the judge determine an appropriate sentence.

Critical Thinking Exercises

1. Several court decisions have attempted to clarify the meaning of "speedy trial." Discuss the importance of the following cases in this context: *Klopfer v. North Carolina* and *Barker v. Wingo*. Why is the concept of a speedy trial so important to defendants?

2. Plea bargaining is an important feature of the criminal justice network. Explain the dynamics of plea bargaining, and discuss the arguments supporting and opposing plea bargaining. Do you see a future without plea bargaining?

Internet Exercises

Finding a good defense attorney and understanding the trial process are both important to criminal defendants.

1. Go to *www.alawyers.com/asn.htm* on the Web. Could you find a criminal defense attorney using this site? An attorney specializing in juvenile justice? How are these attorneys selected for inclusion on this website?

2. If you needed information on previous criminal cases, could you find it using *www.findlaw.com/lawschools/outlines/criminal.html*? Would this website help you locate a law school? Could you find information to help you prepare for law school admissions tests from this same site?

References

Apodaca v. *Oregon*, 406 U.S. 404 (1972).
Baldwin v. *New York*, 399 U.S. 66 (1970).
Ballew v. *Georgia*, 435 U.S. 223 (1978).
Barker v. *Wingo*, 407 U.S. 514 (1972).
Batson v. *Kentucky* 476 U.S. 79 (1986).
Bordenkircher v. *Hayes*, 98 S. Ct. 663 (1978).
Boykin v. *Alabama*, 395 U.S. 238 (1969).
Brady v. *United States*, 397 U.S. 742 (1970).
Burch v. *Louisiana*, 441 U.S. 130, 138 (1979).
Carter, R. M., & Wilkins, L. T. (1967, December). Some factors in sentencing policy. *Journal of Criminal Law, Criminology, and Police Science, 58,* 503–14.
Cole, G. F. (1995). *The American system of criminal justice.* Belmont, CA: Wadsworth.
Dino, G. (2000). Jury verdicts and preference diversity. *American Political Science Review, 94* (2), 395–406.

Duncan v. *Louisiana*, 391 U.S. 145 (1968).

Foot, M. T., Stolberg, A. L., & Shepherd, R. (2000). Attorney and judicial perceptions of the credibility of expert witnesses in child custody cases. *Journal of Divorce and Remarriage, 33* (1/2), 31–45.

Glasser v. *United States*, 315 U.S. 60 (1942).

Gorr, M. (2000). The morality of plea bargaining. *Social Theory and Practice, 26* (1), 129–51.

Illinois Criminal Law and Procedure, 1995. (1995). St. Paul, MN: West.

Johnson v. *Louisiana*, 406 U.S. 356 (1972).

King, N. J. (1999). The American criminal jury. *Law and Contemporary Social Problems, 62* (2), 41–67.

Klopfer v. *North Carolina*, 386 U.S. 213 (1967).

Newman, D. J. (1956). Pleading guilty for consideration: A study of bargain justice. *Journal of Criminal Law, Criminology, and Police Science, 46*, 780–90.

Palermo, G. B., White, M. A., & Wasserman, L. A. (1998). Plea bargaining: Injustice for all? *International Journal of Offender Therapy and Comparative Criminology, 42* (2), 111–21.

Patton v. *United States*, 281 U.S. 276 (1930).

Ricketts v. *Adamson*, 483 U.S. 1 (1987).

Rubinstein, M. L., & White, T. (1979). Plea bargaining: Can Alaska live without it? *Judicature, 62* (6), 266–79.

Santobello v. *New York*, 404 U.S. 257 (1971).

Singer v. *United States*, 380 U.S. 24 (1965).

Songer, D. R., & Crews-Meyer, K. A. (2000). Does judge gender matter? Decision making in state supreme courts. *Social Science Quarterly, 81* (3), 750–62.

Steffensmeier, D., & Demuth, S. (2000). Ethnicity and sentencing outcomes in U. S. federal courts: Who is punished more harshly? *American Sociological Review, 65* (5), 705–29.

Tanaford, S., & Penrod, S. (1986). Jury deliberations: Discussion content and influence processes in jury decision making. *Journal of Applied Social Psychology, 16*, 322–47.

Taylor v. *Louisiana*, 419 U.S. 522 (1975).

United States v. *Monroe*, 404 U.S. 307 (1971).

Williams v. *Florida*, 399 U.S. 78 (1970).

Suggested Readings

Brock, D. F., Sorenson, J., & Marquart, J. W. (2000). Tinkering with the machinery of death: An analysis of the impact of legislative reform on sentencing of capital murders in Texas. *Journal of Criminal Justice, 28* (5), 343–49.

Gorr, M. (2000). The morality of plea bargaining. *Social Theory and Practice, 26* (1), 129–51.

Kaminer, W. (1999, September/October). Games prosecutors play. *American Prospect, 46*, 20–26.

King, N. J. (1999). The American criminal jury. *Law and Contemporary Social Problems, 62* (2), 41–67.

Palermo, G. B., White, M. A., & Wasserman, L. A. (1998). Plea bargaining: Injustice for all? *International Journal of Offender Therapy and Comparative Criminology, 42* (2), 111–23.

Steffensmeier, D., & Demuth, S. (2000). Ethnicity and sentencing outcomes in U.S. federal courts: Who is punished more harshly? *American Sociological Review, 65* (5), 705–29.

Weinreb, L. (1994). *Leading constitutional cases on criminal justice, 1994 edition.* Westbury, NY: Foundation Press.

CHAPTER ELEVEN

Victims and Witnesses in the Criminal Justice Network

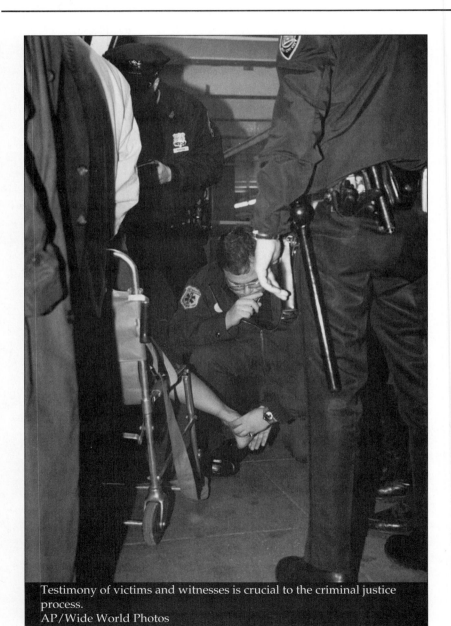

Testimony of victims and witnesses is crucial to the criminal justice process.
AP/Wide World Photos

*J*ulie arrived home after working late one night. As she entered the front door, she saw immediately that something was amiss. A moment later, a man ran through the room and out the patio door. She clearly saw the man's face and could readily identify him if she saw him again. In the next few minutes, Julie locked all the doors and called the police. She inventoried her belongings as she picked up her personal clothing, pictures, and other items that had been scattered around her bedroom. When the police arrived, she told them what was missing and that she could and would identify the burglar if and when he was caught. The investigator told her not to count on recovering the jewelry she reported missing and indicated that the police would inform her of any progress in the case.

For the next several weeks, Julie felt uncomfortable in her home and was fearful about the burglar's returning. On several occasions, she called the police to see if there were any developments in the case. She was told that she need not continue to call, that she would be notified of any changes.

In the meantime, the man who burglarized Julie's house was caught red-handed in the commission of another burglary. He admitted his guilt in several burglaries, including Julie's. None of the merchandise stolen was ever recovered, and a guilty plea was entered to several burglaries as part of a plea agreement. Since Julie's testimony was not needed to convict the burglar, since no stolen items were ever recovered, and since the investigator who handled Julie's case did not handle the cases for which the burglar was prosecuted, Julie was never contacted by the police department or prosecutor. Although the burglar's arrest and sentence was published in the newspaper, Julie had no way of knowing this was the burglar involved in her case. To this day, Julie is very apprehensive when she returns home late at night.

Key Terms

victim compensation

victim restitution

victim impact statements

victim advocacy groups

restorative justice

victim–offender mediation

subpoena

Chapter Outline

Victims in the Criminal Justice Network
Civil Remedies
Restitution
Private Insurance
State-Subsidized Compensation Programs
A Brief Historical Overview of Victim Compensation and Restitution
Restorative Justice Programs
    Victim–Offender Mediation
Consequences of Dissatisfied Victims and Witnesses

VICTIMS IN THE CRIMINAL JUSTICE NETWORK

We have indicated repeatedly that the public plays a crucial role in the criminal justice network. There is, perhaps, no more clear-cut example of the importance of citizen participation than citizen involvement as a victim or witness. The criminal justice network is, to a great extent, dependent on crime victims and witnesses for information regarding criminal behavior. Without such information, arrests, prosecutions, and convictions are extremely difficult. Lack of trust or confidence in the police, prosecutor, judges, and/or the procedures involved in processing defendants through the criminal justice network may lead to a decision on behalf of victims and witnesses not to cooperate with practitioners in the processing of a given case. Such lack of trust or confidence may arise from the belief that criminal law protects offenders more than victims (Jenkins, 1995, p. 84), from inconveniences and/or unpleasant experiences encountered in prior contacts with criminal justice practitioners, or from general confusion and misunderstanding. Whatever the cause, most prosecutors and most police officers regard the lack of cooperation of victims and witnesses in the prosecution of offenders as a very serious problem.

Among the factors that have been associated with lack of cooperation on behalf of victims and witnesses are cold or impersonal treatment by the police or prosecutor, delays in court proceedings, and failure of officials to notify victims concerning their rights to assistance, restitution, or compensation (Conway & Lohr, 1994; Tobolowski, 1993). (See In the News, "Crime Victim's Call Gets Heeded.")

Other factors commonly associated with lack of cooperation in reporting and/or prosecuting include the belief that the police, prosecutor, and judge will not be effective in dealing with the offender; personal knowledge of the offender and an attendant lack of desire to see him or her arrested and prosecuted; and fear of retribution. In addition, some citizens clearly believe that the criminal justice network has an almost total preoccupation with the rights of the criminal and largely ignores the rights of crime victims (Jenkins, 1995).

The defendant has the right to remain silent and to be furnished with a copy of the charges brought against him or her. On a motion by the defendant, the judge will order the prosecutor to furnish the defendant with a list of prosecution witnesses. The defendant also has the right to a speedy trial before an impartial judge and/or jury. Society ultimately pays for the defense of the indigent defendant, as well as for the room, board, counseling, medical treatment, and rehabilitative training or education of the defendant if he or she is incarcerated. The law, however, does not protect the victim from being legally compelled to give testimony that may be embarrassing or self-demeaning, or that may result in considerable pain and suffering. The rights and privileges of the victim, in short, do not appear to be the same as those of the offender, especially from the perspective of the victim (Brown, 1993; Kaminer, 2000).

In the News
_____

CRIME VICTIM'S CALL GETS HEEDED; FREE PHONE PROGRAM AIMS TO HELP KEEP TABS ON OFFENDERS

By Maureen O'Hagan

Crime victims often complain they feel lost in the justice system—a sprawling hodgepodge of bureaucracies, they say, each with its own rules, peculiarities and challenges.

Howard County victims, along with those in seven other counties, will soon get some relief. Under a new program, victims may call a toll-free number of automated information on an offender's court dates and expected release date. In addition, victims can register with the system to receive computer-generated phone calls alerting them when an offender is released.

"It's a powerful tool that will help victims regain their peace of mind and be safe," Lt. Gov. Kathleen Kennedy Townsend (D) said this week when she unveiled the local program at the Howard County Detention Center.

Townsend said she became interested in the idea, which is used in 35 other states, after meeting crime victims across Maryland several years ago.

"I listened to victims complain that they had been victimized twice," she said. For example, she spoke with a victim of domestic violence who learned her attacker had been released only after he knocked at her door.

"I spoke with a woman beaten up by her husband who wakes up with nightmares each night," Townsend said, recalling another case. "She can now call the system and calm her fears."

The program, called Victim Information and Notification Everyday (VINE), works like this: When an alleged offender is booked, jail personnel will enter information about him into a computer. Victims, or anyone who's interested, can retrieve the information by calling a toll-free number, 866-634-8463, 24 hours a day, seven days a week. Using a telephone keypad to punch in an offender's name, people can receive updated information on the offender's custody status. By May, the computer system will be linked to the courts', and information about the trial and other court dates will also be available.

People can also call the same toll-free number to register to receive automated phone calls with updates on the offender.

"The system is victim initiated," said Joe Sviatko, of the Governor's Office of Crime Control and Prevention. "If a victim doesn't take advantage of it, it doesn't work."

The system already has been implemented in Montgomery and Carroll counties, where more than 8,500 victims have used it, according to Townsend's office. It's particularly useful for domestic violence cases because the offender knows his victim, Townsend said.

Continued

"It's sort of a security blanket," said Shirley Haas, director of the Victim/Witness Assistance Unit in Carroll County. A victim can sleep at night knowing the offender is in jail. "If you know he's on the street, you're going to take precautions."

The system, however, has had a few glitches. For example, the notification service will place repeated phone calls, up to every 15 minutes, unless the victim answers the phone and punches in a code that tells the system the message has been received. Chris Jones, a communications specialist with the company that developed VINE, calls that a built-in safety feature.

"It's not going to call a couple times and quit," Jones said. "It's going to keep calling until it gets somebody."

The VINE system at the Howard County Detention Center, along with those in Baltimore, St. Mary's, Worcester, Wicomico, Kent, Queen Anne's and Dorchester counties, went online Monday. All other counties in Maryland, in addition to the state Division of Corrections, are scheduled to join by June.

The startup in Montgomery and Carroll counties was funded with a $150,000 grant from Maryland Victims of Crime Fund, which is operated by the state Board of Victim Services. The fund, which gets money from court fees assessed against defendants, has paid for more than 100 programs, costing $3 million.

The General Assembly authorized $500,000 to expand the VINE program statewide, and Maryland will pay $431,000 a year to a private company to operate it.

The Washington Post, March 8, 2001, p. T3.

It is, of course, quite natural for crime victims to be upset about being victimized. They have been confronted by a deliberate violation of their rights by another. To help them deal with these feelings and to improve the chances that they will assist authorities in the apprehension and prosecution of offenders, they need to know what they can expect to receive in the way of assistance and what is expected of them should they decide to cooperate with the police and/or prosecutor. The victim is as entitled to an explanation and justice as the person wronged (Walker, 1998, pp. 171–72). Each victimization tramples some fundamental personal right of the victim: the right to life, the right to personal security, the right to security of habitation and premises, or the right to retain and enjoy property.

Some believe that victims of crime in the United States occupy, as a class, the same position that racial minorities did years ago. Crime victims are, however, unlike other minorities. They are not a cohesive group unified by religion, race, or language. Crime victims are unified only by fate. Like other minorities, however, crime victims are often misunderstood and ostracized. Just as other minorities are accorded second-class status and are often considered lazy or stupid, crime victims are often blamed for their misfortunes, accused of provoking the criminal, of not resisting strongly enough, or of resisting too strongly. To date, few have recognized that victims do constitute a class that has rights and is entitled to have them enforced. In fact, the United States Senate has been trying to pass a victims' bill of rights for a number of years, but again in April of 2000 the bill was shelved because supporters were far short of the two-thirds majority required to amend the Constitution (Palmer, 2000; Kaminer, 2000).

The ordinary citizen is compelled to depend on the police for protection against bodily harm and loss of property, and must rely on them to effectively ensure the safety of street and home against criminal incursion. Police protection is generally viewed as protection of the public, not of individuals. The protection of an individual does not generally occur until that individual has been victimized (Conway & Lohr, 1994).

Within the framework of an offender-oriented criminal justice network, there is constant pressure for the police to be concerned exclusively with the offender and to view the victim only as an instrument necessary for a successful prosecution.

The decade of the 1960s witnessed a number of U.S. Supreme Court decisions that solidified the rights of alleged offenders. Occasionally dispersed among dissenting opinions are statements noting concern about the impact the decisions might have on future crime victims. For example, in his dissenting opinion in the *Miranda* v. *Arizona* case in 1965 (as it applied to the ability of law enforcement officials to obtain legally admissable confessions from criminal suspects), U.S. Supreme Court Associate Justice Byron R. White predicted that "in some unknown number of cases, the Court's ruling will return a killer, a rapist, or other criminal to the streets and to the environment that produced him, to repeat his crime whenever it pleases him." Finally, White stated, with a great deal of irony, that "there is, of course, a saving factor: the next victims are *uncertain, unnamed, and unrepresented* in this case" (Carrington, 1975, pp. 3–4).

In an attempt to encourage victims to participate in the arrest and prosecution of offenders, a number of victim-oriented programs based on the concepts of compensation and restitution have been developed. These concepts are often used interchangeably, but, in fact, they represent two different points of view. **Victim compensation,** in the criminal–victim relationship, concerns the counterbalancing of a loss suffered by a victim as a result of criminal attack (see In the News, "Restitution Fund"). It is basically payment for the damage or injury caused by the crime. It is an indication of the responsibility of society, and it is civil in character; thus, it represents a noncriminal goal in a criminal case. **Victim restitution** in a criminal–victim relationship involves

In the News

RESTITUTION FUND CAN'T KEEP UP WITH VICTIMS

By Karen Kane

A fund dedicated to compensating Butler County crime victims has been getting bigger and bigger, and not just because collections are increasing.

Payouts from the restitution fund are languishing, and the victims aren't happy.

Jennifer Messick, Butler County victim-witness coordinator, said victims have been complaining since she took the job in August.

"I can't put a number on how many calls there have been, but it's been an issue," she said.

As of Tuesday, the juvenile restitution account totaled $86,180, the highest balance the fund has ever accrued. It's been building dramatically, as these year-end balances indicate: 1995—$4,714; 1996—$6,844; 1997—$13,691; 1998—$31,540; 1999—$58,758; 2000—$85,275.

The numbers caught the attention of county Controller John R. "Jack" McMillin a year ago.

In a March 31, 2000, memo to Juvenile Court Services Director Michael Noyse, McMillin said he had noticed a significant increase in the juvenile restitution account and he wanted to know why.

A month later, Noyse wrote back, acknowledging that he was "surprised" that the balance was "so high"

when the account is intended to be "in-and-out" money.

"The numbers that you have cited seem to indicate that there is a significant time lag between the time we receive restitution payments from our clients and when they are disbursed to the victims," he wrote.

He said he would implement changes that involved monthly disbursements and a decreasing fund balance. But that didn't happen.

Noyse said last week he is certain some distributions were made in 2000, but he said it would take "two weeks or so" to figure out how many and how much.

Noyse blamed the problem on a single employee who failed to implement the improvements he had requested. That employee was moved from the position recently. Noyse had no answer as to why it took so long to notice that the fund balance wasn't going down and was instead increasing.

He confirmed he didn't double-check that his improved procedures were being followed until he received memos from victim-witness advocates who reported complaints from victims who weren't being paid, despite court orders compelling the juveniles to pay.

Continued

Noyse's office is supposed to act as a "middleman," collecting the payments from the juveniles and turning them over to the victims.

Butler County Presiding Judge Thomas Doerr said he's hoping to shift the responsibility for collection of future restitution to the clerk of courts office, which already manages restitution for adult court.

"It just makes sense," Doerr said. He said he would not expect Clerk of Courts Lisa Lotz to "sort out" the existing fund balance.

Lotz said she would want more manpower to handle the extra work.

Noyse said receipts were maintained for all money that was collected from juveniles who were ordered to make restitution to victims. "There's no indication that any money is missing," he said. Likewise, he said there are receipts for disbursements.

But, he said, the process of "cross-referencing court orders for restitution with the receipts" is cumbersome and time-consuming.

Meanwhile, victims go unpaid.

Some offenders are required to make restitution.

Reuters Newsmedia Inc./ Corbis

Doerr said he's not happy with the situation and will make certain it is corrected. He noted, however, that some of the growth in the restitution fund can be attributed to increased collections in recent years.

"We are ordering more restitution now than we ever did before," he said. Now, the challenge is to make sure the victims get the money.

Pittsburgh Post-Gazette, *March 11, 2001, p. N-4.*

restoring the victim to his or her position, which was damaged as a result of a criminal attack. It clearly indicates the responsibility of the offender, is penal in character, and represents a correctional goal in a criminal case. Compensation calls for action by the victim in the form of an application and payment by society; restitution calls for a decision by a criminal court and payment by the offender.

Generally, four methods of monetary recovery are presently available to crime victims: (1) civil remedies, (2) restitution, (3) private insurance, and (4) state-subsidized compensation programs.

CIVIL REMEDIES

As a result of over two centuries of litigation, our criminal justice network has evolved to a stage where crime is regarded as an offense exclusively against the state. The interests of the crime victim have been eroded to the point where they play little or no part in criminal procedure (though in the past few years the movement toward restorative justice in some jurisdictions, discussed below, has called this theory into question). Because of this, the victim must seek legal remedy for his or her injury through the civil courts, where civil procedures apply. The most obvious limitation to such a system of recovery is the relatively low percentage of offenders ultimately apprehended. For the vast majority of crime victims, a tort recovery is a total impossibility. Even if the offender is apprehended, substantial obstacles to a successful civil action remain. The offender generally has few, if any, reserve funds, and most of these will be expended in the process of defense against criminal charges. If sentenced to prison, the offender has little chance to earn an income that could serve as a basis for a civil award. Finally, the civil court process itself is extremely time-consuming for the victim and may result in substantial expenditures of the victim's own funds. Only a small number of victims of crime ever collect damages from the perpetrator.

RESTITUTION

In restitution programs, the criminal is perceived as the appropriate source of benefits for the victim of a crime. The criminal court judge has the alternative of deciding the victim's claim and incorporating a monetary settlement into the final decision. An implicit goal of restitution is to once again make the victim whole (as much as possible) by the direct action of the criminal rather than by a monetary payment by the state. It is sometimes argued that direct repayment by the criminal to the victim has the added benefit of assisting in the rehabilitation of the offender.

As with tort recovery, restitution has proved inadequate for the majority of crime victims, mainly because the offender is either unidentified, unapprehended, or unconvicted; or without assets, employment, or skills.

An additional limitation to restitution programs is the cost involved in administering them. Some have claimed that the costs to the state of administrating a system of offender restitution to the victims of crimes would exceed the sums actually collected to reimburse the victims for their injuries and losses.

The concept of offender restitution has been more popular as a theory than feasible as a practice. As a result, restitution is not used frequently by American judges. One study, for example, found that restitution was imposed in less than half the cases in which it would have been appropriate (Tobolowski, 1993).

PRIVATE INSURANCE

In the absence of a provision to the contrary, an insurance policy covering accidental injuries also covers victims of unforeseen intentional criminal attacks. However, there are a number of significant problems with respect to private insurance against crime. Many individuals cannot afford premiums to procure coverage for their basic health needs, and it is highly doubtful that they are in a position to afford the luxury of coverage against criminal attacks. Such insurance would be beyond the financial means of a substantial number of families, and making such insurance available and meaningful would require limiting the insurer's option to cancel or refuse to renew policies. Since the highest crime rates are in poverty areas, the insurance premiums would be higher for people living in these areas, even though these citizens are least able and least likely to purchase insurance. Moreover, many insurance companies refuse to issue insurance in high-crime areas. Finally, such coverage is generally inadequate to reimburse the victim for any long-term impairment; rarely is full compensation commensurate with damages attained.

STATE-SUBSIDIZED COMPENSATION PROGRAMS

Because of the failure of civil suits, restitution, and private insurance as methods of assisting victims of crime, the concept of compensation by the state has gained favor. Although victim compensation also offers several drawbacks as the principal form of financial aid for victims of crime, it is felt by many to be the most equitable and consistent method of making the victim whole. Unlike civil suits and restitution schemes, compensation provides a remedy without requiring that the assailant either be apprehended and/or convicted, or financially able to repay his or her damages. All states have created victims' compensation programs to repay some of the medical costs and lost income due to victimization (Meadows, 2001, p. 201). Although current programs vary in rationale, scope, and methods, they are sufficiently similar to warrant some general comments concerning their standards and practices. The typical crime victim compensation program serves only as a remedy of last resort to provide reimbursement of certain direct financial costs to certain victims of certain crimes. Payments are almost universally limited to unreimbursed medical expenses, loss of earnings by the victim, loss of support by the victim's dependents, and funeral and burial expenses occurring as a direct result of the criminal incident. Specifically excluded is compensation for property loss resulting from theft or vandalism; in the vast majority of states, also excluded is compensation for pain and suffering. A substantial minority of states forbid their compensation boards from making any award unless the victim would otherwise suffer financial hardship. Every jurisdiction with a compensation program has a statutory maximum award that can be made. This ceiling varies from $10,000 to $50,000. Similarly, most states require that the victim sustain minimum, out-of-pocket losses before becoming eligible for state compensation. Generally, the person must have been an innocent victim of a crime and could not have been related to or living with the offender at the time the incident occurred. After the crime takes place, the victim (or dependent) must report the crime to the police within a specified period of time (usually two to five days) and, thereafter, is obligated to cooperate fully with all law enforcement and judicial officials in the processing of the case. Additionally, the victim must file a "Notice to Apply" for compensation within a certain time interval after the occurrence of the crime (normally within one to two years). The majority of state programs are funded through general tax revenues; however, there are some states that subsidize their programs by imposing an additional fine on all convicted offenders.

Despite the political popularity of providing public assistance to innocent victims of crime, many officials have been reluctant to enact such measures because of apprehension about potential costs. Other criticisms focus on the fear that victims, knowing that they will be reimbursed for losses, may become careless or, conversely, offenders, knowing that victims will be compensated, may be less hesitant about inflicting injury. Finally, there are those critics who believe that a victim compensation plan would encourage fraud. They argue that it will unavoidably result in some citizens' using the compensation plan to either report nonexistent crimes and extract "easy money" from the government, or, taking this argument to its extreme, they fear that people may deliberately injure themselves so that they might collect a check from the state.

A BRIEF HISTORICAL OVERVIEW OF VICTIM COMPENSATION AND RESTITUTION

Historical reference to victim compensation goes back at least as far as the Code of Hammurabi:

> If a man has committed robbery and is caught, that man shall be put to death. If the robber is not caught, the man who has been robbed should formally declare what he has lost and the city shall replace whatever he has lost for him. If it is the life of the owner that is lost, the city or the mayor shall pay one maneh of silver to his kinfolk. (Reiff, 1979, p. 134)

Similarly, the Old Testament indicates that a criminal–victim relationship existed among the early Hebrews. If a person was injured, the perpetrator of the offense was to reimburse him for the time lost from his tasks and to be responsible for seeing to it that he had the resources to be thoroughly healed, if possible (Edelhertz & Geis, 1974, p. 8).

These early systems of compensation/restitution were gradually replaced by state-run criminal prosecution that left the victim only civil remedies by which he or she might collect for injuries. One rationale for this new approach was the claim that these fines underwrote expenses incurred by the authorities in apprehending and prosecuting the offender. Schafer (1972) traces the demise of public compensation to the Middle Ages:

> It was chiefly owing to the violent greed of the feudal barons and the medieval ecclesiastical powers that the rights of the injured party were gradually infringed upon, and finally, appropriated by the authorities. These authorities exacted a double vengeance upon the offender, first by forfeiting his property to themselves instead of to his victim and then by punishing him by the dungeon, the torture, the stake, or the gibbet. But the original victim of the wrong was ignored. (p. 8)

In the 1760s, Cesare Beccaria took issue with the proposition that the primary function of the criminal justice network was to serve as an aid to private action in obtaining recovery from the offender. Since the system had arisen from a social contract, it must serve the interests of society and not the individual victim. Punishment inflicted by the system should serve primarily to deter the offender from further criminal activity and to deter others from committing similar acts. Punishment was not to be imposed to redress private damages. Overall, Beccaria's principles contributed to the already declining role of victims in the criminal justice system (McDonald, 1976).

Lack of consideration for the victim on the part of the state lasted until the twentieth century. This does not mean that there were no advocates of victim rights in the meantime. Nineteenth-century writers such as Jeremy Bentham, Enrico Ferri, and Raffaele Garofalo noted the plight of victims of crime and urged the adoption of public compensation plans. However, the writings of these individuals had little effect on public policy as it applied to reforming the rights of crime victims.

Revival of active interest in compensation from crime victims in contemporary times is attributed to the work of Margaret Fry, an English magistrate and social reformer. Fry, like many others of her day, was primarily interested in restitution for victims being paid by the offender on the assumption that, "although restitution cannot undo the wrong, it will often mitigate the injury, and it has a real educative value for the offender. Repayment is the best first step toward reformation that a dishonest person can take. It is often the ideal solution" (Edelhertz & Geis, 1974, p. 110).

Fry felt that the "state which forbids our going armed in self-defense cannot disown all responsibility for its occasional failure to protect" (Edelhertz & Geis, 1974, p. 10). State compensation, she advocated, should not interfere with the possibility of damage awards against the aggressor.

In 1959, Stephen Schafer, an American criminologist, was given a commission by the British Home Office to work on the problem of restitution/compensation. Thus, after an extended period of dormancy, the needs of crime victims once again came to the attention of governmental bodies and have received increasing attention during the past 40 years.

Since 1982, the state of California has had a Victims' Bill of Rights, spelling out theoretical entitlements for all citizens who suffer injury or loss as the result of a criminal act. All such victims should have the right to immediate emergency aid in the areas of medicine, law, and finances; and all victims should be protected by the police and the courts from threats or coercion on behalf of the offender or his or her supporters. Further, victims should be entitled to participate in, or be represented in, any plea bargaining decisions and should be entitled to the immediate return of any recovered stolen property. Victims should be provided with timely information concerning the course of the investigation of their offense and plans for prosecution (Cole, 1995, pp. 67–68). In addition, victims should have the right to hold law enforcement officers legally responsible for negligence or poor judgment. Finally, victims should be able to exercise the same rights to maintain silence and to have legal representation afforded offenders.

In 1984, Congress passed the Victims of Crime Act, establishing a fund supported by fines, half of which were to support state compensation programs and half of which were to be used for victim assistance programs. In 1992, the U.S. Courts National Fine Center was computerized to help keep track of those fines assessed (Tobolowski, 1993).

In 1994 the Violent Crime Control Act was passed, allowing victims of federal violent and sex crimes to give **victim impact statements** (statements about how their crimes affected them) at the sentencing hearings of their offenders. A number of states also allow such statements (Meadows, 2001, p. 215). In addition, in the 1990s numerous communities established **victim advocacy groups,** which provide services to the victim and/or his or her family. Such services include providing shelter and counseling, support during criminal trials, and information about compensation programs (Meadows, 2001, p. 216).

RESTORATIVE JUSTICE PROGRAMS

Restorative justice advocates employ programs such as victim–offender mediation, victims' impact panels, community service, and community sentencing. The philosophy of **restorative justice** centers on the assertion that *crime affects persons* instead of the traditional notion that *crime affects the state.* In fact, restorative justice defines a "crime [as] an offense against human relationships" (National Victims Center, 1998, p. 52). These programs, aimed at creating or arousing emotions within criminal offenders, appear to be gaining momentum in the criminal justice network in the United States.

Mark Carey, director of community corrections in Dakota County, Minnesota, defines restorative justice as "a philosophical framework for responding to crime and the actions needed to mend this harm. It focuses on crime as an act against another individual or community rather than the state. It is a future-focused model that emphasizes problematic problem solving instead of 'just deserts' " (Wilkinson, 1997, p. 1).

Restorative justice programs have been variously called community conferencing, family group conferencing, community justice, community corrections, balanced and restorative justice, and real justice, depending on the agency applying the concepts. Although community service, victims' impact panels and classes, and victims' impact statements are sometimes referred to as restorative justice programs (because they use restorative justice philosophy), there are four identifiable types of programs practiced under the restorative justice umbrella. Victim–offender mediation, sentencing or peacemaking circles, family group conferencing, and reparative probation or boards are the most popular programs using restorative justice tenets. Each of these programs views crime in the broader sense as affecting the community, the victim, and the offender rather than adhering to the traditional belief that the crime, while it clearly affects the victim, is basically an act against the state. Let's take a closer look at one of these programs.

Victim–Offender Mediation

Victim–offender mediation is perhaps the most widely used restorative justice program. In 1999, there were more than 300 programs in the United States and 900 in Europe, variously called victim–offender meetings, victim–offender mediations, victim–offender reconciliation programs, and victim–offender conferences (Umbreit, 1999). "Victim offender mediation is a process which provides interested victims of primarily property crimes the opportunity to meet the offender, in a safe and structured setting, with the goal of holding the offender directly accountable for [his or her] behavior while providing important assistance and compensation to the victim" (Umbreit, 1999, p. 1). With the help of a mediator, the victim is allowed to tell the offender how the crime has affected his or her life and to listen to any thoughts or feelings that the offender would like to share with the victim. At the close of the mediation, it is hoped that a resolution will be obtained in which the victim receives restitution from the offender.

One of the goals of the mediation is that the victim and the offender are able to reach a mutually agreeable resolution, with little or no help from the mediator. The mediator is responsible primarily for maintaining a safe and secure atmosphere during the mediation, guiding the discussion during the mediation, and ensuring that the negotiated outcome is acceptable to both parties. A survey performed by the Center for Restorative Justice and Peacemaking of programs in 1996 and 1997 found that the most common offenses dealt with through mediation were vandalism, minor assaults, theft, and burglary. A number of the 116 programs surveyed stated that other property offenses and some violent offenses were on occasion dealt with through mediation (Umbreit, 1999).

How well does restorative justice work in practice? Walker (1998) indicates that "evaluations of experimental programs have tended to find slightly lower recidivism rates for offenders receiving restorative justice than for those given traditional sentences of prison or probation. The differences are not always consistent, however, and many questions remain regarding the implementation and outcomes of such programs" (p. 224). According to Schneider (1986), between 40 and 50 percent of victims refused to participate in mediation programs. Davis et al. (1980) found no evidence that mediation reduced levels of future conflict; Roy (1993) found no differences in recidivism rates between court-based programs and victim–offender mediation programs; Niemeyer and Shicor (1996) found mixed recidivism results; and Levrant, Cullen, Fulton, and Wozniak (1999) conclude that there is little reason to hope that restorative justice programs will have a meaningful impact on recidivism. Clearly, further research needs to be done on restorative justice.

CONSEQUENCES OF DISSATISFIED VICTIMS AND WITNESSES

It often occurs that the victim and witnesses in a criminal case are the only participants who have never been in a courtroom before. Frequently, being served with a **subpoena** is the victim's first indication that he or she will be required to testify, and often the victim is poorly prepared to testify because he or she has little or no knowledge of the actual courtroom environment. In many cases, once the victim leaves the courtroom, he or she has little or no further contact with the prosecutor's office. In addition, plea bargaining often allows the accused to plead guilty to some lesser offense in return for dismissal of some or all of the original charges against him or her. Although this procedure speeds up court processes and relieves the court of some scheduling burdens, it essentially neglects the interests of victims, and from the point of view of the victim, it deprives him or her of the opportunity to see justice done. Because the victim is seldom apprised that a plea bargain has been arranged, it is not surprising that many victims fail to understand how offenders are found guilty of both different and lesser charges than those originally and accurately filed. Similarly, victims often fail to understand how sentences resulting from relatively serious charges can be so short or how offenders convicted of such charges can be placed on probation. As a consequence, victims may conclude that cooperation with criminal justice authorities is largely a waste of time; thus, they may fail to cooperate in future cases and/or develop a negative image of the criminal justice network (Newburn, 1993; Conway & Lohr, 1994). Considering the fact that roughly 30 percent of all U.S. households are touched by crime each year, the number of citizens involved as victims is quite large and criminal justice practitioners can ill afford to alienate such large numbers of citizens (Conway & Lohr, 1994). Noncooperation of victims and witnesses, when it indicates a failure of criminal justice practitioners to be responsive to the needs of citizens, then, is a serious problem.

Should the victim of a crime be allowed to intervene in criminal prosecution? Should the victim have the right to participate in hearings before the court on dismissals, guilty pleas, and sentences? The President's Task Force on Victims of Crime advocated allowing some input at the sentencing hearing for victims of violent crimes, and the state of California has a Victims' Bill of Rights that allows victims of any crime (or next of kin if the victim is deceased) to attend all sentencing proceedings and to express their views concerning the crime at such hearings. Judges are to consider these views when imposing sentence.

Most victims probably do want to be kept informed with respect to the disposition of their cases even though they may not be interested in direct participation in the trial and/or sentencing process. The network perspective would lead us to anticipate a number of undesirable consequences if victims desire to be informed and heard, and are not. The criminal justice process is typically initiated by a victim reporting an offense. In many instances the process is interrupted (by plea bargaining or case dismissal) without the victim's knowledge. When this fact becomes known to the victim, he or she often feels that justice has not been done or that initiating criminal proceedings (which victims are encouraged to do by other components of the criminal justice network) is a waste of time. Should such individuals be victimized again, they might well decide not to cooperate in arresting or prosecuting the offender, which makes such arrest and prosecution considerably less likely (Conway & Lohr, 1994). Further, they might well share their experiences and views with others, who might then be less likely to cooperate with the authorities in pursuing criminal cases. At a minimum, keeping victims informed of the progress of their cases would seem a small price to pay for victim cooperation.

Summary

1. Victims and witnesses have often been overlooked by practitioners in the criminal justice network. In many cases they are not informed of important developments in their cases and they are routinely inconvenienced by delays in proceedings.

2. We can summarize current concerns for victims and witnesses in the criminal justice network by concluding that victims and witnesses should not control outcomes in lower criminal courts.

3. But there is a lot of room to institute some sort of role for victims and witnesses in the decision process between the extremes of allowing them to control outcomes and the complete absence of participation that they are now afforded in most cases in most lower criminal courts.

Terms Defined

victim compensation   A payment made by the state to the victim of a crime.

victim restitution   A payment made by an offender to his or her victim.

victim impact statements   Statements made by victims at the sentencing hearings of offenders to show how the crime committed affected their lives.

victim advocacy groups   Groups that lend support to crime victims and/or their families.

restorative justice   A philosophy that asserts that crime affects *people* rather than or in addition to *the state* and that those affected should be restored to wholeness through techniques such as victim confrontation.

victim–offender mediation   One type of restorative justice program in which the victim and offender meet with a mediator in an attempt to resolve the victimization.

subpoena   A court order that directs the recipient to appear in court.

Critical Thinking Exercises

1. How much input into the trial and sentencing of offenders should victims be allowed? What are some of the dangers in allowing too much input? Too little input?

2. Do you think the movement toward restorative justice is a step in the right direction? Do you see any dangers inherent in the process? How could the rights of restorative justice participants best be protected?

Internet Exercises

A number of websites discuss treatment of victims and witnesses by criminal justice practitioners. Many also provide instructions on where to get help, as well as on the judicial process and victim/witness advocates.

1. What type of information in this regard can you find from the website *www.state.ma.us?*

2. Can you find three other websites that provide similar information? How does the information provided compare across jurisdictions?

3. Is there a website that provides information on victim and witness services for the mentally retarded? Is so, identify that source and tell how you located it.

References

Brown, C. G. (1993). *First get mad, then get justice: The handbook for crime victims*. New York: Birch Lane Press.

Carrington, F. G. (1975). *Victims*. New Rochelle, NY: Arlington House.

Cole, G. F. (1995). *The American system of criminal justice*. Belmont, CA: Wadsworth.

Conway, M. R., & Lohr, S. L. (1994). A longitudinal analysis of factors associated with reporting violent crimes to the police. *Journal of Quantitative Criminology, 10* (1), 23–39.

Davis, R., et al. (1980). *Mediation and arbitration as alternatives to prosecution in felony cases: An evaluation of the Brooklyn Dispute Resolution Center*. New York: Vera Institute of Justice.

Edelhertz, H., & Geis, G. (1974). *Public compensation to victims of crime*. New York: Praeger.

Jenkins, P. (1995). Crime control and due process. In D. Close & N. Meier (Eds.), *Morality in criminal justice: An introduction to ethics*, pp. 83–98. Belmont, CA: Wadsworth.

Kaminer, W. (2000). Victims versus suspects (proposed victims' rights amendments). *American Prospect, 11* (9), 18–19.

Levrant, S., Cullen, F. T., Fulton, B., & Wozniak, J. F. (1999). Reconsidering restorative justice: The corruption of benevolence revisited. *Crime and Delinquency, 45*, (1), pp. 3–27.

McDonald, W. (1976). *Criminal justice and the victim*. Beverly Hills, CA: Sage.

Meadows, R. J. (2001). *Understanding violence and victimization* (2nd ed.). Upper Saddle River, NJ: Prentice Hall.

Miranda v. Arizona, 384 U.S. 348 (1965).

National Victims Center. (1998). Promising practices and strategies for victim services in corrections. Online publication: *http://www.nvc.org/ADIR/Compendm.htm*

Newburn, T. (1993). *The long-term needs of victims: A review of the literature*. London: Home Office.

Niemeyer, M., & Shichor, D. (1996). A preliminary study of a large victim/offender reconciliation program. *Federal Probation, 60*, 30–34.

Palmer, E. (2000). Victims' rights amendment supporters beat a tactical retreat. *CQ Weekly, 58* (18), 991–92.

Reiff, R. (1979). *The invisible victim: The criminal justice system's forgotten responsibility*. New York: Basic Books.

Roy, S. (1993). Two types of juvenile restitution programs in two midwestern counties. *Federal Probation, 57*, 48–53.

Schafer, S. (1972). *Compensation and restitution to victims of crime* (2nd ed.). Montclair, NJ: Patterson Smith.

Schneider, A. (1986). Restitution and recidivism rates of juvenile offenders: Results from four experimental studies. *Criminology, 24*, 533–52.

Tobolowski, P. M. (1993). Restitution in the federal criminal justice system. *Judicature, 77* (2), 90–95.

Umbreit, M. (1999). *Victim offender mediation and dialogue: Guidelines for victim sensitive practice*. Center for Restorative Justice and Peacemaking, School of Social Work, University of Minnesota, St. Paul. Unpublished manuscript.

Walker, S. (1998). *Sense and nonsense about crime and drugs: A policy guide* (4th ed.). Belmont, CA: West/Wadsworth.

Wilkinson, R. A. (1997). Back to basics. *Corrections Today, 59*, 6–7.

Suggested Readings

Cohen, M. A., & Miller, T. R. (1998). The cost of mental health care for victims of crime. *Journal of Interpersonal Violence, 13* (1), 93–110.

Felson, R. B., Messner, S. F., & Hoskin, A. (1999). The victim–offender relationship and calling the police in assaults. *Criminology, 37* (4), 931–47.

Meadows, R. J. (2001). *Understanding violence and victimization* (2nd ed.). Upper Saddle River, NJ: Prentice Hall.

Pallone, N. J., & Hennessey, J. J. (1999). Blacks and whites as victims and offenders in aggressive crime in the U.S.: Myths and realities. *Journal of Offender Rehabilitation, 30* (1/2), 1–33.

CHAPTER TWELVE

Corrections

Correctional facilities are used to incapacitate and rehabilitate offenders.
Daniel Grogan/UniPhoto Picture Agency

S tan was a heroin user. He had been addicted to heroin most of his life. He had been arrested on several occasions for possession and been sentenced to probation. While on probation, he tried to steer clear of heroin and even entered several treatment programs, but he inevitably returned to using.

The last time Stan was arrested for possession, he was sentenced to prison as a result of mandatory sentencing laws. He was assigned to a medium security facility but quickly determined that many of the inmates had committed predatory crimes. The more violent offenders ran the cell block when the guards were not present, and they soon frightened Stan into serving as a courier for drugs within the institution. As long as he carried drugs for these violent offenders, they provided him with drugs and protected him from other inmates.

Within a year, Stan contracted AIDS from sharing needles and was caught carrying drugs. The latter led to an additional sentence, so Stan has seen many violent offenders complete their sentences and leave the institution while he still has time to serve. Stan now believes he will die in prison and can't seem to understand how a nonviolent drug user can be sentenced to more time than those who commit violent crimes. Can you?

Key Terms

early release

banishment

transportation

age of enlightenment

hedonism

Walnut Street Jail

Pennsylvania prisons

Auburn prisons

retribution

specific deterrence

general deterrence

supermax security facilities

maximum security facilities

medium security facilities

minimum security facilities

recidivism rates

total institution

warehousing

Chapter Outline

Historical Development
  The Reform Movement
  The American Experience
Correctional Objectives
  Revenge
  Specific Deterrence
  General Deterrence
  Rehabilitation
  Custody
Women in Prison

At the conclusion of the trial process, a number of sentencing alternatives are available to the judge with respect to the guilty party. Among these are probation and incarceration in jail or prison. In recent years, considerable media, public, and political attention has been devoted to corrections in response to reports of overcrowding, drugs, gang violence, and riots in prisons, and in response to early release programs (see In the News, "Jail Inmate Releases Possible"). Here again, the fact that criminal justice is best viewed as a network is apparent. Funds used to build prisons and jails must be appropriated from the public, and prisoners who are released into society must be reintegrated if rehabilitation is one of our goals.

Financial support for alternatives to incarceration also comes from the public. Politicians at all levels (local prosecutors to state governors to the president) have used prison conditions as a political football. In Illinois in recent years, for example, several communities have been involved in the competition as sites for new prisons. Some cities have lost other state facilities (mental hospitals, for instance), and local and state politicians have put pressure on the governor to locate new prisons in those areas. Across the nation, lack of available space to house prisoners has led to **early release** for many inmates to alleviate prison and jail overcrowding (see In the News, "Workhouse Inmates Getting Out Early"). On several occasions, the media focused on stories of atrocities committed by offenders who had been released early (while conveniently overlooking the much larger number of offenders on early release who did not commit further offenses); thus, the media helped shape public opinion against such programs.

In the News

JAIL INMATE RELEASES POSSIBLE; CROWDED CELLS FORCING TOUGH CHOICES

By Scott Williams

WAUKESHA—Jail overcrowding has grown so severe in Waukesha County—with forecasts that it will continue to worsen—that Sheriff's Department officials will consider releasing inmates early and incarcerating fewer people arrested on certain crimes.

A county consultant Thursday listed those steps among potential interim measures the county could take to manage the overflowing jail population while county leaders consider building a new jail or adding to existing buildings.

Sheriff's Inspector Bob Johannik, second in command at the Sheriff's Department, said officials said releasing inmates early and other options suggested by the consultant will be weighed seriously as the department tries to keep the jail population in check.

He acknowledged that the public would probably strongly oppose an early-release program but noted that many taxpayers would also be wary about spending millions of dollars for new jail cells.

"Obviously, everything has its trade-offs," he said.

Johannik attended a briefing Thursday by Dennis Kimme, who outlined options for a special jail study committee, options that would help keep the number of inmates in check until a jail construction project could be completed.

Under the early-release proposal, inmates systematically would be released "out the back door" as new inmates are booked, Kimme said. Those who had served 95% of their sentences could be released first, followed by those who had served 90% of their sentences, and so forth until the congestion is relieved, he said.

In addition to releasing inmates early to make room, Kimme suggested that sheriff's deputies and local police officers could issue tickets with specific court dates for some minor crimes instead of hauling those individuals into jail as is now done.

Kimme also said expanded use of electronic monitoring and quicker sentencings after convictions would be other ways to reduce the jail population.

He acknowledged that the early-release proposal, in particular, would fly in the face of Waukesha County's efforts to maintain a get-tough posture against crime.

"It could be argued this is counter to your current philosophy," he told the committee. "Inevitably, we're going to be forced into something along these lines."

Continued

District Attorney Paul Bucher said that rather than releasing inmates early, he would like the county to provide short-term relief to overcrowding by building a dormitory-style facility that could be constructed quickly and cheaply. Such a building could house enough inmates to relieve pressure on the main jail, he said.

Elm Grove Police Chief Jeffrey Haig said he was "a little uneasy" with the thought of immediately releasing people police arrest, because they might flee prosecution.

"How serious are we about holding people accountable?" Haig said.

Waukesha County officials are confronting several tough questions as they weigh options for handling a jail population that frequently surpasses the jail's capacity of 306 inmates. Last August, the jail reached a record high of 360 inmates.

Sheriff William Kruziki has predicted that the jail population will reach an average of 399 within three years. He was out of the office Thursday and could not be reached for comment.

On Thursday, the population at the main jail was 326.

County Executive Dan Finley has asked the special committee to recommend a new or expanded jail this summer so he can include it in a five-year capital improvements plan later this year.

Finley has projected that it could cost $19 million or more to expand jail facilities.

Whatever expansion plan ultimately is approved, Kimme said, it probably will take at least three years to complete. He said stopgap measures such as those he outlined Thursday will be necessary until the project is completed because overcrowding will only get worse.

In a meeting with the special Justice System Facility Study Committee, the Champaign, Ill., consultant warned that judicial reforms such as the truth-in-sentencing law will only bring more inmates into the jail.

Asked by one committee member if predictions of jail population increases aren't overstated, Kimme said: "Overbuilding has been a problem nowhere."

He said the county's long-term options include renovating the old jail that is attached to the courthouse to create new cells, adding more cells in the Law Enforcement Center that was built seven years ago and constructing a new facility.

If a new jail is built, it should have the potential for future expansion, perhaps in a configuration that could see it grow to eight stories tall, Kimme said.

Milwaukee Journal Sentinel, June 23, 2000, p. 1B.

In the News

WORKHOUSE INMATES GETTING OUT EARLY

By Alison Grant

Cleveland has been granting early release to dozens of minor offenders per month because it does not have enough space for them at the city workhouse.

The House of Corrections, designed for 156 beds, is often packed with 250 or more prisoners, men and women. At night, the workhouse uses cots and portable "stack-a-bunks" to deal with the overflow.

When the population nears 300, Corrections Commissioner Thomas Hardin petitions the Cleveland Municipal Court for relief. Twice a month, Presiding Judge Larry A. Jones signs off on a request by Hardin to grant early release to prisoners, usually 16 to 20 at a time.

Cleveland's campaign to make neighborhoods more livable by arresting people for minor crimes, such as having loud parties and violating curfews, has contributed to the overcrowding.

It was the same picture two years ago, when a state agency charged with enforcing minimum standards at jails and workhouses said the Highland Hills site did not have adequate shower and toilet facilities or ventilation and temperature controls to deal with its inmate population.

"We went back in January and saw some improvement," Deb Stewart, acting administrator of the Bureau of Adult Detention, said yesterday.

The city avoids waiving sentences for prisoners convicted of domestic violence, assault or other violent crimes. It also keeps most drunken-driving offenders for their full sentence.

Prisoners most likely to spring an early release are those who have been arrested for crimes such as disorderly conduct, criminal trespassing, driving without a license or soliciting a prostitute, and who are awaiting trial with a bond of $2,000 or less.

Part of the inmate influx comes from people arrested for crimes targeted since Mayor Michael R. White's administration launched its community policing drive in 1996 that focuses on "quality of life" issues. The result has been more people picked up for violating curfews, being in parks after closing time or having loud parties or open containers.

Jones said the court's overall caseload is up 20 to 30 percent in the last few years.

"This court is in support of community policing, but if you're going to do that on one hand, you have to make adjustments on the other end," Jones said when asked about the overcrowding. "I think this is something that the entire city must deal with—City Council, the administration and the courts."

Councilwoman Merle R. Gordon chairs the Public Health Committee

Continued

that oversees the workhouse. She said the city is right to crack down on minor offenses that disrupt peace and security in the neighborhoods.

"Those are the things constituents complain the loudest about," she said. But she acknowledged there are no easy answers for what to do about the overcrowding.

Council President Michael D. Polensek said the city may have to put more people under house arrest or sentence them to community service instead of the workhouse.

White's budget this year proposes a slight increase of $19,000 over last year's $5.7 million outlay for the Division of Corrections. But the council's finance chairman, Bill W. Patmon, said the council might increase the funding during its March budget hearings.

"Reconciling the budget is yet to take place. This would definitely come up on the radar screen," Patmon said.

The Plain Dealer, *February 12, 2000, p. 1A.*

In addition, correctional officials in the United States have been hampered by our inability to decide precisely what it is we want prisons to accomplish. Currently, we ask prison officials to focus on two, perhaps incompatible, goals—rehabilitation and custody. In the long run, however, the former depends on our willingness to accept those who have served time in prison back into society. To some extent, therefore, rehabilitation is beyond the control of prison authorities. Perhaps a look at the historical development of prisons will help us understand how some of these problems arose.

HISTORICAL DEVELOPMENT

Although prisons are now characteristic of corrections, this has not always been the case. Early codes, such as the Code of Hammurabi and the Sumerian Code, supported the doctrine of an eye for an eye and a tooth for a tooth. With this philosophy as a basis for punishment, sanctions were often swift and severe. Torture and execution were commonplace. The situation improved little under Roman and Greek influence, although changes in the rights of defendants were made during those periods. In the Middle Ages, trial by ordeal, exorcism, and other forms of torture continued. Incarceration was simply a way of holding prisoners until corporal punishment could be administered and was not considered a form of punishment.

Forerunners of incarceration as a form of punishment were banishment and transportation. In some cases, **banishment** (exile) was reserved for the more affluent members of society who were convicted of an offense. The person being banished was pronounced civilly dead and was forced to leave the country. Return meant severe corporal punishment or death. **Transportation** emerged during the sixteenth century and was practiced until the latter part of the nineteenth century. England transported between 300 and 2,000 prisoners to America and Australia annually during this period (Wilson, 1931; Hughes, 1987). Banishment and transportation represented alternatives to corporal and capital punishment, and achieved much the same end as incarceration—the isolation of offenders.

Both the English and the Dutch also developed workhouses. In England, cities or counties were required to construct bridewells to house the poor and convicts, and this practice soon spread to other parts of Europe. Conditions in these workhouses were atrocious, and no attempts were made to segregate inmates by age, gender, or type of offense. Inmates were forced to work long hours, corruption and violence were common among both guards and inmates, and disease was rampant. Nonetheless, workhouses did represent a slight shift in penal philosophy, with society assuming at least minimal responsibility for separating convicts from other citizens.

The Reform Movement

A major turning point in the history of corrections was reached in the late eighteenth and early nineteenth centuries, often referred to as the **age of enlightenment**. Efforts by Montesquieu, Voltaire, Beccaria, Bentham, and Howard were instrumental in bringing reform to the harsh penal philosophy that had existed prior to this period. These individuals and others were concerned with human rights and limiting the coercive power of the state.

Both Montesquieu and Voltaire were concerned with the harsh punishments inflicted on French citizens. Montesquieu's treatise called for an end to such treatment, and Voltaire was actively involved in defending and appealing cases for alleged offenders. Voltaire was eventually imprisoned for his activities and then banished from France. The efforts of both Montesquieu and Voltaire had considerable impact on Beccaria, who was the person most responsible for bringing about changes in the inhumane conditions to which convicts were subjected.

Beccaria anonymously published his famous *Essays on Crimes and Punishments* in 1764, and he is remembered as the individual who directed penal philosophy away from punishment and toward corrections. Beccaria argued that humans are basically rational beings who are calculating in their behavior and controlled by the principle of **hedonism**—the desire to seek pleasurable experiences and avoid painful ones. He contended that prevention should be the goal of punishment and that the punishment should fit the crime. He abhorred torture and capital punishment, and advocated more extensive use of fines, imprisonment, and banishment. In addition, he was concerned with individual rights and with providing procedural safeguards in the trial process (Beccaria, 1953). His principles influenced many of the penologists of his time and remain an important cornerstone of corrections today.

Other contributors to the correctional reform movement include Jeremy Bentham and John Howard. Bentham, an Englishman strongly influenced by Beccaria's work, advocated a system of hedonistic calculus, which would provide graduated penalties based on the seriousness of offenses. Howard was a British sheriff in the latter part of the eighteenth century who was appalled by conditions in British jails and attempted to bring about changes in these conditions. He traveled throughout Europe to observe confinement facilities and conveyed his findings on the inhumane conditions he found everywhere. Partly because of Howard's efforts, Parliament passed the Penitentiary Act of 1779. This act provided for secure and sanitary structures and systematic inspections, among other things (Barnes & Teeters, 1959). Howard's ideas spread to continental Europe and the United States, and his legacy lives on in a contemporary reform organization bearing his name.

The American Experience

As noted, America's involvement with corrections stems from the early days when prisoners were transported here from England. The early settlers employed corporal punishment much like that in their home countries. One of the earliest attempts to humanize treatment of offenders resulted from the efforts of William Penn and his Quaker followers. Penn formulated the Great Law, which replaced corporal and capital punishment with imprisonment and hard labor. After Penn's death, the law was repealed and treatment of offenders once again became inhumane. However, his philosophy did not die. After the Revolution, it surfaced again to become an important part of American correctional philosophy. In fact, the reform efforts of the Quakers led the Pennsylvania legislature to declare a section of the **Walnut Street Jail** as a penitentiary to house convicted felons; thus the Walnut Street Jail became known as the first correctional institution in the United States. While housed in this institution, prisoners were permitted to work and receive wages, and were given religious instruction. Corporal punishment was prohibited, and the guards were not permitted to carry weapons. According to Menninger, the Walnut Street Jail was the birthplace of the prison system (Menninger, 1968). Other states adopted versions of the Walnut Street philosophy, and before long, these institutions became so overcrowded that a new system was developed.

The Pennsylvania and Auburn Systems

As a result of the overcrowding mentioned above, the Pennsylvania legislature was forced to establish new and larger institutions to house prisoners. Two new penitentiaries were established in the 1820s. The architecture of the **Pennsylvania prisons** was unique. They were designed with a central hub and numerous wings radiating from this hub. The design reflected the current attitude toward punishment, which was based on the premise that prison should be a place in which to do penance (thus, the term "penitentiary") and that the best way to achieve this end was through solitary confinement. So each wing of the institution consisted of several cells placed back-to-back, in which inmates worked, ate, slept, and received religious instruction. It was assumed that this arrangement would give each inmate time to contemplate his crimes and repent.

At about the same time, the state of New York was also developing a prison system. The architectural design of the **Auburn prisons** differed substantially from that of the Pennsylvania prisons. The original Auburn structure was built in the shape of a U and consisted of five tiers with numerous cells on each tier. In contrast to the Pennsylvania system, prisoners in the Auburn system ate and worked with other inmates. A code of silence was enforced, and strict punishment was administered to those who violated regulations. Prisoners were placed in their own cells to sleep. Those convicted of the most serious offenses were confined to their cells, and the notion of solitary confinement as a technique for prison discipline emerged from this procedure.

A debate soon ensued over which system was better. Supporters of the Auburn system claimed their choice was more economical and that the congregation of prisoners best suited reform. Advocates of the Pennsylvania system felt their approach was more efficient and orderly. The Pennsylvania system was adopted by several European countries, whereas the Auburn system became more popular in the United States and remains the model for most of our prisons today.

Contemporary Corrections

In 1870, the National Prison Association (now called the American Correctional Association) met in Cincinnati to discuss prison reform. The group developed a list of 36 principles, which led to the establishment of the first reformatory in the United States, at Elmira, New York, under the direction of Z. R. Brockway. Under Brockway's leadership, educational and vocational programs were developed and instituted. Brockway also advocated individual treatment, indeterminate sentencing, and greater use of parole. Although a number of institutions adopted the name "reformatory," most did not adopt all of Brockway's principles. Nonetheless, the Elmira experiment was to have an impact on future correctional efforts. Brockway's attempts at reformation and rehabilitation of prisoners were forerunners of similar attempts in contemporary prisons. Numerous changes have occurred in corrections since Elmira, including the addition of professional staff members and greater reliance on social science research, but the emphasis on both rehabilitation and punishment remains.

CORRECTIONAL OBJECTIVES

It may be said that correctional officials generally pursue two objectives: punishment and rehabilitation. The emphasis shifts from one of the objectives to the other over time with shifts in public opinion and political leadership. In general, rehabilitation received more attention than punishment in the 1960s and 1970s, but the pendulum seems to have swung more toward punishment in recent years.

From a legal viewpoint, the court identified and discussed four objectives of punishment in the case of *Commonwealth* v. *Ritter* (Court of Oyer and Terminer, 1930). These objectives include revenge or retribution, specific deterrence, general deterrence, and rehabilitation or reformation. A brief look at each of these objectives is in order.

Revenge

Revenge, commonly called **retribution,** is one of the oldest known justifications for punishment. It is based on the philosophy that because the victim has suffered, so must the offender (an eye for an eye). Although it is easy to understand why revenge is a motive on the part of victims or their loved ones, how do we determine the severity of the punishment to be inflicted on the offender, and who should make that determination? Suppose Black is the victim of a hit-and-run accident. Do we adhere to a philosophy of punishment in kind? What if Black dies? Do we then execute the driver of the vehicle? What is appropriate punishment if Black is paralyzed? If we decide not to execute the offender, how do we determine an appropriate prison sentence? It should be apparent that making the punishment fit the crime is not always an easy task. If we add to the questions above the additional factors of plea bargaining and prison overcrowding, the issue becomes even more complex. Although revenge may be an ancient and understandable objective, in a practical sense it is difficult to achieve because punishment does not occur in a vacuum.

Specific Deterrence

You may recall from our previous discussion that Beccaria felt that punishment should be severe enough to make the potential offender refrain from engaging in crime. However, not all criminals act in a rational manner (many crimes are committed in the heat of passion, for example), and some who do apparently use a calculus different from that of most people (as may be the case when an angry husband, knowing that he will be apprehended, batters or murders his wife and her lover). In addition, severity of punishment makes a difference to potential offenders only when they believe there is a reasonable chance they will be apprehended for their crimes. According to current clearance rates for most crimes except homicide, the likelihood of detection and apprehension is not particularly great; thus, the proposed punishment, no matter how severe, is unlikely to have any great impact on the potential offender. Further, the effects of **specific deterrence** are very difficult to measure. Would an alternative form of punishment have increased or decreased the likelihood of an offense occurring? Research findings on the effects of punishment as a deterrent are contradictory. Chambliss (1965) argues that punishment affects some categories of shoplifters and traffic offenders, but Pittman and Gordon (1968) contend that punishment has little or no effect on drug addicts and alcoholics. The commonsense appeal of specific deterrence seems to be the basic justification for retaining it as an objective of punishment. However, a good deal of research indicates that punishment is not an effective deterrent to crime (Nagin & Paternoster, 1991).

General Deterrence

The basic premise of **general deterrence** is that punishing one offender for his or her offenses will help dissuade other potential offenders from engaging in criminal conduct. Again, there is a kind of commonsense appeal to the concept, but the value of general deterrence has also been challenged. Numerous studies have been conducted in attempts to measure the deterrent effect of the death penalty as well as other forms of punishment. Most have failed to demonstrate a significant relationship between type of punishment administered and the likelihood that others will commit a similar offense (Nagin & Paternoster, 1991; Wilson & Abrahamse, 1992; Walker, 1998). Despite this lack of scientific support for general deterrence, substantial numbers of practitioners, politicians, and citizens continue to clamor for a get-tough approach to punishment. While any given type of punishment may deter certain individuals from engaging in acts that might lead to such punishment, we currently have too little knowledge of the exact nature of this relationship to determine how best to reach those who are most likely to commit offenses.

Rehabilitation

The basic assumption underlying rehabilitation as a correctional objective is that behavior can be modified if only we know enough about the prior history of the individual involved (and about the causes of the undesirable criminal behavior). For the most part, programs aimed at rehabilitating offenders concentrate on attempting to discover the causes of the aberrant behavior to eliminate or modify the behavior through some form of therapy. Thus, a person identified as committing utilitarian burglary as a result of being a high school dropout and having no vocational skills might be placed in educational and vocational training programs that could provide skills necessary to secure and retain reasonable employment to eliminate the need to commit burglaries. Some segments of the public view rehabilitation programs as catering to criminals and as alternatives that are too lenient. Others have argued that psychological treatment programs reduce inmates to experimental animals (Lewis, 1953). Walker (1998) concludes: "In the end, the evidence on rehabilitation does not look very good. We do not seem to have devised any 'planned intervention' programs that substantially reduce recidivism rates" (p. 225).

Custody

One other, perhaps more general, objective of corrections should be mentioned. Traditionally, prisons have been viewed as institutions in which prisoners are isolated or incapacitated (prevented from committing further crimes). This is the custodial as opposed to the rehabilitative function of correctional authorities, and the contradiction between these two objectives accounts for many of the problems surrounding imprisonment today. Two major problems with the concept of incapacitation are the failure to consider crimes committed by one inmate against another, or against prison staff, as further crimes (and thousands of these are committed annually) and the fact that incapacitation is temporary, because most inmates will eventually be released whether or not they have been rehabilitated.

WOMEN IN PRISON

In December of 1990, there were 44,065 females incarcerated in the United States. This number increased to 87,199 female inmates in June of 1999 (Beck, 2000). During that time period, the number of women convicted of felonies in state courts grew at more than twice the rate for males. In 1998 there were an estimated 950,000 women under the care, custody, or control of correctional, probation, or parole agencies, with about 85 percent supervised in the community (Greenfield & Snell, 1999). A number of states and the Federal Bureau of Prisons have co-correctional facilities that house both men and women (Maguire & Pastore, 1995).

In addition to the costs of creating and staffing new penal institutions for women, society often bears the added cost of rearing the minor children of female inmates (estimated at about 1.3 million in 1998) (Greenfield & Snell, 1999). Traditionally, women's prisons have lagged behind prisons for men in terms of services and programs. As a result, a number of court cases have been filed by female inmates claiming the right to equal protection (treatment). A Supreme Court decision handed down in 1976 (*Craig* v. *Boren*) has often been cited as requiring equal protection for female inmates (Cripe, 1997, p. 21).

CAPITAL PUNISHMENT: TIMELESS CONTROVERSY, ULTIMATE PENALTY

No issue in criminal justice has generated as much debate as capital punishment. Capital punishment is the ultimate sanction, the most symbolic reminder of the state's power to punish its citizens. Although the practice is perhaps as old as human life, it has been particularly controversial in the past 300 years, and the debate has been revived in the past quarter of a century as a result of several heinous and/or spectacular crimes.

When John Hinckley was found not guilty by reason of insanity of attempting to kill President Ronald Reagan, a new wave of concern for criminal justice reform was generated. This concern focuses on getting tougher with

The manner in which capital punishment is carried out is very controversial.

UPI/Bettmann-Corbis

criminals by limiting or abolishing the insanity defense, imposing longer prison terms, limiting or abolishing parole, and, ultimately, making criminals pay for their crimes with their lives. Heinous crimes, such as the murder of Sharon Tate by the Charles Manson "family," the killing of eight student nurses by Richard Speck, or the murders of Nicole Simpson and Ronald Goldman, often lead to a public outcry, which usually includes a call for increased use of the death penalty. Although the details of such crimes may invoke an angry reaction in most of us, the question of whether such offenses justify the ultimate penalty is not easy to resolve.

In 1972, the United States Supreme Court, in the case of *Furman* v. *Georgia*, held that capital punishment, as it was being used, was discriminatory and, therefore, unconstitutional. The court did not rule on the issue of whether capital punishment violated the Eighth Amendment's ban on cruel and unusual punishment. The response to *Furman* was clear-cut. Thirty-eight states passed new legislation concerning the death penalty. Some of this legislation met with the Supreme Court's approval (*Gregg* v. *Georgia*, 1976), and numerous executions have occurred since.

Why has the country with some of the most severe penalties in the civilized world been reluctant to impose the death penalty? If citizens and legislatures approve of capital punishment and the courts accept the practice, why has America averaged so few executions per year? To answer this question, we will examine the history of capital punishment, the argument for retaining or abolishing the death penalty, and the legal guidelines governing its use.

A Brief History of Capital Punishment

Capital punishment, an execution in the name of the state, is one of the most ancient forms of punishment. Early legal codes, such as those of Hammurabi, the Greeks, and the Romans, provided for the death penalty on conviction for a wide range of offenses (Mueller, 1955; Durham, 1994). In more recent times, the practice of banishment was sometimes equivalent to capital punishment. Convicted offenders were forced into the wilderness with very little chance of survival.

Although records are not totally reliable, it is speculated that Henry VIII had as many as 72,000 people executed during his reign. In the 1500s, the British executed convicted offenders for eight offenses: murder, robbery, rape, burglary, larceny, arson, treason, and petty treason. The popularity of the punishment peaked in the 1600s, subsided in the 1700s, and reemerged in the 1800s. Some historians estimate that the British considered as many as 200 or 300 offenses capital offenses during this second peak. Offenses such as shoplifting, cutting down trees, and sacrilege were sometimes accorded capital status. Although the practice was not common, young children and women were occasionally executed during this period. By the 1840s, England had reduced the number of capital offenses to about 20; and in 1965, England joined many other European nations (Netherlands, 1886; Sweden, 1921; Italy, 1944; and West Germany, 1949) in abolishing the death penalty.

Early colonial codes provided for execution of those convicted of rape, man stealing, witchcraft, adultery, and other offenses, but the use of capital punishment was more restricted than in England. It appears that the framers of the Constitution accepted capital punishment as legitimate, and every state permitted the practice at the time the Constitution was ratified.

Beccaria's penal reform philosophy included a stand against the death penalty, and Americans Benjamin Rush and Edward Livingston were influenced by this abolitionist stance. Pennsylvania abolished capital punishment for all crimes except first-degree murder in 1794, and in 1834, it became the first state to ban public executions. In 1846, Michigan was the first state to abolish the death penalty, and by 1918, 11 other states had followed course. In the 1930s and 1940s, some states reinstated the death penalty. The last public execution occurred in Kentucky in 1936. The number of executions declined in the 1960s, and in 1967, a moratorium was declared on capital punishment. A decade later, Gary Gilmore was executed by a firing squad. He was the first of numerous offenders to receive the ultimate punishment in the past 25 years (see Table 12.1). At least 38 states currently have the death penalty, and there are over 3,300 prisoners on death rows in the United States. Still, the controversy between those wishing to abolish the death penalty and those wishing to retain it rages on.

Death Penalty Arguments

There are basically five issues involved in the controversy surrounding capital punishment:

1. Does capital punishment violate constitutional protections against cruel and unusual punishment?
2. Is capital punishment economical?
3. What is the likelihood that an innocent person will be executed?

4. Does it meet the objectives of punishment previously stated?
5. Is it supported by the public?

The Eighth Amendment to the Constitution prohibits the use of cruel and unusual punishment. Is capital punishment cruel and unusual? In the *Furman* decision, the Court held that the death penalty was being administered in discriminatory fashion, with two of the justices (Marshall and Brennan) indicating that they believed capital punishment to be cruel and unusual. In *Gregg* v. *Georgia* (1976), the issue of cruel and unusual punishment was addressed directly, and the court held that the death penalty does not "invariably violate the constitution."

In discussing the relationship between the Eighth Amendment and the death penalty, we must keep in mind that cruelty and unusualness are two distinct issues. Both of these issues have been brought before the courts on numerous occasions. *In Wilkerson* v. *Utah* (1878), the Court held that mandatory public execution of persons who committed premeditated murder was not cruel. Later, when the electric chair was introduced, the court rejected a claim that it was unusual punishment because it had never been used before. In *Weems* v. *United States* (1910), the court struck down a sentence to painful labor because it was excessive (cruel). Historically, it appears, the courts have interpreted the Eighth Amendment to mean a ban on torture or other clearly inhumane treatment. At present, states with the death penalty use different methods of execution, including lethal injection, electrocution, lethal gas, hanging, and firing squads. Electrocution has recently been the subject of debate because there are reported cases of prolonged, agonizing deaths when the electric chairs failed to operate properly. Currently, there are those who are claiming that capital punishment is unusual in view of the fact that there have been relatively few executions since 1967. An additional argument contends that capital punishment is administered in a cruel and unusual fashion because most of those executed are black (90 percent between the years 1930 and 1980). Bowers (1974) examined the characteristics of those executed as far back as the turn of the twentieth century and concluded that blacks have been executed for less serious crimes than whites and that many blacks were executed without appeals.

Given the current cost of incarceration (ranging from $8,000 to $38,000 per year) and the fact that a large number of offenders are sentenced to life terms, many contend that capital punishment should be employed to save money if for no other reason (Stephan, 1999). However, capital punishment does not occur immediately following sentencing. Lengthy and costly appeals are involved, and taxpayers bear the burden of these expenses, thereby reducing whatever cost benefits may be related to capital punishment. In a more general sense, during the past 10 to 20 years, the "get tough on crime" and "lock them up and throw away the key" approaches to dealing with offenders have gained momentum. We have witnessed an overhaul of sentencing procedures, which have addressed truth in sentencing (whereby an inmate is supposed to serve most of the time to which he or she is sentenced) and other issues, such

Table 12.1

Prisoners Executed under Civil Authority by Region and Jurisdiction, 1930–95 (- means zero)

Region and Jurisdiction	Total	1930 to 1934	1935 to 1939	1940 to 1944	1945 to 1949	1950 to 1954	1955 to 1959	1960 to 1964	1965 to 1969	1970 to 1974	1975 to 1979	1980 to 1983	1984	1985	1986	1987	1988	1989	1990	1991	1992	1993	1994	1995
United States	4,172	776	891	645	639	413	304	181	10	3	3	8	21	18	18	25	11	16	23	14	31	38	31	56
Federal	33	1	9	7	6	6	3	1	-	-	-	-	-	-	-	-	-	-	-	-	-	-	-	-
State	4,139	775	882	638	633	407	301	180	10	3	3	8	21	18	18	25	11	16	23	14	31	38	31	56
Northeast	610	155	145	110	74	56	51	17	-	-	-	-	-	-	-	-	-	-	-	-	-	-	-	-
Connecticut	21	2	3	5	5	5	1	-	X	X	X	X	X	X	X	X	X	X	X	X	X	X	X	X
Maine	X	X	X	X	X	X	X	X	X	X	X	X	X	X	X	X	X	X	X	X	X	X	X	X
Massachusetts	27	7	11	6	3	-	X	X	X	X	X	X	X	X	X	X	X	X	X	X	X	X	X	X
New Hampshire	1	-	1	-	-	-	-	-	X	X	X	X	X	X	X	X	X	X	X	X	X	X	X	X
New Jersey	74	24	16	6	8	8	9	3	-	-	-	-	-	-	-	-	-	-	-	-	-	-	-	-
New York	329	80	73	78	36	27	25	10	-	X	X	X	X	X	X	X	X	X	X	X	X	X	X	X
Pennsylvania	154	41	41	15	21	19	12	5	-	-	-	-	-	-	-	-	-	-	-	-	-	-	-	-
Rhode Island	X	X	X	X	X	X	X	X	X	X	X	X	X	X	X	X	X	X	X	X	X	X	X	X
Vermont	4	1	-	1	2	-	X	X	X	X	X	X	X	X	X	X	X	X	X	X	X	X	X	X
Midwest	431	105	113	42	64	42	16	16	5	-	1	1	-	1	-	1	1	5	1	1	4	3	1	2
Illinois	97	34	27	13	5	8	1	2	-	X	X	X	X	X	X	X	1	X	X	X	X	X	1	5
Indiana	44	11	20	1	-	2	1	-	X	X	1	X	1	X	X	X	X	X	X	X	X	1	5	X
Iowa	18	1	7	-	2	2	5	1	X	X	X	X	X	X	X	X	X	X	X	X	X	X	X	X
Kansas	15	X	X	4	5	-	1	2	4	X	X	X	X	X	X	X	X	X	X	X	X	X	X	X
Michigan	X	X	X	X	X	X	X	X	X	X	X	X	X	X	X	X	X	X	X	X	X	X	X	X
Minnesota	X	X	X	X	X	X	X	X	X	X	X	X	X	X	X	X	X	X	X	X	X	X	X	X
Missouri	79	16	20	6	9	5	2	X	X	X	X	X	X	X	X	X	1	-	1	4	1	1	4	6
Nebraska	5	-	-	-	2	1	1	1	-	-	-	-	-	-	-	-	-	-	-	-	-	-	1	-
North Dakota	-	-	-	-	-	-	-	-	-	-	-	-	-	-	-	-	-	-	-	-	-	-	-	-
Ohio	172	43	39	15	36	20	12	7	-	-	-	X	X	X	X	X	X	X	X	X	X	X	X	X
South Dakota	1	X	X	1	X	X	X	X	X	X	X	X	X	X	X	X	X	X	X	X	X	X	X	X
Wisconsin	X	X	X	X	X	X	X	X	X	X	X	X	X	X	X	X	X	X	X	X	X	X	X	X
South	2,569	419	524	413	419	244	183	102	2	2	1	7	21	16	18	24	10	13	17	13	26	30	26	41
Alabama	147	19	41	29	21	14	6	4	2	1	-	1	X	X	X	1	-	1	X	-	1	1	-	X
Arkansas	129	20	33	20	18	11	7	9	1	-	-	X	X	X	X	1	4	1	-	2	2	5	2	2
Delaware	17	2	6	2	2	-	7	-	-	-	-	-	-	-	-	-	-	-	-	1	1	2	-	1
District of Columbia	40	15	5	3	13	3	1	-	-	-	X	X	X	X	X	X	X	X	X	X	X	X	X	X
Florida	206	15	29	38	27	22	27	12	-	-	1	1	8	3	3	2	2	4	2	2	2	3	1	3

Georgia	386	64	73	58	72	51	34	14	-	-	-	1	2	3	1	5	1	1	-	1	-	2	1	2
Kentucky	103	18	34	19	15	8	8	1	-	-	-	-	-	-	-	-	-	-	-	-	-	-	-	-
Louisiana	155	39	19	24	23	14	13	1	-	-	-	1	5	1	-	8	3	-	1	1	-	1	-	1
Maryland	69	6	10	26	19	2	4	1	-	-	-	-	-	-	-	-	-	-	-	-	-	-	1	-
Mississippi	158	26	22	34	26	15	21	10	-	-	-	1	-	-	-	2	-	1	-	-	-	-	-	-
North Carolina	271	51	80	50	62	14	5	1	-	-	-	-	2	-	1	-	-	-	-	1	1	-	1	2
Oklahoma	66	25	9	6	7	4	3	5	1	-	-	-	-	-	-	-	-	-	1	-	2	-	-	3
South Carolina	167	37	30	32	29	16	10	8	-	-	-	-	-	1	1	-	-	-	1	1	-	-	-	1
Tennessee	93	16	31	19	18	1	7	1	-	-	-	-	-	-	-	-	-	-	-	-	-	-	-	-
Texas	401	48	72	38	36	49	25	29	-	-	-	1	3	6	10	6	3	4	4	5	12	17	14	19
Virginia	121	8	20	13	22	15	8	6	-	-	-	1	1	2	1	1	1	1	3	2	4	5	2	5
West Virginia	40	10	10	2	9	5	4	-	X	X	X	X	X	X	X	X	X	X	X	X	X	X	X	X
West	529	96	100	73	76	65	51	45	3	-	2	-	-	1	-	1	1	2	1	-	4	4	2	2
Alaska[a]	X	X	X	X	X	X	X	X	X	X	X	X	X	X	X	X	X	X	X	X	X	X	X	X
Arizona	42	7	10	6	3	2	6	4	-	-	-	-	-	-	-	-	-	-	-	-	1	2	-	1
California	294	51	57	35	45	39	35	29	1	-	-	-	-	-	-	-	-	-	-	-	1	1	-	-
Colorado	47	16	9	6	7	1	2	5	1	-	-	-	-	-	-	-	-	-	-	-	-	-	-	-
Hawaii[a]	X	X	X	X	X	X	X	X	X	X	X	X	X	X	X	X	X	X	X	X	X	X	X	X
Idaho	4	-	-	-	-	2	1	-	-	-	-	-	-	-	-	-	-	-	-	-	-	-	1	-
Montana	7	1	4	1	-	-	-	-	-	-	-	-	-	-	-	-	-	-	-	-	-	-	-	1
Nevada	34	5	3	5	5	9	-	2	-	-	1	-	-	1	-	-	-	2	1	-	-	-	-	-
New Mexico	8	2	-	-	2	2	1	1	-	-	-	-	-	-	-	-	-	-	-	-	-	-	-	-
Oregon	19	1	1	6	6	4	-	1	X	X	-	-	-	-	-	-	-	-	-	-	-	-	-	-
Utah	17	-	2	3	1	2	4	1	-	-	1	-	-	-	-	1	1	-	-	-	1	-	-	-
Washington	49	10	13	9	7	4	2	2	-	-	-	-	-	-	-	-	-	-	-	-	-	1	1	-
Wyoming	8	3	1	2	-	-	-	-	1	-	-	-	-	-	-	-	-	-	-	-	1	-	-	-

Note: In three states, Maine, Minnesota, and Wisconsin, there was no death penalty for the entire period covered by the table. Alaska and Hawaii have not had the death penalty since 1960, when they were first included as states. For other states, the death penalty may have been abolished or declared unconstitutional, and/or subsequently reinstated. In these cases, an X will appear to indicate years when the death penalty was not in effect.

[a] As states, Alaska and Hawaii are included in the series beginning Jan. 1, 1960.

Source: U.S. Department of Justice, Bureau of Justice Statistics, *Correctional Populations in the United States, 1995,* NCJ-163916 (Washington, DC: U.S. Department of Justice, 1997), Table 7.25; and data provided by the U.S. Department of Justice, Bureau of Justice Statistics. Table adapted by SOURCEBOOK staff.

Capital Punishment Statistics Update-1999–2000

In 1999–98 inmates were executed, more than in any year since the early 1950s. Texas executed 35 persons, more than double the number in any other state. Virginia was second with 14 executions. Of those executed in 1999:

61 or 62% were white
33 or 34% were black
4 or 4% were American Indian or Asian.

All of those executed were male. Ninety-four executions were carried out by lethal injection. Thirty-eight states had capital punishment statutes. Some 3,500 inmates were under sentence of death, all for murder. This represented a 2% increase over 1998 yearend. Fifty women were under sentence of death. The youngest inmate on death row was 18, the oldest 84.
In 2000–85 inmates were executed, 13% fewer than in 1999.
Source: U.S. Department of Justice, Bureau of Justice Statistics. *http://www.ojp.usdoj.gov/bjs/glance/exe.htm*

as "three strikes and you're out" legislation, which requires stiff sentences for those who offend repeatedly (see In the News, "Equal Sentencing"). Mandatory sentences for those involved in drug-related offenses are another illustration of this approach. These changes have led to a need for new construction of prisons that the public continues to support through taxes. In 1996, average construction costs per prison bed were $31,184 for minimum security; $50,376 for medium security; and $80,562 for maximum security (no figures were available for the cost per bed of supermax facilities) (Camp & Camp, 1997). In addition, we are currently seeing an increasing population of older inmates. This leads to special housing considerations, additional physical health care considerations, and additional mental health considerations brought on by the emotional stress of prison life among the aging. It has been estimated that the cost of housing an inmate over the age of 60 is about $69,000 per year (Cromwell, 1994, p. 3). It is apparent that some consideration must be given to the needs and costs involved in housing geriatric inmates, as well as to the larger issue of prison construction costs in general.

Defendants in our criminal justice network are, theoretically at least, innocent until proven guilty. It has been said that we would rather allow 100 guilty parties to go free than to convict 1 innocent person. Still, mistakes are possible, and occasionally we find that a person who has been incarcerated for a crime did not, in fact, commit the crime. As might be expected, a major argument against the death penalty is that it is irreversible. With this in mind, Governor George Ryan of Illinois recently announced a moratorium on the death penalty in that state. His concern is based on the fact that more death row inmates have been exonerated than executed since the death penalty was reintroduced in 1977 (Green, 2000). The American Bar Association has also proposed a moratorium on the death penalty for the same reasons (Radlet & Bedau, 1998).

Among the most heated debates concerning the death penalty are those concerning whether or not it achieves the objectives of punishment. Clearly, it precludes the possibility of rehabilitation. Equally clearly, it deters the person executed from further crimes. It also satisfies the revenge motive. But does it deter other potential offenders? Sellin (1967), reviewing the effects of the death penalty, concludes that its abolition does not significantly jeopardize the lives of police officers, correctional personnel, or prison inmates. Bailey (1974), reviewing numerous studies of the death penalty, found no support for the deterrence hypothesis. In fact, Bailey found that in some states that had abolished the death penalty and later reinstated it, homicides actually increased in numbers. In contrast, Phillips (1981) concluded from his study of selected, highly publicized executions in London that they lowered the weekly homicide rate. However, Phillips's conclusions have been criticized because weekly homicide rates rose again two or three weeks later (Ziesel, 1982). According to Walker (1998, p. 102), the safest conclusion at this point is that there is little evidence that the death penalty deters crime.

In the News

EQUAL SENTENCING; TRUTH IN SENTENCING IS THE RIGHT WAY TO GO

By Thomas H. Barland

Truth in sentencing is now law. It will apply to all felony crimes committed on or after Dec. 31, 1999. Under truth in sentencing, anyone sentenced to prison serves 100% of the prison term given. There is no early release.

There is no credit for good behavior.

There will be no release by a parole board.

This is a dramatic and positive change from the present system, which has suffered a loss of credibility and failed to adequately protect the public because most prisoners serve only 40% to 57% of the prison sentence imposed by the judge.

The Criminal Penalties Study Committee was given the task of implementing truth in sentencing by revising the criminal code, creating temporary sentencing guidelines for judges and preparing the way for a sentencing commission that will prepare permanent sentencing guidelines and attempt to bring about a more rational and just sentencing system for Wisconsin.

The committee, after laboring for more than a year, has presented a report to the governor and Legislature, together with proposed legislation that has become Assembly Bill 465. The bill passed the Assembly 83–13 on

Sept. 23 and now awaits scrutiny in the Senate.

Why should the Legislature adopt the recommendations of the committee? The proposals, if adopted, will result in a more rational system of crime classifications; a reduced likelihood of disproportionate, unpredictable, unduly long or bizarre sentences; and sentencing guidelines that will provide judges with a logical and systematic approach to the exercise of sentencing discretion.

The committee further proposes a graduated system of supervision of the defendant when he or she is released from prison, starting first with strict supervision and then requiring the defendant to earn his or her way to less strict levels of supervision.

Finally, the committee sets out the structure for a sentencing commission, which will issue permanent sentencing guidelines, review sentencing practices, conduct studies and make recommendations to improve the system in the future.

Wisconsin badly needs a more fair and rational criminal sentencing system. It needs to significantly improve its methods of punishing and treating criminals. It needs to do this in a more cost-effective way so the

Continued

ballooning Department of Corrections budget does not strangle higher education and other essential services of state government.

Under our present law, our prisons are overcrowded and expensive to maintain. At last count, on Sept 24, we had 19,528 adult prisoners in a system designed for 15,244. Thus far for 1999, our prison population has been increasing at an annual rate of approximately 12%.

Wisconsin now has the third- or fourth-highest rate of prisoner increase of all the states. Without the implementing legislation recommended by committee, the original truth-in-sentencing law—with its 50% increase in maximum prison sentences—could result in a greater increase in prison population or the premature release of possibly dangerous criminals sentenced under our old laws.

Whether we continue under the new or old sentencing systems, the problem of the mushrooming prison population will not be resolved until judges have alternatives to prison that they can use with assurance that the public will be adequately protected. Thus, the committee recommends a new system of enhanced probation and strictly supervised alcohol and drug treatment facilities outside prison, where probation agents will have a stronger lock-up authority than they now have.

Even more urgent is the need to address the racial problems in our society and criminal justice system, which have resulted in a prison population that is 57% minority, and the imprisonment of 3% of all African-Americans living in Wisconsin. These are social ills that can no longer be ignored.

Wisconsin, which prides itself in being progressive and tolerant of diversity in population, has a higher percentage of minority prisoners than the mean for all state and federal prisons. One of the first jobs to be undertaken by the sentencing commission will be the study of race in the criminal justice system.

If the Assembly bill does not pass, or is substantially weakened, Wisconsin will be worse off with an incomplete truth-in-sentencing law than with the laws that exist under its present system. States such as North Carolina, Virginia and Ohio—which have adopted truth in sentencing with a similar structure, including stronger enhanced probation, alternatives to prison and sentencing commission structure—have managed to stabilize their prison populations without an increase in the crime rates.

This bill should be enacted to restore credibility and coherence to criminal sentencing and to deliver a greater measure of public safety to our communities.

Milwaukee Journal Sentinel, *October 3, 1999, p. 1.*

In spite of considerable evidence to the contrary, the American public appears to believe that executions do deter criminals. Public opinion polls have consistently shown that the public favors the death penalty (in 1997, about 75 percent said they believed in capital punishment), and recent polls indicate the American public continues to support capital punishment (Harris, 1997; "Execution Reconsidered," 1999). But opinion polls are just one measure of the public conscience. Some abolitionists argue that prospective jurors may attempt to avoid jury duty in capital cases. It is quite easy to support the death penalty when one is not directly involved or when one is seeking revenge. However, when one must bear the responsibility for assigning the penalty, his or her attitude may be quite different.

Court Decisions and the Death Penalty

As we have noted, there have been several important court cases concerning the death penalty. The effect of *Furman* was to invalidate many existing death penalty statutes and to force legislators to develop more objective criteria while eliminating discrimination. The decision mandated that objective criteria and specialized procedures be incorporated into all future death penalty legislation. Of the 38 states that enacted new death penalty measures following *Furman*, Georgia was the first to have the new statutes tested in the courts. Favorable rulings in *Gregg* v. *Georgia* (1976), *Proffit* v. *Florida* (1976), and *Jurek* v. *Texas* (1976) facilitated the reinstatement of capital punishment. At the same time, however, the Supreme Court has ruled that mandatory death sentences for rape (*Coker* v. *Georgia*, 1972) and murder (*Woodson* v. *North Carolina*, 1976) constitute cruel and unusual punishment. In the 1980s, the court expedited appeal procedures by allowing death penalty appeals to take precedence on federal dockets (*Barefoot* v. *Estelle*, 1983), thereby eliminating the lengthy delays death row inmates have traditionally obtained by appealing their sentences to the Supreme Court. Clearly, capital punishment procedures have been molded slowly over time by both the states and the courts.

CORRECTIONAL ORGANIZATION

Although we commonly use the term "American correctional system," this is a misnomer. Correctional programs in America are actually far more fragmented than unified. There is no central authority controlling these agencies, and to some extent, they pursue different and sometimes conflicting goals.

As is the case with the courts, both the federal government and the states maintain correctional systems. Lack of centralized control is one of the major obstacles to reform, since most jurisdictions provide for autonomy of jails and prisons, which are further segmented by gender, age, and type of offense involved. Similarly, probation, parole, and diversionary programs are also largely autonomous.

The Federal Network

Congress established the Bureau of Prisons in 1930. The legislation that established the federal network resulted from serious overcrowding of existing facilities and the associated practice of leasing space from local and state facilities. Currently, the federal network has been divided into five regions, with headquarters in the following cities: Burlingame, California; Kansas City, Missouri; Dallas; Atlanta; and Philadelphia. Heads of correctional institutions and community facilities report to regional directors who are in turn responsible to the director of the Federal Bureau of Prisons. The Bureau of Prisons has five subdivisions: Correctional Programs, Planning and Development, Medical and Service, Federal Prison Industries, Inc., and the National Institute of Corrections. Each subdivision is responsible for developing and implementing programs that are national in scope, but the daily administration of these programs is left to regional and institutional directors.

Federal institutions vary considerably in size. Those in Atlanta and Leavenworth, Kansas, are quite large, with populations of about 2,000 inmates each, and are reserved for more hardened inmates. The facility in Marion, Illinois, is smaller and houses dangerous and violent offenders. The prison in Terre Haute, Indiana, was designed to house inmates thought to have considerable potential for rehabilitation. The present inmate population of the federal prisons is about 113,000, with about 8,300 of these being females.

New federal institutions have been built in Brooklyn; Guaynabo, Puerto Rico; and Los Angeles. These metropolitan correctional centers are designed to house federal offenders serving short sentences and pretrial detainees. Built near federal courts, these new high-rise institutions stand in sharp contrast to older prisons, with unbreakable glass replacing bars, and dormitory or private rooms as opposed to cells.

Through the National Institute of Corrections, the Federal Bureau of Prisons provides assistance to state and local networks through grants, by conducting research, by disseminating research materials, and by conducting training seminars.

State Networks

The bulk of the corrections network is located at the state level. At midyear 1999, the nation's prisons and jails incarcerated 1,860,520 persons (Beck, 2000). During the year 2000, this number surpassed 2,000,000. We are witnessing annual prison population increases of between 5 and 6 percent. As we continue to incarcerate more and more people, the costs for construction, operation, and personnel continue to escalate. State spending for correctional facilities has been increasing at an average of about 7 percent per year. This increase represents about twice the annual increase for state education (3.6 percent) and more than twice the increase for state natural resources (2.5 percent) (Stephan, 1999). The question we must ask ourselves is whether we can afford to pay for facilities to house and treat this increasing population. Perhaps we need to do more to prevent individuals from becoming involved in crime and to reintegrate those who have been incarcerated back in to society. These issues will be discussed in greater detail later in the text.

While some states have only 1 or 2 correctional facilities, more heavily populated states such as Texas, California, and Illinois have 10 or more facilities. Originally, many prisons were constructed near large urban industrial areas, and industry made use of the cheap labor available. When this contract system was abolished, prison officials were faced with the task of making work for inmates. This work often consisted of menial tasks invented solely for the purpose of keeping the inmates occupied.

In rural areas, prison farms were built. The stated intent of these farms was to use prison labor to produce agricultural products, thereby increasing the economic feasibility of the institutions. However, abuses occurred, and prisoners were leased to farmers as a source of cheap labor. This practice has been abolished in some states because with the advent of mechanized farming, prison officials found it more profitable to lease prison lands to farmers than to force prisoners to tend the land.

TYPES OF INSTITUTIONS

A major problem with correctional facilities concerns the opportunity they provide for inmates to become more antisocial as a result of their exposure to more hardened offenders. In an attempt to deal with this problem, most jurisdictions have developed classification systems based on the amount of security required for inmates. Most commonly, prisons are divided into maximum, medium, and minimum security categories. In some cases, supermax security facilities have also been developed.

Supermax Security Facilities

Supermax security facilities house offenders who are extremely violent or dangerous and/or who are considered serious escape risks. They reflect the goals of revenge and incapacitation. Perimeter security typically consists of double fences and razor ribbon, electronic surveillance systems, and electric fences or walls. Movement inside these prisons is tightly controlled; inmates are placed in restraints and escorted by several staff. Contact with the outside world is restricted, the emphasis is on security and control, and treatment and rehabilitation programs are limited. Inmates may be locked down for as many as 23 hours per day.

Maximum Security Facilities

Maximum security facilities also reflect the goals of revenge and incapacitation. They are generally characterized by high concrete walls that are typically occupied by armed guards and equipped with floodlights. These institutions are generally reserved for dangerous offenders and those serving long sentences. Because of the emphasis on custody, rehabilitation programs are often present in name only in such institutions.

Medium Security Facilities

Medium security facilities have become more popular over the years in the United States. These prisons are usually smaller than maximum security prisons. Physically, they often resemble their maximum security counterparts, but they generally provide for more freedom of movement internally. These institutions house younger and less dangerous offenders and place more emphasis on rehabilitation than do maximum security facilities.

Minimum Security Facilities

Minimum security facilities house nonviolent and nontraditional offenders, for the most part. They are characterized by dormitory-style living, private rooms, and the absence of armed guards and walls. Most have been built relatively recently in comparison with maximum and medium security facilities, and they generally house fewer inmates than either of the other two types. Work and educational release are integral parts of minimum security programs, and home furlough is used frequently. These facilities, although criticized as being country clubs for white-collar and political offenders, are thought to provide better opportunities for rehabilitation than other types of prisons because they tend to maximize contact between inmates and the outside world in which they must survive after release from prison.

JAILS

In terms of sheer numbers, jails are one of the most important features of the correctional network. In 1997, there were some 567,000 inmates in jails across the United States (Bureau of Justice Statistics, 1997). Jails are usually the first, and sometimes the only, contact offenders have with corrections. Although jails have often been ignored by those interested in corrections, recent criticisms of the deplorable conditions existing in many of these facilities have increased their visibility somewhat (Thompson, 1986; Mays, 1992).

History of Jails

Earlier we noted that pretrial detention existed in Europe in the sixteenth century. Champion (2001 p. 82) describes these early detention facilities as providing substandard food and shelter and being plagued by malnutrition, disease, and death. These facilities were basically holding tanks rather than correctional institutions. As indicated earlier, the Walnut Street Jail was the first institution in America to be used for correctional purposes. In the seventeenth century, jails were built for the general detention of prisoners awaiting monthly court session in Jamestown, Virginia (Champion, 1998, p. 306). Although Fishman documented the poor conditions existing in American jails in 1923, little public attention was devoted to them until 1970, when the first national jail census was conducted (Fishman, 1969).

In the 1980s and 1990s, many jails were cited for failure to meet jail standards relating to fire safety, health and sanitation, and various other areas. As a means to relieve overcrowding, court-ordered reductions in the number of jail inmates have become common in the past two decades.

Control and Organization

Jails have been very difficult to reform because they are normally financed and administered at the local or county level. This local autonomy has allowed jails to escape many state and federal reform movements and frequently involves jails in local politics. They have been traditionally low-priority items in county budgets, and they are generally under the direct supervision of the sheriff, an elected official subject to political pressures, which is important because local constituents seldom consider jails the most desirable place to expend funds. In addition, the sheriff is both a law enforcement official and the chief correctional officer in the county, and law enforcement duties traditionally have been considered more important than jail supervision. Jail staffs frequently have little correctional training and are generally not well paid. Further, inmate–staff ratios of 40 to 1 are not uncommon in jails. It is not difficult to see why jails—with little supervision, inadequate staff, and high inmate–staff ratios—contribute little to correctional efforts.

Jail Problems

Beginning with the first jail census, investigations have consistently shown that jail populations are basically male (89 percent), under 35 years of age (68 percent), under- or unemployed, below the poverty level, and disproportionately from minority groups (58 percent) (Bureau of Justice Statistics, 1997, p. 6). Jails are institutions in which the powerless are housed until the time of their trial, until they have served their sentences, or until the charges against them are dropped.

In 1975, Goldfarb referred to the jail as "the ultimate ghetto." (While this label may sound extreme, many who have studied American jails agree wholeheartedly. Many of these institutions are antiquated, with 25 percent having been constructed more than 50 years ago, and another 6 percent more than 100 years ago. There are, to be sure, some modern jails, but these are the exception rather than the rule. Because of the bad state of repair, jails have been plagued by fires. In 1991, a jail fire in Missouri killed four inmates ("Four Prisoners Trapped," 1991). Previous fires in Biloxi, Mississippi, and Jersey City, New Jersey, also resulted in inmate deaths (Patterson, 1983). Many of the older structures are without emergency exits, do not have fire extinguishers that are in working order, and have antiquated locking systems so that inmates are virtually doomed if fire breaks out. Heating, ventilation, and lighting are also problems in many jails, as is outdated or inoperative plumbing.

Despite regulations, convicted offenders are frequently not segregated from pretrial detainees, and juveniles are frequently placed in cell blocks with adults. Many jails also house drunks and vagrants on a short-term basis. As a result of inadequate funding, constant turnover, and the lack of authority to require pretrial detainees (who, after all, have not been convicted of any offense) to participate, treatment programs are virtually nonexistent in most jails.

Health problems are also common in jail settings. Poor or poorly prepared food characterizes many such institutions. Recent research has found intravenous drug use and the transmission of HIV to be problems among inmates in rural jails (Kane & Dotson, 1997), and tuberculosis rates in jails may be five times higher than in the general population (Mueller, 1996). Virtually all contagious diseases, from hepatitis to the common cold, can easily become epidemics in jail facilities.

Some efforts to improve jail conditions have been made. Some states have established new and stricter standards for local jails, but follow-up inspections may or may not be mandated and carried out (Mueller, 1996). Inmates have also sought redress through the courts (*Brenneman* v. *Madigan*, 1972). However, without proper policies, funding, and mandated inspections, the jails are likely to remain problematic (Kane & Dotson, 1997).

EVALUATING PRISON REHABILITATION PROGRAMS

How do we determine whether or not prison rehabilitation programs are successful? Most commonly, we look at **recidivism rates,** which are based on the proportion of offenders released from prison who become involved in reported criminal behavior after their release. Many criminal justice officials believe that recidivism rates range from 50 to 75 percent, that is, that one-half to three-fourths of all offenders released from prison commit additional offenses (Maguire & Pastore, 1995; Camp & Camp, 1995). Such high estimates have been challenged by a number of researchers (Beck & Shipley, 1989). Among the first to challenge traditional conceptions of recidivism was Daniel Glaser (1964), whose research indicated that a figure of 35 percent is more reasonable. Glaser argues that recidivism rates depend on a number of factors, including the characteristics of offenders sentenced to prison, the manner in which parole is employed, and the type of institution involved. For example, in a jurisdiction that relies heavily on probation, only those offenders considered poor risks may be sentenced to prison. Similarly, if parole or early release is used extensively, some inmates may be released prematurely. Finally, when we sentence offenders to maximum instead of medium or minimum security facilities, we are making some assumptions about the likelihood of rehabilitation, and this affects recidivism rates in each of these types of institutions. Glaser makes the additional point that many ex-convicts are returned to prison not because they commit new crimes but because they commit technical violations of parole requirements, which do not necessarily indicate a return to criminal behavior.

The debate concerning recidivism rates continues, with some supporting Glaser's approach and others continuing to believe that recidivism is considerably higher than Glaser would have us believe. The problems of measuring recidivism are complex, but if we are to improve our performance in the area of rehabilitation, accurate measures of recidivism for different types of programs must be developed. What we have learned is that a number of obstacles to rehabilitation exist in the prison setting, and it is to these obstacles that we now turn our attention.

The Prison Society

The potential for successful rehabilitation in prison depends on a number of factors. Two of the most important factors are the presence of qualified staff members in sufficient numbers and creation of an atmosphere conducive to rehabilitation. Under present conditions in most prisons, neither of these conditions exists. The lack of adequately trained staff in sufficient numbers reflects the fact that prisons have not traditionally received high priority when it comes to allocation of resources. The inability of prison officials to create conditions favorable to rehabilitation results partly from inadequate staff, but equally important is the fact that most of the time spent by inmates is in the company of other inmates. Life inside prison is radically different from the prior experiences of the new inmate. In Goffman's (1961) terms, prison is a **total institution.** The inmate's identity is stripped away, and decisions that the inmate previously made concerning eating, sleeping, working, and so forth are now made by the institutional staff. Yet, when we release the offender from prison, we expect him or her to assume full responsibility for these and other decisions in the outside world. Additionally, while the inmate is in prison, he or she is subject to what may be called the inmates' code. Sykes and Messinger (1970) point out that even if the prison administration strongly supports rehabilitation, it is difficult to achieve because peer group pressure forces inmates not to support the goals of the administration (Lambropoulou, 1999). In some prisons, inmate gangs have become so powerful that they actually control the institution and the staff, making rehabilitation unlikely.

Robert Martinson (1974), after studying correctional programs, argued that very few rehabilitation programs work. Unfortunately, his remarks have been interpreted to mean that nothing can work, even though he later admitted that under certain circumstance some programs might be effective. Others have found similar evidence that rehabilitation can be effective under certain conditions, which, unfortunately, are seldom met (Walker, 1998). This debate has accompanied the accusation and perhaps rationalization that prisons have simply become warehouses. That is, the manifest goal of corrections has become the incapacitation of the convicted and the protection of the public.

In the late 1990s, state and federal prisons in the United States were operating at about 125 percent of capacity (Gilliard & Beck, 1996). The causes and ramifications of **warehousing** are severe. When warehousing occurs, the administrative agenda, the means of evaluation, and the goals are all redefined. The overcrowding resulting from warehousing leads to tension, limits the opportunity for rehabilitation (Conklin, 1998, p. 516), and creates a sense of abandonment on the part of the inmate. Prisons that have experienced violent riots are frequently overcrowded, highly authoritarian, and understaffed (Useem & Reisig, 1999).

The problem of warehousing can be explained by the network approach. First, the public, and perhaps some criminal justice officials, complain that too many convicted offenders are on the streets or are not receiving appropriate punishment. The legislatures respond by enacting laws requiring longer sentences and limiting other alternatives. The courts are forced to sentence more defendants to prison and for longer periods of time. Correction officials are often caught in the middle: they must accommodate the increase in prison population, but they do not receive concomitant funding to comply with prison regulations. Once the warehousing is revealed through civil suits or a riot, the public is appalled by what has happened. Although they are shocked, do they want to fund a bond issue or increase taxes to provide adequate prison care? There are no easy solutions. The issue of warehousing is extremely complex, and one can see how actions and reactions in one portion of the network affect other components (Conklin, 1998, pp. 465–66).

Rehabilitation versus Custody

Another obstacle to rehabilitation is the conflict that often occurs between therapeutic and correctional staff. In many institutions, the staff of one persuasion has little or no respect for those of the other, and inmates sometimes use this lack of trust and respect among staff members to their advantage. Therapeutic staff frequently regard themselves as above correctional staff and are far better paid in most cases. Correctional staff often resent the fact that they take most of the risks in dealing with inmates 24 hours a day, but are not regarded as professionals and are not well paid.

Group and some individual therapy occur in most prisons, some also have social-skills training programs, and others offer family intervention and educational programs (Conklin, 1998, pp. 515–16). But costs for these types of treatment are high, and success is hampered by insufficient knowledge of the causes of crime, the fact that inmates might see a therapist/counselor less than one hour per week (the rest of the time is spent with other inmates under the supervision of correctional staff), and a lack of followup after the offender is released from prison. It is also somewhat ironic that we continue to provide psychological therapy to inmates when a great deal of the available evidence suggests that they are no more in need of such therapy than most of the rest of us.

Education and Vocational Training in Prison

As early as the 1830s, education was defined as one means of assisting prisoner rehabilitation, and most prisons currently offer educational programs of one type or another. Many inmates do not have high school educations, and some estimates indicate that as many as 80 percent are illiterate. The quality of educational programs in prisons varies considerably, and some of the most outspoken critics of prison education argue that such programs are merely tools to occupy the inmates' time and that under conditions of confinement, they have little chance to succeed. An additional problem plaguing educational programs in prison is the negative experience that many inmates have had with education in the outside world. Still, it appears that some prison education programs do benefit participants by helping them deal with the stress of prison overcrowding, by helping create more positive feelings about other inmates, and by improving inmate self-esteem (Lawrence, 1995; Parker, 1990).

In theory, most prison work programs are designed to provide inmates with job skills that may help them secure employment on the outside. In reality, something quite different often occurs. Many of the skills prisoners are taught are obsolete by the time they are released (and some are obsolete at the time they are taught). Even when the skills they learned are current, ex-convicts often find that the stigma of having served time in prison is more important than the skills they possess. In short, no matter how skilled they are, they can't find employment because of their records.

In reviewing the increase in prison population over the past quarter of a century, Clear (1994) concludes that the expansion of the prison system in the United States has not reduced crime and has produced few other social benefits. Walker (1998) states that "no conclusive evidence indicates that locking up a lot of people actually produces the promised reduction in crime. Finally, even where some crime reduction does occur, it is not clear that it is worth the enormous dollar cost to society" (p. 140). Alternatives to the current emphasis on building new prisons must be found, and we turn our attention to some of these alternatives in the next chapter.

Summary

1. Overcrowding of prisons and jails, the high costs of incarceration, and high recidivism rates indicating the failure of correctional rehabilitation programs have all attracted the attention of the public and politicians in recent years.

2. Jail and prison populations continue to skyrocket, and rehabilitation continues to be an elusive goal.

3. Questions concerning the effectiveness of punishment as a deterrent remain basically unanswered, but the public continues to support the use of incarceration as a means of retribution or revenge.

overall conditions in jails and prisons may be better today than in afety and health continue to be major issues in these institutions.

...les, gangs, and staff differences of opinion continue to make re- ...ation difficult, if not impossible, in most cases.

6. Educational and vocational training programs leave a good deal to be desired.

7. Capital punishment continues to be supported by the majority of the public even though a number of states have imposed, or are considering impos- ing, a moratorium on the death penalty, because of evidence that many of the inmates on death row may be innocent of the crimes for which they were sentenced.

Key Terms Defined

early release The release of a prisoner before he or she has served the mini- mum period of time required for the offense.

banishment The process of pronouncing a person civilly dead and forcing him or her to leave the country.

transportation The practice of transporting convicts to a country other than the one in which they are citizens.

age of enlightenment The period during the late eighteenth and early nine- teenth centuries when humanitarian reforms occurred with respect to the mentally ill, prisoners, juveniles, and others.

hedonism The seeking of pleasurable experiences.

Walnut Street Jail The first correctional institution in the United States.

Pennsylvania prisons Prisons designed with a central hub and numerous wings radiating from this hub, with cells in each wing placed back-to- back for the purpose of isolating prisoners from one another.

Auburn prisons U-shaped prisons with several tiers of cells; prisoners worked and ate together, and a code of silence was enforced.

retribution Exacting repayment (often with a motive of revenge); making the punishment fit the crime.

specific deterrence The notion that punishment will prevent the criminal from repeating his or her crimes.

general deterrence The notion that punishment of some will prevent others from committing crimes.

supermax security facilities Prisons housing extremely violent or dangerous offenders and/or those who are considered major escape risks.

maximum security facilities Prisons designed to isolate and maintain cus- tody of dangerous offenders and those serving long sentences.

medium security facilities Similar to maximum security facilities, but more freedom of movement is generally allowed inmates.

minimum security facilities Prisons without walls and armed guards characteristic of medium, maximum, and supermax facilities, with emphasis on rehabilitation as opposed to custody.

recidivism rates Rates based on the proportion of offenders released from prison who become involved in reported criminal behavior after their release.

total institution An institution (such as a prison) in which all decisions concerning working, eating, sleeping, and freedom of movement are made by the staff instead of the inmates.

warehousing Placing offenders in institutions with little regard for treatment or prisoners' rights.

Critical Thinking Exercises

1. Trace the historical development of corrections in America. What have been the most significant contributions to reform of American penal institutions?
2. American jails have been called a national scandal. Why? Suggest reforms that might improve jails. How likely are these reforms to be implemented? Why?
3. Why do rehabilitation programs prove unsuccessful with many, if not most, inmates? What changes would have to occur for such programs to be more effective?
4. Discuss the pros and cons of capital punishment. Do you support capital punishment? Why or why not?

Internet Exercises

We have discussed a number of problems related to corrections in the United States. Examine some of the latest information available on the Internet on the following corrections issues:

1. Correctional education (*www.corrections.com/*).
2. HIV and AIDS in prisons (what websites did you use to obtain your information?).
3. Jail overcrowding (what websites did you use to obtain your information?).
4. Privatization of prisons (what websites did you use to obtain your information?).

References

Bailey, W. C. (1974, September). Murder and the death penalty. *Journal of Criminal Law, Criminology, and Police Science, 65,* 416–22.

Barefoot v. *Estelle,* 77 Led. 2d. 1090 (1983).

Barnes, H. E., & Teeters, N. K. (1959). *New horizons in criminology* (3rd ed.). Englewood Cliffs, NJ: Prentice Hall.

Beccaria, C. (1953). *Essays on crimes and punishments.* Stanford, CA: Academic Reprints.

Beck, A. J. (2000, April). *Prison and jail inmates at midyear 1999.* Bureau of Justice Statistics. Washington, DC: U.S. Government Printing Office.

Beck, A. J., & Shipley, B. E. (1989, April). *Recidivism of prisoners released in 1983.* Washington, DC: U.S. Department of Justice.

Bowers, W. J. (1974). *Executions in America.* Lexington, MA: D.C. Heath.

Brenneman v. *Madigan,* 343 F. Supp. 128 (1972).

Bureau of Justice Statistics. (1997). *Prison and jail inmates at midyear 1997.* Washington, DC: U.S. Department of Justice.

Camp, G. M., & Camp, C. G. (1995). *The corrections yearbook: Adult corrections.* South Salem: NY: Criminal Justice Institute.

Camp, G. M., & Camp, C. G. (1997). *The corrections yearbook, 1997.* South Salem, NY: Criminal Justice Institute.

Chambliss, W. J. (1965). *Crime and the legal process.* New York: McGraw-Hill.

Champion, D. J. (1998). *Criminal justice in the United States* (2nd ed.). Chicago: Nelson-Hall.

Champion, D. J. (2001). *Corrections in the United States: A contemporary perspective.* (3rd ed.). Upper Saddle River, NJ. Prentice Hall.

Clear, T. (1994). *Harm in American penology: Offenders, victims, and their communities.* Albany, NY: New York University Press.

Coker v. *Georgia,* 433 U.S. 584 (1972).

Conklin, J. E. (1998). *Criminology* (6th ed.). Boston: Allyn and Bacon.

Court of Oyer and Terminer, Philadelphia, 13 DJC 285 (1930).

Craig v. *Boren,* 429 U.S. 190 (1976).

Cripe, C. A. (1997). *Legal aspects of corrections management.* Gaithersburg, MD: Aspen.

Cromwell, P. (1994, June). The graying of America's prisons. *Overcrowded Times, 3.*

Durham, A. M. (1994). *Crisis and reform: Current issues in American punishment.* Boston: Little, Brown.

Execution Reconsidered: Move toward Moratoriums in State Executions. [Editorial]. (1999, July 24). *Economist,* 27.

Fishman, J. F. (1969). *Crucibles of crime: The shocking story of the American jail.* Montclair, NJ: Patterson Smith.

Four prisoners trapped in their cells are killed by smoke from fire at Missouri jail. (1991, September 15). *New York Times,* p. 18.

Furman v. *Georgia,* 408 U.S. 238 (1972).

Gilliard D. K., & Beck, A. J. (1996, August). *Prison and jail inmates, 1995.* Washington, DC: U.S. Department of Justice.

Glaser, D. (1964). *The effectiveness of a prison and parole system.* Indianapolis: Bobbs-Merrill.

Goffman, E. (1961). *Asylums.* Garden City, NY: Doubleday.

Goldfarb, R. (1975). *Jails: The ultimate ghetto.* New York: Archer Press.

Green, J. (2000). Second thoughts on the death penalty: Governor of Illinois halts all executions. *American Prospect, 11* (10), 10–11.

Greenfield, L. A., & Snell, T. (1999, December). *Women offenders.* Bureau of Justice Statistics special report. Washington, DC: U.S. Government Printing Office.

Gregg v. *Georgia,* 428 U.S. 153 (1976).

Harris, L., et al. (1997, June 11). *The Harris poll.* Los Angeles: Creators Syndicate.

Hughes, R. (1987). *The fatal shore*. New York: Knopf.

Jurek v. *Texas*, 428 U.S. 262 (1976).

Kane, S., & Dotson, C. J. (1997). HIV risk and injecting drug use: Implications for rural jails. *Crime and Delinquency, 43*, 169–85.

Lambropoulou, E. (1999). The sociology of prison and the self-referential approach to prison organization and to correctional reforms. *Systems Research and Behavioral Science, 16*, (3), 239–52.

Lawrence, R. A. (1995). Classrooms vs. prison cells: Funding policies for education and corrections. *Journal of Crime and Justice, 18*, 113–26.

Lewis, C. S. (1953). The humanitarian theory of punishment. *Res Judicatae, 6*.

Maguire, K., and Pastore, A. L. (1995). *Bureau of justice statistics sourcebook of criminal justice statistics–1994*. Albany, NY: Hindelang Criminal Justice Research Center.

Martinson, R. R. (1974, Spring). What works? Questions and answers about prison reform. *The Public Interest*, 22–55.

Mays, G. L. (1992). *Setting the jail research agenda for the 1990s*. Proceedings from a special meeting. Washington, DC: National Institute of Corrections.

Menninger, K. (1968). *The crime of punishment*. New York: Viking Press.

Mueller, G. O. W. (1955). Tort, crime, and the primitive law. *Journal of Criminal Law, Criminology, and Police Science, 46*, 16–19.

Mueller, J. (1996). Locking up tuberculosis. *Corrections Today, 58*, 100–101.

Nagin, D. S., & Paternoster, R. (1991). The preventive effects of perceived risk of arrest: Testing an expanded conception of deterrence. *Criminology, 29*, 561–87.

Parker, E. A. (1990). The social psychological impact of a college education on the prison inmate. *Journal of Correctional Education, 41*, 140–46.

Patterson, M. J. (1983). The price of neglect is tragedy. *Corrections Magazine, 9* (1), 6–21.

Phillips, D. P. (1981). The deterrent effect of capital punishment: New evidence on an old controversy. *American Journal of Sociology, 86*, 139–48.

Pittman, D. J., & Gordon, C. W. (1968). *Revolving door*. New York: Free Press.

Profitt v. *Florida*, 428 U.S. 242 (1976).

Radlet, M. L., & Bedau, H. A. (1998). The execution of the innocent. *Law and Contemporary Problems, 61* (4), 105–24.

Sellin, T. (Ed.) (1967). *Capital punishment*. New York: Harper and Row.

Stephan, J. J. (1999, August). *State prison expenditures, 1996*. Washington, DC: Bureau of Justice Statistics.

Sykes, G., & Messinger, S. (1970). The inmate social code. In N. Johnson et al. (Eds.), *The sociology of punishment and corrections*, pp. 401–408. New York: Wiley.

Thompson, J. A. (1986). The American jail: Problems, politics, prospects. *American Journal of Criminal Justice, 10*, 205–21.

Useem, B., & Reisig, M. D. (1999). Collective action in prisons: Protests, disturbances, and riots. *Criminology, 37* (4), 735–59.

Walker, S. (1998). Sense and nonsense about crime and drugs: A policy guide (4th ed.). Belmont, CA: Wadsworth.

Weems v. *United States*, 217 U.S. 349 (1910).

Wilkerson v. *Utah*, 99 U.S. 130 (1878).

Wilson, J. Q., & Abrahamse, A. (1992). Does crime pay? *Justice Quarterly, 9*, 359–77.

Wilson, M. (1931). *The crime of punishment*. New York: Harcourt Brace and World.

Woodson v. *North Carolina*, 428 U.S. 280 (1976).

Ziesel, H. (1982). A comment on the 'deterrent effect of capital punishment' by Phillips. *American Journal of Sociology, 88*, 167–69.

Suggested Readings

Allen, H. E., & Simonsen, C. E. (2001). *Corrections in America: An introduction* (9th ed.). Upper Saddle River, NJ: Prentice Hall.

Lambropoulou, E. (1999). The sociology of prison and the self-referential approach to prison organization and to correctional reforms. *Systems Research and Behavioral Science, 16* (3), 239–52.

Phillips, M. (2000, June 3). Landmark rulings and laws on death. *CQ Weekly, 58* (23), 1326–27.

Sykes, G. M. (1958). *The society of captives: A study of a maximum security prison.* Princeton, NJ: Princeton University Press.

Wall, J. (1998). Elder care: Louisiana initiates program to meet the needs of aging population. *Corrections Today, 60* (2), 136–38.

CHAPTER THIRTEEN

Prisoners' Rights and Alternatives to Incarceration

Inmates typically look forward to visits from family and friends.
Spencer Grant/Photo Edit

J ulie is a convicted murderer. In spite of numerous early attempts to rehabilitate her through intermediate sanctions (including probation and boot camp), her behavior became increasingly violent and she eventually took the life of one of her boyfriend's lovers.

Convicted of murder, Julie was sentenced to life in prison without the possibility of parole. Good time meant nothing to her because she would never leave prison, so she continued her violent behavior in prison. Eventually, Julie was moved to a supermaximum security prison where she is locked down 23 hours per day. She continues to claim that she will kill anyone who gets in her way. She says she has nothing to lose and will never cooperate with prison authorities.

Key Terms

civil death

hands-off doctrine

cruel and unusual punishment

good time

intermediate sanctions

boot camps

community corrections

probation

intensive probation

parole

Chapter Outline

Freedom of Speech
Freedom of Religion
Cruel and Unusual Punishment
Due Process
Alternatives to Incarceration
   Probation
   Community Correctional Programs
   Parole

In the previous chapter, we noted that, historically, persons convicted of crime suffered a civil death. This practice was continued through the development of the penitentiary and reformatory systems and was recognized by state courts as recently as 1871 (*Ruffin* v. *Commonwealth*, 1871).

Under the doctrine of **civil death,** convicted offenders were denied the right to vote, to hold public office, or to enter into contracts. Until the 1960s, the courts would not hear suits from incarcerated offenders, and inmates had no means of challenging the conditions imposed by their keepers. This refusal to hear suits from prison inmates concerning prison officials is commonly referred to as the **hands-off doctrine.** The basic assumption behind this doctrine was that corrections was not a judicial province and that convicted persons were civilly dead and had relinquished constitutional rights and privileges.

In *Cooper* v. *Pate* (1964), the Supreme Court ended the hands-off doctrine by ruling that inmates are protected by the Civil Rights Act, which states, in part:

> Every person who, under color of any statute, ordinance, regulation, custom or usage of any State or Territory subjects, or causes to be subjected, any citizen of the United States or other person within the jurisdiction thereof to the deprivation of any rights, privileges, or immunities secured by the Constitution and laws shall be liable to the party injured in an action at law, suit in equity or other proper proceeding for redress. (Civil Rights Act, 42 U.S.C. 1983)

The result of this decision was a major change in correctional philosophy, commonly referred to as the prisoners' rights movement. The practice of allowing inmates to file actions concerning their confinement has led to numerous suits and has drastically altered some traditional correctional practices. For example, during the 1960s there were only a few hundred lawsuits filed by prisoners, but by the mid-1990s that number had swelled to nearly 40,000 cases per year. Although there was a dramatic increase in prisoner cases filed, nearly 70 percent of those cases were rejected by the courts as being frivolous. In response to this boom in prison litigation, Congress passed the Prison Litigation Reform Act, which became effective in 1996. The purpose of the act was to limit case filings, to limit federal court jurisdiction, to order changes in prison conditions, and to return more freedom to the states to manage their prisons. While the Supreme Court attempted to curb prisoner's lawsuits, it also ruled in *Casey* v. *Lewis* (1996) that inmates should have access to state and federal court systems and that correctional facilities should offer them law library facilities or persons trained to help illiterate offenders prepare their legal pleadings.

Although very few of the suits filed produce major changes in corrections, some have had dramatic effects. Let us look at some specific changes resulting from suits in the areas of freedom of speech, freedom of religion, freedom from cruel and unusual punishment, and due process.

FREEDOM OF SPEECH

Historically, prison officials have engaged in practices that denied inmates the use of mail service, censored both incoming and outgoing mail, and denied inmates access to media sources when access might have been embarrassing to such officials. Court decisions have required that such practices be altered. In *Procunier* v. *Martinez* (1974), the Supreme Court struck down the blanket practice of censoring all incoming and outgoing mail. The Court held that censorship could be practiced, but only if there was a substantial belief that the contents of the mail threatened security. Prior to this decision, the First Circuit Court of Appeals had outlawed a Massachusetts practice that prohibited inmates from sending letters to the news media (*Nolan* v. *Fitzpatrick*, 1971).

In contrast, in *Saxbe* v. *Washington Post* (1974), the right of an inmate to grant press interviews was denied on the grounds that it would lead to notoriety, which would undermine the attempts of authorities to provide equal treatment. In 1987, the Supreme Court ruled that inmates do not have the right to receive mail from another person and that such mail may be banned if it violates legitimate correctional interests (*Turner* v. *Safley*, 1987). In a related case, the Supreme Court held that prisons do not violate the First Amendment if they prohibit receipt of publications if those publications violate legitimate penalogical interests (*Thornburgh* v. *Abbott*, 1989).

FREEDOM OF RELIGION

Historically, religion has been an important feature of prison life, yet restrictions have been placed on its exercise for economic reasons, for security reasons, and for the sake of prison officials' maintaining of authority. Most restrictions have been aimed at religious rituals rather than religious beliefs. Several of the suits filed were in connection with the Black Muslim religion, with the most important being *Cooper* v. *Pate* (1964). In this decision, the Court prohibited prison officials from completely banning religious services but did permit restricting participation for those who abuse the privilege. In *Walker* v. *Blackwell* (1969) and *Khan* v. *Carlson* (1975), federal courts upheld prison officials' refusals to provide special diets for all religious sects.

There have been contrasting decisions concerning what constitutes a religion. In *Theriault* v. *Carlson* (1974), the Fifth Circuit Court of Appeals ruled that the Church of the New Song and Universal Life did not constitute a religion but amounted to a mockery and a sham. However, the Eighth Circuit Court of Appeals recognized the same religion and held that its members were protected under the First Amendment (*Reemers* v. *Brewer*, 1974). The Supreme Court ruled (*O'Lone* v. *Estate of Shabazz*, 1987) that Black Muslims' rights were not violated when work assignments made it impossible for them to attend religious services.

CRUEL AND UNUSUAL PUNISHMENT

The Eighth Amendment's prohibition of **cruel and unusual punishment** has served as a basis for inmates' contesting the legality of prison conditions. Perhaps the most famous of these cases is *Holt* v. *Sarver* (1970), in which the Court ruled that conditions in the Cummings Prison Farm constituted cruel and unusual punishment. Later, in *Pugh* v. *Locke* (1976) and *Ruiz* v. *Estelle* (1982), courts threatened to close prison systems in Alabama and Texas, respectively, unless changes were made.

Concerning overcrowding as a form of cruel and unusual punishment, in *Bell* v. *Wolfish* (1979) and *Rhodes* v. *Chapman* (1981), the courts have upheld the practice of double bunking as long as it does not lead to filth or disease or limit the inmate's participation in prison programs. Additional Eighth Amendment decisions have prohibited the use of corporal punishment and restricted the use of solitary confinement.

DUE PROCESS

A number of inmate suits have been concerned with the loss of privileges or **good time**. In *Wolff* v. *McDonnell* (1974), the Supreme Court held that loss of good time or privileges was important enough to justify some due process requirements. As a result, prison officials must now provide advance notice of charges against inmates, hold a hearing, and allow time for the inmate to call witnesses and obtain assistance in preparing a defense. In a related decision, the Court held, however, that inmates have no right to counsel in a disciplinary hearing (*Baxter* v. *Palmigiano*, 1976).

The requirements of due process do not apply to all prison practices. In the companion cases of *Meachurn* v. *Fano* (1976) and *Montaye* v. *Haymes* (1976), the Court upheld the practice of not providing due process in the transfer of an inmate from one institution to another. In a 1995 decision, the Supreme Court held that due process claims are limited to restraints on freedom that impose an atypical and significant hardship on an inmate in relation to the ordinary incidents of prison life (*Sandin* v. *Conner*, 1995). Thus a prisoner doesn't have a due process right to prevent transfer to another facility. As you can see, the prisoners' rights movement has had important implications for prison practices. Administrative practices have been altered and prison conditions improved by some of the suits filed by inmates.

ALTERNATIVES TO INCARCERATION

In our discussion of prisons, we noted that conditions in these institutions are often less than ideal. Incarceration is also very expensive. Conservative estimates place the annual cost of incarcerating one offender at between $20,000 and $30,000. As an alternative to the expensive, generally ineffective, and sometimes inhumane practice of incarceration, the concepts of intermediate sanctions and community corrections have evolved.

Intermediate sanctions are those that are less severe than incarceration but more restrictive than probation (Cole, 1995, p. 449). Such sanctions include home confinement/electronic monitoring, intensive probation, community service, boot camps, restitution, forfeiture, and fines. Of these, **boot camps** have received the most media attention. These camps are based on the assumption that rigorous physical training and discipline can "shock" young offenders out of criminal behavior. Sentences are typically short (less than six months), and inmates are dealt with in much the same manner as military recruits. Evaluations of these camps are now being done, and the results appear to be mixed, at best (Jones, 1996).

Therapeutic treatment centers are residential centers designed to stimulate major behavioral changes. These centers deliver highly structured treatment 24 hours a day but generally for shorter stays, of 120 days. While the major emphasis is on drug- and alcohol-related behaviors, the centers also deal with violence and anger management.

Community corrections programs include probation, parole, work release centers, halfway houses, and other community-based programs (see In the News, "How Norfolk County Aims to Curb Recidivism"). The assumption underlying community corrections is that rehabilitation can best be achieved if contacts are maintained between offenders and the community and family to which he or she must eventually return. Note that many intermediate sanctions are administered in community settings. Although research indicates that community corrections is about as effective as prison in terms of recidivism rates, the former has the advantage of being less expensive.

The newest community-based approach is the movement toward restorative justice, a program with the emphasis on restitution rather than punishment. As indicated in Chapter 11, the restorative justice approach attempts to resolve differences between criminals and their victims using victim–offender mediation and other techniques.

Probation

Probation is the supervised, conditional, and revocable release of an offender into the community in lieu of incarceration. It is a sanction that is served in the community instead of in prison, and if the conditions of probation are violated, the judge may modify the conditions of probation or sentence the offender to prison or jail.

Probation, as we know it, began in 1841 when a cobbler named John Augustus requested that judges let him pay fines for and supervise minor offenders. Partly because of his success, Massachusetts passed the first probation law in 1878; all states now have some form of probation.

Currently, probation may be granted in as many as 80 percent of the cases coming to the attention of the courts. Supporters believe that probation gives offenders a second chance and allows them to avoid the effects of incarceration while maintaining ties in the community to which they would eventually return if incarcerated, under the supervision of a probation officer. In addition, supporters point out that probation, even if no more effective than incarceration, costs a great deal less. Opponents claim that probation is equivalent to no punishment at all, is too widely granted, and is ineffective because most probation officers provide little or no actual supervision to probationers. In response to these charges and to the recognition that a small number of high-risk offenders commit a disproportionate amount of crime, many communities have developed the practice of **intensive probation,** which requires daily contact between probation officers and their charges. Caseloads are cut to allow probation officers to focus their efforts on a small number of offenders. Intensive probation has both positive and negative consequences. On the positive side, preliminary results show intensive supervision probation (ISP) reduces rearrest rates for probationers, reduces the costs (as compared with incarceration), and reduces the prison population (see In the News, "Intensive Probation Pays Off"). It was designed to improve the rehabilitative efforts of probation

In the News

HOW NORFOLK COUNTY AIMS TO CURB RECIDIVISM

By Michael G. Bellotti

Statistics show that two-thirds of all released convicts land back in jail. So the real challenge for lawenforcement officials isn't simply keeping criminals off the streets but giving them the tools they need to stop reoffending.

According to a study released last week by Boston's Community Resources for Justice, recidivism is more likely than ever because of a decline in reintegration programs in our prisons and county jails since the 1980s.

The group's chief executive officer, John J. Larivee, told the *Globe* recently that correctional facilities are sending convicts out to the streets "without preparation and without supervision."

While the study accurately reflects a general trend, the Norfolk County Sheriff's Office has developed a model approach aimed at bringing down the rate of recidivism by creating structure and accountability inside prison walls. That means continual education and drug-addiction treatment for inmates in every category from incarceration to prerelease to probation.

The fact is that 80 percent of all reoffenders have a drug or alcohol problem. That's why the focus on treatment and education is so important.

The Norfolk County Sheriff's Office meets the challenge head-on with its reintegration unit inside the 500-inmate Norfolk County Correctional Center in Dedham.

Through counseling and education, the unit helps inmates with drug addiction recovery. It also provides accountability through self-help groups as Alcoholics Anonymous and Narcotics Anonymous.

Inmates who complete the programs are sent to recovery homes or halfway houses after they finish their sentences. In these settings, they are required to work 40-hour weeks, pay rent, eat family-style home meals, and continue treatment and education programs.

As an inmate prepares to be released, the education and treatment continues from the main facility to the Dedham Alternative Center.

Here, minimum-security inmates participate in intensive substance-abuse and relapse prevention education. Basic life skills are also taught, such as how to write a resume and fill out a job application.

The sheriff's office has also committed itself to extending programs and education to probationers and parolees. The office's Community Corrections Center in Quincy opened in the summer of 1999 to help people on probation and parole avoid returning to jail.

Continued

The center is one of the first of its kind in the state and is a collaborative project among the courts, the Probation Department, the Parole Board, and the Sheriff's Office.

Under the program, probationers and parolees are required to report to the center for drug and alcohol testing, counseling, and education. In fact, the Community Corrections Center has a 100 percent success rate for GED enrollees. Since the center opened, all 34 students have graduated.

The goal of these programs is to create a productive atmosphere of structure and accountability for every classification of inmate so each person has a better chance of successful reintegration once he is released.

And it can be done without extra cost to the public. In its last fiscal year, the Norfolk County Sheriff's Office cut nearly $800,000 from its operating budget while expanding programming and reintegration initiatives with approximately $600,000 in grant funding.

And more will be done. The office recently secured a $1.3 million federal grant from the U.S. Department of Education to establish an inmate reintegration initiative called the Moving Ahead Program.

The program is a partnership between the Sheriff's Office, St. Francis House, the Education Development Center, and Harvard Medical School that will help prepare prerelease inmates for employment.

The 14-week training program will offer life-skills training, career development assistance, job placement services, and treatment for drug and alcohol addiction.

With efforts like these applied across the state, we can break the reoffender mold, turn back the tide of recidivism, and make our communities safer.

The Boston Globe, January 27, 2001, p. A15.

officers and to increase public protection by enhancing surveillance. At least two negative consequences have been identified. First, constant supervision of the probationer is likely to lead to discovery of more technical violations of probation. Second, reintegration into the workforce may be made more difficult by constant supervision, especially if it occurs on the work site.

When a judge sentences an offender to probation, he or she specifies the maximum period of time involved, which is established by statute. Probation can be terminated early if the probationer makes satisfactory progress. The probationer is notified by the judge of the conditions of his or her probation, which are, at least in theory, tailored to the specific needs of the probationer. Common conditions of probation include the requirement to refrain from violating any criminal statute, to report or appear in person before a probation officer at certain times, to refrain from possessing a firearm, to make restitution to the injured party, to secure and retain employment, to undergo therapy, and to remain in the county or state of residence unless permitted to leave by the probation officer.

In the News

INTENSIVE PROBATION PAYS OFF, PANEL TOLD; N.O. OFFICIALS BACK ALTERNATIVE SENTENCES

By Michael Perlstein

The state Senate Judiciary B Committee made a stop in New Orleans Wednesday, where lawmakers got a firsthand look at several alternative sentencing options and heard testimony from local officials seeking to expand the programs.

The group toured Criminal Sheriff Charles Foti's "About Face" boot camp program, watched a session of Judge Calvin Johnson's drug court, then finished with a hearing that focused on the city's intensive probation program. New Orleans court officials also touted their use of drug-testing, community service and monitoring of domestic violence cases.

To ease the state corrections budget, the legislative panel is looking at alternatives to prison time for nonviolent first-offenders and ways to cut the sentences of elderly inmates. The committee chairman, Sen. Don Cravins, D-Lafayette, kicked off the hearings last month with a session at the Louisiana State Penitentiary at Angola. The backdrop for Wednesday's hearing was a bit more regal—the polished oak courtroom of Judge Arthur Hunter—but the issues were basically the same.

"There are ways to reduce the prison population without reducing public safety," Magistrate Judge Gerard Hansen told the committee. "There are alternatives that work."

As an example, Hansen, the court's chief judge, said a court-run intensive probation program has been successful at cutting corrections costs while keeping recidivism rates low. He said it costs about $2,000 a year to monitor a defendant on intensive probation, compared to $36,000 a year to keep the same defendant behind bars.

With intensive probation, defendants must report to court once a week, compared to once a month under state supervision. In addition, judges and court-appointed case officers require participants to undergo regular drug-testing, work toward a GED and bring pay stubs to prove they are working. Drug court, established only in a few sections of criminal court, has similarly strict requirements.

Byron Stewart of the Orleans Parish Judicial Administrator's Office said the programs are effective because of the face-to-face relationships forged between judges and defendants.

"It works because the judges don't talk to them like criminals, they talk to them like family. The key is hands-on personal interaction," Stewart said.

Judge Leon Cannizzaro, a supporter of sentencing alternatives, told the panel that years of "locking people up and throwing away the key doesn't work. We've tried that. For years, Louisiana has locked up more

Continued

people per capita than any other state and it hasn't made the public any more safe."

Cannizzaro said strict probation programs can help reverse a would-be criminal career before it escalates from drug and property crimes to violent crimes. "What we're doing is instilling pride in people. It works because we're holding the probationer accountable."

Cannizzaro encouraged lawmakers to expand the programs to other parts of the state, but even more urgent, he said, is the need for money to keep the New Orleans programs running. Drug court and intensive probation were launched several years ago with federal grants that are now running dry, he explained.

The Times Picayune *(New Orleans), October 12, 2000, p. 2.*

Each probationer is assigned to a probation officer, who is responsible for supervising and assisting probationers in activities such as locating employment and housing, managing finances, and dealing with other problems as they arise. Given the fact that many probation officers have caseloads of 50 to 100 probationers at any given time, the actual amount of supervision provided may be negligible, leading to some of the criticisms mentioned above.

Offenders who violate the conditions of their probation run the risk of having it revoked. The most common ground for revocation is the commission of another offense. The probation officer notifies the judge of the alleged violation, and a revocation hearing is held. In *Gagnon* v. *Scarpelli* (1973), the Supreme Court ruled that revocation hearings must be public. In an earlier decision, the Court held that an accused had the right to counsel during revocation proceedings but had avoided the issue of whether a revocation hearing was mandatory (*Mempa* v. *Rhay*, 1967).

Revocation hearings require that the state prove that violations of probation occurred, usually by a preponderance of evidence. Evidence is presented in open court, and the probationer has the right to be represented by counsel, to cross-examine witnesses, and to call his or her own witnesses. If the judge finds the allegations unfounded, the probationer is returned to probation under present conditions. If the allegations are substantiated, the court may modify probation conditions or send the offender to prison or jail to serve his or her original sentence.

Community Correctional Programs

Community correctional programs are designed to help reintegrate the offender into the community, and they take the form of halfway houses, prerelease guidance centers, home confinement, and work release programs. While the offender is in residence, he or she is temporarily released to work, attend school, participate in therapy, and visit family. Although great hope has been held for such programs, their overall success rate has not been much better (in terms of recidivism) than that achieved by prisons, and, compared with probation, they are quite costly. In addition, it is often difficult to find neighborhoods or communities willing to support such programs because of fears that inmates will become involved in further crime and endanger area residents.

Parole

Parole and probation are sometimes confused by the general public. Like probation, **parole** is supervised, revocable release; but unlike probation, it occurs after part of the original sentence has already been served in prison or jail. If the parolee violates the conditions of his or her parole, the parolee can be returned to prison or jail to serve the remainder of the original sentence. Whereas roughly 80 percent of all felons formerly left prison on discretionary release by parole, today only about 40 percent are released by decision of a parole board. Determinate sentencing and mandatory release have lessened the role of the parole board in many states. Still, in those jurisdictions retaining discretionary parole boards, parole represents an important means of controlling overcrowding in prisons, which leads to frequent criticisms that release on parole depends more on the number of offenders awaiting incarceration than on the behavior of the offender released on parole.

The authority to grant parole is usually delegated by statute to some formal body. Most states now delegate this authority to the judge who presides over the case, but in some a semi-autonomous parole board appointed by the governor is maintained. Qualifications for membership on parole boards vary by jurisdiction. In some areas, board members must have professional experience in corrections, law enforcement, or some other human service. In others, appointment is through patronage, and the composition of the board is highly questionable.

In those states with determinate sentencing, the duties of the parole board are minimal. Offenders serve their time minus time off for good behavior and are released automatically. In the remaining states, the parole board has far greater latitude in deciding the release date and conditions of parole.

What factors should be considered in the parole decision? Obviously, the statutory minimum of the sentence must have been completed, but beyond this, the criteria to be employed are considerably more difficult to specify. How much weight, for example, should we give to the offender's behavior in prison, the availability of employment, family support, and support services available in the community in which the parolee will reside? Should prison overcrowding be a consideration in granting parole? Should the nature of the offense for which the prisoner was incarcerated be a determining factor? These and other questions make parole decisions difficult. In the final analysis, the reaction of citizens on the outside will determine the success or failure of parole, assuming that the parolee meets the conditions established to successfully complete parole.

Are parolees entitled to due process? Like probation, parole is conditional and revocable. Inmates released on parole risk revocation if they are caught violating the stipulated conditions of their parole. One year prior to the Supreme Court's decision in *Gagnon* v. *Scarpelli*, the court ruled that parolees were entitled to fundamental due process during revocation proceedings (*Morrissey* v. *Brewer*, 1972). The parole officer maintains discretion in determining if probable cause exists that a violation has occurred. If probable cause is found, the parolee is entitled to such fundamental due process rights as notice of charges, disclosure of evidence, a hearing before a neutral and detached body, the right to appear and testify, the right to cross-examine witnesses, and written notification outlining the ruling body's decision. These rights were further extended to inmates released to relieve prison overcrowding who were not officially placed on parole, (*Young* v. *Harper*, 1997).

The current problem of prison overcrowding has placed greater demands on intermediate sanctions, probation, parole, and other forms of community corrections. Some prisons are legally forced to release inmates to avoid exceeding maximum daily population levels. The result is that some inmates may be paroled before the prison staff feel they are prepared to reenter society. This places increased pressure on the parole officer, who may already have a heavy caseload. One must question the quantity and quality of supervision the parolee receives under these conditions.

In conclusion, we would like to emphasize the importance of viewing alternatives to incarceration from the network perspective. Political decisions, public opinion, the attitudes and practices of criminal justice practitioners, and the behavior of each individual offender all play a part in determining whether alternatives to incarceration will succeed or fail and to what extent.

Summary

1. The prisoners' rights movement and alternatives to incarceration have led to changes in our traditional conceptions of corrections.

2. A number of court decisions have improved conditions in prisons and jails, although many remain substandard.

3. In general, freedom of speech, freedom of religion, immunity from cruel and unusual punishment, and due process guarantees are the areas in which inmate suits have helped define more clearly what constitutes acceptable treatment in institutions.

4. Probation, parole, and other alternatives to incarceration have been tried in the hope that they would prove more successful than imprisonment in reintegrating offenders and in preventing recidivism. Research findings generally fail to indicate the superiority of these alternatives over incarceration, perhaps partly because alternative programs are still relatively new.

civil death   Denial of the right to vote, the right to hold public office, and the right to enter into contracts.

hands-off doctrine   Refusal of the courts to hear suits on behalf of prison inmates.

cruel and unusual punishment   Punishment administered by the government that is prohibited by the Constitution.

good time   Time during which an inmate abides by the rules of the institution, which is then subtracted from his or her sentence.

intermediate sanctions   Sanctions less severe than incarceration but more restrictive than probation.

boot camps   An intermediate sanction designed to "shock" young offenders out of criminal behavior by imposing rigorous physical activity and harsh, military-style discipline.

community corrections   Correctional programs, such as probation, parole, work release, and halfway houses, in which prisoners are allowed and encouraged to maintain community and family ties.

probation   The supervised, conditional, and revocable release of an offender into the community in lieu of incarceration.

intensive probation   Probation requiring daily or very frequent face-to-face meetings between a probation officer and his or her probationers.

parole   The supervised, conditional, and revocable release of an offender into the community after he or she has served part of a sentence.

Critical Thinking Exercises

1. What do programs such as probation, parole, and other types of community corrections attempt to accomplish? What is the rationale for such programs? What are some of the obstacles to developing successful community corrections programs? Do you believe these programs are as effective as imprisonment?

2. What kinds of changes do you think we can look forward to in the next few years in prisoners' rights and alternatives to incarceration? Will building more prisons solve the crime problem in the United States? Why or why not?

Internet Exercises

Our discussion of prisoners' rights has raised a number of issues. Many of these issues are addressed by the American Civil Liberties Union (ACLU), Human Rights Watch (HRW), and other organizations.

1. What are the latest highlights from the ACLU website (*www.aclu.org*)?
2. What types of information are available from the HRW site (*www.hrw.org*)?
3. What are the expressed goals of Free World Friends (*www.freeworldfriends. com*) as related to prisoners?

References

Baxter v. *Palmigiano*, 96 S. Ct. 1551 (1976).
Bell v. *Wolfish*, 99 S. Ct. 1873 (1979).
Casey v. *Lewis*, 518 U.S. 343 S. Ct. 2174 (1996).
Civil Rights Act, 42 U.S.C. (1983).
Cole, G. F. (1995). *The American system of criminal justice* (7th ed.). Belmont, CA.: Wadsworth.
Cooper v. *Pate*, 378 U.S. 546 (1964).
Gagnon v. *Scarpelli*, 411 U.S. 471 (1973).
Holt v. *Sarver*, 300 F. Supp. 825 (1970).
Jones, M. (1996). Do boot camp graduates make better probationers? *Journal of Crime and Justice,* *19* (1), 1–14.
Khan v. *Carlson*, 527 F. 2d 492 (1975).
Meacham v. *Fano*, 427 U.S. 215 (1976).
Mempa v. *Rhay*, 389 U.S. 128 (1967).
Montaye v. *Haymes*, 427 U.S. 236 (1976).
Morrissey v. *Brewer*, 408 U.S. 471 (1972).
Nolan v. *Fitzpatrick*, 451 F. 2d 545 (1971).
O'Lone v. *Estate of Shabazz*, 482 U.S. 342 (1987).
Procunier v. *Martinez*, 416 U.S. 396 (1974).
Pugh v. *Locke*, 406 F Supp. 318 (1976).
Reemers v. *Brewer*, 494 F. 2d 1227 (1974).
Rhodes v. *Chapman*, 452 U.S. 337 (1981).
Ruffin v. *Commonwealth*, 62 Va. 780 (1871).
Ruiz v. *Estelle*, 503 F. Supp. 1265 (1982).
Sandin v. *Conner*, 515 U.S. 472 (1995).
Saxbe v. *Washington Post*, 417 U.S. 843 (1974).
Theriault v. *Carlson*, 339 F. Supp. 375 (1974).
Thornburgh v. *Abbott*, 109 S. Ct. 1874 (1989).
Turner v. *Safley*, 107 S. Ct. 2254 (1987).
Walker v. *Blackwell*, 411 F. 2d 23 (1969).
Wolff v. *McDonnell*, 418 U.S. 539 (1974).
Young v. *Harper* 520 U.S. 143 (1997).

Suggested Readings

Alexander, R., Jr. (1998). The impact of the Religious Freedom Restoration Act on prisons. *Journal of Criminal Justice, 26* (5), 385–98.

Collins, W. C., & Grant, D. C. (1998). The Prison Litigation Reform Act. *Corrections Today, 60* (5), 60–62.

Evans, D. (1999). Building hope through community justice. *Corrections Today, 61* (1), 73.

Lee, R. D., Jr. (1996). Prioners' rights to recreation: Quantity, quality, and other aspects. *Journal of Criminal Justice, 24,* (2), 167–78.

Lutz, F. E., & Brody, D. C. (1999). Mental abuse as cruel and unusual punishment: Do boot camps violate the Eighth Amendment? *Crime and Delinquency, 45* (2), 242–55.

Maxwell, S. R., & Gray, M. K. (2000). Deterrence: Testing the effects of perceived sanction certainty on probation violations (intensive supervision probation programs). *Sociological Inquiry, 70,* (2), 117–36.

Modley, P. (2000). NIC assists corrections with managing female offenders in the community. *Corrections Today, 62* (4), 152, 154.

Teles, S. M., & Kleiman, M. (2000). Escape from America's prison policy. *American Prospect, 11* (20), 30–34.

Wilhelmus, D. W. (1999). Where have all the law libraries gone? Offenders' rights to access the courts in the wake of *Casey* v. *Lewis. Corrections Today, 61* (7), 122–24.

CHAPTER FOURTEEN

Juvenile Justice

Serious juvenile offenses are often forerunners to adult crimes.
Jerry Lara/San Antonio Exp./Corbis Sygma

*J*ohn dropped out of school at age 16. Within a month he had joined a gang and participated in spray painting obscenities on the school. Within hours he was apprehended by the police on the basis of eyewitness testimony. John admitted his role in spray painting, and the arresting officer attempted to reach a station house adjustment between John, his parents, and school officials. Despite repeated efforts, John's parents could not be located. A juvenile probation officer was notified of the offense, and she tried to arrange a preliminary conference of interested parties to settle the issue without going to court. Again, John's parents failed to appear, and school officials refused to settle without their input. A petition was filed in juvenile court, and John and his parents were notified of the date, time, and location of the adjudicatory hearing. In the meantime, an attorney was appointed to represent John at the hearing. The attorney contacted John and spoke to him for five minutes on the phone. The next time John saw the attorney was at the adjudicatory hearing. John's parents did not show up for the hearing.

Given John's confession and the eyewitness testimony, the prosecutor had no trouble proving that John committed the offense. The judge placed John on six months probation and ordered him to pay the cost of removing the spray paint. The probation officer ordered John to stay away from members of the gang and to report to him weekly. At the weekly meetings, the probation officer spent 5 to 10 minutes with John, basically telling him to stay away from gang members and out of trouble. Still, within a month, John was associating with members of the gang again. Six months later, John was arrested again, this time for burglary. Again John received probation and was ordered to observe a number of conditions to remain in the community. Absent any family ties, relying on gang members for company, and unable to locate a good-paying job, John again turned to burglary. This time, having turned 18, John was sentenced to prison. John is currently serving time in prison, this time for armed robbery committed with another ex-inmate during his most recent release.

John, now 21, still has no family ties, has never earned a GED, and has no job skills. What do you see in John's future?

Key Terms

age of responsibility

mens rea

parens patriae

in loco parentis

era of socialized juvenile justice

legalists

adjudicatory hearing

delinquent acts

status offenders

petition

preliminary conference

street corner or station house adjustments

ward of the state

dispositional hearing

diversion programs

Chapter Outline

Juvenile Justice: A Historical Overview
Defining and Measuring Delinquency
Purpose and Scope of Juvenile Court Acts
Juvenile Justice Procedures
Current Dilemmas in Juvenile Justice

The juvenile justice network in the United States is distinct from, but not independent of, the criminal justice network. The network approach would lead us to believe that what happens to juveniles as they are processed through the juvenile justice system would have important consequences for other components of the network. For example, if such juveniles are successfully rehabilitated, they will not become problems for the police, courts, and corrections at the adult level, nor will they continue to prey on other citizens. If our efforts to assist youthful offenders fail, the consequences are equally apparent.

The juvenile justice network in the United States is just over 100 years old. Since its inception, it has been controversial with respect to objectives and procedures, because major gaps between theory and practice have emerged in the period since 1899, when the first family court was established in Cook County, Illinois. The reasons for the controversy surrounding the juvenile court and the distinction between theory and practice are apparent on review of the history of the juvenile court.

JUVENILE JUSTICE: A HISTORICAL OVERVIEW

Over 4,000 years ago, the Code of Hammurabi contained references to runaway children and youth who disowned their parents. About 2,000 years ago, Roman civil law and canon (church) law made distinctions between juveniles and adults based on the concept of **age of responsibility.** During the eleventh and twelfth centuries, distinctions were made in British common law between youth and adults. For example, children under 7 years of age were not subject to criminal sanctions because they were presumed to be incapable of forming criminal intent, or **mens rea;** children between the ages of 7 and 14 were exempt from criminal prosecution unless it could be demonstrated that they had formed criminal intent, could distinguish right from wrong, and understood the consequences of their actions (Blackstone, 1803). These issues remain important in juvenile court proceedings today. At what age is a child capable of understanding right from wrong? At what age can a child understand the consequences of his or her actions?

In the fifteenth century, chancery courts (under the direction of the king's chancellor) were created in England to grant relief and assistance to needy parties, including women and children, who were left to fend for themselves as a result of the death of a husband or father, abandonment, or divorce. The king, exercising the right of **parens patriae** (parent of the country), permitted these courts to act **in loco parentis** (in the place of parents) to provide necessary services to such women and children.

By the sixteenth century, British children could be separated from their pauper parents and apprenticed to others (Rendleman, 1974, p. 77). This practice was based on the assumption that the state has a primary interest in the welfare of children and has a right to ensure such welfare.

At about the same time, attempts were being made in England to settle disputes involving juveniles in a confidential fashion and to segregate youths requiring confinement from adult offenders. The former practice was to help juveniles avoid public shame and stigmatization; the latter, to avoid the harmful consequences of association with more hardened offenders. Although juveniles continued to be incarcerated in adult institutions throughout most of the 1700s, they were often segregated from adult offenders. In 1788, Robert Young established a separate institution for young offenders that was to "educate and instruct in some useful trade or occupation the children of convicts or other such infant poor as are engaged in a vagrant and criminal course of life" (Sanders, 1974, p. 48).

In the United States during the 1700s, numerous juveniles were imprisoned, but few seemed to benefit from the experience. As a result, several institutions for juveniles were established in the early and mid-1800s. These institutions were oriented toward education and treatment, and away from punishment. By the mid-1800s, these institutions were declared a great success by those who ran them (Simonsen & Gordon, 1991, p. 23). Others, however, were less enthusiastic about the institutions, and in the second half of the nineteenth century, it was widely recognized that such institutions failed to reform or rehabilitate delinquents. Reform schools became the new means of dealing with delinquents, but they too failed to rehabilitate most delinquents.

Court decisions in the last half of the nineteenth century were in conflict over the necessity of due process for juveniles, but by the time the first family court appeared in Chicago in 1899, "the delinquent child had ceased to be a criminal and had the status of a child in need of care, protection, and discipline directed toward rehabilitation" (Cavan, 1969, p. 362).

The period between 1899 and 1967 has been called the **era of socialized juvenile justice.** Emphasis on obtaining a complete picture of the delinquent to determine appropriate care, regardless of legal requirements, became paramount. Informality became the rule and was confirmed by the decision of the Supreme Court not to hear the *Holmes* case in 1955 on the basis that juvenile courts are not criminal courts and, therefore, the constitutional rights guaranteed to accused adults do not apply to juveniles (*In re Holmes*, 1955).

Twelve years later, however, forces opposing the extreme informality and license of the juvenile court won a major victory in the case of Gerald Gault (see Appendix). The problems created by extreme informality and lack of concern for constitutional guarantees became abundantly clear in the *Gault* case. Neither Gault nor his parents were notified properly of the charges against him, of their right to counsel, of their right to cross-examine witnesses, of their right to remain silent, of their right to a transcript of the proceedings, or of their right to appeal (*In re Gault*, 1967). The Supreme Court decision in this case left no doubt that juveniles are protected by these guarantees and brought an end to the era of socialized justice. It did not, however, end the debate between those favoring more formal juvenile court proceedings (the **legalists**) and those favoring a more informal, casework approach (the caseworkers or therapists). That debate rages today, with a variety of consequences for juvenile justice practitioners, as we shall see.

DEFINING AND MEASURING DELINQUENCY

One of the major problems facing students of delinquency is that of arriving at a suitable definition. Without such a definition, measurement is impossible; and without accurate measurement, prevention and treatment are extremely difficult.

Two different types of definitions of delinquency have emerged over the years: legal and behavioral. Strict legal definitions hold that only those juveniles who have been officially labeled by the courts are delinquents. Such definitions are problematic because, according to self-report studies and victim survey research, the definitions do not include the vast majority of all juveniles who commit delinquent acts and, therefore, may lead us to seriously underestimate the number of delinquents. In addition, legal definitions vary from state to state and time to time. Behavioral definitions hold that juveniles who have violated or attempted to violate statutes are delinquent whether or not they are apprehended; thus, the juvenile who engages in acts of vandalism is considered delinquent even though he or she has not been officially labeled by the court. Such definitions can provide a more comprehensive picture of the extent and nature of delinquency, provided we are able to collect accurate data from unofficial as well as official sources (Cox, Conrad, & Allen, 2001).

PURPOSE AND SCOPE OF JUVENILE COURT ACTS

Juvenile court acts authorize the creation of juvenile courts with the legal authority to hear certain types of cases, including delinquency, dependency, neglect or abuse, and other cases requiring authoritative intervention (a minor in need of supervision, for example). These acts establish both procedural guidelines and substantive law relative to juveniles, which are to be administered in the interests of juveniles and in the spirit of parental concern. A separate nomenclature has been developed for juvenile procedures to ensure that these goals are pursued (see Figure 14.1). An examination of the figure shows that juveniles typically have a petition filed in their interests rather than a complaint filed against them. They may be taken into custody instead of arrested, may have a preliminary conference instead of a preliminary hearing, are accused of having committed a delinquent act rather than a crime (with some exceptions), go through an **adjudicatory hearing** rather than a criminal

Adult	Juvenile
Arrest	Take into custody
Preliminary hearing	Preliminary conference/detention hearing (both optional)
Grand jury/information/indictment	Petition
Arraignment	
Criminal trial	Adjudicatory hearing
Sentencing hearing	Dispositional hearing
Sentence: probation, incarceration, etc.	Disposition: probation, incarceration, etc.
Appeal	Appeal

Figure 14.1

Comparison of Adult Criminal Justice and Juvenile Justice Systems

trial, may be found delinquent rather than guilty, and participate in a dispositional hearing instead of a sentencing hearing.

In addition to establishing such guidelines and a distinct language, juvenile court acts specify the age limits within which the juvenile court has jurisdiction and the nature of the acts over which the court has authority. For example, **delinquent acts** are normally defined as acts designated criminal in terms of local, state, or federal law committed by youth under a certain age. Similarly, those considered **status offenders** are typically juveniles who commit acts that are offenses only because of their age—running away from home, being beyond the control of parents, or being incorrigible.

JUVENILE JUSTICE PROCEDURES

Court proceedings concerning juveniles officially begin with the filing of a petition alleging that the juvenile is delinquent or in need of authoritative intervention of some kind (we will exclude from consideration here children who are dependent or neglected). Prior to the filing of the **petition**, the youth may have been taken into custody by the police and, in some states, may have been involved in a **preliminary conference** arranged by the juvenile probation officer in an attempt to settle the dispute out of court without filing a petition. Such a conference brings all parties to the dispute together (if they agree to attend), and the parties attempt to reach a settlement agreeable to all. If such a settlement cannot be reached or if the victim demands that a petition be filed, the case may be taken into juvenile court.

In any case, it is likely that delinquents who are about to have petitions filed on them will come into contact with the police. This contact may be in the form of an arrest, or may involve taking the juvenile into custody, which does not constitute an arrest (usually for the welfare of the youth involved). Typically, statutes require that the police attempt to contact the parents of any juvenile taken into custody, ensure the constitutional rights of the juvenile while he or she is in custody (including the right to counsel), and release the youth from custody as soon as possible unless they intend to detain him or her, which requires a detention hearing involving the juvenile court judge if the detention is to be for more than a few hours. It should be noted here that the majority of juvenile cases are settled either at a preliminary conference or through the use of **street corner** or **station house adjustments** on behalf of the police. Such adjustments allow the police to process most juveniles by obtaining agreement on behalf of their parents to see that the victim is compensated in some way for any damages he or she incurred.

When a detention hearing is necessary, the state generally must prove that detention is required to protect the youth, to protect society, or to prevent flight. If the judge agrees that detention is necessary, a specified time period is involved, at the end of which the juvenile must be brought before the court or released.

If the case cannot be settled out of court, a petition is filed alleging that the youth in question is delinquent or in need of authoritative intervention. Generally speaking, any adult who has knowledge of a delinquent act or has reason to believe a delinquent act has been committed by the youth in question may file a petition. The petition gives the name and age of the juvenile and usually the names and address(es) of the parents. It includes a statement of the facts that bring the youth under the jurisdiction of the juvenile court. The petition is then filed with the prosecutor, who decides, often in conjunction with the juvenile probation officer, whether or not to prosecute the case.

If the prosecutor decides to prosecute, proper notice must be given to the juvenile and his or her parents or guardian, as well as to all other concerned parties. The court typically issues a summons specifying the date, place, and time of the adjudicatory hearing and of the right of all parties to counsel. Notification by certified mail or publication are acceptable if the summons cannot be delivered personally.

On the date indicated on the summons, the adjudicatory hearing is held. All parties to the proceedings have the right to attend, but the public is typically excluded. Unlike adults, juveniles under the jurisdiction of the juvenile court have no right to trial by jury or to a public hearing because the courts have ruled that adjudicatory hearings are not adversary proceedings. Although this may be true in theory, it is often not true in reality, and debate continues as to the legitimacy of these restrictions. Most adjudicatory hearings are conducted by a juvenile court judge who decides matters of fact, matters of law, and proper disposition of those found delinquent. The Supreme Court has ruled that the same standard of proof employed in adult criminal trials (guilt beyond reasonable doubt) must be adhered to in delinquency proceedings (*In re Gault*, 1967; *In re Winship*, 1970).

After hearing the evidence, the juvenile court judge makes a decision as to whether the juvenile is delinquent. If the juvenile is adjudicated delinquent, he or she becomes a **ward of the state** and the court becomes the juvenile's legal guardian. At this point, the judge asks the juvenile probation officer to conduct a social background investigation, which will be used to assist in determining an appropriate disposition. The judge may also set the date for the **dispositional hearing,** which is typically separate from the adjudicatory hearing.

The social background investigation focuses on evidence, including written and oral reports, relating to the juvenile's family, environment, school history, friends, and other material that may be helpful in obtaining an accurate picture of the juvenile's circumstances. In some instances, the probation officer makes a written dispositional recommendation to the judge; in others, the probation officer simply provides the judge with his or her report without making any recommendations. In any case, the juvenile and his or her legal representative have access to the social background investigation, because there is no irrefutable presumption of accuracy attached to the investigation (*Kent v. United States,* 1966). In fact, such reports often focus on the negative aspects of the juvenile's environment and overlook positive information.

The dispositional alternatives available to the juvenile court judge are specified in each state's juvenile court act. In general, these include placement in a foster home, placement in a private or public detention facility, probation (while the child remains in his or her parent's home or while in a foster home), and commitment to a state correctional facility for juveniles. After reaching a dispositional alternative, the judge issues a dispositional order.

Probation is by far the most common disposition in juvenile cases, perhaps accounting for 75 to 85 percent of all such dispositions. As we have indicated previously, probation is a sentence served in the community, under specified conditions, and under the supervision of the probation officer. Conditions commonly imposed on juvenile probationers require that they must attend school regularly, must not leave the county or state without the approval of the probation officer, must keep regular appointments with the probation officer, must avoid certain places or types of places (pool halls or other game rooms, for example), must find and retain part-time employment, and so on. If the conditions of probation are violated or if the youth commits another offense while on probation, then probation may be revoked. At the revocation hearing, the judge decides whether such violations occurred and, if they did, whether to revoke probation and send the youth to a private or public detention facility to serve the remainder of his or her time. The length of probation varies, but seldom exceeds two to three years, although in most states it may be continued until the age at which the youth is no longer under the jurisdiction of the juvenile court.

Private and public detention facilities vary tremendously in terms of size, length and type of program, and cost. Some, such as boot camps, employ behavior modification or peer pressure programs, others concentrate mostly on education and vocational training, and some are basically warehouses with few if any rehabilitation programs. Some allow home visits and some encourage parents to visit and participate in rehabilitation efforts, while others do little along these lines. These institutions are difficult to inspect and control, and some have become infamous because of the brutality and abuse that sometimes occur under these conditions.

The use of foster home placement as a disposition would appear to hold some promise for delinquents, but a variety of factors combine to limit such placement. First, many parents of teenagers are reluctant to bring a delinquent youth into their homes for fear that their children will pick up the delinquent's habits. Second, some individuals become foster parents because they mistakenly believe that they can profit financially from the experience. However, for the most part, the subsidy provided by the state or county for each youth placed in a foster home is seldom enough to totally support the youth, let alone supplement the income of the foster parents. Third, foster parents are dealing with "high risk of failure" youth when they agree to work with delinquents and not infrequently become discouraged when their efforts at rehabilitation are less successful than they intended. As a result, they may decide to withdraw from foster home programs.

The least desirable (from the point of view of most juvenile court officials) and the least frequently employed disposition is commitment to a state correctional facility for juveniles. As a rule, only those delinquents regarded as unsalvageable are so committed. Such youth include those who commit violent offenses against others, repeatedly appear in juvenile court for relatively serious offenses, and most often have failed to benefit from probation or detention of other types. Many judges believe that sending a delinquent to a state correctional facility virtually guarantees that the youth will pursue a criminal career as an adult.

Regardless of the disposition handed down by the juvenile court judge, juveniles, like adults, have the right to appeal, although in practice, appeals from juvenile courts have been rare.

CURRENT DILEMMAS IN JUVENILE JUSTICE

Among the many dilemmas plaguing the juvenile court network is the perception that there has been a major increase in the past few years in violent crimes committed by juveniles (though in fact the number of violent crimes committed by juveniles has dropped considerably since 1995). Other factors are an increase in the visibility of street gang youth, a number of highly publicized school shootings, and fear on behalf of many adults. This environment makes reintegration of juveniles who have been found delinquent difficult at best and has led to the passage of legislation intended to get tough with juveniles by making transfer to adult court easier and such transfer a possibility for younger juveniles who commit violent offenses (see In the News, "Is Child Saving Dead?").

There continues to be a belief that practitioners at all levels of the juvenile justice network are something less than real criminal justice officials. Police officers assigned to juvenile bureaus are often regarded as kiddie cops by other police officers, even though special dedication and expertise are required of such officers. (This perception tends to be less prevalent in areas where juvenile officers deal on a regular basis with street gang members.) Prosecutors often dislike handling juvenile cases because they are unlikely to lead to posi-

In the News

Is Child Saving Dead?

By M. M. Moon *et al.*

At the close of the nineteenth century, the United States witnessed an unprecedented movement to save its children from physical and moral harm. The "child savers," as champions of this movement have come to be known, sought wide-reaching reforms . . . [with] the establishment of a system of juvenile justice. Now, a century after its creation, the juvenile court has experienced a period of sustained criticism. . . .

The foundation of this system of justice was an overriding belief that juvenile delinquents could be saved. . . . Beginning in the 1960s . . . the benevolent principles on which the system was based stood in stark and ironic contrast to the punitive reality of the juvenile justice system. . . . In the 100-year anniversary of the juvenile court, serious concerns remain about

the viability of this system. . . . At the end of 1997, 17 states had redefined their juvenile court purpose clauses to emphasize public safety, certain sanctions, and/or offender accountability. . . . It is frequently suggested that the changes in the juvenile court have been precipitated by two factors: high rates of serious crime and a shift in public attitudes toward youthful offenders. . . . Contemporary discussions about youthful offenders have taken a decidedly punitive flavor in the past ten years . . . [but] despite sweeping reforms aimed at altering the juvenile court to reflect retributive and punitive goals, it is uncertain that the public wants a juvenile justice system based exclusively, or even primarily, on punishment.

Moon et al., 2000, pp. 38–41

tive publicity even when an adjudication of delinquent is returned, and because preparation of such cases means time away from other cases that may be perceived as more serious or important. Defense attorneys sometimes fail to regard juvenile cases as worthy of the same preparation as adult criminal cases. Juvenile court judges are sometimes assigned this duty on a part-time basis and are sometimes unfamiliar with the requirements of the juvenile court act under which they are to operate, and many tend to overlook procedural requirements at the adjudicatory hearing on the grounds that they are interested in the total picture of the alleged delinquent. As a result, proper cross-examination of witnesses is sometimes impossible, especially if the witness happens to be an authority figure such as a teacher or a police officer, and hearsay evidence is sometimes considered. It is somewhat ironic that this should be the case when, as we have seen, it is the courts that have decided that the total picture of the delinquent may be considered only if it is obtained using the same legal procedures as are required for adults. As is the case in adult court, few judges are properly trained to decide which of the dispositional alternatives would be most beneficial to the youth in question and so, in spite of good intentions, operate on a trial-and-error basis with little attempt to do follow-up research to determine the effectiveness of the dispositions they hand down (see In the News, "A Boy Caught in a Legal Travesty").

In the News

A BOY CAUGHT IN A LEGAL TRAVESTY

Editorial

A Florida judge's outrageous decision last week to sentence a 14-year-old to life in prison without parole for the murder of a 6-year-old playmate is but the last act in a train wreck of justice system failures in this wrenching case.

In January a Miami jury convicted Lionel Tate of first-degree murder in the horrific beating death of Tiffany Eunick. Lionel was just 12 years old at the time of the 1999 murder, and despite his adult size—he then weighed 166 pounds—he was a child with juvenile impulses and boyish fantasies. The boy was obsessed with professional wrestling, and he later claimed he was just imitating his television idols when he threw and punched the girl.

Tiffany's death, while senseless and preventable, was an accident, defense attorneys claimed. Prosecutors argued it was murder, and even the defense medical experts who testified agreed that the gruesome injuries to the 48-pound girl—more than 30 of them, including a skull fracture, internal hemorrhaging and liver lacerations—were

anything but the results of horseplay. The jury came to the same conclusion, and on Friday the judge threw the book at Lionel, imposing the maximum penalty allowable in the case. The judge went as far as lambasting both the defense attorney and the prosecutor, who had each sensibly argued against life imprisonment for the teenager.

The case should stand out as the inevitable, shameful consequence of bad law begetting bad lawyering, of a judge who clearly lost his way, of one tragedy giving rise to others.

Florida is one of about 40 states, including California, that lets prosecutors try juveniles as adults for some violent crimes. And in Florida, as elsewhere, lawmakers have handed prosecutors much more discretion in recent years to make decisions that constrain the choices juries and judges can make later about culpability and punishment.

So a 12-year-old Lionel Tate was indicted for first-degree murder despite psychological evidence that chil-

Continued

dren don't have the maturity to control their impulses or understand the consequences of their actions. Add to that, defense lawyers served their client poorly. Before Lionel's trial, his mother rejected several offers to have her son plead guilty to second-degree murder and receive a sentence of three years in a juvenile facility and 10 years of probation. Little wonder, then, that some jurors, after sifting the overwhelming evidence of Lionel's violent behavior, said they felt legally bound not to return a conviction on a lesser charge. Finally, throw in a judge who angrily rejected dozens of entreaties for leniency.

There's a long line of Lionel Tates to come. Another 14-year-old Florida boy, Nathaniel Brazil, is scheduled to be tried as an adult on a first-degree murder charge next month. And last week Charles Andrew Williams, 15, was in court to face murder charges in the shooting rampage at Santana High School in Santee, Calif. Although prosecutors have ruled out the death penalty, Williams, if tried as an adult under California's Proposition 21, could be sentenced to life in prison.

Tiffany Eunick's awful murder cannot be undone, but the destruction of another child's life can be prevented. Gov. Jeb Bush should commute the life sentence to a punishment more appropriate for a child gone wrong.

Los Angeles Times, *March 13, 2001, p. 8.*

By contacting youth early, police officers hope to keep them out of trouble.
Kevin R. Morris/Corbis

Juvenile probation officers face the same dilemmas as their counterparts working with adults. They are officers of the court and must occasionally discipline their charges, but to be effective in helping probationers, they must gain their confidence. As a result, the probation officer must maintain a delicate balance between the roles of counselor/friend and disciplinarian. Recognizing the difficulty of this task, a number of states now require a college degree (some jurisdictions seek those with graduate degrees) for juvenile probation officers, provide mandated annual training for such officers, and subsidize their salaries in the hope of attracting and retaining qualified personnel.

Numerous attempts have been and are being made to ensure better-qualified juvenile personnel. A number of states now require specialized training and specific designation for juvenile police officers. Prosecutors and juvenile court judges have their own associations, complete with national and regional meetings that address key issues confronting the juvenile justice system. In addition, specialized training programs and seminars for both judges and prosecutors are available and are frequently well attended.

Attempts to divert youth from the juvenile justice network have also been popular in recent years. **Diversion programs** are of two basic types: those that attempt to divert youth from initial involvement in delinquency and those that attempt to divert youth who have already been involved in delinquent activities from becoming further involved. Although some diversion programs claim considerable success, it is difficult to determine whether such reported success is due to selection procedures or to the programs themselves. In addition, diversion programs have been criticized for keeping youth under a microscope, that is, monitoring their behavior so closely that they become defined as delinquent for engaging in behaviors similar to those of other youth who are not defined as delinquent simply because no one is monitoring their behavior. It is doubtful that many of us could escape the label "delinquent" if our behaviors were closely monitored all the time. Electronic surveillance devices and intensive supervision by probation officers are two examples of such monitoring. The intent of these innovations is to reduce or maintain the cost of supervising youth in trouble while providing close supervision for those who appear to need it most.

The dilemma in juvenile corrections on whether to emphasize custody or rehabilitation is much the same as in adult corrections, and the same staff controversies exist. Further, the inmate subculture is at least as pervasive in juvenile institutions as in adult facilities, and some, if not most, juvenile correctional facilities are literally run by gangs. There is little doubt that one of the things the delinquent committed to a correctional facility learns is a wide variety of delinquent activities.

In an attempt to change the behavior of problem youth without the consequences of long-term institutionalization, boot camps, similar to those for adults, have been developed. These camps promote discipline through physical conditioning and teamwork while attempting to improve academic achievement and instill moral values. After evaluating three such programs, Bourque et al. (1996) conclude: "The evaluation team could not draw any conclusions about the programs' long-term ability to change offenders' behavior or to save money and space for the country's overburdened juvenile justice system. . . . Until more information is available on recidivism and the cost of alternatives to institutionalization, the impact of juvenile camps on correctional crowding and skyrocketing costs will be difficult to determine" (p. 9).

Although the language and structure of the juvenile justice network is intended to prevent stigmatization, in practice, it occurs routinely. Although the public is excluded from juvenile court proceedings, the press may attend, and not infrequently, the identities of delinquents are disclosed through this medium either directly or indirectly. Further, in the case of youth adjudicated delinquent, school officials and other public agency officials are routinely informed of this decision. In many cases, youth involved publicize their adjudication as a symbol of their toughness. Even in the case of youth who avoid such publicity, weekly visits to or from the probation officer make it difficult to conceal the label.

The public has become increasingly concerned about violent offenses committed by juveniles. We have become, to some extent, afraid of our own children. As a result, the public has called for more severe penalties for youth involved in violent offenses. It is increasingly easy to automatically transfer youth who commit such offenses to adult court, thereby negating the philosophy of treat, educate, and rehabilitate instead of punish. As indicated above, there is precious little evidence to indicate that such transfers or increasingly severe punishment have any major impact on juvenile offenders, but as the network approach would indicate, when there is a perceived threat, any or all components of the network may react. In this case, public fear has resulted in pressure on legislators to pass laws mandating severe punishment for violent youth. To the extent that judges impose more severe sentences on youth or waive them to adult courts, which may lead to incarceration, correctional officials have larger numbers of inmates to deal with. Already overcrowded facilities, combined with federal and state standards for jails and prisons, may lead to cursory attempts at rehabilitation or outright early release of some offenders. When such offenders recidivate, the press focuses attention on them, public concern is once again aroused, and the cycle begins again.

In some jurisdictions, the decision to transfer youth to adult court rests with the prosecutor rather than the judge. While this action may help streamline the transfer process, once such a transfer occurs, the protections offered in juvenile court cease to exist. The juvenile's trial is public, as are records related to the case. Long-term incarceration and loss of civil rights are possibilities, and individualized treatment and rehabilitation become less likely. Opportunities to associate with, and learn from, hardened criminals increase. As a result of such risks, a full hearing before a judge who makes the final waiver decision is probably in the best interests of juveniles. Nonetheless, community pressure supporting the current concept of transfer is considerable because many observers believe that juvenile offenders are coddled by the juvenile justice network, even when they commit serious violations.

A number of remedies have been put forth for the problems confronting the juvenile justice network. Many of these remedies are based on overreaction to the inaccurate perception that there has been a recent increase in violent juvenile crime. Get-tough policies have been adopted in a number of states as a result of the mistaken belief that the more severe the punishment, the less likely the offender is to commit an offense. As noted above, there is little evidence to indicate that this return to the classical approach (based on assumptions of free will, the rationality of human beings, and a relationship between severity of punishment and likelihood of crime) will produce the desired results. In the meantime, the goals of the juvenile justice network may be set aside or overlooked.

It is likely that major changes in juvenile delinquency will occur as there is a shift in demographics leading to a larger proportion of the population in the 12- to 18-year old age range. Positive changes that would provide more and better opportunities for educational and vocational success for minority youth, thus lessening the likelihood of involvement with the delinquent subculture, are clearly needed. Frankly, changes of the latter type seem less likely now than two decades ago as the result of the prevailing political and economic climate of the 1990s. Reassessing the basic values and institutions in a society is a difficult undertaking, and instituting quick fixes is much more attractive than seeking long-term solutions to chronic problems.

At the beginning of the twenty-first century, those interested in the juvenile court can be divided into two basic groups: those who believe the juvenile court should be abolished and those who believe it should be reformed. Some of those in the former group believe that the juvenile court has never fulfilled the promise of the original juvenile court to protect and rehabilitate youth. Others believe the court has failed to guarantee the constitutional rights of juveniles. Still others believe the court is incapable of dealing with contemporary youth, who differ in many ways from the clients envisioned by the original framers of the juvenile court. "There is little argument that the current juvenile justice system is indeed in turmoil and lacks the foresight and preventive measures required for lasting reform. . . . The challenge before us is to move from the rhetoric to the reality of what we are going to do to save their [juveniles'] lives and our collective futures" (Hatchett, 1998, pp. 83–84).

Bilchik (1998) concludes: "A revitalized juvenile justice system needs to be put into place and brought to a scale that will ensure immediate and appropriate sanctions, provide effective treatment, reverse trends in juvenile violence, and rebuild public confidence in and support for the juvenile justice system" (p. 89). Such a system would include swift intervention with early offenders, an individualized comprehensive needs assessment, transfer of serious or chronic offenders, and intensive aftercare. This system would require the coordinated efforts of law enforcement, treatment, correctional, judicial, and social service personnel. This approach to delinquency control represents a form of community programming that might help reintegrate troubled youth into mainstream society rather than further isolate and alienate them (Basemore & Washington, 1995; Zaslaw & Balance, 1996). Accomplishing this goal will require the best efforts of the various components of the adult and juvenile justice networks as well as the support of the public.

Summary

1. The juvenile justice network in the United States is a separate network just over 100 years old.

2. The underlying philosophy of the juvenile justice network is based on principles developed in England and transported to this country.

3. These principles include parens patriae, in loco parentis, chancery/equity or protection, treatment, and rehabilitation of women and children.

4. The first family court in the United States was established in 1899 in Cook County, Illinois.

5. Since the inception of the juvenile justice network, there has been debate about how official or informal the proceedings should be, and the courts have taken first one position and then the other.

6. At present, the legalists appear to have the advantage because the courts now require a considerable degree of formality in delinquency proceedings.

7. Protection of juveniles from stigmatization; recruitment, training, and retention of qualified personnel; and a current wave of public fear of violent youth are problems confronting the juvenile justice network as we enter the twenty-first century.

Key Terms Defined

age of responsibility   The age at which children are assumed to be responsible (in a legal sense) for their actions.

mens rea   A criminal or guilty state of mind.

parens patriae   The right of the government to take care of those who cannot legally care for themselves.

in loco parentis   In the place of parents.

era of socialized juvenile justice   The period between 1899 and 1967, during which juvenile courts emphasized getting the total picture of the juvenile as opposed to adhering only to legal requirements.

legalists   Those favoring a formal approach to juvenile justice.

adjudicatory hearing   A hearing in juvenile cases at which the judge determines whether the youth in question is delinquent, dependent, abused, or otherwise in need of intervention.

delinquent acts   Acts committed by youth under a specified age that violate a federal, state, or municipal law.

status offenders   Those who commit acts that constitute an offense only because of the age of the offender.

petition   A written request for action directed to the juvenile court.

preliminary conference   A conference of interested parties at which a juvenile probation officer attempts to adjust juvenile cases without taking official action.

street corner or **station house adjustments**   Adjustments in juvenile cases made by a police officer and other interested parties in lieu of taking further official action.

ward of the state   A juvenile whose guardian is the court.

dispositional hearing   A hearing in juvenile cases at which the judge decides on appropriate placement for the juvenile in question.

diversion programs   Programs intended to divert (redirect) youth from the official juvenile justice network.

Critical Thinking Exercises

1. Do you think the juvenile justice system is capable of handling the kinds of cases presented before it today? Is juvenile court the appropriate place for youth who commit violent offenses in which several people lose their lives? If not, at what age do you think youth should be transferred to adult court and for what kinds of offenses?

2. How important are the concepts of rehabilitation, treatment, and education as applied to juveniles today? Can get-tough policies and harsh punishment accomplish the goals of the juvenile court? Present both sides of the argument regarding these types of policies. Which arguments do you find most persuasive?

Internet Exercises

Juveniles are often treated differently from adults in the justice network because they have unique problems and unique status.

1. Can you find a website that provides information for troubled teens and/or their parents?

2. What types of recent information concerning delinquents are available from *www.crime-times.org*?

3. If you wanted to know more about the processing of juveniles in the federal system, could you find that information from *www.ojd.usdoj.gov?* What other information concerning juveniles is available from this source?

References

Bazemore, G., & Washington, C. (1995, Spring). Charting the future of the juvenile justice system: Reinventing mission and management. *Spectrum, 68,* 51–66.

Bilchik, S. (1998). A juvenile justice system for the 21st century. *Crime and Delinquency, 44,* (1), 89–101.

Blackstone, W. (1803). *Commentaries on the laws of England* (12th ed.). London: Strahan.

Bourque, B. B., et al. (1996). Boot camps for juvenile offenders: An implementation evaluation of three demonstration programs. *Research in Brief.* Washington, DC: National Institute of Justice.

Cavan, R. S. (1969). *Juvenile delinquency: Development, treatment, control* (2nd ed.). Philadelphia: Lippincott.

Cox, S. M., Conrad, J. J., & Allen, J. M. (2002). *Juvenile justice: A guide to practice and theory* (5th ed.). Boston: McGraw-Hill.

Hatchett, G. (1998). Why we can't wait: The juvenile court in the new millenium. *Crime and Delinquency, 44,* (1), 83–88.

In re Gault, 387 U.S. 1, 49–50; 87 S. Ct. 1428, 1455 (1967).

In re Holmes, 379 Pa. 599, 109 A. 2d. 523 (1954); cert denied, 348 U.S. 973, 75 S. Ct. 535 (1955).

In re Winship, 397 U.S. 358, 90 S. Ct. 1068 (1970).

Kent v. *United States,* 383 U.S. 541, 86 S. Ct. 1045, 16 L. Ed. 2d. 84 (1966).

Moon, M. M., Sundt, J. L., Cullen, F. T., & Wright, J. P. (2000). Is child saving dead? Public support for juvenile rehabilitation. *Crime and Delinquency, 46,* (1), 38–60.

Rendleman, D. R. (1974). Parens patriae: From chancery to the juvenile court. In F. L. Faust & P. J. Brantingham (Eds.), *Juvenile justice philosophy,* pp. (72–117). St. Paul, MN: West.

Sanders, W. B. (1974). Some early beginnings of the children's court movement in England. In F. L. Faust & P. J. Brantingham (Eds.), *Juvenile justice philosophy,* pp. 46–47. St. Paul, MN: West.

Simonsen, C. E., & Gordon, M. S. (1991). *Juvenile justice in America* (2nd ed.). New York: Macmillan.

Zaslaw, J. G., & Balance, G. S. (1996, February). The socio-legal reponse: A new approach to juvenile justice in the '90s. *Corrections Today, 58,* 72.

Suggested Readings

Cox, S. M., Conrad, J. J., & Allen, J. M. (2002). *Juvenile justice: A guide to practice and theory* (5th ed.). Boston: McGraw-Hill.

Dorne, C., & Gewerth, K. (1998). *American juvenile justice: Cases, legislation, comments.* San Francisco: Austin and Winfield.

Mays, G. L., & Winfree, L. T., Jr. (2000). *Juvenile justice.* Boston: McGraw-Hill.

Wooden, W. S., & Blazak, R. (2001). *Renegade kids, suburban outlaws.* Belmont, CA: Wadsworth.

The U.S. Constitution and Selected Landmark Decisions:

*Constitution of the United States of America**

PREAMBLE

We, the People of the United States, in Order to form a more perfect Union, establish justice, insure domestic tranquility, provide for the common defence, promote the general welfare, and secure the blessings of liberty to ourselves and our posterity, do ordain and establish this Constitution for the United States of America.

ARTICLE I

Section 1

All legislative Powers herein granted shall be vested in a Congress of the United States, which shall consist of a Senate and House of Representatives.

Section 2

The House of Representatives shall be composed of Members chosen every second Year by the People of the several States, and the Electors in each State shall have the Qualifications requisite for Electors of the most numerous Branch of the State Legislature.

No Person shall be a Representative who shall not have attained to the Age of twenty-five Years, and been seven Years a Citizen of the United States, and who shall not, when elected, be an Inhabitant of that State in which he shall be chosen.

Representatives and *direct Taxes shall be apportioned* among the several States which may be included within this Union, according to their respective Numbers, *which shall be determined by adding to the whole Number of free Persons, including those bound to Service for a Term of Years,* and excluding Indians not

---

*Effective March 4, 1789

taxed, *three-fifths of all other Persons.* The actual Enumeration shall be made within three Years after the first Meeting of the Congress of the United States, and within every subsequent Term of ten Years, in such Manner as they shall by Law direct. The Number of Representatives shall not exceed one for every thirty Thousand, but each State shall have at Least one Representative; *and until such enumeration shall be made, the State of New Hampshire shall be entitled to choose three, Massachusetts eight, Rhode-Island and Providence Plantations one, Connecticut five, New-York six, New Jersey four, Pennsylvania eight, Delaware one, Maryland six, Virginia ten, North Carolina five, South Carolina five, and Georgia three.*

When vacancies happen in the Representation from any State, the Executive Authority thereof shall issue Writs of Election to fill such Vacancies.

The House of Representatives shall choose their Speaker and other Officers; and shall have the sole Power of Impeachment.

Section 3

The Senate of the United States shall be composed of two Senators from each State, *chosen by the Legislature thereof,* for six Years; and each Senator shall have one Vote.

Immediately after they shall be assembled in Consequence of the first Election, they shall be divided as equally as may be into three Classes. The Seats of the Senators of the first Class shall be vacated at the Expiration of the second Year, of the second Class at the Expiration of the fourth Year, and of the third Class at the Expiration of the sixth Year, so that one-third may be chosen every second Year; *and if Vacancies happen by Resignation, or otherwise, during the Recess of the Legislature of any State, the Executive thereof may make temporary Appointment until the next Meeting of the Legislature, which shall then fill such Vacancies.*

No Person shall be a Senator who shall not have attained to the Age of thirty Years, and been nine Years a Citizen of the United States, and who shall not, when elected, be an Inhabitant of that State for which he shall be chosen.

The Vice-President of the United States shall be President of the Senate, but shall have no Vote, unless they be equally divided.

The Senate shall choose their other Officers, and also a President pro tempore, in the Absence of the Vice-President, or when he shall exercise the Office of President of the United States.

The Senate shall have the sole Power to try all Impeachments. When sitting for that Purpose, they shall be on Oath or Affirmation. When the President of the United States is tried, the Chief Justice shall preside: And no Person shall be convicted without the Concurrence of two-thirds of the Members present.

Judgment in Cases of Impeachment shall not extend further than to removal from Office, and disqualification to hold and enjoy any Office of honor, Trust or Profit under the United States: but the Party convicted shall nevertheless be liable and subject to Indictment, Trial, Judgment and Punishment, according to Law.

Section 4

The Times, Place and Manner of holding Elections for Senators and Representatives, shall be prescribed in each State by the Legislature thereof; but the Congress may at any time by Law make or alter such Regulations, except as to the Places of choosing Senators.

The Congress shall assemble at least once in every Year, and such Meeting shall be on the first Monday of December, unless they shall by Law appoint a different day.

Section 5

Each House shall be the Judge of the Elections, Returns and Qualifications of its own Members, and a Majority of each shall constitute a Quorum to do Business; but a smaller Number may adjourn from day to day, and may be authorized to compel the Attendance of absent Members, in such Manner, and under such Penalties as each House may provide.

Each House may determine the Rules of its Proceedings, punish its Members for disorderly Behaviour, and, with the Concurrence of two-thirds, expel a Member.

Each House shall keep a Journal of its Proceedings, and from time to time publish the same, excepting such Parts as may in their Judgment require Secrecy; and the Yeas and Nays of the Members of either House on any question shall, at the Desire of one-fifth of those Present, be entered on the Journal.

Neither House, during the Session of Congress, shall, without the Consent of the other, adjourn for more than three days, nor to any other Place than that in which the two Houses shall be sitting.

Section 6

The Senators and Representatives shall receive a Compensation for their Services, to be ascertained by Law, and paid out of the Treasury of the United States. They shall in all Cases, except Treason, Felony and Breach of the Peace, be privileged from Arrest during their Attendance at the Session of their respective Houses, and in going to and returning from the same; and for any Speech or Debate in either House, they shall not be questioned in any other Place.

No Senator or Representative shall, during the Time for which he was elected, be appointed to any civil Office under the Authority of the United States, which shall have been created, or the Emoluments whereof shall have been increased during such time; and no Person holding any Office under the United States, shall be a Member of either House during his Continuance in Office.

Section 7

All Bills for raising Revenue shall originate in the House of Representatives; but the Senate may propose or concur with Amendments as on other Bills.

Every Bill which shall have passed the House of Representatives and the Senate shall, before it becomes a Law, be presented to the President of the United States; if he approve, he shall sign it, but if not, he shall return it, with his Objections, to that House in which it shall have originated, who shall enter the Objections at large on their Journal, and proceed to reconsider it. If after such Reconsideration two-thirds of the House shall agree to pass the Bill, it shall be sent, together with the Objections, to the other House, by which it shall likewise be reconsidered, and if approved by two-thirds of that House, it shall become a Law. But in all such Cases the Votes of both Houses shall be determined by Yeas and Nays and the Names of the Persons voting for and against the Bill shall be entered on the Journal of each House respectively. If any Bill shall not be returned by the President within ten Days (Sundays excepted) after it shall have been presented to him, the Same shall be a Law, in like Manner as if he had signed it, unless the Congress by their Adjournment prevent its Return, in which Case it shall not be a law.

Every Order, Resolution, or Vote to which the Concurrence of the Senate and House of Representatives may be necessary (except on a question of Adjournment) shall be presented to the President of the United States; and before the Same shall take Effect, shall be approved by him, or being disapproved by him, shall be repassed by two-thirds of the Senate and House of Representatives, according to the Rules and Limitations prescribed in the Case of a Bill.

Section 8

The Congress shall have Power: To lay and collect Taxes, Duties, Imposts and Excises, to pay the Debts and provide for the common Defence and general Welfare of the United States; but all Duties, Imposts and Excises shall be uniform throughout the United States.

> To borrow Money on the credit of the United States;
> To regulate Commerce with foreign Nations, and among the several States, and with the Indian Tribes;
> To establish a uniform Rule of Naturalization, and uniform Laws on the subject of Bankruptcies throughout the United States;
> To coin Money, regulate the Value thereof, and of foreign Coin, and fix the Standard of Weights and Measures;
> To provide for the Punishment of counterfeiting the Securities and current Coin of the United States;
> To establish Post Offices and post Roads;

To promote the Progress of Science and useful Arts, by securing for limited Times to Authors and Inventors the exclusive Right to their respective Writings and Discoveries;

To constitute Tribunals inferior to the Supreme Court;

To define and punish Piracies and Felonies committed on the high Seas, and Offences against the Law of Nations;

To declare War, grant Letters of Marque and Reprisal, and make Rules concerning Captures on Land and Water;

To raise and support Armies, but no Appropriation of Money to the Use shall be for a longer Term than two Years;

To provide and maintain a Navy;

To make Rules for the Government and Regulation of the land and naval Forces;

To provide for calling forth the Militia to execute the Laws of the Union, suppress Insurrections and repel Invasions;

To provide for organizing, arming, and disciplining the Militia, and for governing such Part of them as may be employed in the Service of the United States, reserving to the States respectively, the Appointment of the Officers, and the Authority of training the Militia according to the Discipline prescribed by Congress;

To exercise exclusive Legislation in all Cases whatsoever, over such District (not exceeding ten Miles square) as may, by Cession of particular States, and the Acceptance of Congress, become the Seat of Government of the United States, and to exercise like Authority over all Places purchased by the Consent of the Legislature of the State in which the Same shall be, for the Erection of Forts, Magazines, Arsenals, dock-Yards, and other needful Buildings;—And

To make all Laws which shall be necessary and proper for carrying into Execution the foregoing Powers, and all other Powers vested by this Constitution in the Government of the United States, or in any Department or Officer thereof.

Section 9

The Migration or Importation of such Persons as any of the States now existing shall think proper to admit, shall not be prohibited by the Congress prior to the Year one thousand eight hundred and eight, but a Tax or duty may be imposed on such Importation, not exceeding ten dollars for each Person.

The Privilege of the Writ of Habeas Corpus shall not be suspended, unless when in Cases of Rebellion or Invasion the public Safety may require it.

No Bill of Attainder or ex post facto Law shall be passed.

No Capitation, or other direct, Tax shall be laid, unless in Proportion to the Census or Enumeration herein before directed to be taken.

No Tax on Duty shall be laid on Articles exported from any State.

No Preference shall be given by any Regulation of Commerce or Revenue to the Ports of one State over those of another; nor shall Vessels bound to, or from, one State, be obliged to enter, clear, or pay Duties in another.

No Money shall be drawn from the Treasury, but in Consequence of Appropriations made by Law; and a regular Statement and Account of the Receipts and Expenditures of all public Money shall be published from time to time.

No Title of Nobility shall be granted by the United States; And no Person holding any Office of Profit or Trust under them, shall, without the Consent of the Congress, accept of any present, Emolument, Office, or Title, of any kind whatever, from any King, Prince, or foreign State.

Section 10

No State shall enter into any Treaty, Alliance, or Confederation; grant Letters of Marque and Reprisal; coin Money; emit Bills of Credit; make any Thing but gold and silver Coin a Tender in Payment of Debts; pass any Bill of Attainder, ex post facto Law, or Law impairing the Obligation of Contracts, or grant any Title of Nobility.

No State shall, within the Consent of the Congress, lay any Imposts or Duties on Imports or Exports, except what may be absolutely necessary for executing its inspection Laws; and the net Produce of all Duties and Imposts, laid by any State on Imports or Exports, shall be for the Use of the Treasury of the United States; and all such Laws shall be subject to the Revision and Control of the Congress.

No State shall, without the Consent of Congress, lay any Duty of Tonnage, keep Troops, or Ships of War in Time of Peace, enter into any Agreement or Compact with another State, or with a foreign Power, or engage in War, unless actually invaded, or in such imminent Danger as will not admit of Delay.

ARTICLE II

Section 1

The executive Power shall be vested in a President of the United States of America. He shall hold his Office during the Term of four Years, and, together with the Vice-President, chosen for the same Term, be elected, as follows:

Each State shall appoint, in such Manner as the Legislature thereof may direct, a Number of Electors, equal to the whole Number of Senators and Representatives to which the State may be entitled in the Congress: but no Senator or Representative, or Person holding an Office of Trust or Profit under the United States, shall be appointed an Elector.

The Electors shall meet in their respective States, and vote by Ballot for two Persons, of whom one at least shall be an Inhabitant of the same State with themselves. And they shall make a List of all the Persons voted for, and of the Number of Votes for each; which List they shall sign and certify, and transmit sealed to the Seat of the Government of the United States, directed to the President of the Senate. The President of the Senate shall, in the Presence of the Senate and House of Representatives, open all the Certificates, and the Votes shall then be counted. The Person having the greatest Number of Votes shall be the President, if such Number be a Majority of the whole Number of Electors appointed; and if there be more than one who have such Majority, and have an equal Number of Votes, then the House of Representatives shall immediately choose by Ballot one of them for President; and if no Person have a Majority, then from the five highest on the List the said House shall in like Manner choose the President. But in choosing the President, the Votes shall be taken by States, the Representation from each State having one Vote. A Quorum for this Purpose shall consist of a Member or Members from two-thirds of the States, and a Majority of all the States shall be necessary to a Choice. In every Case, after the Choice of the President, the Person having the greatest Number of Votes of the Electors shall be the Vice-President. But if there should remain two or more who have equal Votes, the Senate shall choose from them by Ballot the Vice-President.

The Congress may determine the Time of choosing the Electors, and the Day on which they shall give their Votes; which Day shall be the same throughout the United States.

No Person except a natural born Citizen, or a Citizen of the United States, at the time of the Adoption of this Constitution, shall be eligible to the Office of President; neither shall any Person be eligible to that Office who shall not have attained to the Age of thirty-five Years, and been fourteen Years a Resident within the United States.

In Case of the Removal of the President from Office, or of his Death, Resignation, or Inability to discharge the Powers and Duties of the said Office, the Same shall devolve on the Vice-President, and the Congress may by Law provide for the Case of Removal, Death, Resignation or Inability, both of the President and Vice-President, declaring what Officer shall then act as President, and such Officer shall act accordingly, until the Disability be removed, or a President shall be elected.

The President shall, at stated Times, receive for his Services, a Compensation which shall neither be increased nor diminished during the Period for which he shall have been elected, and he shall not receive within that Period any other Emolument from the United States, or any of them.

Before he enter on the Execution of his Office, he shall take the following Oath or Affirmation—"I do solemnly swear (or affirm) that I will faithfully execute the office of the President of the United States, and will, to the best of my Ability, preserve, protect and defend the Constitution of the United States."

Section 2

The President shall be Commander in Chief of the Army and Navy of the United States, and of the Militia of the several States, when called into actual Service of the United States; he may require the Opinion, in writing, of the principal Office in each of the executive Departments, upon any Subject relating to the Duties of their respective Offices, and he shall have Power to grant Reprieves and Pardons for Offences against the United States, except in Cases of Impeachment.

He shall have Power, by and with the Advice and Consent of the Senate, to make Treaties, provided two-thirds of the Senators present concur; and he shall nominate, and by and with the Advice and Consent of the Senate, shall appoint Ambassadors, other public Ministers and Consuls, Judges of the Supreme Court, and all other Officers of the United States, whose Appointments are not herein otherwise provided for, and which shall be established by Law: but the Congress may by Law vest the Appointment of such inferior Officers, as they think proper, in the President alone, in the Courts of Law, or in the Heads of Departments.

The President shall have Power to fill up all Vacancies that may happen during the Recess of the Senate, by granting Commissions which shall expire at the End of their next Session.

Section 3

He shall from time to time give to the Congress Information of the State of the Union, and recommend to their Consideration such Measures as he shall judge necessary and expedient; he may, on extraordinary Occasions, convene both Houses, or either of them, and in Case of Disagreement between them, with Respect to the Time of Adjournment, he may adjourn them to such Time as he shall think proper; he shall receive Ambassadors and other public Ministers; he shall take Care that the Laws be faithfully executed, and shall Commission all the Officers of the United States.

Section 4

The President, Vice-President and all civil Officers of the United States, shall be removed from Office on Impeachment for, and Conviction of, Treason, Bribery, or other high Crimes and Misdemeanors.

ARTICLE III

Section 1

The judicial Power of the United States shall be vested in one Supreme Court, and in such inferior Courts as the Congress may from time to time ordain and establish. The Judges, both of the Supreme and inferior Courts, shall hold their Offices during good Behavior, and shall, at stated Times, receive for their Services, a Compensation, which shall not be diminished during their Continuance in Office.

Section 2

The judicial Power shall extend to all Cases, in Law and Equity, arising under this Constitution, the Laws of the United States, and Treaties made, or which shall be made, under their Authority;—to all Cases affecting Ambassadors, other public Ministers and Consuls;—to all Cases of admiralty and maritime Jurisdiction;—to Controversies to which the United States shall be a Party;—to Controversies between two or more States;—*between a State and Citizens of another State;*—between Citizens of different States;—between Citizens of the same State claiming Lands under Grants of different States, *and between a State, or the Citizens thereof, and foreign States, Citizens or Subjects.*

In all Cases affecting Ambassadors, other public Ministers and Consuls, and those in which a State shall be Party, the Supreme Court shall have original Jurisdiction. In all the other Cases before mentioned, the Supreme Court shall have appellate Jurisdiction, both as to Law and Fact, with such Exceptions, and under such Regulations as the Congress shall make.

The Trial of all Crimes, except in Cases of Impeachment, shall be by Jury; and such Trial shall be held in the State where the said Crimes shall have been committed; but where not committed within any State, the Trial shall be at such Place or Places as the Congress may by Law have directed.

Section 3

Treason against the United States, shall consist only in levying War against them, or in adhering to their Enemies, giving them Aid and Comfort. No Person shall be convicted of Treason unless on the Testimony of two Witnesses to the same overt Act, or of Confession in open Court.

The Congress shall have Power to declare the Punishment of Treason, but no Attainder of Treason shall work Corruption of Blood, or Forfeiture except during the Life of the Person attained.

ARTICLE IV

Section 1

Full Faith and Credit shall be given in each State to the public Acts, Records and judicial Proceedings of every other State. And the Congress may by general Laws prescribe the Manner in which such Acts, Records and Proceedings shall be proved, and the Effect thereof.

Section 2

The Citizens of each State shall be entitled to all Privileges and Immunities of Citizens in the several States.

A Person charged in any State with Treason, Felony, or other Crime, who shall flee from Justice, and be found in another State, shall on Demand of the executive Authority of the State from which he fled, be delivered up, to be removed to the State having Jurisdiction of the Crime.

No Person held to Service or Labour in one State, under the Laws thereof, escaping into another, shall, in Consequence of any Law or Regulation therein, be discharged from such Service or Labour, but shall be delivered up on Claim of the Party to whom such Service of Labour may be due.

Section 3

New States may be admitted by the Congress into this Union; but no new States shall be formed or erected within the Jurisdiction of any other State; nor any State be formed by the Junction of two or more States, or Parts of States, without the Consent of the Legislatures of the States concerned as well as of the Congress.

The Congress shall have Power to dispose of and make all needful Rules and Regulations respecting the Territory or other Property belonging to the United States; and nothing in this Constitution shall be so construed as to prejudice any Claims of the United States, of any particular State.

Section 4

The United States shall guarantee to every State in this Union a Republican Form of Government, and shall protect each of them against Invasion; and on Application of the Legislature, or of the Executive (when the Legislature cannot be convened) against domestic Violence.

ARTICLE V

The Congress, whenever two-thirds of both Houses shall deem it necessary, shall propose Amendments to this Constitution, or, on the Application of the Legislatures of two-thirds of the several States, shall call a Convention for proposing Amendments, which, in either Case, shall be valid to all Intents and Purposes, as Part of this Constitution, when ratified by the Legislatures of three-fourths of the several States, or by Conventions in three-fourths thereof, as the one or the other Mode of Ratification may be proposed by the Congress; Provided *that no Amendment which may be made prior to the Year One thousand eight hundred and eight shall in any Manner affect the first and fourth Clauses in the Ninth Section of the first Article;* and that no State, without its Consent, shall be deprived of its equal Suffrage in the Senate.

ARTICLE VI

All Debts contracted and Engagements entered into, before the Adoption of this Constitution, shall be as valid against the United States under this Constitution, as under the Confederation.

This Constitution, and the Laws of the United States which shall be made in Pursuance thereof and all Treaties made, or which shall be made, under the Authority of the United States, shall be the supreme Law of the Land; and the Judges in every State shall be bound thereby, any Thing in the Constitution or Laws of any State to the Contrary notwithstanding.

The Senators and Representatives before mentioned, and the Members of the several State Legislatures, and all executive and judicial Officers, both of the United States and of the several States, shall be bound by Oath or Affirmation, to support this Constitution; but no religious Test shall ever be required as a Qualification to any Office or public Trust under the United States.

ARTICLE VII

The Ratification of the Conventions of nine States, shall be sufficient for the Establishment of this Constitution between the States so ratifying the Same.

DONE in Convention by the Unanimous Consent of the States present the Seventeenth Day of September in the Year of our Lord one thousand seven hundred and Eighty-seven and of the Independence of the United States of America the Twelfth. In witness whereof We have hereunto subscribed our Names, Attest William Jackson
Secretary

> G° Washington—
> Presidt. and deputy
> from Virginia

New Hampshire	John Langdon
	Nicholas Gilman
Massachusetts	Nathaniel Gorham
	Rufus King
Connecticut	Wm. Saml. Johnson
	Roger Sherman
New York	{Alexander Hamilton
New Jersey	Wil: Livingston
	David Brearley.
	Wm. Paterson.
	Jona: Dayton

Pennsylvania	B. Franklin
	Thomas Mifflin
	Robt. Morris
	Geo. Clymer
	Thos. FitzSimons
	Jared Ingersoll
	James Wilson
	Gouv Morris
Delaware	Geo: Read
	Gunning Bedford Jun
	John Dickinson
	Richard Bassett
	Jaco: Broom
Maryland	James McHenry
	Dan of St. Thos Jenifer
	Danl. Carroll
Virginia	John Blair—
	James Madison Jr.
North Carolina	Wm. Blount
	Richd. Dobbs Spaight.
	Hu Williamson
South Carolina	J. Rutledge
	Charles Cotesworth Pinckney
	Charles Pinckney
	Pierce Butler
Georgia	William Few
	Abr Baldwin

AMENDMENTS TO THE CONSTITUTION OF THE UNITED STATES OF AMERICA

AMENDMENT I

Congress shall make no law respecting an establishment of religion, or prohibiting the free exercise thereof; abridging the freedom of speech, or of the press; or of the right of the people peaceably to assemble and to petition the Government for a redress of grievances.

AMENDMENT II

A well regulated Militia, being necessary to the security of a free State, the right of the people to keep and bear Arms, shall not be infringed.

AMENDMENT III

No Soldier shall, in time of peace be quartered in any house, without the consent of the Owner, nor in time of war, but in a manner to be prescribed by law.

AMENDMENT IV

The right of the people to be secure in their persons, houses, papers, and effects, against unreasonable searches and seizures, shall not be violated, and no Warrants shall issue, but upon probable cause, supported by Oath or affirmation and particularly describing the place to be searched, and the persons or things to be seized.

AMENDMENT V

No person shall be held to answer for a capital, or otherwise infamous crime, unless on a presentment or indictment of a Grand Jury, except in cases arising in the land or naval forces, or in the Militia, when in actual service in time of War or public danger; nor shall any person be subject for the same offence to be twice put in jeopardy of life or limb; nor shall be compelled in any criminal case to be a witness against himself, nor be deprived of life, liberty, or property, without due process of law; nor shall private property be taken for public use, without just compensation.

AMENDMENT VI

In all criminal prosecutions, the accused shall enjoy the right to a speedy and public trial, by an impartial jury of the State and district wherein the crime shall have been committed, which district shall have been previously ascertained by law, and to be informed of the nature and cause of the accusation: to be confronted with the witnesses against him; to have compulsory process for obtaining witnesses in his favor, and to have the Assistance of Counsel for his defence.

AMENDMENT VII

In suits at common law, where the value in controversy shall exceed twenty dollars, the right of trial by jury shall be preserved, and no fact tried by jury, shall be otherwise reexamined in any Court of the United States, than according to the rules of the common law.

AMENDMENT VIII

Excessive bail shall not be required, nor excessive fines imposed, nor cruel and unusual punishments inflicted.

AMENDMENT IX

The enumeration in the Constitution, of certain rights, shall not be construed to deny or disparage others retained by the people.

AMENDMENT X

The powers not delegated to the United States by the Constitution, nor prohibited by it to the States, are reserved to the States respectively, or to the people. (Ratification of first ten amendments completed December 15, 1791.)

AMENDMENT XI

The Judicial power of the United States shall not be construed to extend to any suit in law or equity, commenced or prosecuted against one of the United States by Citizens of another State, or by Citizens or Subjects of any Foreign State.
(Declared ratified January 8, 1798.)

AMENDMENT XII

The electors shall meet in their respective states and vote by ballot for President and Vice-President, one of whom, at least, shall not be an inhabitant of the same state with themselves; they shall name in their ballots the person voted for as President, and in distinct ballots the person voted for as Vice-President, and they shall make distinct lists of all persons voted for as President, and of all persons voted for as Vice-President, and of the number of votes for each, which lists they shall sign and certify, and transmit sealed to the seat of the government of the United States, directed to the President of the Senate;—The President of the Senate shall, in presence of the Senate and House of Representatives, open all the certificates and the votes shall then be counted;—The person having the greatest number of votes for President, shall be the President, if such number be a majority of the whole number of Electors appointed; and if no person have such majority, then from the persons having the highest numbers not exceeding three on the list of those voted for as President, the House of Representatives shall choose immediately, by ballot, the President. But in choosing the President, the votes shall be taken by states, the representation from each state having one vote; a quorum for this purpose shall consist of a member or members from two-thirds of the states, and a majority of all the states shall be necessary to a choice.

*[and if the House of Representatives shall not choose a President whenever the right of choice shall devolve upon them, before the fourth day of March next following, then the Vice-President shall act as President, as in the case of the death or other constitutional disability of the President.]—The person having the greatest number of votes as Vice-President, shall be the Vice-President, if such number be a majority of the whole number of Electors appointed, and if no person have a majority, then from the two highest numbers on the list, the Senate shall choose the Vice-President; a quorum for the purpose shall consist of two-thirds of the whole number of Senators, and a majority of the whole number shall be necessary to a choice. But no person constitutionally ineligible to the office of President shall be eligible to that of Vice-President of the United States.

(Declared ratified September 25, 1804.)

AMENDMENT XIII

Section 1

Neither slavery nor involuntary servitude, except as a punishment for crime whereof the party shall have been duly convicted, shall exist within the United States, or any place subject to their jurisdiction.

Section 2

Congress shall have power to enforce this article by appropriate legislation.

(Declared ratified December 18, 1865.)

AMENDMENT XIV

Section 1

All persons born or naturalized in the United States, and subject to the jurisdiction thereof, are citizens of the United States and of the State wherein they reside. No State shall make or enforce any law which shall abridge the privileges or immunities of citizens of the United States; nor shall any State deprive any person of life, liberty, or property, without due process of law; nor deny to any person within its jurisdiction the equal protection of the laws.

Section 2

Representatives shall be apportioned among the several States according to their respective numbers, counting the whole number of persons in each State,

---

*See Amendments XX and XXV.

excluding Indians not taxed. But when the right to vote at any election for the choice of electors for President and Vice-President of the United States, Representatives in Congress, the Executive and Judicial officers of a State, or the members of the Legislature thereof, is denied to any of the male inhabitants of such State, being twenty-one years of age, and citizens of the United States, or in any way abridged, except for participation in rebellion, or other crime, the basis of representation therein shall be reduced in the proportion which the number of such male citizens shall bear to the whole number of male citizens twenty-one years of age in such State.

Section 3

No person shall be a Senator or Representative in Congress, or elector of President and Vice-President, or hold any office, civil or military, under the United States, or under any State, who, having previously taken an oath, as a member of Congress, or as an officer of the United States, or as a member of any State legislature, or as an executive or judicial officer of any State, to support the Constitution of the United States, shall have engaged in insurrection or rebellion against the same, or given aid or comfort to the enemies thereof. But Congress may by a vote of two-thirds of each House, remove such disability.

Section 4

The validity of the public debt of the United States, authorized by law, including debts incurred for payment of pensions and bounties for services in suppressing insurrection or rebellion, shall not be questioned. But neither the United States nor any State shall assume or pay any debt or obligation incurred in aid of insurrection or rebellion against the United States, or any claim for the loss or emancipation of any slave; but all such debts, obligations and claims shall be held illegal and void.

Section 5

The Congress shall have power to enforce, by appropriate legislation, the provisions of this article.

(Declared ratified July 28, 1868.)

AMENDMENT XV

Section 1

The right of citizens of the United States to vote shall not be denied or abridged by the United States or by any State on account of race, color, or previous condition of servitude—

Section 2

The Congress shall have power to enforce this article by appropriate legislation.
(Declared ratified March 30, 1870.)

AMENDMENT XVI

The Congress shall have power to lay and collect taxes on incomes, from whatever source derived, without apportionment among the several States, and without regard to any census or enumeration.
(Declared ratified February 25, 1913.)

AMENDMENT XVII

The Senate of the United States shall be composed of two Senators from each State, elected by the people thereof, for six years; and each Senator shall have one vote. The electors in each State shall have the qualifications requisite for electors of the most numerous branch of the State legislatures.

When vacancies happen in the representation of any State in the Senate, the executive authority of such State shall issue writs of election to fill such vacancies: *Provided,* That the legislature of any State may empower the executive thereof to make temporary appointments until the people fill the vacancies by election as the legislature may direct.

This amendment shall not be so construed as to affect the election or term of any Senator chosen before it becomes valid as part of the Constitution.
(Declared ratified May 31, 1913.)

AMENDMENT XVIII

Section 1

After one year from the ratification of this article the manufacture, sale, or transportation of intoxicating liquors within, the importation thereof into, or the exportation thereof from the United States and all territory subject to the jurisdiction thereof for beverage purposes is hereby prohibited.

Section 2

The Congress and the several States shall have concurrent power to enforce this article by appropriate legislation.

Section 3

This article shall be inoperative unless it shall have been ratified as an amendment to the Constitution by the legislatures of the several States, as provided in the Constitution, within seven years from the date of submission hereof to the States by the Congress]*

(Declared ratified January 29, 1919.)

AMENDMENT XIX

The right of citizens of the United States to vote shall not be denied or abridged by the United States or by any State on account of sex.

Congress shall have power to enforce this article by appropriate legislation. (Declared ratified August 26, 1920.)

AMENDMENT XX

Section 1

The terms of the President and Vice-President shall end at noon on the 20th day of January, and the terms of Senators and Representatives at noon on the 3d day of January, of the years in which such terms would have ended if this article had not been ratified; and the terms of their successors shall then begin.

Section 2

The Congress shall assemble at least once in every year, and such meeting shall begin at noon on the 3d day of January, unless they shall by law appoint a different day.

Section 3

If, at the time for the beginning of the term of the President, the President elect shall have died, the Vice-President elect shall become President. If a President shall not have been chosen before the time fixed for the beginning of his term, or if the President elect shall have failed to qualify, then the Vice-President elect shall act as President until a President shall have qualified; and the Congress may by law provide for the case wherein neither a President elect nor a Vice-President elect shall have qualified, declaring who shall then act as President, or the manner in which one who is to act shall be selected, and such person shall act accordingly until a President or Vice-President shall have qualified.

Section 4

The Congress may by law provide for the case of the death of any of the persons from whom the House of Representatives may choose a President when-

---

*Amendment XVIII was repealed by section 1 of amendment XXI.

ever the right of choice shall have devolved upon them and for the case of the death of any of the persons from whom the Senate may choose a Vice-President whenever the right of choice shall have devolved upon them.

Section 5

Sections 1 and 2 shall take effect on the 15th day of October following the ratification of this article.

Section 6

This article shall be inoperative unless it shall have been ratified as an amendment to the Constitution by the legislatures of three-fourths of the several States within seven years from the date of its submission.
(Declared ratified February 6, 1933.)

AMENDMENT XXI

Section 1

The eighteenth article of amendment to the Constitution of the United States is hereby repealed.

Section 2

The transportation or importation into any State, Territory, or possession of the United States for delivery or use therein of intoxicating liquors, in violation of the laws thereof, is hereby prohibited.

Section 3

This article shall be inoperative unless it shall have been ratified as an amendment to the Constitution by conventions in the several States, as provided in the Constitution, within seven years from the date of the submission hereof to the States by the Congress.
(Declared ratified December 5, 1933.)

AMENDMENT XXII

Section 1

No person shall be elected to the office of the President more than twice, and no person who has held the office of President, or acted as President, for more than two years of a term to which some other person was elected President shall be elected to the office of the President more than once. But this article shall not apply to any person holding the office of President when this Article was proposed by the Congress, and shall not prevent any person who may be holding the office of President, or acting as President, during the term within which this Article becomes operative from holding the office of President or acting as President during the remainder of such term.

Section 2

This article shall be inoperative unless it shall have been ratified as an amendment to the Constitution by the legislatures of three-fourths of the several States within seven years from the date of its submission to the States by the Congress.
(Declared ratified March 1, 1951.)

AMENDMENT XXIII

Section 1

The District constituting the seat of Government of the United States shall appoint in such manner as the Congress may direct:
A number of electors of President and Vice President equal to the whole number of Senators and Representatives in Congress to which the District would be entitled if it were a State, but in no event more than the least populous State; they shall be in addition to those appointed by the States, but they shall be considered, for the purposes of the election of President and Vice President, to be electors appointed by a State; and they shall meet in the District and perform such duties as provided by the twelfth article of amendment.

Section 2

The Congress shall have power to enforce this article by appropriate legislation.
(Declared ratified April 3, 1961.)

AMENDMENT XXIV

Section 1

The right of citizens of the United States to vote in any primary or other election for President or Vice President, for electors for President or Vice President, or for Senator or Representative in Congress, shall not be denied or abridged by the United States or any State by reason of failure to pay any poll tax or other tax.

Section 2

The Congress shall have power to enforce this article by appropriate legislation.
(Declared ratified February 4, 1962.)

AMENDMENT XXV

Section 1

In case of the removal of the President from office or of his death or resignation, the Vice President shall become President.

Section 2

Whenever there is a vacancy in the office of the Vice President, the President shall nominate a Vice President who shall take office upon confirmation by a majority vote of both Houses of Congress.

Section 3

Whenever the President transmits to the President pro tempore of the Senate and the Speaker of the House of Representatives his written declaration that he is unable to discharge the powers and duties of his office, and until he transmits to them a written declaration to the contrary, such powers and duties shall be discharged by the Vice President as Acting President.

Section 4

Whenever the Vice President and a majority of either the principal officers of the executive departments or of such other body as Congress may by law provide, transmit to the President pro tempore of the Senate and the Speaker of the House of Representatives their written declaration that the President is unable to discharge the powers and duties of his office, the Vice President shall immediately assume the powers and the duties of the office as Acting President.

Thereafter, when the President transmits to the President pro tempore of the Senate and the Speaker of the House of Representatives his written declaration that no inability exists, he shall resume the power and duties of his office unless the Vice President and a majority of either the principal officers of the executive department or of such other body as Congress may by law provide, transmit within four days to the President pro tempore of the Senate and the Speaker of the House of Representatives their written declaration that the President is unable to discharge the powers and duties of his office. Thereupon Congress shall decide the issue, assembling within forty-eight hours for that purpose if not in session. If the Congress, within twenty-one days after receipt of the latter written declaration, or, if Congress is not in session, within twenty-one days after Congress is required to assemble, determines by two-thirds vote of both Houses that the President is unable to discharge the powers and duties of his office, the Vice President shall continue to discharge the same as Acting President; otherwise, the President shall resume the powers and duties of his office.

(Declared ratified February 10, 1967.)

AMENDMENT XXVI

Section 1

The right of citizens of the United States, who are eighteen years of age or older, to vote shall not be denied or abridged by the United States or by any state on account of age.

Section 2

The Congress shall have the power to enforce this article by appropriate legislation. (Declared Ratified, 1971.)

AMENDMENT XXVII

No law, varying the compensation for the services of the Senators and Representatives, shall take effect, until an election of Representatives shall have intervened.

MAPP V. OHIO

Supreme Court of the United States.
367 U.S. 643, 81 S.Ct. 1684, 6 L.Ed.2d 1081 (1961).

Mr. Justice CLARK delivered the opinion of the Court. . . .

On May 23, 1957, three Cleveland police officers arrived at appellant's residence in that city pursuant to information that "a person [was] hiding out in the home, who was wanted for questioning in connection with a recent bombing, and that there was a large amount of police paraphernalia being hidden in the home." . . . Upon their arrival at that house, the officers knocked on the door and demanded entrance but appellant, after telephoning her attorney, refused to admit them without a search warrant. They advised their headquarters of the situation and undertook a surveillance of the house.

The officers again sought entrance three hours later when four or more additional officers arrived on the scene. When Miss Mapp did not come to the door immediately, at least one of the several doors to the house was forcibly opened and the policemen gained admittance. Meanwhile Miss Mapp's attorney arrived, but the officers, having secured their own entry, and continuing in their defiance of the law, would permit him neither to see Miss Mapp nor to enter the house. It appears that Miss Mapp was halfway down the stairs from the upper floor to the front door when the officers, in this high-handed manner, broke into the hall. She demanded to see the search warrant. A paper, claimed to be a warrant, was held up by one of the officers. She grabbed the "warrant" and placed it in her bosom. A struggle ensued in which the officers recovered the piece of paper and as a result of which they handcuffed appellant because she had been "belligerent" in resisting their official rescue of the "warrant" from her person. Running roughshod over appellant, a policeman "grabbed" her, "twisted [her] hand," and she "yelled [and] pleaded with him" because "it was hurting." Appellant, in handcuffs, was then forcibly taken upstairs to her bedroom where the officers searched a dresser, a chest of drawers, a closet and some suitcases. They also looked into a photo album and through personal papers belonging to the appellant. The search spread to the rest of the second floor including the child's bedroom, the living room, the kitchen and a dinette. The basement of the building and a trunk found therein were also searched. The obscene materials for possession of which she was ultimately convicted were discovered in the course of that widespread search.

At the trial no search warrant was produced by the prosecution, nor was the failure to produce one explained or accounted for. At best, "There is, in the record, considerable doubt as to whether there ever was any warrant for the search of defendant's home." . . .

. . . [T]his Court in *Weeks v. United States,* 232 U.S. 383, 34 S.Ct. 341, 58 L.Ed. 652 (1914), stated that

> "the Fourth Amendment . . . put the courts of the United States and Federal officials, in the exercise of their power and authority, under limitations and

restraints [and] . . . . forever secure[d] the people, their persons, houses, papers
and effects against all unreasonable searches and seizures under the guise of law
. . . and the duty of giving to it force and effect is obligatory upon all entrusted
under our Federal system with the enforcement of the laws." At pp. 391–392.

Specifically dealing with the use of the evidence unconstitutionally seized, the
Court concluded:

"If letters and private documents can thus be seized and held and used in evidence
against a citizen accused of an offense, the protection of the Fourth Amendment
declaring his right to be secure against such searches and seizures is of no value,
and, so far as those thus placed are concerned, might as well be stricken from the
Constitution. The efforts of the courts and their officials to bring the guilty to
punishment, praiseworthy as they are, are not to be aided by the sacrifice of those
great principles established by years of endeavor and suffering which have
resulted in their embodiment in the fundamental law of the land." At p. 393.

"The striking outcome of the *Weeks* case and those which followed it was the
sweeping declaration that the Fourth Amendment, although not referring to
or limiting the use of evidence in courts, really forbade its introduction if obtained by government officers through a violation of the Amendment." . . .
   In 1949, 35 years after *Weeks* was announced, this Court, in
                                        . . .
Wolf v. Colorado, . . . , again for the first time, discussed the effect of the Fourth
Amendment upon the States through the operation of the Due Process Clause
of the Fourteenth Amendment. It said:

"[W]e have no hesitation in saying that were a State affirmatively to sanction
such police incursion into privacy it would run counter to the guaranty of the
Fourteenth Amendment." . . .

Nevertheless, . . . the Court decided that the *Weeks* exclusionary rule would
not then be imposed upon the States as "an essential ingredient of the right."
. . . While in 1949, prior to the *Wolf* case, almost two-thirds of the States were
opposed to the use of the exclusionary rule, now, despite the *Wolf* case, more
than half of those since passing upon it, by their own legislative or judicial decision, have wholly or partly adopted or adhered to the *Weeks* rule. . . . Significantly, among those now following the rule is California, which, according
to its highest court, was "compelled to reach that conclusion because other
remedies have completely failed to secure compliance with the constitutional
provisions. . . ."
                                        . . .
   Today we once again examine *Wolf's* constitutional documentation of the
right to privacy free from unreasonable state intrusion, and, after its dozen years
on our books, are led by it to close the only courtroom door remaining open to
evidence secured by official lawlessness in flagrant abuse of that basic right, reserved to all persons as a specific guarantee against that very same unlawful
conduct. We hold that all evidence obtained by searches and seizures in violation of the Constitution is, by that same authority, inadmissible in a state court.

Since the Fourth Amendment's right of privacy has been declared enforceable against the States through the Due Process Clause of the Fourteenth, it is enforceable against them by the same sanction of exclusion as is used against the Federal Government. Were it otherwise, then just as without the *Weeks* rule the assurance against unreasonable federal searches and seizures would be "a form of words," valueless and undeserving of mention in a perpetual charter of inestimable human liberties, so too, without that rule the freedom from state invasions of privacy would be so ephemeral and so neatly severed from its conceptual nexus with the freedom from all brutish means of coercing evidence as not to mend this Court's high regard as a freedom "implicit in the concept of ordered liberty." . . . In short, the admission of the new constitutional right by *Wolf* could not consistently tolerate denial of its most important constitutional privilege, namely, the exclusion of the evidence which an accused had been forced to give by reason of the unlawful seizure. To hold otherwise is to grant the right but in reality to withhold its privilege and enjoyment. Only last year the Court itself recognized that the purpose of the exclusionary rule "is to deter—to compel respect for the constitutional guaranty in the only effectively available way—by removing the incentive to disregard it."

. . .

There are those who say, as did Justice (then Judge) Cardozo, that under our constitutional exclusionary doctrine "[t]he criminal is to go free because the constable has blundered." *People v. Defore*, 242 N.Y., at 21, 150 N.E., at 587. In some cases this will undoubtedly be the result. But, as was said in *Elkins*, "there is another consideration—the imperative of judicial integrity." 364 U.S., at 222. The criminal goes free, if he must, but it is the law that sets him free. Nothing can destroy a government more quickly than its failure to observe its own laws, or worse, its disregard of the charter of its own existence. As Mr. Justice Brandeis, dissenting, said in *Olmstead v. United States*, 277 U.S. 438, 485, 48 S.Ct. 564, 72 L.Ed. 944 (1928): "Our Government is the potent, the omnipresent teacher. For good or for ill, it teaches the whole people by its example. . . . If the Government becomes a lawbreaker, it breeds contempt for law; it invites every man to become a law unto himself; it invites anarchy." Nor can it lightly be assumed that, as a practical matter, adoption of the exclusionary rule fetters law enforcement. . . .

The ignoble shortcut to conviction left open to the State tends to destroy the entire system of constitutional restraints on which the liberties of the people rest. Having once recognized that the right to privacy embodied in the Fourth Amendment is enforceable against the States, and that the right to be secure against rude invasions of privacy by state officers, is, therefore, constitutional in origin, we can no longer permit that right to remain an empty promise. Because it is enforceable in the same manner and to like effect as other basic rights secured by the Due Process Clause, we can no longer permit it to be revocable at the whim of any police officer who, in the name of law enforcement itself, chooses to suspend its enjoyment. Our decision, founded on reason and truth, gives to the individual no more than that which the Constitution guarantees him, to the police officer no less than that to which honest law enforcement is entitled, and, to the courts, that judicial integrity so necessary in the true administration of justice.

The judgement of the Supreme Court of Ohio is reversed and the cause remanded for further proceedings not inconsistent with this opinion.

Reversed and remanded.

MIRANDA V. ARIZONA

Supreme Court of the United States, 1966.
384 U.S. 436, 86 S.Ct. 1602, 16 L.Ed.2d 694.

Mr. CHIEF JUSTICE WARREN delivered the opinion of the Court.

The cases before us raise questions which go to the roots of our concepts of American criminal jurisprudence: the restraints society must observe consistent with the Federal Constitution in prosecuting individuals for crime. More specifically, we deal with the admissibility of statements obtained from an individual who is subjected to custodial police interrogation and the necessity for procedures which assure that the individual is accorded his privilege under the Fifth Amendment to the Constitution not to be compelled to incriminate himself.

We dealt with certain phases of this problem recently in *Escobedo v. State of Illinois*, 378 U.S. 478, 84 S.Ct. 1758, 12 L.Ed.2d 977 (1964). There, as in the four cases before us, law enforcement officials took the defendant into custody and interrogated him in a police station for the purpose of obtaining a confession. The police did not effectively advise him of his right to remain silent or of his right to consult with his attorney. Rather, they confronted him with an alleged accomplice who accused him of having perpetrated a murder. When the defendant denied the accusation and said "I didn't shoot Manuel, you did it," they handcuffed him and took him to an interrogation room. There, while handcuffed and standing, he was questioned for four hours until he confessed. During this interrogation, the police denied his request to speak to his attorney, and they prevented his retained attorney, who had come to the police station, from consulting with him. At his trial, the State, over his objection, introduced the confession against him. We held that the statements thus made were constitutionally inadmissible.

This case has been the subject of judicial interpretation and spirited legal debate since it was decided two years ago. Both state and federal courts, in assessing its implications, have arrived at varying conclusions. A wealth of scholarly material has been written tracing its ramifications and underpinnings. Police and prosecutor have speculated on its range and desirability. We granted certiorari in these cases, 382 U.S. 924, 925, 937, 86 S.Ct. 318, 320, 395, 15 L.Ed.2d 338, 339, 348, in order further to explore some facets of the problems, thus exposed, of applying the privilege against self-incrimination to in-custody interrogation, and to give concrete constitutional guidelines for law enforcement agencies and courts to follow.

. . .

Our holding will be spelled out with some specificity in the pages which follow but briefly stated it is this: the prosecution may not use statements, whether exculpatory or inculpatory, stemming from custodial interrogation of the defendant unless it demonstrates the use of procedural safeguards effective to secure the privilege against self-incrimination. By custodial interrogation, we mean questioning initiated by law enforcement officers after a person has been taken into custody or otherwise deprived of his freedom of action in any significant way. As for the procedural safeguards to be employed, unless other fully effective means are devised to inform accused persons of their right of silence and to assure a continuous opportunity to exercise it, the following measures are required. Prior to any questioning, the person must be warned that he has a right to remain silent, that any statement he does make may be used as evidence against him, and that he has a right to the presence of an attorney, either retained or appointed. The defendant may waive effectuation of these rights, provided the waiver is made voluntarily, knowingly and intelligently. If, however, he indicates in any manner and at any stage of the process that he wishes to consult with an attorney before speaking there can be no questioning. Likewise, if the individual is alone and indicates in any manner that he does not wish to be interrogated, the police may not question him. The mere fact that he may have answered some questions or volunteered some statements on his own does not deprive him of the right to refrain from answering any further inquiries until he has consulted with an attorney and thereafter consents to be questioned.

I

The constitutional issue we decide in each of these cases is the admissibility of statements obtained from a defendant questioned while in custody or otherwise deprived of his freedom of action in any significant way. In each, the defendant was questioned by police officers, detectives, or a prosecuting attorney in a room in which he was cut off from the outside world. In none of these cases was the defendant given a full and effective warning of his rights at the outset of the interrogation process. In all the cases, the questioning elicited oral admissions, and in three of them, signed statements as well which were admitted at their trials. They all thus share salient features—incommunicado interrogation of individuals in a police-dominated atmosphere, resulting in self-incriminating statements without full warnings of constitutional rights.

An understanding of the nature and setting of this in-custody interrogation is essential to our decisions today. The difficulty in depicting what transpires at such interrogations stems from the fact that in this country they have largely taken place incommunicado. From extensive factual studies undertaken in the early 1930's, including the famous Wickersham Report to Congress by a Presidential Commission, it is clear that police violence and the "third degree" flourished at that time. In a series of cases decided by this

Court long after these studies, the police resorted to physical brutality—beatings, hanging, whipping—and to sustained and protracted questioning incommunicado in order to extort confessions. The Commission on Civil Rights in 1961 found much evidence to indicate that "some policemen still resort to physical force to obtain confessions," 1961 Comm'n on Civil Rights Rep., Justice, pt. 5, 17. The use of physical brutality and violence is not, unfortunately, relegated to the past or to any part of the country. Only recently in Kings County, New York, the police brutally beat, kicked and placed lighted cigarette butts on the back of a potential witness under interrogation for the purpose of securing a statement incriminating a third party. *People v. Portelli,* 15 N.Y.2d 235, 257 N.Y.S.2d 931, 205 N.E.2d 857 (1965).

The examples given above are undoubtedly the exception now, but they are sufficiently widespread to be the object of concern. Unless a proper limitation upon custodial interrogation is achieved—such as these decisions will advance—there can be no assurance that practices of this nature will be eradicated in the foreseeable future.

. . .

Again we stress that the modern practice of in-custody interrogation is psychologically rather than physically oriented. As we have stated before, "Since *Chambers v. State of Florida,* 309 U.S. 227, 60 S.Ct. 472, 84 L.Ed. 716, this Court has recognized that coercion can be mental as well as physical, and that the blood of the accused is not the only hallmark of an unconstitutional inquisition." *Blackburn v. State of Alabama,* 361 U.S. 199, 206, 80 S.Ct. 274, 279, 4 L.Ed.2d 242 (1960). Interrogation still takes place in privacy. Privacy results in secrecy and this in turn results in a gap in our knowledge as to what in fact goes on in the interrogation rooms. A valuable source of information about present police practices, however, may be found in various police manuals and texts which document procedures employed with success in the past, and which recommend various other effective tactics. These texts are used by law enforcement agencies themselves as guides. It should be noted that these texts professedly present the most enlightened and effective means presently used to obtain statements through custodial interrogation. By considering these texts and other data, it is possible to describe procedures observed and noted around the country.

The officers are told by the manuals that the "principal psychological factor contributing to a successful interrogation is privacy—being alone with the person under interrogation." The efficacy of this tactic has been explained as follows:

"If at all practicable, the interrogation should take place in the investigator's office or at least in a room of his own choice. The subject should be deprived of every psychological advantage. In his own home he may be confident, indignant, or recalcitrant. He is more keenly aware of his rights and more reluctant to tell of his indiscretions or criminal behavior within the walls of his home. Moreover his family and other friends are nearby, their presence lending moral support. In his office, the investigator possesses all the advantages. The atmosphere suggests the invincibility of the forces of the law."

To highlight the isolation and unfamiliar surroundings, the manuals instruct the police to display an air of confidence in the suspect's guilt and from outward appearance to maintain only an interest in confirming certain details. The guilt of the subject is to be posited as a fact. The interrogator should direct his comments toward the reasons why the subject committed the act, rather than court failure by asking the subject whether he did it. Like other men, perhaps the subject has had a bad family life, had an unhappy childhood, had too much to drink, had an unrequited desire for women. The officers are instructed to minimize the moral seriousness of the offense, to cast blame on the victim or on society. These tactics are designed to put the subject in a psychological state where his story is but an elaboration of what the police purport to know already—that he is guilty. Explanations to the contrary are dismissed and discouraged.

The texts thus stress that the major qualities an interrogator should possess are patience and perseverance. One writer describes the efficacy of these characteristics in this manner:

"In the preceding paragraphs emphasis has been placed on kindness and stratagems. The investigator will, however, encounter many situations where the sheer weight of his personality will be the deciding factor. Where emotional appeals and tricks are employed to no avail, he must rely on an oppressive atmosphere of dogged persistence. He must interrogate steadily and without relent, leaving the subject no prospect of surcease. He must dominate his subject and overwhelm him with his inexorable will to obtain the truth. He should interrogate for a spell of several hours pausing only for the subject's necessities in acknowledgement of the need to avoid a charge of duress that can be technically substantiated. In a serious case, the interrogation may continue for days, with the required intervals for food and sleep, but with no respite from the atmosphere of domination. It is possible in this way to induce the subject to talk without resorting to duress or coercion. The method should be used only when the guilt of the subject appears highly probable."

The manuals suggest that the suspect be offered legal excuses for his actions in order to obtain an initial admission of guilt. Where there is a suspected revenge-killing, for example, the interrogator may say:

"Joe, you probably didn't go out looking for this fellow with the purpose of shooting him. My guess is, however, that you expected something from him and that's why you carried a gun—for your own protection. You knew him for what he was, no good. Then when you met him he probably started using foul, abusive language and he gave some indication that he was about to pull a gun on you, and that's when you had to act to save your own life. That's about it, isn't it, Joe?"

Having then obtained the admission of shooting, the interrogator is advised to refer to circumstantial evidence which negates the self-defense explanation. This should enable him to secure the entire story. One text notes that "Even if he fails to do so, the inconsistency between the subject's original denial of the shooting and his present admission of at least doing the shooting will serve to deprive him of a self-defense 'out' at the time of trial."

When the techniques described above prove unavailing, the texts recommend they be alternated with a show of some hostility. One ploy often used has been termed the "friendly-unfriendly" or the "Mutt and Jeff" act:

> "In this technique, two agents are employed. Mutt, the relentless investigator, who knows the subject is guilty and is not going to waste any time. He's sent a dozen men away for this crime and he's going to send the subject away for the full term. Jeff, on the other hand, is obviously a kindhearted man. He has a family himself. He has a brother who was involved in a little scrape like this. He disapproves of Mutt and his tactics and will arrange to get him off the case if the subject will cooperate. He can't hold Mutt off for very long. The subject would be wise to make a quick decision. The technique is applied by having both investigators present while Mutt acts out his role. Jeff may stand by quietly and demur at some of Mutt's tactics. When Jeff makes his plea for cooperation, Mutt is not present in the room."

The interrogators sometimes are instructed to induce a confession out of trickery. The technique here is quite effective in crimes which require identification or which run in series. In the identification situation, the interrogator may take a break in his questioning to place the subject among a group of men in a line-up. "The witness or complainant (previously coached, if necessary) studies the line-up and confidently points out the subject as the guilty party." Then the questioning resumes "as though there were now no doubt about the guilt of the subject." A variation on this technique is called the "reverse line-up":

> "The accused is placed in a line-up, but this time he is identified by several fictitious witnesses or victims who associated him with different offenses. It is expected that the subject will become desperate and confess to the offense under investigation in order to escape from the false accusations."

The manuals also contain instructions for police on how to handle the individual who refuses to discuss the matter entirely or who asks for an attorney or relatives. The examiner is to concede him the right to remain silent. "This usually has a very undermining effect. First of all, he is disappointed in his expectation of an unfavorable reaction in the part of the interrogator. Secondly, a concession of this right to remain silent impresses the subject with the apparent fairness of his interrogator." After this psychological conditioning, however, the officer is told to point out the incriminating significance of the suspect's refusal to talk:

> "Joe, you have the right to remain silent. That's your privilege and I'm the last person in the world who'll try to take it away from you. If that's the way you want to leave this, O.K. But let me ask you this. Suppose you were in my shoes and I were in yours and you called me in to ask me about this and I told you, 'I don't want to answer any of your questions.' You'd think I had something to hide, and you'd probably be right in thinking that. That's exactly what I'll have to think about you, and so will everybody else. So let's sit here and talk this whole thing over."

Few will persist in their initial refusal to talk, it is said, if this monologue is employed correctly.

In the event that the subject wishes to speak to a relative or an attorney, the following advice is tendered:

> "[T]he interrogator should respond by suggesting that the subject first tell the truth to the interrogator himself rather than get anyone else involved in the matter. If the request is for an attorney, the interrogator may suggest that the subject save himself or his family the expense of any such professional service, particularly if he is innocent of the offense under investigation. The interrogator may also add, 'Joe, I'm only looking for the truth, and if you're telling the truth, that's it. You can handle this by yourself.' "

From these representative samples of interrogation techniques, the setting prescribed by the manuals and observed in practice becomes clear. In essence, it is this: To be alone with the subject is essential to prevent distraction and to deprive him of any outside support. The aura of confidence in his guilt undermines his will to resist. He merely confirms the preconceived story the police seek to have him describe. Patience and persistence, at times relentless questioning, are employed. To obtain a confession, the interrogator must "patiently maneuver himself or his quarry into a position from which the desired objective may be attained." When normal procedures fail to produce the needed result, the police may resort to deceptive stratagems such as giving false legal advice. It is important to keep the subject off balance, for example, by trading on his insecurity about himself or his surroundings. The police then persuade, trick, or cajole him out of exercising his constitutional rights.

Even without employing brutality, the "third degree" or the specific stratagems described above, the very fact of custodial interrogation exacts a heavy toll on individual liberty and trades on the weakness of individuals. This fact may be illustrated simply by referring to three confession cases decided by this Court in the Term immediately preceding our *Escobedo* decision. In *Townsend v. Sain*, 372 U.S. 293, 83 S.Ct. 745, 9 L.Ed.2d 770 (1963), the defendant was a 19-year-old heroin addict, described as a "near mental defective," id., at 307–310, 83 S.Ct. at 754–755. The defendant in *Lynumn v. State of Illinois*, 372 U.S. 528, 83 S.Ct. 917, 9 L.Ed.2d 922 (1963), was a woman who confessed to the arresting officer after being importuned to "cooperate" in order to prevent her children from being taken by relief authorities. This Court as in those cases reversed the conviction of a defendant in *Haynes v. State of Washington*, 373 U.S. 503, 83 S.Ct. 1336, 10 L.Ed.2d 513 (1963), whose persistent request during his interrogation was to phone his wife or attorney. In other settings, these individuals might have exercised their constitutional rights. In the incommunicado police-dominated atmosphere, they succumbed.

In the cases before us today, given this background, we concern ourselves primarily with this interrogation atmosphere and the evils it can bring. In No. 759, *Miranda v. Arizona*, the police arrested the defendant and took him to a special interrogation room where they secured a confession. In No. 760,

Vignera v. New York, the defendant made oral admissions to the police after interrogation in the afternoon, and then signed an inculpatory statement upon being questioned by an assistant district attorney later the same evening. In No. 761, *Westover v. United States*, the defendant was handed over to the Federal Bureau of Investigation by local authorities after they had detained and interrogated him for a lengthy period, both at night and the following morning. After some two hours of questioning, the federal officers had obtained signed statements from the defendant. Lastly, in No. 584, *California v. Stewart*, the local police held the defendant five days in the station and interrogated him on nine separate occasions before they secured his inculpatory statement.

In these cases, we might find the defendants' statements to have been involuntary in traditional terms. Our concern for adequate safeguards to protect precious Fifth Amendment rights is, of course, not lessened in the slightest. In each of the cases, the defendant was thrust into an unfamiliar atmosphere and run through menacing police interrogation procedures. The potentiality for compulsion is forcefully apparent, for example, in *Miranda*, where the indigent Mexican defendant was a seriously disturbed individual with pronounced sexual fantasies, and in *Stewart*, in which the defendant was an indigent Los Angeles Negro who had dropped out of school in the sixth grade. To be sure, the records do not evince overt physical coercion or patent psychological ploys. The fact remains that in none of these cases did the officers undertake to afford appropriate safeguards at the outset of the interrogation to insure that the statements were truly the product of free choice.

It is obvious that such an interrogation environment is created for no purpose other than to subjugate the individual to the will of his examiner. This atmosphere carries its own badge of intimidation. To be sure, this is not physical intimidation, but it is equally destructive of human dignity. The current practice of incommunicado interrogation is at odds with one of our Nation's most cherished principles—that the individual may not be compelled to incriminate himself. Unless adequate protective devices are employed to dispel the compulsion inherent in custodial surroundings, no statement obtained from the defendant can truly be the product of his free choice.

. . .

III

Today, then, there can be no doubt that the Fifth Amendment privilege is available outside of criminal court proceedings and serves to protect persons in all settings in which their freedom of action is curtailed in any significant way from being compelled to incriminate themselves. We have concluded that without proper safeguards the process of in-custody interrogation of persons suspected or accused of crime contains inherently compelling pressures which work to undermine the individual's will to resist and to compel him to speak where he would not otherwise do so freely. In order to combat these pressures and to permit a full opportunity to exercise the privilege against self-incrimination, the accused must be adequately and effectively apprised of his rights and the exercise of those rights must be fully honored.

It is impossible for us to foresee the potential alternatives for protecting the privilege which might be devised by Congress or the States in the exercise of their creative rule-making capacities. Therefore we cannot say that the Constitution necessarily requires adherence to any particular solution for the inherent compulsions of the interrogation process as it is presently conducted. Our decision in no way creates a constitutional strait-jacket which will handicap sound efforts at reform, nor is it intended to have this effect. We encourage Congress and the States to continue their laudable search for increasingly effective ways of protecting the rights of the individual while promoting efficient enforcement of our criminal laws. However, unless we are shown other procedures which are at least as effective in apprising accused persons of their right of silence and in assuring a continuous opportunity to exercise it, the following safeguards must be observed.

At the outset, if a person in custody is to be subjected to interrogation, he must first be informed in clear and unequivocal terms that he has the right to remain silent. For those unaware of the privilege, the warning is needed simply to make them aware of it—the threshold requirement for an intelligent decision as to its exercise. More important, such a warning is an absolute prerequisite in overcoming the inherent pressures of the interrogation atmosphere. It is not just the subnormal or woefully ignorant who succumb to an interrogator's imprecations, whether implied or expressly stated, that the interrogation will continue until a confession is obtained or that silence in the face of accusation is itself damning and will bode ill when presented to a jury. Further, the warning will show the individual that his interrogators are prepared to recognize his privilege should he choose to exercise it.

The Fifth Amendment privilege is so fundamental to our system of constitutional rule and the expedient of giving an adequate warning as to the availability of the privilege so simple, we will not pause to inquire in individual cases whether the defendant was aware of his rights without a warning being given. Assessments of the knowledge the defendant possessed, based on information as to his age, education, intelligence, or prior contact with authorities, can never be more than speculation; a warning is a clearcut fact. More important, whatever the background of the person interrogated, a warning at the time of the interrogation is indispensable to overcome its pressures and to insure that the individual knows he is free to exercise the privilege at that point in time.

The warning of the right to remain silent must be accompanied by the explanation that anything said can and will be used against the individual in court. This warning is needed in order to make him aware not only of the privilege, but also of the consequences of forgoing it. It is only through an awareness of these consequences that there can be any assurance of real understanding and intelligent exercise of the privilege. Moreover, this warning may serve to make the individual more acutely aware that he is faced with a phase of the adversary system—that he is not in the presence of persons acting solely in his interest.

The circumstances surrounding in-custody interrogation can operate very quickly to overbear the will of one merely made aware of his privilege by his interrogators. Therefore, the right to have counsel present at the interrogation is indispensable to the protection of the Fifth Amendment privilege under the system we delineate today. Our aim is to assure that the individual's right to choose between silence and speech remains unfettered throughout the interrogation process. A once-stated warning, delivered by those who will conduct the interrogation, cannot itself suffice to that end among those who most require knowledge of their rights. A mere warning given by the interrogators is not alone sufficient to accomplish that end. Prosecutors themselves claim that the admonishment of the right to remain silent without more "will benefit only the recidivist and the professional." Brief for the National District Attorneys Association as *amicus curiae*, p. 14. Even preliminary advice given to the accused by his own attorney can be swiftly overcome by the secret interrogation process. Cf. *Escobedo v. State of Illinois*, 378 U.S. 478, 485, n. 5, 84 S.Ct. 1758, 1762. Thus, the need for counsel to protect the Fifth Amendment privilege comprehends not merely a right to consult with counsel prior to questioning, but also to have counsel present during any questioning if the defendant so desires.

The presence of counsel at the interrogation may serve several significant subsidiary functions as well. If the accused decides to talk to his interrogators, the assistance of counsel can mitigate the dangers of untrustworthiness. With a lawyer present the likelihood that the police will practice coercion is reduced, and if coercion is nevertheless exercised the lawyer can testify to it in court. The presence of a lawyer can also help to guarantee that the accused gives a fully accurate statement to the police and that the statement is rightly reported by the prosecution at trial. See *Crooker v. State of California*, 357 U.S. 433, 443–448, 78 S.Ct. 1287, 1293–1296, 2 L.Ed.2d 1448 (1958) (Douglas, J., dissenting).

An individual need not make a pre-interrogation request for a lawyer. While such request affirmatively secures his right to have one, his failure to ask for a lawyer does not constitute a waiver. No effective waiver of the right to counsel during interrogation can be recognized unless specifically made after the warnings we here delineate have been given. The accused who does not know his rights and therefore does not make a request may be the person who most needs counsel. As the California Supreme Court has aptly put it:

> "Finally, we must recognize that the imposition of the requirement for the request would discriminate against the defendant who does not know his rights. The defendant who does not ask for counsel is the very defendant who most needs counsel. We cannot penalize a defendant who, not understanding his constitutional rights, does not make the formal request and by such failure demonstrates his helplessness. To require the request would be to favor the defendant whose sophistication or status had fortuitously prompted him to make it." *People v. Dorado*, 62 Cal.2d 338, 351, 42 Cal.Rptr. 169, 177–178, 398 P.2d 361, 369–370, (1965) (Tobriner, J.).

In *Carnley v. Cochran*, 369 U.S. 506, 513, 82 S.Ct. 884, 889, 8 L.Ed.2d 70 (1962), we stated: "[I]t is settled that where the assistance of counsel is a constitutional requisite, the right to be furnished counsel does not depend on a request." This proposition applies with equal force in the context of providing counsel to protect an accused's Fifth Amendment privilege in the face of interrogation. Although the role of counsel at trial differs from the role during interrogation, the differences are not relevant to the question whether a request is a prerequisite.

Accordingly we hold that an individual held for interrogation must be clearly informed that he has the right to consult with a lawyer and to have the lawyer with him during interrogation under the system for protecting the privilege we delineate today. As with the warnings of the right to remain silent and that anything stated can be used in evidence against him, this warning is an absolute prerequisite to interrogation. No amount of circumstantial evidence that the person may have been aware of this right will suffice to stand in its stead. Only through such a warning is there ascertainable assurance that the accused was aware of this right.

If an individual indicates that he wishes the assistance of counsel before any interrogation occurs, the authorities cannot rationally ignore or deny his request on the basis that the individual does not have or cannot afford a retained attorney. The financial ability of the individual has no relationship to the scope of the rights involved here. The privilege against self-incrimination secured by the Constitution applies to all individuals. The need for counsel in order to protect the privilege exists for the indigent as well as the affluent. In fact, were we to limit these constitutional rights to those who can retain an attorney, our decisions today would be of little significance. The cases before us as well as the vast majority of confession cases with which we have dealt in the past involve those unable to retain counsel. While authorities are not required to relieve the accused of his poverty, they have the obligation not to take advantage of indigence in the administration of justice. Denial of counsel to the indigent at the time of interrogation while allowing an attorney to those who can afford one would be no more supportable by reason or logic than the similar situation at trial and on appeal struck down in *Gideon v. Wainwright*, 372 U.S. 335, 83 S.Ct. 792, 9 L.Ed.2d 799 (1963), and *Douglas v. People of State of California*, 372 U.S. 353, 83 S.Ct. 814, 9 L.Ed.2d 811 (1963).

In order fully to apprise a person interrogated of the extent of his rights under this system then, it is necessary to warn him not only that he has the right to consult with an attorney, but also that if he is indigent a lawyer will be appointed to represent him. Without this additional warning, the admonition of the right to consult with counsel would often be understood as meaning only that he can consult with a lawyer if he has one or has the funds to obtain one. The warning of a right to counsel would be hollow if not couched in terms that would convey to the indigent—the person most often subjected to interrogation—the knowledge that he too has a right to have counsel present. As with the warnings of the right to remain silent and of the general right to counsel, only by effective and express explanation to the indigent of this right can there be assurance that he was truly in a position to exercise it.[5]

Once warnings have been given, the subsequent procedure is clear. If the individual indicates in any manner, at any time prior to or during questioning, that he wishes to remain silent, the interrogation must cease.[6] At this point he has shown that he intends to exercise his Fifth Amendment privilege; any statement taken after the person invokes his privilege cannot be other than the product of compulsion, subtle or otherwise. Without the right to cut off questioning, the setting of in-custody interrogation operates on the individual to overcome free choice in producing a statement after the privilege has been once invoked. If the individual states that he wants an attorney, the interrogation must cease until an attorney is present. At that time, the individual must have an opportunity to confer with the attorney and to have him present during any subsequent questioning. If the individual cannot obtain an attorney and he indicates that he wants one before speaking to police, they must respect his decision to remain silent.

This does not mean, as some have suggested, that each police station must have a "station house lawyer" present at all times to advise prisoners. It does mean, however, that if police propose to interrogate a person they must make known to him that he is entitled to a lawyer and that if he cannot afford one, a lawyer will be provided for him prior to any interrogation. If authorities conclude that they will not provide counsel during a reasonable period of time in which investigation in the field is carried out, they may refrain from doing so without violating the person's Fifth Amendment privilege so long as they do not question him during that time.

If the interrogation continues without the presence of an attorney and a statement is taken, a heavy burden rests on the government to demonstrate that the defendant knowingly and intelligently waived his privilege against self-incrimination and his right to retained or appointed counsel. *Escobedo v. State of Illinois*, 378 U.S. 478, 490, n. 14, 84 S.Ct. 1758, 1764, 12 L.Ed.2d 977. This Court has always set high standards of proof for the waiver of constitutional rights, *Johnson v. Zerbst*, 304 U.S. 458, 58 S.Ct. 1019, 82 L.Ed. 1461 (1938), and we reassert these standards as applied to in-custody interrogation. Since the State is responsible for establishing the isolated circumstances under which the interrogation takes place and has the only means of making available corroborated evidence of warnings given during incommunicado interrogation, the burden is rightly on its shoulders.

---

[5]While a warning that the indigent may have counsel appointed need not be given to the person who is known to have an attorney or is known to have ample funds to secure one, the expedient of giving a warning is too simple and the rights involved too important to engage in *ex post facto* inquiries into financial ability when there is any doubt at all on that score.

[6]If an individual indicates his desire to remain silent, but has an attorney present, there may be some circumstances in which further questioning would be permissible. In the absence of evidence of overbearing, statements then made in the presence of counsel might be free of the compelling influence of the interrogation process and might fairly be construed as a waiver of the privilege for purposes of these statements.

An express statement that the individual is willing to make a statement and does not want an attorney followed closely by a statement could constitute a waiver. But a valid waiver will not be presumed simply from the silence of the accused after warnings are given or simply from the fact that a confession was in fact eventually obtained. A statement we made in *Carnley v. Cochran*, 369 U.S. 506, 516, 82 S.Ct. 884, 890, 8 L.Ed.2d 70 (1962), is applicable here:

> "Presuming waiver from a silent record is impermissible. The record must show, or there must be an allegation and evidence which show, that an accused was offered counsel but intelligently and understandingly rejected the offer. Anything less is not waiver."

See also *Glasser v. United States*, 315 U.S. 60, 62 S.Ct. 457, 86 L.Ed. 680 (1942). Moreover, where in-custody interrogation is involved, there is no room for the contention that the privilege is waived if the individual answers some questions or gives some information on his own prior to invoking his right to remain silent when interrogated.

Whatever the testimony of the authorities as to waiver of rights by an accused, the fact of lengthy interrogation or incommunicado incarceration before a statement is made is strong evidence that the accused did not validly waive his rights. In these circumstances the fact that the individual eventually made a statement is consistent with the conclusion that the compelling influence of the interrogation finally forced him to do so. It is inconsistent with any notion of a voluntary relinquishment of the privilege. Moreover, any evidence that the accused was threatened, tricked, or cajoled into a waiver will, of course, show that the defendant did not voluntarily waive his privilege. The requirement of warnings and waiver of rights is a fundamental with respect to the Fifth Amendment privilege and not simply a preliminary ritual to existing methods of interrogation.

The warnings required and the waiver necessary in accordance with our opinion today are, in the absence of a fully effective equivalent, prerequisites to the admissibility of any statement made by a defendant. No distinction can be drawn between statements which are direct confessions and statements which amount to "admissions" of part or all of an offense. The privilege against self-incrimination protects the individual from being compelled to incriminate himself in any manner; it does not distinguish degrees of incrimination. Similarly, for precisely the same reason, no distinction may be drawn between inculpatory statements and statements alleged to be merely "exculpatory." If a statement made were in fact truly exculpatory it would, of course, never be used by the prosecution. In fact, statements merely intended to be exculpatory by the defendant are often used to impeach his testimony at trial or to demonstrate untruths in the statement given under interrogation and thus to prove guilt by implication. These statements are incriminating in any meaningful sense of the word and may not be used without the full warnings and effective waiver required for any other statement. In *Escobedo* itself, the defendant fully intended his accusation of another as the slayer to be exculpatory as to himself.

The principles announced today deal with the protection which must be given to the privilege against self-incrimination when the individual is first subjected to police interrogation while in custody at the station or otherwise deprived of his freedom of action in any significant way. It is at this point that our adversary system of criminal proceedings commences, distinguishing itself at the outset from the inquisitorial system recognized in some countries. Under the system of warnings we delineate today or under any other system which may be devised and found effective, the safeguards to be erected about the privilege must come into play at this point.

Our decision is not intended to hamper the traditional function of police officers in investigating crime. See *Escobedo v. State of Illinois,* 378 U.S. 478, 492, 84 S.Ct. 1758, 1765. When an individual is in custody on probable cause, the police may, of course, seek out evidence in the field to be used at trial against him. Such investigation may include inquiry of persons not under restraint. General on-the-scene questioning as to facts surrounding a crime or other general questioning of citizens in the fact-finding process is not affected by our holding. It is an act of responsible citizenship for individuals to give whatever information they may have to aid in law enforcement. In such situations the compelling atmosphere inherent in the process of in-custody interrogation is not necessarily present.

In dealing with statements obtained through interrogation, we do not purport to find all confessions inadmissible. Confessions remain a proper element in law enforcement. Any statement given freely and voluntarily without any compelling influences is, of course, admissible in evidence. The fundamental import of the privilege while an individual is in custody is not whether he is allowed to talk to the police without the benefit of warnings and counsel, but whether he can be interrogated. There is no requirement that police stop a person who enters a police station and states that he wishes to confess to a crime, or a person who calls the police to offer a confession or any other statement he desires to make. Volunteered statements of any kind are not barred by the Fifth Amendment and their admissibility is not affected by our holding today.

To summarize, we hold that when an individual is taken into custody or otherwise deprived of his freedom by the authorities in any significant way and is subjected to questioning, the privilege against self-incrimination is jeopardized. Procedural safeguards must be employed to protect the privilege and unless other fully effective means are adopted to notify the person of his right of silence and to assure that the exercise of the right will be scrupulously honored, the following measures are required. He must be warned prior to any questioning that he has the right to remain silent, that anything he says can be used against him in a court of law, that he has the right to the presence of an attorney, and that if he cannot afford an attorney one will be appointed for him prior to any questioning if he so desires. Opportunity to exercise these rights must be afforded to him throughout the interrogation. After such warnings have been given, and such opportunity afforded him, the individual may knowingly and intelligently waive these rights and agree to answer questions or make a statement. But unless and until such warnings and waiver are demonstrated by the prosecution at trial, no evidence obtained as a result of interrogation can be used against him.

IV

A recurrent argument made in these cases is that society's need for interrogation outweighs the privilege. This argument is not unfamiliar to this Court. See, e.g., *Chambers v. State of Florida*, 309 U.S. 227, 240–241, 60 S.Ct. 472, 478–479, 84 L.Ed. 716 (1940). The whole thrust of our foregoing discussion demonstrates that the Constitution has prescribed the rights of the individual when confronted with the power of government when it provided in the Fifth Amendment that an individual cannot be compelled to be a witness against himself. That right cannot be abridged. As Mr. Justice Brandeis once observed:

> "Decency, security, and liberty alike demand that government officials shall be subjected to the same rules of conduct that are commands to the citizen. In a government of laws, existence of the government will be imperilled if it fails to observe the law scrupulously. Our government is the potent, the omnipresent teacher. For good or for ill, it teaches the whole people by its example. Crime is contagious. If the government becomes a lawbreaker, it breeds contempt for law; it invites every man to become a law unto himself; it invites anarchy. To declare that in the administration of the criminal law the end justifies the means . . . would bring terrible retribution. Against that pernicious doctrine this court should resolutely set its face." *Olmstead v. United States*, 277 U.S. 438, 485, 48 S.Ct. 564, 575, 72 L.Ed. 944 (1928) (dissenting opinion).[7] In this connection, one of our country's distinguished jurists has pointed out: "The quality of a nation's civilization can be largely measured by the methods it uses in the enforcement of its criminal law."

If the individual desires to exercise his privilege, he has the right to do so. This is not for the authorities to decide. An attorney may advise his client not to talk to police until he has had an opportunity to investigate the case, or he may wish to be present with his client during any police questioning. In doing so an attorney is merely exercising the good professional judgment he has been taught. This is not cause for considering the attorney a menace to law enforcement. He is merely carrying out what he is sworn to do under his oath—to protect to the extent of his ability the rights of his client. In fulfilling this responsibility the attorney plays a vital role in the administration of criminal justice under our Constitution.

In announcing these principles, we are not unmindful of the burdens which law enforcement officials must bear, often under trying circumstances. We also fully recognize the obligation of all citizens to aid in enforcing the criminal laws. This Court, while protecting individual rights, has always given

---

[7]In quoting the above from the dissenting opinion of Mr. Justice Brandeis we, of course, do not intend to pass the constitutional questions involved in the *Olmstead* case.

ample latitude to law enforcement agencies in the legitimate exercise of their duties. The limits we have placed on the interrogation process should not constitute an undue interference with a proper system of law enforcement. As we have noted, our decision does not in any way preclude police from carrying out their traditional investigatory functions. Although confessions may play an important role in some convictions, the cases before us present graphic examples of the overstatement of the "need" for confessions. In each case authorities conducted interrogations ranging up to five days in duration despite the presence, through standard investigating practices, of considerable evidence against each defendant.

. . .

It is also urged that an unfettered right to detention for interrogation should be allowed because it will often redound to the benefit of the person questioned. When police inquiry determines that there is no reason to believe that the person has committed any crime, it is said, he will be released without need for further formal procedures. The person who has committed no offense, however, will be better able to clear himself after warnings with counsel present than without. It can be assumed that in such circumstances a lawyer would advise his client to talk freely to police in order to clear himself.

Custodial interrogation, by contrast, does not necessarily afford the innocent an opportunity to clear themselves. A serious consequence of the present practice of the interrogation alleged to be beneficial for the innocent is that many arrests "for investigation" subject large numbers of innocent persons to detention and interrogation. In one of the cases before us, No. 584, *California v. Stewart*, police held four persons, who were in the defendant's house at the time of the arrest, in jail for five days until defendant confessed. At that time they were finally released. Police stated that there was "no evidence to connect them with any crime." Available statistics on the extent of this practice where it is condoned indicate that these four are far from alone in being subjected to arrest, prolonged detention, and interrogation without the requisite probable cause.

Over the years the Federal Bureau of Investigation has compiled an exemplary record of effective law enforcement while advising any suspect or arrested person, at the outset of an interview, that he is not required to make a statement, that any statement may be used against him in court, that the individual may obtain the services of an attorney of his own choice and, more recently, that he has a right to free counsel if he is unable to pay. A letter received from the Solicitor General in response to a question from the Bench makes it clear that the present pattern of warnings and respect for the rights of the individual followed as a practice by the FBI is consistent with the procedure which we delineate today. It states:

> "At the oral argument of the above cause, Mr. Justice Fortas asked whether I could provide certain information as to the practices followed by the Federal Bureau of Investigation. I have directed these questions to the attention of the

Director of the Federal Bureau of Investigation and am submitting herewith a statement of the questions and of the answers which we have received.

" '(1) When an individual is interviewed by agents of the Bureau, what warning is given to him?

" 'The standard warning long given by Special Agents of the FBI to both suspects and persons under arrest is that the person has a right to say nothing and a right to counsel, and that any statement he does make may be used against him in court. Examples of this warning are to be found in the *Westover* case at 342 F.2d 684 (1965), and *Jackson v. United States,* [119 U.S.App.D.C. 100] 337 F.2d 136 (1964), cert. den. 380 U.S.935, 85 S.Ct. 1353.

" 'After passage of the Criminal Justice Act of 1964, which provides free counsel for Federal defendants unable to pay, we added to our instructions to Special Agents the requirement that any person who is under arrest for an offense under FBI jurisdiction, or whose arrest is contemplated following the interview, must also be advised of his right to free counsel if he is unable to pay, and the fact that such counsel will be assigned by the Judge. At the same time, we broadened the right to counsel warning to read counsel of his own choice, or anyone else with whom he might wish to speak.

" '(2) When is the warning given?

" 'The FBI warning is given to a suspect at the very outset of the interview, as shown in the *Westover* case, cited above. The warning may be given to a person arrested as soon as practicable after the arrest, as shown in the *Jackson* case, also cited above, and in *United States v. Konigsberg,* 336 F.2d 844 (1964), cert. den. [*Celso v. United States*] 379 U.S. 933 [85 S.Ct. 327, 13 L.Ed.2d 342] but in any event it must precede the interview with the person for a confession or admission of his own guilt.

" '(3) What is the Bureau's practice in the event that (a) the individual requests counsel and (b) counsel appears?

" 'When the person who has been warned of his right to counsel decides that he wishes to consult with counsel before making a statement, the interview is terminated at that point, *Schultz v. United States,* 351 F.2d 287 ([10 Cir.] 1965). It may be continued, however, as to all matters *other* than the person's own guilt or innocence. If he is indecisive in his request for counsel, there may be some question on whether he did or did not waive counsel. Situations of this kind must necessarily be left to the judgment of the interviewing Agent. For example, in *Hiram v. United States,* 354 F.2d 4 ([9 Cir.] 1965), the Agent's conclusion that the person arrested had waived his right to counsel was upheld by the courts.

" 'A person being interviewed and desiring to consult counsel by telephone must be permitted to do so, as shown in *Caldwell v. United States,* 351 F.2d 459 ([1 Cir.] 1965). When counsel appears in person, he is permitted to confer with his client in private.

" '(4) What is the Bureau's practice if the individual requests counsel, but cannot afford to retain an attorney?

" 'If any person being interviewed after warning of counsel decides that he wishes to consult with counsel before proceeding further the interview is terminated, as shown above. FBI Agents do not pass judgment on the ability of the person to pay for counsel. They do, however, advise those who have been arrested for an offense under FBI jurisdiction, or whose arrest is contemplated following the interview, of a right to free counsel *if* they are unable to pay, and the availability of such counsel from the Judge.' "[8]

The practice of the FBI can readily be emulated by state and local enforcement agencies. The argument that the FBI deals with different crimes than are dealt with by state authorities does not mitigate the significance of the FBI experience.

The experience in some other countries also suggests that the danger to law enforcement in curbs on interrogation is overplayed. The English procedure since 1912 under the Judges' Rules is significant. As recently strengthened, the Rules require that a cautionary warning be given an accused by a police officer as soon as he has evidence that affords reasonable grounds for suspicion; they also require that any statement made be given by the accused without questioning by police. The right of the individual to consult with an attorney during this period is expressly recognized.

The safeguards present under Scottish law may be even greater than in England. Scottish judicial decisions bar use in evidence of most confessions obtained through police interrogation. In India, confessions made to police not in the presence of a magistrate have been excluded by rule of evidence since 1872, at a time when it operated under British law. Identical provisions appear in the Evidence Ordinance of Ceylon, enacted in 1895. Similarly, in our country the Uniform Code of Military Justice has long provided that no suspect may be interrogated without first being warned of his right not to make a statement and that any statement he makes may be used against him. Denial of the right to consult counsel during interrogation has also been proscribed by military tribunals. There appears to have been no marked detrimental effect on criminal law enforcement in these jurisdictions as a result of these rules. Conditions of law enforcement in our country are sufficiently similar to permit reference to this experience as assurance that lawlessness will not result from warning an individual of his rights or allowing him to exercise them. Moreover, it is consistent with our legal system that we give at least as much protection to these rights as is given in the jurisdictions described. We deal in our country with rights grounded in a specific requirement of the Fifth Amendment of the Constitution, whereas other jurisdictions arrived at their conclusions on the basis of principles of justice not so specifically defined.

It is also urged upon us that we withhold decision on this issue until state legislative bodies and advisory groups have had an opportunity to deal with these problems by rule making. We have already pointed out that the Constitution does not require any specific code of procedures for protecting the privilege against self-incrimination during custodial interrogation. Congress and

---

[8]We agree that the interviewing agent must exercise his judgment in determining whether the individual waives his right to counsel. Because of the constitutional basis of the right, however, the standard for waiver is necessarily high. And, of course, the ultimate responsibility for resolving this constitutional question lies with the courts.

the States are free to develop their own safeguards for the privilege, so long as they are fully as effective as those described above in informing accused persons of their right of silence and in affording a continuous opportunity to exercise it. In any event, however, the issues presented are of constitutional dimensions and must be determined by the courts. The admissibility of a statement in the face of a claim that it was obtained in violation of the defendant's constitutional rights is an issue the resolution of which has long since been undertaken by this Court. See *Hopt v. People of Territory of Utah,* 110 U.S. 574, 4 S.Ct. 202, 28 L.Ed. 262 (1884). Judicial solutions to problems of constitutional dimension have evolved decade by decade. As courts have been presented with the need to enforce constitutional rights, they have found means of doing so. That was our responsibility when *Escobedo* was before us and it is our responsibility today. Where rights secured by the Constitution are involved, there can be no rule making or legislation which would abrogate them.

V

Because of the nature of the problem and because of its recurrent significance in numerous cases, we have to this point discussed the relationship of the Fifth Amendment privilege to police interrogation without specific concentration on the facts of the cases before us. We turn now to these facts to consider the application to these cases of the constitutional principles discussed above. In each instance, we have concluded that statements were obtained from the defendant under circumstances that did not meet constitutional standards for protection of the privilege.

No. 759. *Miranda v. Arizona.*

On March 13, 1963, petitioner, Ernesto Miranda, was arrested at his home and taken into custody to a Phoenix police station. He was there identified by the complaining witness. The police then took him to "Interrogation Room No. 2" of the detective bureau. There he was questioned by two police officers. The officers admitted at trial that Miranda was not advised that he had a right to have an attorney present.[9] Two hours later, the officers emerged from the interrogation room with a written confession signed by Miranda. At the top of the statement was a typed paragraph stating that the confession was made voluntarily, without threats or promises of immunity and "with full knowledge of my legal rights, understanding any statement I make may be used against me."[10]

---

[9]Miranda was also convicted in a separate trial on an unrelated robbery charge not presented here for review. A statement introduced at that trial was obtained from Miranda during the same interrogation which resulted in the confession involved here. At the robbery trial, one officer testified that during the interrogation he did not tell Miranda that anything he said would be held against him or that he could consult with an attorney. The other officer stated that they had both told Miranda that anything he said would be used against him and that he was not required by law to tell them anything.

[10]One of the officers testified that he read this paragraph to Miranda. Apparently, however, he did not do so until after Miranda had confessed orally.

At his trial before a jury, the written confession was admitted into evidence over the objection of defense counsel, and the officers testified to the prior oral confession made by Miranda during the interrogation. Miranda was found guilty of kidnapping and rape. He was sentenced to 20 to 30 years' imprisonment on each count, the sentences to run concurrently. On appeal, the Supreme Court of Arizona held that Miranda's constitutional rights were not violated in obtaining the confession and affirmed the conviction. 98 Ariz. 18, 401 P.2d 721. In reaching its decision, the court emphasized heavily the fact that Miranda did not specifically request counsel.

We reverse. From the testimony of the officers and by the admission of respondent, it is clear that Miranda was not in any way apprised of his right to consult with an attorney and to have one present during the interrogation, nor was his right not to be compelled to incriminate himself effectively protected in any other manner. Without these warnings the statements were inadmissible. The mere fact that he signed a statement which contained a typed-in clause stating that he had "full knowledge" of his "legal rights" does not approach the knowing and intelligent waiver required to relinquish constitutional rights.

· · ·

No. 760. *Vignera v. New York.*

Petitioner, Michael Vignera, was picked up by New York police on October 14, 1960, in connection with the robbery three days earlier of a Brooklyn dress shop. They took him to the 17th Detective Squad headquarters in Manhattan. Sometime thereafter he was taken to the 66th Detective Squad. There a detective questioned Vignera with respect to the robbery. Vignera orally admitted the robbery to the detective. The detective was asked on cross-examination at trial by defense counsel whether Vignera was warned of his right to counsel before being interrogated. The prosecution objected to the question and the trial judge sustained the objection. Thus, the defense was precluded from making any showing that warnings had not been given. While at the 66th Detective Squad, Vignera was identified by the store owner and a saleslady as the man who robbed the dress shop. At about 3 P.M. he was formally arrested. The police then transported him to still another station, the 70th Precinct in Brooklyn, "for detention." At 11 P.M. Vignera was questioned by an assistant district attorney in the presence of a hearing reporter who transcribed the questions and Vignera's answers. This verbatim account of these proceedings contains no statement of any warnings given by the assistant district attorney. At Vignera's trial on a charge of first degree robbery, the detective testified as to the oral confession. The transcription of the statement taken was also introduced in evidence. At the conclusion of the testimony, the trial judge charged the jury in part as follows:

> "The law doesn't say that the confession is void or invalidated because the police officer didn't advise the defendant as to his rights. Did you hear what I said? I am telling you what the law of the State of New York is."

Vignera was found guilty of first degree robbery. He was subsequently adjudged a third-felony offender and sentenced to 30 to 60 years' imprisonment. The conviction was affirmed without opinion by the Appellate Division, Second Department, 21 A.D.2d 752, 252 N.Y. S.2d 19, and by the Court of Appeals, also without opinion, 15 N.Y.2d 970, 259 N.Y.S.2d 857, 207 N.E.2d 527, remittitur amended, 16 N.Y. 2d 614, 261 N.Y.S.2d 65, 209 N.E.2d 110. In argument to the Court of Appeals, the State contended that Vignera had no constitutional right to be advised of his right to counsel or his privilege against self-incrimination.

We reverse. The foregoing indicates that Vignera was not warned of any of his rights before the questioning by the detective and by the assistant district attorney. No other steps were taken to protect these rights. Thus he was not effectively apprised of his Fifth Amendment privilege or of his right to have counsel present and his statements are inadmissible. No. 761. *Westover v. United States.*

At approximately 9:45 P.M. on March 20, 1963, petitioner, Carl Calvin Westover, was arrested by local police in Kansas City as a suspect in two Kansas City robberies. A report was also received from the FBI that he was wanted on a felony charge in California. The local authorities took him to a police station and placed him in a line-up on the local charges, and at about 11:45 P.M. he was booked. Kansas City police interrogated Westover on the night of his arrest. He denied any knowledge of criminal activities. The next day local officers interrogated him again throughout the morning. Shortly before noon they informed the FBI that they were through interrogating Westover and that the FBI could proceed to interrogate him. There is nothing in the record to indicate that Westover was ever given any warning as to his rights by local police. At noon, three special agents of the FBI continued the interrogation in a private interview room of the Kansas City Police Department, this time with respect to the robbery of a savings and loan association and a bank in Sacramento California. After two or two and one-half hours, Westover signed separate confessions to each of these two robberies which had been prepared by one of the agents during the interrogation. At trial one of the agents testified, and a paragraph on each of the statements state that the agents advised Westover that he did not have to make a statement, that any statement he made could be used against him, and that he had the right to see an attorney.

Westover was tried by a jury in federal court and convicted of the California robberies. His statements were introduced at trial. He was sentenced to 15 years' imprisonment on each count, the sentences to run consecutively. On appeal, the conviction was affirmed by the Court of Appeals for the Ninth Circuit. 342 F.2d 684.

We reverse. On the facts of this case we cannot find that Westover knowingly and intelligently waived his rights to remain silent and his right to consult with counsel prior to the time he made the statement. At the time the FBI agents began questioning Westover, he had been in custody for over 14 hours and had been interrogated at length during that period. The FBI interrogation began immediately upon the conclusion of the interrogation by Kansas City police and was conducted in local police headquarters. Although the two law enforcement authorities are legally distinct and the crimes for which they interrogated Westover were different, the impact on him was that of a continuous period of questioning. There is no evidence of any warning given prior to the FBI interrogation nor is there any evidence of an articulated waiver of rights after the FBI commenced its interrogation. The record simply shows that the defendant did in fact confess a short time after being turned over to the FBI following interrogation by local police. Despite the fact that the FBI agents gave warnings at the outset of their interview, from Westover's point of view the warnings came at the end of the interrogation process. In these circumstances an intelligent waiver of constitutional rights cannot be assumed.

We do not suggest that law enforcement authorities are precluded from questioning any individual who has been held for a period of time by other authorities and interrogated by them without appropriate warnings. A different case would be presented if an accused were taken into custody by the second authority removed both in time and place from his original surroundings, and then adequately advised of his rights and given an opportunity to exercise them. But here the FBI interrogation was conducted immediately following the state interrogation in the same police station—in the same compelling surroundings. Thus, in obtaining a confession from Westover the federal authorities were the beneficiaries of the pressure applied by the local in-custody interrogation. In these circumstances the giving of warnings alone was not sufficient to protect the privilege.

No. 584. *California v. Stewart.*

In the course of investigating a series of purse-snatch robberies in which one of the victims had died of injuries inflicted by her assailant, respondent, Roy Allen Stewart, was pointed out to Los Angeles police as the endorser of dividend checks taken in one of the robberies. At about 7:15 P.M., January 31, 1963, police officers went to Stewart's house and arrested him. One of the officers asked Stewart if they could search the house, to which he replied, "Go ahead." The search turned up various items taken from the five robbery victims. At the time of Stewart's arrest, police also arrested Stewart's wife and three other persons who were visiting him. These four were jailed along with Stewart and were interrogated. Stewart was taken to the University Station of the Los Angeles Police Department where he was placed in a cell. During the next five days, police interrogated Stewart on nine different occasions. Except during the first interrogation session, when he was confronted with an accusing witness, Stewart was isolated with his interrogators.

During the ninth interrogation session, Stewart admitted that he had robbed the deceased and stated that he had not meant to hurt her. Police then brought Stewart before a magistrate for the first time. Since there was no evidence to connect them with any crime, the police then released the other four persons arrested with him.

Nothing in the record specifically indicates whether Stewart was or was not advised of his right to remain silent or his right to counsel. In a number of instances, however, the interrogating officers were asked to recount everything that was said during the interrogations. None indicated that Stewart was ever advised of his rights.

Stewart was charged with kidnapping to commit robbery, rape, and murder. At his trial, transcripts of the first interrogation and the confession at the last interrogation were introduced in evidence. The jury found Stewart guilty of robbery and first degree murder and fixed the penalty as death. On appeal, the Supreme Court of California reversed. 62 Cal.2d 571, 43 Cal.Rptr. 201, 400 P.2d 97. It held that under this Court's decision in *Escobedo*, Stewart should have been advised of his right to remain silent and of his right to counsel and that it would not presume in the face of a silent record that the police advised Stewart of his rights.

We affirm. In dealing with custodial interrogation, we will not presume that a defendant has been effectively apprised of his rights and that his privilege against self-incrimination has been adequately safeguarded on a record that does not show that any warnings have been given or that any effective alternative has been employed. Nor can a knowing and intelligent waiver of these rights be assumed on a silent record. Furthermore, Stewart's steadfast denial of the alleged offenses through eight of the nine interrogations over a period of five days is subject to no other construction than that he was compelled by persistent interrogation to forego his Fifth Amendment privilege.

Therefore, in accordance with the foregoing, the judgments of the Supreme Court of Arizona in No. 759, of the New York Court of Appeals in No. 760, and of the Court of Appeals for the Ninth Circuit in No. 761 are reversed. The judgment of the Supreme Court of California in No. 584 is affirmed. It is so ordered.

Judgments of Supreme Court of Arizona in No. 759, of New York Court of Appeals in No. 760, and of the Court of Appeals for the Ninth Circuit in No. 761 reversed.

Judgment of Supreme Court of California in No. 584 affirmed.

CHIMEL V. CALIFORNIA

Supreme Court of the United States, 1969.
395 U.S. 752, 89 S. Ct. 2034, 23 L. Ed. 2d 685.

Mr. Justice STEWART delivered the opinion of the Court.

. . .

Approval of a warrantless search incident to a lawful arrest seems first to have been articulated by the Court in 1914 as dictum in *Weeks v. United States* . . . in which the Court stated:

> "What then is the present case? Before answering that inquiry specifically it may be well by a process of exclusion to state what it is not. It is not an assertion of the

right on the part of the Government, always recognized under English and American law, to search the person of the accused when legally arrested to discover and seize the fruits of evidences of crime." . . .

That statement made no reference to any right to search the *place* where an arrest occurs, but was limited to a right to search the "person." Eleven years later the case of *Carroll v. United States,* 267 U.S. 132 (1925), brought the following embellishment of the Weeks statement:

"When a man is legally arrested for an offense, whatever is found upon his person *or in his control* which it is unlawful for him to have and which may be used to prove the offense may be seized and held as evidence in the prosecution." (Emphasis added.) . . .

Still, that assertion too was far from a claim that the "place" where one is arrested may be searched so long as the arrest is valid. Without explanation, however, the principle emerged in expanded form a few months later in *Agnello v. United States,* 269 U.S. 20 (1925)—although still by way of dictum:

"The right without a search warrant contemporaneously to search persons lawfully arrested while committing crime and to search the place where the arrest is made in order to find and seize things connected with the crime as its fruits or as the means by which it was committed, as well as weapons and other things to effect an escape from custody, is not to be doubted." And in *Marron v. United States* two years later, the dictum of Agnello appeared to be the foundation of the Court's decision. In that case federal agents had secured a search warrant authorizing the seizure of liquor and certain articles used in its manufacture. When they arrived at the premises to be searched, they say "that the place was used for retailing and drinking intoxicating liquors." They proceeded to arrest the person in charge and to execute the warrant. In searching a closet for the items listed in the warrant they came across an incriminating ledger, concededly not covered by the warrant, which they also seized. The Court upheld the seizure of the ledger by holding that since the agents had made a lawful arrest, "[t]hey had a right without a warrant contemporaneously to search the place in order to find and seize the things used to carry on the criminal enterprise." . . .

That the Marron opinion did not mean all that it seemed to say became evident, however, a few years later in *Go-Bart Importing Company v. United States,* 282 U.S. 344 (1931), and *United States v. Lefkowitz,* 285 U.S. 452 (1932). . . . In *Go-Bart,* agents had searched the office of persons whom they had lawfully arrested and had taken several papers from a desk, a safe, and other parts of the office. The Court noted that no crime had been committed in the agents' presence, and that although the agent in charge "had an abundance of information and time to swear out a valid [search] warrant, he failed to do so." . . . In holding the search and seizure unlawful, the Court stated:

"Plainly the case before us is essentially different from *Marron v. United States.* . . . There, officers executing a valid search warrant for intoxicating liquors found and arrested one Birdsall who in pursuance of a conspiracy was actually engaged in running a saloon. As an incident to the arrest they seized a ledger in a closet where the liquor or some of it was kept and some bills beside the cash register. These things were visible and accessible and in the offender's immediate custody. There was no threat of force or general search or rummaging of the place." . . .

This limited characterization of Marron was reiterated in Lefkowitz, a case in which the Court held unlawful a search of desk drawers and cabinet despite the fact that the search had accompanied a lawful arrest. . . .

The limiting views expressed in Go-Bart and Lefkowitz were thrown to the winds, however, in *Harris v. United States*, 331 U.S. 145, decided in 1947. In that case, officers had obtained a warrant for Harris' arrest on the basis of his alleged involvement with the cashing and interstate transportation of a forged check. He was arrested in the living room of his four-room apartment, and in an attempt to recover two canceled checks thought to have been used in effecting the forgery, the officers undertook a thorough search of the entire apartment. Inside a desk drawer they found a sealed envelope marked "George Harris, personal papers." The envelope, which was then torn open, was found to contain altered Selective Service documents, and those documents were used to secure Harris' conviction for violating the Selective Training and Service Act of 1940. The Court rejected Harris' Fourth Amendment claim, sustaining the search as "incident to arrest." . . .

Only a year after Harris, however, the pendulum swung again. In *Trupiano v. United States*, 334 U.S. 699 (1948), agents raided the site of an illicit distillery, saw one of several conspirators operating the still, and arrested him, contemporaneously "seiz[ing] the illicit distillery." . . . The Court held that the arrest and others made subsequently had been valid, but that the unexplained failure of the agents to procure a search warrant—in spite of the fact that they had had more than enough time before the raid to do so—rendered the search unlawful. The opinion stated:

"It is a cardinal rule that, in seizing goods and articles, law enforcement agents must secure and use search warrants wherever reasonably practicable. . . . This rule rests upon the desirability of having magistrates rather than police officers determine when searches and seizures are permissible and what limitations should be placed upon such activities. . . ." To provide the necessary security against unreasonable intrusions upon the private lives of individuals, the framers of the Fourth Amendment required adherence to judicial processes wherever possible. And subsequent history has confirmed the wisdom of that requirement.

. . .

"A search or seizure without a warrant as an incident to a lawful arrest had always been considered to be a strictly limited right. It grows out of the inherent necessities of the situation at the time of the arrest. But there must be something more in the way of necessity than merely a lawful arrest." . . .

In 1950, two years after Trupiano, came *United States v. Rabinowitz,* 339 U.S. 56, the decision upon which California primarily relies in the case now before us. In Rabinowitz, federal authorities had been informed that the defendant was dealing in stamps bearing forged overprints. On the basis of that information they secured a warrant for his arrest, which they executed at his one-room business office. At the time of the arrest, the officers "searched the desk, safe, and file cabinets in the office for about an hour and a half" . . . and seized 573 stamps with forged overprints. The stamps were admitted into evidence at the defendant's trial, and this Court affirmed his conviction, rejecting the contention that the warrantless search had been unlawful. The Court held that the search in its entirety fell within the principle giving law enforcement authorities "[t]he right 'to search the place where the arrest is made in order to find and seize things connected with the crime. . . .' " . . . Harris was regarded as "ample authority" for that conclusion. . . . The opinion rejected the rule of Trupiano that "in seizing goods and articles, law enforcement agents must secure and use search warrants wherever reasonably practicable." The test, said the Court, "is not whether it is reasonable to procure a search warrant, but whether the search was reasonable." . . .

Rabinowitz has come to stand for the proposition, *inter alia,* that a warrantless search "incident to a lawful arrest" may generally extend to the area that is considered to be in the "possession" or under the "control" of the person arrested. And it was on the basis of that proposition that the California courts upheld the search of the petitioner's entire house in this case. That doctrine, however, at least in the broad sense in which it was applied by the California courts in this case, can withstand neither historical nor rational analysis.

Even limited to its own facts, the Rabinowitz decision was, as we have seen, hardly founded on an unimpeachable line of authority. As Mr. Justice Frankfurter commented in dissent in that case, the "hint" contained in Weeks was, without persuasive justification, "loosely turned into dictum and finally elevated to a decision." . . . And the approach taken in cases such as Go-Bart, Lefkowitz, and Trupiano was essentially disregarded by the Rabinowitz Court.

Nor is the rationale by which the State seeks here to sustain the search of the petitioner's house supported by a reasoned view of the background and purpose of the Fourth Amendment. Mr. Justice Frankfurter wisely pointed out in his Rabinowitz dissent that the Amendment's proscription of "unreasonable searches and seizures" must be read in light of "the history that gave rise to the words"—history of "abuses so deeply felt by the Colonies as to be one of the potent causes of the Revolution. . . ." The Amendment was in large part a reaction to the general warrants and warrantless searches that had so alienated the colonists and had helped speed the movement for independence. In the scheme of the Amendment, therefore, the requirement that "no Warrants shall issue, but upon probable cause," plays a crucial part. As the Court put it in *McDonald v. United States,* 335 U.S. 451 (1948):

"We are not dealing with formalities. The presence of a search warrant serves a high function. Absent some grave emergency, the Fourth Amendment has interposed a magistrate between the citizen and the police. This was done not to shield criminals nor to make the home a safe haven for illegal activities. It was done so that an objective mind might weigh the need to invade that privacy in order to enforce the law. The right of privacy was deemed too precious to entrust to the discretion of those whose job is the detection of crime and the arrest of criminals. . . . And so the Constitution requires a magistrate to pass on the desires of the police before they violate the privacy of the home. We cannot be true to that constitutional requirement and excuse the absence of a search warrant without a showing by those who seek exemption from the constitutional mandate that the exigencies of the situation made that course imperative." . . . Even in the Agnello case the Court relied upon the rule that "[b]elief, however well founded, that an article sought is concealed in a dwelling house, furnishes no justification for a search of that place without a warrant. And such searches are held unlawful notwithstanding facts unquestionably showing probable cause." . . . Clearly, the general requirement that a search warrant be obtained is not lightly to be dispensed with, and "the burden is on those seeking [an] exemption [from the requirement] to show the need for it. . . ."

. . .

. . . When an arrest is made, it is reasonable for the arresting officer to search the person arrested in order to remove any weapons that the latter might seek to use in order to resist arrest or effect his escape. Otherwise, the officer's safety might well be endangered, and the arrest itself frustrated. In addition, it is entirely reasonable for the arresting officer to search for and seize any evidence on the arrestee's person in order to prevent its concealment or destruction. And the area into which an arrestee might reach in order to grab a weapon or evidentiary items must, of course, be governed by a like rule. A gun on a table or in a drawer in front of one who is arrested can be as dangerous to the arresting officer as one concealed in the clothing of the person arrested. There is ample justification, therefore, for a search of the arrestee's person and the area "within his immediate control"—construing that phrase to mean the area from within which he might gain possession of a weapon or destructible evidence.

There is no comparable justification, however, for routinely searching any room other than that in which an arrest occurs—or, for that matter, for searching through all the desk drawers or other closed or concealed areas in that room itself. Such searches, in the absence of well-recognized exceptions, may be made only under the authority of a search warrant. The "adherence to judicial processes" mandated by the Fourth Amendment requires no less.

. . .

It is argued in the present case that it is "reasonable" to search a man's house when he is arrested in it. But that argument is founded on little more than a subjective view regarding the acceptability of certain sorts of police conduct, and not on considerations relevant to Fourth Amendment interests.

Under such an unconfined analysis, Fourth Amendment protection in this area would approach the evaporation point. It is not easy to explain why, for instance, it is less subjectively "reasonable" to search a man's house when he is arrested on his front lawn—or just down the street—than it is when he happens to be in the house at the time of arrest.

. . .

It would be possible, of course, to draw a line between Rabinowitz and Harris on the one hand, and this case on the other. For Rabinowitz involved a single room, and Harris a four-room apartment, while in the case before us an entire house was searched. But such a distinction would be highly artificial. The rationale that allowed the searches and seizures in Rabinowitz and Harris would allow the searches and seizures in this case. No consideration relevant to the Fourth Amendment suggests any point of rational limitation, once the search is allowed to go beyond the area from which the person arrested might obtain weapons or evidentiary items. The only reasoned distinction is one between a search of the person arrested and the area within his reach on the one hand, and more extensive searches on the other.

The petitioner correctly points out that one result of decisions such as Rabinowitz and Harris is to give law enforcement officials the opportunity to engage in searches not justified by probable cause, by the simple expedient of arranging to arrest suspects at home rather than elsewhere. We do not suggest that the petitioner is necessarily correct in his assertion that such a strategy was utilized here, but the fact remains that had he been arrested earlier in the day, at his place of employment rather than at home, no search of his house could have been made without a search warrant. In any event, even apart from the possibility of such police tactics, the general point so forcefully made by Judge Learned Hand in *United States v. Kirschenblatt* remains:

> "After arresting a man in his house, to rummage at will among his papers in search of whatever will convict him, appears to us to be indistinguishable from what might be done under a general warrant; indeed, the warrant would give more protection, for presumably it must be issued by a magistrate. True, by hypothesis the power would not exist, if the supposed offender were not found on the premises; but it is small consolation to know that one's papers are safe only so long as one is not at home." . . .

Rabinowitz and Harris have been the subject of critical commentary for many years, and have been relied upon less and less in our own decisions. It is time, for the reasons we have stated, to hold that on their own facts, and insofar as the principles they stand for are inconsistent with those that we have endorsed today, they are no longer to be followed.

Application of sound Fourth Amendment principles to the facts of this case produces a clear result. The search here went far beyond the petitioner's person and the area from within which he might have obtained either a weapon or something that could have been used as evidence against him. There was no constitutional justification, in the absence of a search warrant, for extending the search beyond that area. The scope of the search was, therefore, "unreasonable" under the Fourth and Fourteenth Amendments and the petitioner's conviction cannot stand.

Reversed.

[Mr. Justice HARLAN wrote a concurring opinion.]

[Mr. Justice WHITE, with whom Mr. Justice BLACK joined, dissented.]

IN RE GAULT

Supreme Court of the United States, 1967.
387 U.S. 1, 87 S.Ct. 1428, 18 L.Ed.2d 527.

Mr. Justice Fortas delivered the opinion of the Court.

This is an appeal under 28 U.S.C. § 1257(2) from a judgment of the Supreme Court of Arizona affirming the dismissal of a petition for a writ of habeas corpus. 99 Ariz. 181, 407 P.2d 760 (1965). The petition sought the release of Gerald Francis Gault, appellants' 15-year-old son, who had been committed as a juvenile delinquent to the State Industrial School by the Juvenile Court of Gila County, Arizona. The Supreme Court of Arizona affirmed dismissal of the writ against various arguments which included an attack upon the constitutionality of the Arizona Juvenile Code because of its alleged denial of procedural due process rights to juveniles charged with being "delinquents." The Court agreed that the constitutional guarantee of due process of law is applicable in such proceedings. It held that Arizona's Juvenile Code is to be read as "impliedly" implementing the "due process concept." It then proceeded to identify and describe "the particular elements which constitute due process in a juvenile hearing." It concluded that the proceedings ending in commitment of Gerald Gault did not offend those requirements. We do not agree, and we reverse. We begin with a statement of the facts.

I

On Monday, June 8, 1964, at about 10 A.M., Gerald Francis Gault and a friend, Ronald Lewis, were taken into custody by the Sheriff of Gila County. Gerald was then still subject to a six months' probation order which had been entered on February 25, 1964, as a result of his having been in the company of another boy who had stolen a wallet from a lady's purse. The police action on June 8 was taken as the result of a verbal complaint by a neighbor of the boys, Mrs. Cook, about a telephone call made to her in which the caller or callers made lewd or indecent remarks. It will suffice for purposes of this opinion to say that the remarks or questions put to her were of the irritatingly offensive, adolescent, sex variety.

At the time Gerald was picked up, his mother and father were both at work. No notice that Gerald was being taken into custody was left at the home. No other steps were taken to advise them that their son had, in effect, been arrested. Gerald was taken to the Children's Detention Home. When his mother arrived home at about 6 o'clock, Gerald was not there. Gerald's older brother was sent to look for him at the trailer home of the Lewis family. He apparently learned then that Gerald was in custody. He so informed his mother. The two of them went to the Detention Home. The deputy probation officer, Flagg, who was also superintendent of the Detention Home, told Mrs. Gault "why Jerry was there" and said that a hearing would be held in Juvenile Court at 3 o'clock the following day, June 9.

Officer Flagg filed a petition with the court on the hearing day, June 9, 1964. It was not served on the Gaults. Indeed, none of them saw this petition until the habeas corpus hearing on August 17, 1964. The petition was entirely formal. It made no reference to any factual basis for the judicial action which it initiated. It recited only that "said minor is under the age of eighteen years, and is in need of the protection of this Honorable Court; [and that] said minor is a delinquent minor." It prayed for a hearing and an order regarding "the care and custody of said minor." Officer Flagg executed a formal affidavit in support of the petition.

On June 9, Gerald, his mother, his older brother, and Probation Officers Flagg and Henderson appeared before the Juvenile Judge in chambers. Gerald's father was not there. He was at work out of the city. Mrs. Cook, the complainant, was not there. No one was sworn at this hearing. No transcript or recording was made. No memorandum or record of the substance of the proceedings was prepared. Our information about the proceedings and the subsequent hearing on June 15, derives entirely from the testimony of the Juvenile Court Judge, Mr. and Mrs. Gault and Officer Flagg at the habeas corpus proceeding conducted two months later. From this, it appears that at the June 9 hearing Gerald was questioned by the judge about the telephone call. There was conflict as to what he said. His mother recalled that Gerald said he only dialed Mrs. Cook's number and handed the telephone to his friend, Ronald. Officer Flagg recalled that Gerald had admitted making the lewd remarks. Judge McGhee testified that Gerald "admitted making one of these [lewd] statements." At the conclusion of the hearing, the judge said he would "think about it." Gerald was taken back to the Detention Home. He was not sent to his own home with his parents. On June 11 or 12, after having been detained since June 8, Gerald was released and driven home. There is no explanation in the record as to why he was kept in the Detention Home or why he was released. At 5 P.M. on the day of Gerald's release, Mrs. Gault received a note signed by Officer Flagg. It was on plain paper, not letterhead. Its entire text was as follows:

> "Mrs. Gault:
> "Judge McGHEE has set Monday June 15, 1964 at 11:00 A.M. as the date and time for further Hearings on Gerald's delinquency"
> "/s/Flagg"

At the appointed time on Monday, June 15, Gerald, his father and mother, Ronald Lewis and his father, and Officers Flagg and Henderson were present before Judge McGhee. Witnesses at the habeas corpus proceeding differed in their recollections of Gerald's testimony at the June 15 hearing. Mr. and Mrs. Gault recalled that Gerald again testified that he had only dialed the number and that the other boy had made the remarks. Officer Flagg agreed that at this hearing Gerald did not admit making the lewd remarks. But Judge McGhee recalled that "there was some admission again of some of the lewd statements. He—he didn't admit any of the more serious lewd statements." Again, the complainant, Mrs. Cook, was not present. Mrs. Gault asked that Mrs. Cook be present "so she could see which boy that done the talking, the dirty talking over the phone." The Juvenile Judge said "she didn't have to be present at that hearing." The judge did not speak to Mrs. Cook or communicate with her at any time. Probation Officer Flagg had talked to her once—over the telephone on June 9.

At this June 15 hearing a "referral report" made by the probation officers was filed with the court, although not disclosed to Gerald or his parents. This listed the charge as "Lewd Phone Calls." At the conclusion of the hearing, the judge committed Gerald as a juvenile delinquent to the State Industrial School "for the period of his minority [that is, until 21], unless sooner discharged by due process of law." An order to that effect was entered. It recites that "after a full hearing and due deliberation the Court finds that said minor is a delinquent child, and that said minor is of the age of 15 years."

No appeal is permitted by Arizona law in juvenile cases. On August 3, 1964, a petition for a writ of habeas corpus was filed with the Supreme Court of Arizona and referred by it to the Superior Court for hearing.

At the habeas corpus hearing on August 17, Judge McGhee was vigorously cross-examined as to the basis for his actions. He testified that he had taken into account the fact that Gerald was on probation. He was asked "under what section of . . . the code you found the boy delinquent?"

His answer is set forth in the margin.[1] In substance, he concluded that Gerald came within ARS § 8—201, subsec. 6(a), which specifies that a "delinquent child" includes one "who has violated a law of the state or an ordinance or regulation of a political subdivision thereof." The law which Gerald was found to have violated is ARS § 13—377. This section of the Arizona Criminal Code provides that a person who "in the presence or hearing of any woman or child . . . uses vulgar, abusive or obscene language, is guilty of a misdemeanor. . . ." The penalty specified in the Criminal Code, which would apply to an adult, is $5 to $50, or imprisonment for not more than two months. The judge also testified that he acted under ARS § 8—201, subsec. 6(d) which

---

[1]"Q. All right. Now, Judge, would you tell me under what section of the law or tell me under what section of— of the code you found the boy delinquent?

"A. Well, there is a—I think it amounts to disturbing the peace. I can't give you the section, but I can tell you the law, that when one person uses lewd language in the presence of another person, that it can amount to— and I consider that when a person makes it over the phone, that it is considered in the presence. I might be wrong, that is one section. The other section upon which I consider the boy delinquent is Section 8—201, Subsection (d), habitually involved in immoral matters."

includes in the definition of a "delinquent child" one who, as the judge phrased it, is "habitually involved in immoral matters."[2]

Asked about the basis for his conclusion that Gerald was "habitually involved in immoral matters," the judge testified, somewhat vaguely, that two years earlier, on June 2, 1962, a "referral" was made concerning Gerald, "where the boy had stolen a baseball glove from another boy and lied to the Police Department about it." The judge said there was "no hearing," and "no accusation" relating to this incident, "because of lack of material foundation." But it seems to have remained in his mind as a relevant factor. The judge also testified that Gerald had admitted making other nuisance phone calls in the past which, as the judge recalled the boy's testimony, were "silly calls, or funny calls, or something like that."

The Superior Court dismissed the writ, and appellants sought review in the Arizona Supreme Court. That court stated that it considered appellants' assignments of error as urging (1) that the Juvenile Code, ARS § 8—201 to § 8—239, is unconstitutional because it does not require that parents and children be apprised of the specific charges, does not require proper notice of a hearing, and does not provide for an appeal; and (2) that the proceedings and order relating to Gerald constituted a denial of due process of law because of the absence of adequate notice of the charge and the hearing; failure to notify appellants of certain constitutional rights including the rights to counsel and to confrontation, and the privilege against self-incrimination; the use of unsworn hearsay testimony; and the failure to make a record of the proceedings. Appellants further asserted that it was [an] error for the Juvenile Court to remove Gerald from the custody of his parents without a showing and finding of their unsuitability, and alleged a miscellany of other errors under state law.

The Supreme Court handed down an elaborate and wide-ranging opinion affirming dismissal of the writ and stating the court's conclusions as to the issues raised by appellants and other aspects of the juvenile process. In their jurisdictional statement and brief in this Court, appellants do not urge upon us all of the points passed upon by the Supreme Court of Arizona. They urge that we hold the Juvenile Code of Arizona invalid on its face or as applied in this case because, contrary to the Due Process Clause of the Fourteenth Amendment, the juvenile is taken from the custody of his parents and committed to a state institution pursuant to proceedings in which the Juvenile Court has virtually unlimited discretion, and in which the following basic rights are denied:

---

[2]ARS § 8—201. subsec. 6, the section of the Arizona Juvenile Code which defines a delinquent child, reads:
" 'Delinquent child' includes:
"(a) A child who has violated a law of the state or an ordinance or regulation of a political subdivision thereof.
"(b) A child who, by reason of being incorrigible, wayward or habitually disobedient, is uncontrolled by his parent, guardian or custodian.
"(c) A child who is habitually truant from school or home.
"(d) A child who habitually so deports himself as to injure or endanger the morals or health of himself or others."

1. Notice of the charges;
2. Right to counsel;
3. Right to confrontation and cross-examination;
4. Privilege against self-incrimination;
5. Right to a transcript of the proceedings; and
6. Right to appellate review.

We shall not consider other issues which were passed upon by the Supreme Court of Arizona. We emphasize that we indicate no opinion as to whether the decision of that court with respect to such other issues does or does not conflict with requirements of the Federal Constitution.

II

The Supreme Court of Arizona held that due process of law is requisite to the constitutional validity of proceedings in which a court reaches the conclusion that a juvenile has been at fault, has engaged in conduct prohibited by law, or has otherwise misbehaved with the consequence that he is committed to an institution in which his freedom is curtailed. This conclusion is in accord with the decisions of a number of courts under both federal and state constitutions.

This Court has not heretofore decided the precise question. In *Kent v. United States*, 383 U.S. 541, 86 S.Ct. 1045, 16 L.Ed.2d 84 (1966), we considered the requirements for a valid waiver of the "exclusive" jurisdiction of the Juvenile Court of the District of Columbia so that a juvenile could be tried in the adult criminal court of the District. Although our decision turned upon the language of the statute, we emphasized the necessity that "the basic requirements of due process and fairness" be satisfied in such proceedings. *Haley v. State of Ohio*, 332 U.S. 596, 68 S.Ct. 302, 92 L.Ed. 224 (1948), involved the admissibility, in a state criminal court of general jurisdiction, of a confession by a 15-year-old boy. The Court held that the Fourteenth Amendment applied to prohibit the use of the coerced confession. Mr. Justice Douglas said, "Neither man nor child can be allowed to stand condemned by methods which flout constitutional requirements of due process of law." To the same effect is *Gallegos v. State of Colorado*, 370 U.S. 49, 82 S.Ct. 1209, 8 L.Ed.2d 325 (1962). Accordingly, while these cases relate only to restricted aspects of the subject, they unmistakably indicate that, whatever may be their precise impact, neither the Fourteenth Amendment nor the Bill of Rights is for adults alone.

We do not in this opinion consider the impact of these constitutional provisions upon the totality of the relationship of the juvenile and the state. We do not even consider the entire process relating to juvenile "delinquents." For example, we are not here concerned with the procedures or constitutional rights applicable to the prejudicial stages of the juvenile process, nor do we direct our attention to the post-adjudicative or dispositional process. We consider only the problems presented to us by this case. These relate to the proceedings by which a determination is made as to whether a juvenile is a "delinquent" as a result of alleged misconduct on his part, with the consequence that he may be committed to a state institution. As to these proceedings, there appears to be little current dissent from the proposition that the Due Process Clause has a role to play. The problem is to ascertain the precise impact of the due process requirement upon such proceedings.

In view of this, it would be extraordinary if our Constitution did not require the procedural regularity and the exercise of care implied in the phrase "due process." Under our Constitution, the condition of being a boy does not justify a kangaroo court. The traditional ideas of Juvenile Court procedure, indeed, contemplated that time would be available and care would be used to establish precisely what the juvenile did and why he did it—was it a prank of adolescence or a brutal act threatening serious consequences to himself or society unless corrected? Under traditional notions, one would assume that in a case like that of Gerald Gault, where the juvenile appears to have a home, a working mother and father, and an older brother, the Juvenile Judge would have made a careful inquiry and judgment as to the possibility that the boy could be disciplined and dealt with at home, despite his previous transgressions.[3] Indeed, so far as appears in the record before us, except for some conversation with Gerald about his school work and his "wanting to go to . . . Grand Canyon with his father," the points to which the judge directed his attention were little different from those that would be involved in determining any charge of violation of a penal statute. The essential difference between Gerald's case and a normal criminal case is that safeguards available to adults were discarded in Gerald's case. The summary procedure as well as the long commitment was possible because Gerald was 15 years of age instead of over 18.

If Gerald had been over 18, he would not have been subject to Juvenile Court proceedings. For the particular offense immediately involved, the maximum punishment would have been a fine of $5 to $50, or imprisonment in jail for not more than two months. Instead, he was committed to custody for a maximum of six years. If he had been over 18 and had committed an offense to which such a sentence might apply, he would have been entitled to substantial rights under the Constitution of the United States as well as under Arizona's laws and constitution. The United States Constitution would guarantee him rights and protections with respect to arrest, search, and seizure, and pretrial interrogation. It would assure him of specific notice of the charges and ade-

---

[3]The Juvenile Judge's testimony at the habeas corpus proceeding is devoid of any meaningful discussion of this. He appears to have centered his attention upon whether Gerald made the phone call and used lewd words. He was impressed by the fact that Gerald was on six months' probation because he was with another boy who allegedly stole a purse—a different sort of offense, sharing the feature that Gerald was "along." And he even referred to a report which he said was not investigated because "there was no accusation" "because of lack of material foundation." With respect to the possible duty of a trial court to explore alternatives to involuntary commitment in a civil proceeding, cf. *Luke v. Cameron*, 124 U.S. App.D.C. 264, 364 F.2d 657 (1966), which arose under statutes relating to treatment of the mentally ill.

quate time to decide his course of action and to prepare his defense. He would be entitled to clear advice that he could be represented by counsel, and, at least if a felony were involved, the State would be required to provide counsel if his parents were unable to afford it. If the court acted on the basis of his confession, careful procedures would be required to assure its voluntariness. If the case went to trial, confrontation and opportunity for cross-examination would be guaranteed. So wide a gulf between the State's treatment of the adult and of the child requires a bridge sturdier than mere verbiage, and reasons more persuasive than cliche can provide. As Wheeler and Cottrell have put it, "The rhetoric of the juvenile court movement has developed without any necessarily close correspondence to the realities of court and institutional routines."

In *Kent v. United States,* supra, we stated that the Juvenile Court Judge's exercise of the power of the state as *parens patriae* was not unlimited. We said that "the admonition to function in a 'parental' relationship is not an invitation to procedural arbitrariness." With respect to the waiver by the Juvenile Court to the adult court of jurisdiction over an offense committed by a youth, we said that "there is no place in our system of law for reaching a result of such tremendous consequences without ceremony—without hearing, without effective assistance of counsel, without a statement of reasons." We announced with respect to such waiver proceedings that while "We do not mean . . . to indicate that the hearing to be held must conform with all of the requirements of a criminal trial or even of the usual administrative hearing; but we do hold that the hearing must measure up to the essentials of due process and fair treatment." We reiterate this view, here in connection with a juvenile court adjudication of "delinquency," as a requirement which is part of the Due Process Clause of the Fourteenth Amendment of our Constitution.[4]

We now turn to the specific issues which are presented to us in the present case.

III. *Notice of Charges*

Appellants allege that the Arizona Juvenile Code is unconstitutional or alternatively that the proceedings before the Juvenile Court were constitutionally defective because of failure to provide adequate notice of the hearings. No notice was given to Gerald's parents when he was taken into custody on Monday, June 8. On that night, when Mrs. Gault went to the Detention Home, she

---

[4]The Nat'l Crime Comm'n Report recommends that "Juvenile courts should make fullest feasible use of preliminary conferences to dispose of cases short of adjudication." Id., at 84. See also D.C. Crime Comm'n Report, pp. 662–665. Since this "consent decree" procedure would involve neither adjudication of delinquency nor institutionalization, nothing we say in this opinion should be construed as expressing any views with respect to such procedure. The problems of preadjudication treatment of juveniles, and of post-adjudication disposition, are unique to the juvenile process; hence what we hold in this opinion with regard to the procedural requirements at the adjudicatory stage has no necessary applicability to other steps of the juvenile process.

was orally informed that there would be a hearing the next afternoon and was told the reason why Gerald was in custody. The only written notice Gerald's parents received at any time was a note on plain paper from Officer Flagg delivered on Thursday or Friday, June 11 or 12, to the effect that the judge had set Monday, June 15, "for further Hearings on Gerald's delinquency."

A "petition" was filed with the court on June 9 by Officer Flagg, reciting only that he was informed and believed that "said minor is a delinquent minor and that it is necessary that some order be made by the Honorable Court for said minor's welfare." The applicable Arizona statute provides for a petition to be filed in Juvenile Court, alleging in general terms that the child is "neglected, dependent or delinquent." The statute explicitly states that such a general allegation is sufficient, "without alleging the facts." There is no requirement that the petition be served and it was not served upon, given to, or shown to Gerald or his parents.

The Supreme Court of Arizona rejected appellants' claim that due process was denied because of inadequate notice. It stated that "Mrs. Gault knew the exact nature of the charge against Gerald from the day he was taken to the detention home." The court also pointed out that the Gaults appeared at the two hearings "without objection." The court held that because "the policy of the juvenile law is to hide youthful errors from the full gaze of the public and bury them in the graveyard of the forgotten past," advance notice of the specific charges or basis for taking the juvenile into custody and for the hearing is not necessary. It held that the appropriate rule is that "the infant and his parents or guardian will receive a petition only reciting a conclusion of delinquency. But no later than the initial hearing by the judge, they must be advised of the facts involved in the case. If the charges are denied, they must be given a reasonable period of time to prepare."

We cannot agree with the court's conclusion that adequate notice was given in this case. Notice, to comply with due process requirements, must be given sufficiently in advance of scheduled court proceedings so that reasonable opportunity to prepare will be afforded, and it must "set forth the alleged misconduct with particularity." It is obvious, as we have discussed above, that no purpose of shielding the child from the public stigma of knowledge of his having been taken into custody and scheduled for hearing is served by the procedure approved by the court below. The "initial hearing" in the present case was a hearing on the merits. Notice at that time is not timely; and even if there were a conceivable purpose served by the deferral proposed by the court below, it would have to yield to the requirements that the child and his parents or guardian be notified, in writing, of the specific charge or factual allegations to be considered at the hearing, and that such written notice be given at the earliest practicable time, and in any event sufficiently in advance of the hearing to permit preparation. Due process of law requires notice of the sort we have described—that is, notice which would be deemed constitutionally adequate in a civil or criminal proceeding. It does not allow a hearing to be held in which a youth's freedom and his parents' right to his custody are at stake without giving them timely notice, in advance of the hearing, of the specific issues that they must meet. Nor, in the circumstances of this case, can it reasonably be said that the requirement of notice was waived.

IV. Right to Counsel

Appellants charge that the Juvenile Court proceedings were fatally defective because the court did not advise Gerald or his parents of their right to counsel, and proceeded with the hearing, the adjudication of delinquency and the order of commitment in the absence of counsel for the child and his parents or an express waiver of the right thereto. The Supreme Court of Arizona pointed out that "[t]here is disagreement [among the various jurisdictions] as to whether the court must advise the infant that he has a right to counsel." It noted its own decision in *Arizona State Dept. of Public Welfare v. Barlow*, 80 Ariz. 249, 296 P.2d 298 (1956), to the effect "that *the parents* of an infant in a juvenile proceeding cannot be denied representation by counsel of their choosing." (Emphasis added.) It referred to a provision of the Juvenile Code which it characterized as requiring "that the probation officer shall look after the interests of neglected, delinquent and dependent children," including representing their interests in court. The court argued that "The parent and the probation officer may be relied upon to protect the infant's interests." Accordingly it rejected the proposition that "due process requires that an infant have a right to counsel." It said that juvenile courts have the discretion, but not the duty, to allow such representation; it referred specifically to the situation in which the Juvenile Court discerns conflict between the child and his parents as an instance in which this discretion might be exercised. We do not agree. Probation officers, in the Arizona scheme, are also arresting officers. They initiate proceedings and file petitions which they verify, as here, alleging the delinquency of the child; and they testify, as here, against the child. And here the probation officer was also superintendent of the Detention Home. The probation officer cannot act as counsel for the child. His role in the adjudicatory hearing, by statute and in fact, is as arresting officer and witness against the child. Nor can the judge represent the child. There is no material difference in this respect between adult and juvenile proceedings of the sort here involved. In adult proceedings, this contention has been foreclosed by decisions of this Court. A proceeding where the issue is whether the child will be found to be "delinquent" and subjected to the loss of his liberty for years is comparable in seriousness to a felony prosecution. The juvenile needs the assistance of counsel to cope with problems of law, to make skilled inquiry into the facts, to insist upon regularity of the proceedings, and to ascertain whether he has a defense and to prepare and submit it. The child "requires the guiding hand of counsel at every step in the proceedings against him." Just as in *Kent v. United States*, supra, 383 U.S., at 561–562, 86 S.Ct., at 1057–1058, we indicated our agreement with the United States Court of Appeals for the District of Columbia Circuit that the assistance of counsel is essential for purposes of waiver proceedings, so we hold now that it is equally essential for the determination of delinquency, carrying with it the awesome prospect of incarceration in a state institution until the juvenile reaches the age of 21.[5]

During the last decade, court decisions, experts, and legislatures have demonstrated increasing recognition of this view. In at least one-third of the States, statutes now provide for the right of representation by retained counsel in juvenile delinquency proceedings, notice of the right, or assignment of counsel, or a combination of these. In other States, court rules have similar provisions.

The President's Crime Commission has recently recommended that in order to assure "procedural justice for the child," it is necessary that "Counsel . . . be appointed as a matter of course wherever coercive action is a possibility, without requiring any affirmative choice by child or parent."[6] As stated by

---

[5]This means that the commitment, in virtually all cases, is for a minimum of three years since jurisdiction of juvenile courts is usually limited to age 18 and under.

[6]Nat'l Crime Comm'n Report, pp. 86–87. The Commission's statement of its position is very forceful:

"The Commission believes that no single action holds more potential for achieving procedural justice for the child in the juvenile court than provision of counsel. The presence of an independent legal representative of the child, or of his parent, is the keystone of the whole structure of guarantees that a minimum system of procedural justice requires. The rights to confront one's accusers, to cross-examine witnesses, to present evidence and testimony of one's own, to be unaffected by prejudicial and unreliable evidence, to participate meaningfully in the dispositional decision, to take an appeal have substantial meaning for the overwhelming majority of persons brought before the juvenile court only if they are provided with competent lawyers who can invoke those rights effectively. The most informal and well-intentioned of judicial proceedings are technical; few adults without legal training can influence or even understand them; certainly children cannot. Papers are drawn and charges expressed in legal language. Events follow one another in a manner that appears arbitrary and confusing to the uninitiated. Decisions, unexplained, appear too official to challenge. But with lawyers come records of proceedings; records make possible appeals which, even if they do not occur, impart by their possibility a healthy atmosphere of accountability.

"Fears have been expressed that lawyers would make juvenile court proceedings adversary. No doubt this is partly true, but it is partly desirable. Informality is often abused. The juvenile courts deal with cases in which facts are disputed and in which, therefore, rules of evidence, confrontation of witnesses, and other adversary procedures are called for. They deal with many cases involving conduct that can lead to incarceration or close supervision for long periods, and therefore juveniles often need the same safeguards that are granted to adults. And in all cases children need advocates to speak for them and guard their interest, particularly when disposition decisions are made. It is the disposition stage at which the opportunity arises to offer individualized treatment plans and in which the danger inheres that the court's coercive power will be applied without adequate knowledge of the circumstances. "Fears also have been expressed that the formality lawyers would bring into juvenile court would defeat the therapeutic aims of the court. But informality has no necessary connection with therapy; it is a device that has been used to approach therapy, and it is not the only possible device. It is quite possible that in many instances lawyers, for all their commitment to formality, could do more to further therapy for their clients than can the small, overworked social staffs of the courts.

. . .

"The Commission believes it is essential that counsel be appointed by the juvenile court for those who are unable to provide their own. Experience under the prevailing systems in which children are free to seek counsel of their choice reveals how empty of meaning the right is for those typically the subjects of juvenile court proceedings. Moreover, providing counsel only when the child is sophisticated enough to be aware of his need and to ask for one or when he fails to waive his announced right [is] not enough, as experience in numerous jurisdictions reveal.

"*The Commission recommends:*

"COUNSEL SHOULD BE APPOINTED AS A MATTER OF COURSE WHEREVER COERCIVE ACTION IS A POSSIBILITY, WITHOUT REQUIRING ANY AFFIRMATIVE CHOICE BY CHILD OR PARENT."

the authoritative "Standards for Juvenile and Family Courts," published by the Children's Bureau of the United States Department of Health, Education, and Welfare:

> "As a component part of a fair hearing required by due process guaranteed under the 14th amendment, notice of the right to counsel should be required at all hearings and counsel provided upon request when the family is financially unable to employ counsel." Standards, p. 57.

This statement was "reviewed" by the National Council of Juvenile Court Judges at its 1965 Convention and they "found no fault" with it. The New York Family Court Act contains the following statement:

> "This act declares that minors have a right to the assistance of counsel of their own choosing or of law guardians in neglect proceedings under article three and in proceedings to determine juvenile delinquency and whether a person is in need of supervision under article seven. This declaration is based on a finding that counsel is often indispensable to a practical realization of due process of law and may be helpful in making reasoned determinations of fact and proper orders of disposition."

The Act provides that "At the commencement of any hearing" under the delinquency article of the statute, the juvenile and his parent shall be advised of the juvenile's "right to be represented by counsel chosen by him or his parent . . . or by a law guardian assigned by the court. . . ." The California Act (1961) also requires appointment of counsel.

We conclude that the Due Process Clause of the Fourteenth Amendment requires that in respect of proceedings to determine delinquency which may result in commitment to an institution in which the juvenile's freedom is curtailed, the child and his parents must be notified of the child's right to be represented by counsel retained by them, or if they are unable to afford counsel, that counsel will be appointed to represent the child.

At the habeas corpus proceeding, Mrs. Gault testified that she knew that she could have appeared with counsel at the juvenile hearing. This knowledge is not a waiver of the right to counsel which she and her juvenile son had, as we have defined it. They had a right expressly to be advised that they might retain counsel and to be confronted with the need for specific consideration of whether they did or did not choose to waive the right. If they were unable to afford to employ counsel, they were entitled in view of the seriousness of the charge and the potential commitment, to appointed counsel, unless they chose waiver. Mrs. Gault's knowledge that she could employ counsel was not an "intentional relinquishment or abandonment" of a fully known right.[7]

---

[7]Johnson v. Zerbst, 304 U.S. 458, 464, 58 S.Ct. 1019, 1023, 82 L.Ed. 1461 (1938); Carnley v. Cochran, 369 U.S. 506, 82 S.Ct. 884, 8 L.Ed.2d 70 (1962); United States ex rel. Brown v. Fay, 242 F.Supp. 273 (D.C.S.D.N.Y. 1965).

V. Confrontation, Self-Incrimination, Cross-Examination

Appellants urge that the writ of habeas corpus should have been granted because of the denial of the rights of confrontation and cross-examination in the Juvenile Court hearings, and because the privilege against self-incrimination was not observed. The Juvenile Court Judge testified at the habeas corpus hearing that he had proceeded on the basis of Gerald's admission at the two hearings. Appellants attack this on the ground that the admissions were obtained in disregard of the privilege against self-incrimination. If the confession is disregarded, appellants argue that the delinquency conclusion, since it was fundamentally based on a finding that Gerald had made lewd remarks during the phone call to Mrs. Cook, is fatally defective for failure to accord the rights of confrontation and cross-examination which the Due Process Clause of the Fourteenth Amendment of the Federal Constitution guarantees in state proceedings generally.

Our first question, then, is whether Gerald's admission was improperly obtained and relied on as the basis of decision, in conflict with the Federal Constitution. For this purpose, it is necessary briefly to recall the relevant facts.

Mrs. Cook, the complainant, and the recipient of the alleged telephone call, was not called as a witness. Gerald's mother asked the Juvenile Court Judge why Mrs. Cook was not present and the judge replied that "she didn't have to be present." So far as appears, Mrs. Cook was spoken to only once, by Officer Flagg, and this was by telephone. The judge did not speak with her on any occasion. Gerald had been questioned by the probation officer after having been taken into custody. The exact circumstances of this questioning do not appear but any admissions Gerald may have made at this time do not appear in the record. Gerald was also questioned by the Juvenile Court Judge at each of the two hearings. The judge testified in the habeas corpus proceeding that Gerald admitted making "some of the lewd statements . . . [but not] any of the more serious lewd statements." There was conflict and uncertainty among the witnesses at the habeas corpus proceeding—the Juvenile Court Judge, Mr. and Mrs. Gault, and the probation officer—as to what Gerald did or did not admit.

We shall assume that Gerald made admissions of the sort described by the Juvenile Court Judge, as quoted above. Neither Gerald nor his parents were advised that he did not have to testify or make a statement, or that an incriminating statement might result in his commitment as a "delinquent."

The Arizona Supreme Court rejected appellants' contention that Gerald had a right to be advised that he need not incriminate himself. It said: "We think the necessary flexibility for individualized treatment will be enhanced by a rule which does not require the judge to advise the infant of a privilege against self-incrimination."

In reviewing this conclusion of Arizona's Supreme Court, we emphasize again that we are here concerned only with a proceeding to determine whether a minor is a "delinquent" and which may result in commitment to a state institution. Specifically, the question is whether, in such a proceeding, an admission by the juvenile may be used against him in the absence of clear and unequivocal evidence that the admission was made with knowledge that he was not obliged to speak and would not be penalized for remaining silent. In light of *Miranda v. State of Arizona*, 384 U.S. 436, 86 S.Ct. 1602, 16 L.Ed.2d 694 (1966), we must also consider whether, if the privilege against self-incrimination is available, it can effectively be waived unless counsel is present or the right to counsel has been waived.

It has long been recognized that the eliciting and use of confessions or admissions require careful scrutiny. Dean Wigmore states:

"The ground of distrust of confessions made in certain situations is, in a rough and indefinite way, judicial experience. There has been no careful collection of statistics of untrue confessions, nor has any great number of instances been even loosely reported . . . but enough have been verified to fortify the conclusion, based on ordinary observation of human conduct, that under certain stresses a person, especially one of defective mentality or peculiar temperament, may falsely acknowledge guilt. This possibility arises wherever the innocent person is placed in such a situation that the untrue acknowledgment of guilt is at the time the more promising of two alternatives between which he [is] obliged to choose; that is, he chooses any risk that may be in falsely acknowledging guilt, in preference to some worse alternative associated with silence.

"The principle, then, upon which a confession may be excluded is that it is, under certain conditions, *testimonially untrustworthy*. . . . [T]he essential feature is that the principle of exclusion is a testimonial one, analogous to the other principles which exclude narrations as untrustworthy. . . ."

This Court has emphasized that admissions and confessions of juveniles require special caution. In *Haley v. State of Ohio*, 332 U.S. 596, 68 S.Ct. 302, 92 L.Ed. 224, where this Court reversed the conviction of a 15-year-old boy for murder, Mr. Justice Douglas said:

"What transpired would make us pause for careful inquiry if a mature man were involved. And when, as here, a mere child—an easy victim of the law—is before us, special care in scrutinizing the record must be used. Age 15 is a tender and difficult age for a boy of any race. He cannot be judged by the more exacting standards of maturity. That which would leave a man cold and unimpressed can overawe and overwhelm a lad in his early teens. This is the period of great instability which the crisis of adolescence produces. A 15-year-old lad, questioned through the dead of night by relays of police, is a ready victim of the inquisition. Mature men possibly might stand the ordeal from midnight to 5 a.m. But we cannot believe that a lad of tender years is a match for the police in such a contest. He needs counsel and support if he is not to become the victim first of fear, then of panic. He needs someone on whom to lean lest the overpowering presence of the law, as he knows it, crush him. No friend stood at the side of this 15-year-old boy as the police, working in relays, questioned him hour after hour, from midnight until dawn. No lawyer stood guard to make sure that the police went so far and no farther, to see to it that they stopped short of the point where he became the victim of coercion. No counsel or friend was called during the critical hours of questioning."

In *Haley*, as we have discussed, the boy was convicted in an adult court, and not a juvenile court. In notable decisions, the New York Court of Appeals and the Supreme Court of New Jersey have recently considered decisions of Juvenile Courts in which boys have been adjudged "delinquent" on the basis of confessions obtained in circumstances comparable to those in *Haley*. In both instances, the State contended before its highest tribunal that constitutional requirements governing inculpatory statements applicable in adult courts do not apply to juvenile proceedings. In each case, the State's contention was rejected, and the juvenile court's determination of delinquency was set aside on the grounds of inadmissibility of the confession. *In Matters of W. and S.*, 19 N.Y.2d 55, 277 N.Y.S.2d 675, 224 N.E.2d 102 (1966) (opinion by Keating, J.), and *In Interests of Carlo and Stasilowicz*, 48 N.J. 224, 225 A.2d 110 (1966) (opinion by Proctor, J.).

The privilege against self-incrimination is, of course, related to the question of the safeguards necessary to assure that admissions or confessions are reasonably trustworthy, that they are not the mere fruits of fear or coercion, but are reliable expressions of the truth. The roots of the privilege are, however, far deeper. They tap the basic stream of religious and political principle because the privilege reflects the limits of the individual's attornment to the state and—in a philosophical sense—insists upon the equality of the individual and the state. In other words, the privilege has a broader and deeper thrust than the rule which prevents the use of confessions which are the product of coercion because coercion is thought to carry with it the danger of unreliability. One of its purposes is to prevent the state, whether by force or by psychological domination, from overcoming the mind and will of the person under investigation and depriving him of the freedom to decide whether to assist the state in securing his conviction.

It would indeed be surprising if the privilege against self-incrimination were available to hardened criminals but not to children. The language of the Fifth Amendment, applicable to the States by operation of the Fourteenth Amendment, is unequivocal and without exception. And the scope of the privilege is comprehensive. As Mr. Justice White, concurring, stated in *Murphy v. Waterfront Commission*, 378 U.S. 52, 94, 84 S.Ct. 1594, 1611, 12 L.Ed.2d 678 (1964):

> "The privilege can be claimed in *any proceeding*, be it criminal or civil, administrative or judicial, investigatory or adjudicatory . . . it protects *any disclosures* which the witness may reasonably apprehend *could be used in a criminal prosecution or which could lead to other evidence that might be so used*." (Emphasis added.)

With respect to juveniles, both common observation and expert opinion emphasize that the "distrust of confessions made in certain situations" to which Dean Wigmore referred in the passage quoted supra, at 1453, is imperative in the case of children from an early age through adolescence. In New York, for example, the recently enacted Family Court Act provides that the juvenile and his parents must be advised at the start of the hearing of his right to remain silent. The New York statute also provides that the police must attempt to communicate with the juvenile's parents before questioning him, and that absent "special circumstances" a confession may not be obtained from the child prior to notifying his parents or relatives and releasing the child either to them or to the Family Court. In *In Matters of W. and S.*, referred to above, the New York Court of Appeals held that the privilege against self-incrimination applies in juvenile delinquency cases and requires the exclusion of involuntary confessions, and that *People v. Lewis*, 260 N.Y. 171, 183 N.E. 353, 86 A.L.R. 1001 (1932), holding the contrary, had been specifically overruled by statute.

The authoritative "Standards for Juvenile and Family Courts" concludes that, "Whether or not transfer to the criminal court is a possibility, certain procedures should always be followed. Before being interviewed [by the police], the child and his parents should be informed of his right to have legal counsel present and to refuse to answer questions or be fingerprinted if he should so decide."

Against the application to juveniles of the right to silence, it is argued that juvenile proceedings are "civil" and not "criminal," and therefore the privilege should not apply. It is true that the statement of the privilege in the Fifth Amendment, which is applicable to the States by reason of the Fourteenth Amendment, is that no person "shall be compelled in any *criminal case* to be a witness against himself." However, it is also clear that the availability of the privilege does not turn upon the type of proceeding in which its protection is invoked, but upon the nature of the statement or admission and the exposure which it invites. The privilege may, for example, be claimed in a civil or administrative proceeding, if the statement is or may be inculpatory.

It would be entirely unrealistic to carve out of the Fifth Amendment all statements by juveniles on the ground that these cannot lead to "criminal" involvement. In the first place, juvenile proceedings to determine "delinquency," which may lead to commitment to a state institution, must be regarded as "criminal" for purposes of the privilege against self-incrimination. To hold otherwise would be to disregard substance because of the feeble enticement of the "civil" label-of-convenience which has been attached to juvenile proceedings. Indeed, in over half of the States, there is not even assurance that the juvenile will be kept in separate institutions, apart from adult "criminals." In those States juveniles may be placed in or transferred to adult penal institutions after having been found "delinquent" by a juvenile court. For this purpose, at least, commitment is a deprivation of liberty. It is incarceration against one's will, whether it is called "criminal" or "civil." And our Constitution guarantees that no person shall be "compelled" to be a witness against himself when he is threatened with deprivation of his liberty—a command which this Court has broadly applied and generously implemented in accordance with the teaching of the history of the privilege and its great office in mankind's battle for freedom.

In addition, apart from the equivalence for this purpose of exposure to commitment as a juvenile delinquent and exposure to imprisonment as an adult offender, the fact of the matter is that there is little or no assurance in Arizona, as in most if not all of the States, that a juvenile apprehended and interrogated by the police or even by the Juvenile Court itself will remain outside of the reach of adult courts as a consequence of the offense for which he has been taken into custody. In Arizona, as in other States, provision is made for Juvenile Courts to relinquish or waive jurisdiction to the ordinary criminal courts. In the present case, when Gerald Gault was interrogated concerning violation of a section of the Arizona Criminal Code, it could not be certain that the Juvenile Court Judge would decide to "suspend" criminal prosecution in court for adults by proceeding to an adjudication in Juvenile Court.

It is also urged, as the Supreme Court of Arizona here asserted, that the juvenile and presumably his parents should not be advised of the juvenile's right to silence because confession is good for the child as the commencement of the assumed therapy of the juvenile court process, and he should be encouraged to assume an attitude of trust and confidence toward the officials of the juvenile process. This proposition has been subjected to widespread challenge on the basis of current reappraisals of the rhetoric and realities of the handling of juvenile offenders.

In fact, evidence is accumulating that confessions by juveniles do not aid in "individualized treatment," as the court below put it, and that compelling the child to answer questions, without warning or advice as to his right to remain silent, does not serve this or any other good purpose. In light of the observations of Wheeler and Cottrell, and others, it seems probable that where children are induced to confess by "paternal" urgings on the part of officials and the confession is then followed by disciplinary action, the child's reaction is likely to be hostile and adverse—the child may well feel that he has been led or tricked into confession and that despite his confession, he is being punished.

Further, authoritative opinion has cast formidable doubt upon the reliability and trustworthiness of "confessions" by children. This Court's observations in *Haley v. State of Ohio* are set forth above. The recent decision of the New York Court of Appeals referred to above, *In Matters of W. and S.* deals with a dramatic and, it is to be hoped, extreme example. Two 12-year-old Negro boys were taken into custody for the brutal assault and rape of two aged domestics, one of whom died as the result of the attack. One of the boys was schizophrenic and had been locked in the security ward of a mental institution at the time of the attacks. By a process that may best be described as bizarre, his confession was obtained by the police. A psychiatrist testified that the boy would admit "whatever he thought was expected so that he could get out of the immediate situation." The other 12-year-old also "confessed." Both confessions were in specific detail, albeit they contained various inconsistencies. The Court of Appeals, in an opinion by Keating, J., concluded that the confessions were products of the will of the police instead of the boys. The confessions were therefore held involuntary and the order of the Appellate Division affirming the order of the Family Court adjudging the defendants to be juvenile delinquents was reversed.

A similar and equally instructive case has recently been decided by the Supreme Court of New Jersey. *In Interests of Carlo and Stasilowicz, supra.* The body of a 10-year-old girl was found. She had been strangled. Neighborhood boys who knew the girl were questioned. The two appellants, aged 13 and 15, confessed to the police, with vivid detail and some inconsistencies. At the Juvenile Court hearing, both denied any complicity in the killing. They testified that their confessions were the product of fear and fatigue due to extensive police grilling. The Juvenile Court Judge found that the confessions were voluntary and admissible. On appeal, in an extensive opinion by Proctor, J., the Supreme Court of New Jersey reversed. It rejected the State's argument that the constitutional safeguard of voluntariness governing the use of confessions does not apply in proceedings before the Juvenile Court. It pointed out that under New Jersey court rules, juveniles under the age of 16 accused of committing a homicide are tried in a proceeding which "has all of the appurtenances of a criminal trial," including participation by the county prosecutor, and requirements that the juvenile be provided with counsel, that a stenographic record be made, etc. It also pointed out that under New Jersey law, the confinement of the boys after reaching age 21 could be extended until they had served the maximum sentence which could have been imposed on an adult for such a homicide, here found to be second-degree murder carrying up to 30 years' imprisonment. The court concluded that the confessions were involuntary, stressing that the boys, contrary to statute, were placed in the police station and there interrogated; that the parents of both boys were not allowed to see them while they were being interrogated; that inconsistencies appeared among the various statements of the boys and with the objective evidence of the crime; and that there were protracted periods of questioning. The court noted the State's contention that both boys were advised of their constitutional rights before they made their statements, but it held that this should not be given "significant weight in our determination of voluntariness." Accordingly, the judgment of the Juvenile Court was reversed.

In a recent case before the Juvenile Court of the District of Columbia, Judge Ketcham rejected the proffer of evidence as to oral statements made at police headquarters by four juveniles who had been taken into custody for alleged involvement in an assault and attempted robbery. *In the Matter of Four Youths,* Nos. 28—776—J, 28—778—J, 28—783—J, 28—859—J. Juvenile Court of the District of Columbia, April 7, 1961. The court explicitly stated that it did not rest its decision on a showing that the statements were involuntary, but because they were untrustworthy. Judge Ketcham said:

> "Simply stated, the Court's decision in this case rests upon the considered opinion—after nearly four busy years on the Juvenile Court bench during which the testimony of thousands of such juveniles has been heard—that the statements of adolescents under 18 years of age who are arrested and charged with violations of law are frequently untrustworthy and often distort the truth."

We conclude that the constitutional privilege against self-incrimination is applicable in the case of juveniles as it is with respect to adults. We appreciate that special problems may arise with respect to waiver of the privilege by or on behalf of children, and that there may well be some differences in technique—but not in principle—depending upon the age of the child and the presence and competence of parents. The participation of counsel will, of course, assist the police, juvenile courts and appellate tribunals in administering the privilege. If counsel was not present for some permissible reason when an admission was obtained, the greatest care must be taken to assure that the admission was voluntary, in the sense not only that it was not coerced or suggested, but also that it was not the product of ignorance of rights or of adolescent fantasy, fright or despair.

The "confession" of Gerald Gault was first obtained by Officer Flagg, out of the presence of Gerald's parents, without counsel and without advising him of his right to silence, as far as appears. The judgment of the Juvenile Court was stated by the judge to be based on Gerald's admissions in court. Neither "admission" was reduced to writing, and, to say the least, the process by which the "admissions," were obtained and received must be characterized as lacking the certainty and order which are required of proceedings of such formidable consequences. Apart from the "admission," there was nothing upon which a judgment or finding might be based. There was no sworn testimony. Mrs. Cook, the complainant, was not present. The Arizona Supreme Court held that "sworn testimony must be required of all witnesses including police officers, probation officers and others who are part of or officially related to the juvenile court structure." We hold that this is not enough. No reason is suggested or appears for a different rule in respect of sworn testimony in juvenile courts than in adult tribunals. Absent a valid confession adequate to support the determination of the Juvenile Court, confrontation and sworn testimony by witnesses available for cross-examination were essential for a finding of "delinquency" and an order committing Gerald to a state institution for a maximum of six years.

The recommendations in the Children's Bureau's "Standards for Juvenile and Family Courts" are in general accord with our conclusions. They state that testimony should be under oath and that only competent, material and relevant evidence under rules applicable to civil cases should be admitted in evidence. The New York Family Court Act contains a similar provision.

As we said in *Kent v. United States*, 383 U.S. 541, 554, 86 S.Ct. 1045, 1053, 16 L.Ed.2d 84 (1966), with respect to waiver proceedings, "there is no place in our system of law for reaching a result of such tremendous consequences without ceremony. . . ." We now hold that, absent a valid confession, a determination of delinquency and an order of commitment to a state institution cannot be sustained in the absence of sworn testimony subjected to the opportunity for cross-examination in accordance with our law and constitutional requirements.

VI. *Appellate Review and Transcript of Proceedings*

Appellants urge that the Arizona statute is unconstitutional under the Due Process Clause because, as construed by its Supreme Court, "there is no right of appeal from a juvenile court order. . . ." The court held that there is no right to a transcript because there is no right to appeal and because the proceedings are confidential and any record must be destroyed after a prescribed period of time. Whether a transcript or other recording is made, it held, is a matter for the discretion of the juvenile court.

This Court has not held that a State is required by the Federal Constitution "to provide appellate courts or a right to appellate review at all." In view of the fact that we must reverse the Supreme Court of Arizona's affirmance of the dismissal of the writ of habeas corpus for other reasons, we need not rule on this question in the present case or upon the failure to provide a transcript or recording of the hearings—or, indeed, the failure of the Juvenile Judge to state the grounds for his conclusion. Cf. *Kent v. United States,* supra, 383 U.S., at 561, 86 S.Ct., at 1057, where we said, in the context of a decision of the juvenile court waiving jurisdiction to the adult court, which by local law, was permissible: ". . . it is incumbent upon the Juvenile Court to accompany its waiver order with a statement of the reasons or considerations therefor." As the present case illustrates, the consequences of failure to provide an appeal, to record the proceedings, or to make findings or state the grounds for the juvenile court's conclusion may be to throw a burden upon the machinery for habeas corpus, to saddle the reviewing process with the burden of attempting to reconstruct a record, and to impose upon the Juvenile Judge the unseemly duty of testifying under cross-examination as to the events that transpired in the hearings before him.

For the reasons stated, the judgment of the Supreme Court of Arizona is reversed and the cause remanded for further proceedings not inconsistent with this opinion. It is so ordered.

Judgment reversed and cause remanded with directions.

Name and Case Index

Subject Index

J

"Jail Inmate Releases Possible" (Williams), 267–268
Jails, 288–290
Judges
See also Court system
administrative duties of, 166
appointment of, 7, 28–30, 159
career ladder of, 28
chief judges, 187
en banc, 159, 168
judicial discretion, 36–37
role of, 185
Judges' Rules, 376
Judicial Act of 1789, 158
Judiciary Act of 1789, 195
"Juries, Their Powers under Siege, Find Their Role Is Being Eroded" (Glaberson), 227–230
Jurisdiction, 153, 158, 168
Jury trials
bench trials and, 223
hung jury, 234
jury pool, 224, 240
jury selection, 224–227
order of trial, 231–234
plea bargaining and, 222–223
rights and, 221
sequestered juries, 234
Justice, definition of, 15, 19
Justice of the peace courts, 155–156
Justifiable homicide, 65
Juvenile justice
adjudicatory hearings, 320–321, 331
age of responsibility and, 318, 331
appellate review and, 404–405
boot camps and, 328
confrontation rights, 397–404
cross-examination and, 397–404
current dilemmas in, 324–331
delinquent acts, 320, 321, 332
dispositional hearings, 323, 332
diversion programs, 328, 332
economic status and, 83
era of socialized juvenile justice, 319
foster homes and, 324
history of, 318–320
juvenile court acts, 320–321
in loco parentis, 319, 331
mental state and, 52
notice of charges and, 393–394
parens patriae and, 318–319, 331, 392–393
probation and, 323

procedures in, 321–324
right to counsel and, 394–397
station house adjustments, 322, 332
status offenders, 321, 332
unofficial probation and, 14–15
U.S. Supreme Court rulings on, 387–405
wards of the state, 322–323, 332

K

Kerner Commission, 113
Kickbacks, 139
"King Claims Drugs Led to Jasper Death" (Stewart), 78
Knapp Commission, 138
Ku Klux Klan, 78

L

Larceny/theft, 74–75, 85, 99–101, 378
Law
See also specific laws
case law, 49
civil law, 50
common law, 53
conflict model, 48
criminal law, 50–52
definition of, 46, 57
federalization of, 54, 163
federal law, 53–54
functions of, 57
history of, 52–53
law enforcement procedures, 117–122
origins of, 46–50
politics and, 48
procedural law, 49
state law, 53–54
statutory law, 49
substantive law, 49
Leadership Conference on Civil Rights, 79
Leading questions, 233, 240
Legalists, 320, 331
"Legislators Hear Testimony about Racial Profiling on State's Roads" (Walsh), 120
Life without possibility of parole, 68
Lindbergh Act, 54
London Metropolitan Police, 111
Los Angeles Police Department, 13, 16, 102, 113
Lower courts, 155, 158

M

McArthur Justice Center, 179
Mafia, 101
Magistrate judges, 157–158, 168

Probation
  definition of, 305, 307, 312
  juvenile justice, 323
  probation officers, 30, 37, 185–186
Problem-oriented policing, 114–115
Procedural law, definition of, 49, 58
Property crimes
  arson, 76–77, 85, 278
  burglary, 75–76, 85, 278
  larceny/theft, 74–75, 85, 99–101, 378
  mediation and, 257
  robbery, 73–74, 85, 278
Prosecutors
  career ladder, 28, 177
  crime statistics and, 82
  defense counsel's relationship with, 181–184
  discretion and, 36, 175
  independent counsel, 26, 174
  influence of, 26
  politics and, 26, 175
  prosecutorial abuse, 175
  role in court system, 174–177
"Prosecutors Undermine Cases by Failure to
    Heed Rules of Law" (Francke), 210–213
Prostitution, 92, 93, 105
Protection of illegal activities, 139
Public
  definition of, 19
  political influence of, 24
  public discretion, 32–33
  role in criminal justice network, 12–13
Public defenders, 177–180
Public executions, 278

Q
Quakers, 272

R
Race. *See* Minorities
Racial profiling, 176
Racketeer Influenced and Corrupt
    Organizations (RICO), 102, 104
Rape
  capital punishment and, 278
  definition of, 69–70, 85
  sexual predators, 71
  statutory rape, 73, 85
Real evidence, 231, 240
Receiving stolen goods, 74
Recidivism, 257–258, 290, 295, 306–307
Recross-examination, 231, 240

Redirect examination, 231, 240
Reformatories, 273
Rehabilitation, 275, 282, 290–293
Released on recognizance (ROR), 200, 214
Religious freedom, 303
*Report of the National Advisory Committee on
    Civil Disorders* (Kerner Commission), 113
"Restitution Fund Can't Keep Up with
    Victims" (Kane), 250
Restorative justice, 249–251, 252, 254–258,
    260, 304
Retardation, 52, 70
Retribution, 274, 294
Revenge, 274
RICO. *See* Racketeer Influenced and Corrupt
    Organizations (RICO)
Right to counsel, 195, 359–381, 394–397
Right to speedy trial, 160–161, 163, 166–167, 168
Riots, 292
Robbery, 73–74, 85, 278
Roman Catholic church, 52
Roman law, 52, 318
ROR. *See* Released on recognizance (ROR)
Ruby Ridge, 25

S
Sanctions, definition of, 47, 57
SARA process, 114, 144
School shootings, 17, 324
Scotland, 376
Search and seizure, 7, 356–359, 381–386
Selective enforcement, definition of, 33
Self-report studies, 83–84, 86
Sentencing, 68, 185, 234–239, 256–257, 258, 266
Sequestered juries, 234, 240
Serious case, 223
Sexual exploitation of child, 73
Sexual predators, 71
Shakedowns, 139
"Sheriff's Dispatcher Suspected of Internet
    Fraud" (Spice and Sink), 97–98
Sixth Amendment
  jury trials and, 221, 222
  rights granted by, 53, 195, 206, 231, 347
  speedy trial and, 160–161, 163, 166–167, 220
  statement of, 347
Smith and Wesson, 17
Social control, definition of, 110, 144
Sodomy, 17, 70, 85
Solitary confinement, 273
Specific deterrence, 274–275, 294

V

Venire, 224, 240
Venue, 153, 168, 208
Vera Foundation, 200
Victims
  advocacy groups for, 256–257, 260
  civil remedies for, 252
  in criminal justice system, 246–251
  dissatisfaction of, 258–259
  impact statements of, 256, 260
  monetary recovery for, 249–251
  private insurance and, 253
  restitution for, 249–251, 252, 254–258, 260
  state subsidized compensation programs
    for, 253–254
  victim compensation, 249–251, 254–256, 260
  victim-offender mediation, 257–258, 260
Victims of Crime Act of 1984, 256
Victim survey research, 82–83, 86
Violent Crime Control Act of 1994, 256
Violent Crime Control and Law Enforcement
    Act of 1994, 54
Voir dire, 224, 240
Voluntary manslaughter, 65, 66, 67

W

Waco, Texas, 25
Walnut Street Jail, 272, 288, 294
Wardens, 30
Wards of the state, 322–323, 332
Warehousing, 292, 295
Washington, Denzel, 10
Watchmen, 111
West Germany, 278
"White Blasts Police Union for Filing Suit"
    (Grant), 128–129
White-collar crime, 18, 96, 98, 105
Wickersham Commission, 113, 361
Women, 126, 133, 276
"Women Confront Police Challenge"
    (Robinson), 127
"Workhouse Inmates Getting Out Early"
    (Grant), 269–270
Workhouses, 271
Writ of certiorari, 159, 168